Business Law

putyourknowledgeinto practice

● **Business Law**
J. Scott Slorach and Jason G. Ellis

● **Legislation for Business Law**
Rachel Cooper

● **Foundations for the LPC**
George Miles *et al.*

● **Lawyers' Skills**
Julian Webb *et al.*

● **Solicitors' Accounts**
Dale Kay and Janet Baker

● **Criminal Litigation Handbook**
Martin Hannibal and Lisa Mountford

● **Civil Litigation Handbook**
Susan Cunningham-Hill and Karen Elder

● **Property Law Handbook**
Robert Abbey and Mark Richards

● **A Practical Approach
to Civil Procedure**
Stuart Sime

● **A Practical Approach
to Conveyancing**
Robert Abbey and Mark Richards

● **Family Law Handbook** (*coming soon*)
Jane Sendall

Commercial Law
Robert Bradgate and Fidelma White

● **Employment Law**
James Holland and Stuart Burnett

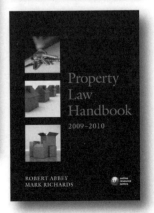

Business Law

Professor J. Scott Slorach MA (Oxon), Solicitor

Board Member: Programme Design and Production, The College of Law,
Visiting Professor, Strathclyde University

Jason G. Ellis MA (Oxon), LLM, Solicitor

Director of Curriculum Design, The College of Law

OXFORD
UNIVERSITY PRESS

OXFORD

UNIVERSITY PRESS

Great Clarendon Street, Oxford OX2 6DP

Oxford University Press is a department of the University of Oxford.
It furthers the University's objective of excellence in research, scholarship,
and education by publishing worldwide in

Oxford New York

Auckland Cape Town Dar es Salaam Hong Kong Karachi
Kuala Lumpur Madrid Melbourne Mexico City Nairobi
New Delhi Shanghai Taipei Toronto

With offices in

Argentina Austria Brazil Chile Czech Republic France Greece
Guatemala Hungary Italy Japan Poland Portugal Singapore
South Korea Switzerland Thailand Turkey Ukraine Vietnam

Oxford is a registered trademark of Oxford University Press
in the UK and in certain other countries

Published in the United States
by Oxford University Press Inc., New York

First published 1993
Eleventh edition 2003
Twelfth edition 2004
Thirteenth edition 2005
Fourteenth edition 2006
Fifteenth edition 2007
Sixteenth edition 2008
Seventeenth edition 2009

British Library Cataloguing in Publication Data
Data available

Typeset by Laserwords Private Limited, Chennai, India
Printed in Great Britain
on acid-free paper by
Ashford Colour Press Ltd, Gosport, Hampshire

ISBN 978–0–19–957161–1

10 9 8 7 6 5 4 3 2 1

OUTLINE CONTENTS

DETAILED CONTENTS

PREFACE

Raymond Chandler gave the sage advice about writing which was when in doubt have a man come through the door with a gun in his hand. As such we thought it would be appropriate in this latest edition to include such an event. We hope readers have a happy time hunting this down.

Jason Ellis
J. Scott Slorach

May 2009

ONLINE RESOURCES TO ACCOMPANY
THIS BOOK ...

Online Resource Centres are developed to provide students and lecturers with ready-to-use teaching and learning resources. They are free of charge, designed to complement the textbook and offer additional materials that are suited to electronic delivery. The Online Resource Centre to accompany this book can be found at:

www.oxfordtextbooks.co.uk/orc/business09–10/

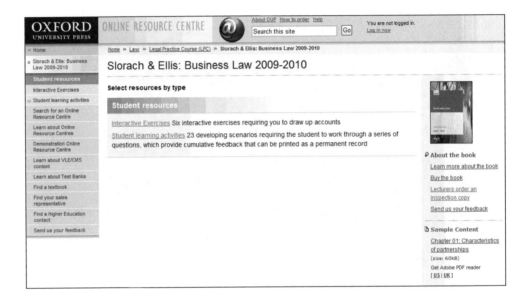

Student resources

Student learning activities

Freely accessible with no need for a password, this book is accompanied by student learning activities designed to help students to test their knowledge and understanding of the practical application of business law. Made up of several developing scenarios, the activities require the student to work through a series of questions which provide cumulative feedback that can be printed out as a permanent record.

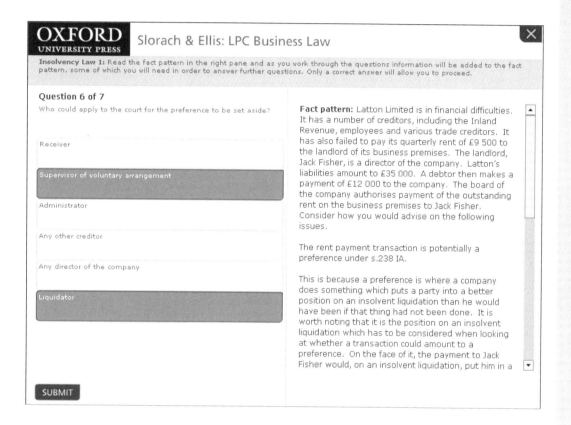

Lecturer resources

Lecturers can download the student learning activities for use in their own virtual learning environment. This part of the site is password protected to ensure that only lecturers adopting this book can access it.

Registering for a password is simple: click on 'Lecturer Resources' on the Online Resource Centre, complete a simple registration form which allows you to choose your own user name and password, and access will be granted within 48 hours (subject to verification).

Using your lecturer password, you can import the student learning activities into Blackboard, WebCT and most other virtual learning environments so that your students can access the activities direct from your VLE system.

ACKNOWLEDGEMENTS

Chapter 35 was originally based on the following articles:

'Distributorships—Low Risk Expansion into New Markets' by Michael Arnold (a partner in Evershed Wells & Hind) (*PLC Magazine*, Volume IV, Number 2, March 1993).

'Agency Agreements—New Protection for Commercial Agents' by Jeremy Scholes and Nick Blane (*PLC Magazine*, Volume IV, Number 10, November 1993, pp. 31–46).

'Agency Agreements—EC Competition Law, Drafting and Termination', by Jeremy Scholes and Nick Blane (*PLC Magazine*, Volume IV, Number 11, December 1993, pp. 39–48).

'Commercial Agents Regulations: Postscript—DTI's Last Minute Amendments' by Jeremy Scholes and Nick Blane (*PLC Magazine*, Volume V, Number 2, March 1994, pp. 39–44).

The authors would like to thank Michael Arnold, Jeremy Scholes, Nick Blane, and *PLC Magazine* for their help with this chapter.

TABLE OF CASES

TABLE OF STATUTES

TABLE OF SECONDARY LEGISLATION

European Secondary Legislation

Partnerships

Characteristics of partnerships

1

This chapter covers the following topics:

1.1 Introduction

1.1.1 Types of business medium

The established business media in the United Kingdom are sole traders, partnerships and companies. Sole traders by definition tend to be relatively small concerns, as do partnerships, although a number of professional partnerships overturn this assumption. Companies cover the full spectrum of business sizes.

Chapters 1 to **6** of this Guide cover partnerships; **Chapters 7** to **16** cover companies. Since 6 April 2001, a new business medium has been in existence, known as the 'limited liability partnership'. This is discussed in **Chapter 31**. As limited liability partnerships are a hybrid of company and partnership law concepts, it is recommended that they are not studied until partnerships and companies have been covered.

In this chapter, we will look at the rules for determining whether a partnership has come into existence as well as the formalities with which businesses which will be run through partnerships must comply. (This Guide will not consider the rules relating to limited partnerships created under the Limited Partnership Act 1907.)

We will not look separately in this chapter, or in the ones which follow, at sole proprietorships. However, many of the formalities to which partnerships are subject (for example, in relation to the choice of a business name) apply equally to sole proprietors.

1.2   Relevant law

Much of the law relating to partnership is to be found in the Partnership Act (PA) 1890. The Act was mainly declaratory of the law of partnership as it had developed up to 1890. The Act does not provide a complete code of partnership law, and indeed s. 46 specifically provides that: 'The rules of equity and of common law applicable to partnership shall continue in force except so far as they are inconsistent with the express provisions of this Act.'

1.3   Definition of partnership

The definition of a partnership is to be found in s. 1(1) PA 1890 which states: 'Partnership is the relation which subsists between persons carrying on a business in common with a view of profit.' (A registered company is specifically excluded from the definition by s. 1(2).) To satisfy the definition, two or more persons must be carrying on a business. It follows from this that an agreement to run a business in the future does not constitute an immediate partnership, nor does the taking of preliminary steps to enable a business to be run. 'Business' is defined by s. 45 PA 1890 as including 'every trade, occupation or profession'.

Section 2 PA 1890 lays down certain 'rules for determining the existence of a partnership'. These provide that:

(a)   Joint or common ownership of property 'does not of itself create a partnership' even where profits from the property are shared (s. 2(1)).

(b)   The sharing of *gross* returns does not of itself create a partnership (s. 2(2)). A person is not, therefore, a partner in a business merely because he receives commission on sales which he has introduced.

(c)   The receipt of a share of *profits* is prima facie evidence of partnership (s. 2(3)). This topic is dealt with in **2.6**.

It should be noted that a written partnership agreement is *not* a prerequisite for the existence of a partnership. The existence of a partnership is *always* a question of fact.

1.4   Nature of partnership and terminology

A partnership is, in law, a very different type of institution from a company. The most significant difference is that partners have unlimited liability for the debts of the partnership, whereas the liability of shareholders for a company's debts is limited. (The liability of partners to creditors is considered in **Chapter 3**.) Partnerships, unlike companies, are not required to go through any registration process when they are formed and, again unlike companies, they are under no obligation to make their accounts public.

A partnership is not a separate legal entity from its partners (in contrast to companies, which are legally distinct from their shareholders). However, to a limited extent in relation to litigation (see **Chapter 3**) and taxation (see **Chapter 17**), the existence of the partnership is recognised as being independent of the individual members.

As a means of recognising the differences which exist between a partnership and a company, the former is commonly referred to as a *firm*.

1.5 Number of partners

Until quite recently, the maximum number of persons who could be members of a particular partnership was usually 20 (s. 716 Companies Act (CA) 1985). Numerous exemptions to this limit existed, in particular for certain professions, including solicitors and accountants. This rule was abolished completely in late 2002, so that no limits apply in any circumstances.

1.6 Capacity

Generally speaking, any person including a minor (person under 18) is legally capable of forming a partnership with any other person. Companies as well as individuals can, provided their objects clause gives them the power to do so, enter into a partnership with other companies or with individuals. (This Guide will not consider any rules applicable where one or more companies are members of a partnership.)

1.7 Duration of partnership

Most partnerships are partnerships 'at will'. This means that no particular period is agreed upon as being the time during which the partnership is to last. A partnership at will can be dissolved by notice by any partner unless there is an agreement to the contrary (see ss. 26(1) and 32(c) PA 1890).

A partnership for a fixed term or for a term defined by reference to some event (e.g., the completion of some particular job) is also possible. Such a partnership cannot generally be dissolved by notice.

There may sometimes be difficulty in deciding when a partnership begins. Because of the way partnership is defined, this is essentially a question of fact. The terms of a partnership agreement as to commencement may be evidence (though not conclusive) of when a partnership begins.

1.8 Partnership name and publicity of information

A partnership is entitled (subject to what is said below) to choose any name which it wishes. There is nothing in partnership law corresponding with the requirement that a company should have a corporate name which is registered with the Registrar of Companies (see **8.6.3.1**).

The law relating to partnership names is now contained in the Business Names Act (BNA) 1985. The Act permits the free use of certain names and requires approval for others. In addition it contains rules requiring publicity as to the membership of partnerships in certain circumstances.

1.8.1 Automatically permitted names

If the business of a partnership is carried on under a name which consists of the surnames of all the partners, no restrictions apply (s. 1 BNA 1985). This is also the case where the name consists of the partners' surnames together with 'permitted additions' and nothing else. The permitted additions are:

(a) the forenames or initials of the partners;

(b) the addition of an 's' to a surname to signify that there is more than one partner with that name; and/or

(c) a statement that the business is being carried on in succession to the business of a former owner.

Where the name of the partnership does not consist solely of the surnames of the partners, or of the surnames of the partners together with permitted additions, then the disclosure requirements of s. 4 BNA 1985 will apply and in some cases approval of the name is required under ss. 2 and 3.

1.8.2 Disclosure requirements of s. 4 BNA 1985

Any partnership which uses a business name (other than one permitted under s. 1 BNA 1985) is required to state the name of each partner (together with an address for service in Great Britain) on every:

(a) business letter;

(b) order for goods or services;

(c) invoice;

(d) receipt; and

(e) written demand for payment of a debt (s. 4(1)(a) BNA 1985).

The same information must also be given by a notice in a prominent position at each place of business of the partnership (s. 4(1)(b) BNA 1985). The same information must also be given (in writing) to anyone with whom the partnership has had dealings or negotiations and who asks for the information (s. 4(2) BNA 1985).

The requirement of including names and addresses in letters, etc., does not apply to a partnership with more than 20 members provided that, instead of the partners' names, the letter states the address of the principal place of business and that the names and addresses of the partners can be inspected there.

1.8.3 Approval under ss. 2 and 3 BNA 1985

Section 2 BNA 1985 makes it an offence to carry on business (without the approval of the Secretary of State) under a name which suggests a connection with the Government or a local authority, or which includes a word specified in regulations made under the Act. Section 3 gives the Secretary of State power to make such regulations. Regulations have been made under the Act which specify scores of words for which approval is required.

Partners who are starting a business and who wish to use a business name should consult the regulations. If they find that their name includes a word covered by the regulations they should first write to the government department or other body (if any) which is to be consulted in relation to that word asking it whether it objects. They should then apply to the Secretary of State for approval stating that they have made such a request and enclosing a copy of any reply that they have received from the government department or other body that they have consulted.

online resource centre

Interactive online exercises (Student Learning Activities) which complement the topics covered in this chapter are available at www.oxfordtextbooks.co.uk/orc/business09_10/.

Partnership management and finance

This chapter covers the following topics:

2.1 Introduction

In this chapter we will look at:

(a) the ways a partnership can be managed;

(b) the relationship of the partners to each other and the obligations which partners owe to each other; and

(c) how the finances of a partnership can be handled, both in terms of raising capital to finance the business and distribution of profits the business makes.

2.2 The legal relationship between the partners (s. 24)

Section 24 PA 1890 lays down a number of rules which regulate the relationship between partners and the management of their business. These rules '. . . may be varied by the consent of all the partners, and such consent may be express or inferred from a course of conduct'. The most common way in which the rules in s. 24 are varied is where the partners enter into a partnership agreement (see **Chapter 6**).

If partners do not wish specific provisions of s. 24 to apply to their business then, for certainty, contrary provisions should be incorporated in their partnership agreement.

Several of the subsections of s. 24 deal with the relationship of the partners in respect of the distribution of profits and losses made by the partnership; these subsections are dealt with in 2.6.

2.2.1 Management of the business

Section 24(5) provides that (subject to contrary agreement, express or implied) 'Every partner may take part in the management of the partnership business'.

If the management structure of a particular partnership is to be different from the equality of partners presumed by s. 24(5), then express agreement should be made. For example, a large partnership may have different grades of partners, major decisions being taken only by the senior grade. Similarly, some partners may be 'sleeping partners', that is, partners who have contributed capital but who do not take an active part in management or decision-making.

2.2.2 Decisions of the partners

Section 24(8) says that (subject to contrary agreement, express or implied):

Any differences arising as to ordinary matters connected with the partnership business may be decided by a majority of the partners, but no change may be made in the nature of the partnership business without the consent of all the partners.

In most circumstances, therefore, a simple majority of the partners is required to take a decision. If there is an equality of votes a decision has not been taken and the status quo is preserved.

2.2.3 Restrictions on majority rule

There are three main limitations imposed on the ability of the majority of the partners to bind the whole firm. First, partners are under a fiduciary duty to each other and so must exercise their powers for the benefit of the firm as a whole. For example, in *Blisset v Daniel* (1853) 10 Hare 493, a power was given (by the partnership agreement) to the majority of the partners permitting them to expel a partner. The majority exercised this power with a view to obtaining cheaply the expelled partner's shares in the partnership. This was held to be an illegal use of the power to expel as it amounted to a breach of the duty of good faith required of a fiduciary.

Secondly, the majority may not impose their views on the minority without first consulting them (*Const v Harris* (1824) T & R 496). However, there is no requirement that consultation should take the form of a meeting (unless the partnership agreement so provides).

Thirdly, the following provisions of the Partnership Act limit majority rule:

(a) Section 24(8) requires unanimity for a change in the partnership business. This is so that a partner who has decided to invest in one particular type of business will not be forced to invest in something else against his wishes.

(b) Section 24(7) provides that: 'No person may be introduced as a partner without the consent of all the existing partners'. Such a rule is vital to the running of a small partnership where each partner will wish to ensure that his fellow partners cannot force him to go into partnership with someone of whom he disapproves. In a large partnership it may be considered appropriate that s. 24(7) should not apply (so that, for example, the senior partners may be given power to decide who to take on as junior partners and who to promote to senior partnership), in which case the partnership agreement must exclude the requirement of unanimity in this respect.

(c) Unanimity is required by s. 19 for an alteration to the partnership agreement. The agreement of the partners to an alteration can be inferred from a course of dealings.

(d) Section 25 prevents expulsion of a partner by a majority of the partners unless all the partners have *expressly* agreed to such a power being conferred.

2.2.4 Other provisions

Other provisions of s. 24 which affect the relationship between the partners are as follows:

(a) Section 24(2) gives a partner a right to be indemnified by the firm in respect of payments made and personal liabilities incurred 'in the ordinary and proper conduct of the business of the firm or in or about anything necessarily done for the preservation of the business or property of the firm'.

(b) Section 24(9) gives all the partners a right to inspect and copy the partnership accounts.

2.3 The duty of good faith

2.3.1 Equitable provisions

The contract of partnership is a contract *uberrimae fidei* (of the utmost good faith), so that a partner is required to disclose all relevant information in his possession to his partners. If he fails to do so his partners may set aside transactions which they have entered into with him as a result of the non-disclosure.

Similarly, a partner owes a fiduciary duty to his fellow partners; that is, he owes the duty of good faith to his partners in his dealings with them which a trustee owes to a beneficiary.

2.3.2 Statutory provisions

The requirement of good faith in dealings between partners is of general application, but three particular aspects of the duty are dealt with in ss. 28–30 PA 1890.

2.3.2.1 Duty to disclose information

Section 28 provides that: 'Partners are bound to render true accounts and full information of all things affecting the partnership to any partner or his legal representative.' This is really just a formulation in statutory language of the duty of disclosure imposed by equity. A good illustration of the working of the rule is given by *Law v Law* [1905] 1 Ch 140. In that case one partner offered to buy the share of another at a price which seemed fair to the vendor who was not actively engaged in running the business. The purchaser, however, knew of facts which made the vendor's share more valuable than the vendor realised. When the vendor discovered this it was held that he was entitled to rescind the contract of sale on the ground of non-disclosure.

2.3.2.2 Duty to account for secret profits

Section 29 states that:

(1) Every partner must account to the firm for any benefit derived by him without the consent of the other partners from any transaction concerning the partnership, or from any use by him of the partnership property, name or business connection.

(2) This section applies also to transactions undertaken after a partnership has been dissolved by the death of a partner, and before the affairs thereof have been completely wound up, either by any surviving partner or by the representative of the deceased partner.

This section imposes similar restrictions and duties on partners as apply to company directors (see **9.7**). Any profit made in breach of the section is held on trust for the benefit of the partnership as a whole. The rule applies to transactions entered into by a partner where the opportunity came to him as a result of the partnership, to commissions received on contracts introduced to the partnership, to sales of property to the partnership by a partner and to profits derived from sales of partnership property. A partner may retain any such profit if his partners consent following full disclosure of the circumstances.

2.3.2.3 Duty to account for profits from competing business

Section 30 PA 1890 provides that:

If a partner, without the consent of the other partners, carries on any business of the same nature as and competing with that of the firm, he must account for and pay over to the firm all profits made by him in that business.

The provisions of s. 30 are quite narrow. In order to succeed under this section the partners must show that the businesses are of the same nature and that they are in fact competing for the same customers. Thus in *Aas v Benham* [1891] 2 Ch 244, a partner in a firm of shipbrokers was held not to be accountable for profits he had made from shipbuilding. However, in *Glassington v Thwaites* (1823) 1 Sim & St 124, a partner in a morning newspaper who set up an evening newspaper was held to be accountable. It should be noted that there is overlap between s. 30 and s. 29(1) (see **2.3.2.2** above)—a partner may be held accountable because he is competing with his partners or because he is using 'the partnership property name or business connection'; often a partner who sets up a new business will be doing both these things.

2.3.2.4 Preventing a partner from setting up a non-competing business

A partner who sets up a non-competing business and who does not use the partnership property, name or business connection is not liable to his partners in any way under the Act. Many partnership agreements, therefore, provide that the partners are to devote their whole time to the partnership and specify that the partners are not to start any other businesses. With such an agreement the partners may be able to obtain an injunction, damages or dissolution of the partnership against the partner who sets up a new business, even though it does not compete with the firm's business. They will not, however, have any right to make him contribute his profits in the other business to the partnership.

2.4 The partnership's finances

2.4.1 Sources of finance

The sources of finance for a partnership are basically the same as those available to any business. A partnership will need assets and cash in order to run its business. Money (or in some cases assets) may be contributed in the form of a permanent investment by the partners or it may be borrowed from either the partners or outside sources. Once the business of the partnership has started further finance may also be provided by retention of profits.

2.4.2 Partners' capital

The permanent investment of a partner is described as his 'capital'. The capital of a partner may be contributed by him in the form of cash or property (including, for example, business premises or the goodwill of an existing business). The term 'capital' is somewhat ambiguous. It refers to the actual cash or other assets contributed to the partnership by a partner and the indebtedness of the partnership as a whole to the partner resulting from this investment. A partner's capital in this latter sense should be contrasted with other debts which the firm owes to the partner, as repayment of the capital cannot normally be claimed from the firm until dissolution (see **5.2.2.3**). Other indebtedness to a partner (for example, a loan) may be repaid before dissolution.

2.5 The distinction between a partner and a lender

As we saw in **Chapter 1**, the essential nature of a partnership is that two or more people are sharing profits of a business. A person who merely lends to a partnership is not a partner. The distinction between a partner and a lender is extremely important as a partner bears unlimited liability for the debts of the partnership whereas the lender only stands to lose the money invested if the business fails (if he has taken security for his loan, his risk of losing even that much may be small). However, if a business is successful a partner stands to earn a great deal of profit whereas a lender will receive only interest on his loan.

Many investors would like to have the best of both worlds, i.e., limited liability and a share of profits. This can be achieved by investing in a company. However, in the case of partnerships, s. 2(3) PA 1890 effectively restricts this type of investment. It provides that: 'The receipt by a person of a share of profits . . . is prima facie evidence that he is a partner . . . but does not of itself make him a partner . . . '. The subsection then sets out some particular rules which provide that:

(a) A person does not become a partner merely because a debt or other liquidated sum is paid to him by instalments out of profits.

(b) A servant or agent does not become a partner merely because his remuneration varies with profits.

(c) A widow or child of a partner is not a partner merely because a proportion of profits is paid to that person as an annuity.

(d) A lender whose interest varies with profits is not automatically a partner if the contract is in writing and signed by all the parties.

(e) A vendor who receives payment for his business in the form of an annuity varying with profits is not automatically a partner.

Sharing of profits is only prima facie evidence of partnership and particular types of contract are covered by the five rules mentioned above. However, there remains a risk that anyone who receives a share of profits *may* be held to be a partner and therefore personally liable for debts. Anyone entering into such an arrangement who does not wish to take on the risk of unlimited liability should take steps to ensure that he or she does not become a partner, e.g., by avoiding any suggestion that he has a right to take part in management and by having a written agreement setting out the terms of his involvement with the firm.

2.6   Division of profits and sharing of losses between partners

Section 24 PA 1890 lays down a number of rules as to division of profits. These rules may be varied by an express or implied agreement of the partners, and for the avoidance of doubt it is preferable to state in a partnership agreement how both profits and losses are to be shared even if the agreement follows some or all of the statutory presumptions. Section 24 deals with the division of both income and capital profits.

2.6.1   Share of profits and losses (s. 24(1))

Section 24(1) states:

All the partners are entitled to share equally in the capital and profits of the business, and must contribute equally towards the losses whether of capital or otherwise sustained by the firm.

This rule may be broken down into three parts which will be examined in turn.

2.6.1.1   Sharing of capital

The first part of the rule states that 'all the partners are entitled to share equally in the capital'. On the face of it this means that when a partner leaves the firm or when the firm is dissolved he is entitled to take out a part of the capital corresponding with the total amount of capital divided by the number of partners. However, in practice this is unlikely to be so. All the rules in s. 24 are subject to contrary agreement express or implied. Where the partners have contributed unequally to the capital, there is an *implied* agreement that they are entitled to withdraw capital unequally. For example, if A contributes £10,000, B £20,000 and C £30,000, those are the sums which each can withdraw on leaving in the absence of any express agreement to the contrary.

2.6.1.2   Sharing of profits

The second part of the rule in s. 24(1) states that 'all the partners are entitled to share equally in the profits of the business'. The provision of capital in unequal shares *does not* give rise to the implication that this part of the rule has been displaced. Thus in the example given above if the profits of the firm were £9,000, A, B and C would each be entitled to £3,000. If a partner is to receive more than an equal share of profits because of his capital contribution or the work he does, this must be specifically agreed to and should be expressly stated in the partnership agreement.

The rule as to share of profits applies to capital as well as income profits. 'Capital profits' is the term for amounts remaining following the payment of all creditors and repayment of capital contributions to partners on the dissolution of a partnership. When the firm in our example is dissolved, any capital profit will be shared equally even though the capital was not contributed equally. Thus after A has received £10,000, B £20,000 and

C £30,000, any surplus will be divided equally. The partners are, of course, free to agree to the contrary. It may well be decided that capital profits should be divided in the same ratio as capital was provided. The ratio in which capital profits are divided (sometimes called the 'asset surplus ratio') is often different from the income profit–sharing ratio.

2.6.1.3   Sharing of losses

The third part of the rule in s. 24(1) states that losses of capital and income are prima facie to be shared equally. However, if the partners share profits unequally (because of an express or implied agreement to do so), then s. 44 PA 1890 says that losses will also be shared unequally unless there is an agreement to the contrary.

2.6.2   Interest on capital

Section 24(4) provides that: 'A partner is not entitled . . . to interest on capital.' Where capital is contributed unequally, it may be considered appropriate to make provision in the partnership agreement for interest on capital to compensate the partner who has contributed more. The agreement should specify the rate of interest or the method by which the rate is to be determined. Interest on capital is *not* a deductible expense of the business in determining its net profits (see **17.5.2**). It is merely a preferential appropriation of profits. This means that once the net profit of the partnership has been ascertained the partners' first entitlement will be to interest and then the remaining net profit will be allocated in accordance with the agreed profit-sharing ratio.

2.6.3   Interest on loans

In the absence of contrary agreement a loan by a partner to the partnership carries only 5% interest (s. 24(3)). It should be noted that this rate of interest is paid only on 'actual payments or advances'. Interest is not payable under s. 24(3) on a share of profits which is simply left in the business. The partners are, of course, free to agree that interest will be paid on undrawn profits if they wish.

2.6.4   Remuneration of partners

Section 24(6) provides that: 'No partner shall be entitled to remuneration for acting in the partnership business.' In many partnerships the division of work between the partners is unequal, and therefore it will have to be expressly agreed that some of the partners be paid a salary to compensate them for the extra work which they have done. As with interest on capital, a salary payable to a partner is *not* a deductible expense but is merely a preferential appropriation of profit.

EXAMPLE   In a partnership with three members it might be agreed that:

(a) the profit-sharing ratio will be D 20%, E 40%, F 40%;

(b) interest on capital will be paid at a rate of 10% p.a. (D's capital is £10,000, E's £20,000 and F's £30,000); and

(c) D is to have a salary of £20,000 p.a.

If profits of £100,000 are made they will be divided as follows:

			£	£
Profit				100,000
Interest:	D		1,000	
	E		2,000	
	F		3,000	
				6,000
Salary:	D			20,000
Share of profits:	D (20%)		14,800	
	E (40%)		29,600	
	F (40%)		29,600	
				74,000
				100,000

In some partnerships (particularly professional partnerships) there may be relatively junior partners who are entitled to a salary to the exclusion of any other share of profits. At first sight it is hard to see how such 'salaried partners' can be regarded as partners at all, as partnership requires that the partners are 'carrying on business in common with a view of profit' (s. 1(1) PA 1890). Nevertheless, in *Stekel v Ellice* [1973] 1 WLR 191, it was held that a salaried partner could be, in law, a full partner with all the rights and duties which that entails.

2.6.5   Drawings

The amount to which a partner is entitled from the profits in a firm (as salary and interest, if agreed to, and share of profits) will not be known until the profit and loss account has been drawn up after the end of the partnership's financial year. The partnership agreement will, therefore, usually provide that a partner is to have the right to take a specified amount of money on account of his expected profits during the course of the year. Sums taken on account in this way are called 'drawings'. If at the end of the year the partner has taken less than he was entitled to he can draw the balance; if he has taken more than it turns out he was entitled to then the partnership agreement will probably require him to pay back the excess and/or pay interest on it. The partnership agreement may provide that each partner is to leave undrawn in the business a proportion of his entitlement to profit. This is because businesses normally need to retain funds to meet increased costs of trading and to fund any future expansion.

2.7   Payment of interest

A payment of interest by a partnership to a creditor will usually be a business expense. This is because the interest payment will satisfy the test for deduction of expenses, that is, that the payment is incurred 'wholly and exclusively for the purposes of the trade'. (As mentioned above, payment of interest on capital to a partner is *not* a business expense, it is an allocation of profits to the partner.)

Where a partnership *receives* interest this is treated as income of the partners.

2.8 Partnership property

2.8.1 Introduction

There is a major reason why it may be important to decide what property is and what is not partnership property. When the firm is dissolved each partner is entitled to retain any property which is his own personal property; property which is partnership property is used first to pay creditors of the firm and then any surplus is distributed among the partners in accordance with the terms of the partnership agreement (equally in the absence of contrary agreement). This is so, once it is decided that an asset is partnership property, even though the asset was introduced by one particular partner and the asset has risen in value thus creating a capital profit for the partnership.

2.8.2 Definition

Partnership property is partly defined by s. 20(1) PA 1890 as:

> All property and rights and interests in property originally brought into the partnership stock or acquired, whether by purchase or otherwise, on account of the firm, or for the purposes and in the course of the partnership business . . .

Section 21 deals with a slightly different situation and states:

> Unless the contrary intention appears, property bought with money belonging to the firm is deemed to have been bought on account of the firm.

2.8.3 The test

Whether property is partnership property or remains the separate property of a partner depends on the intention of the partners, express or implied. Property is not partnership property merely because it is used by the firm. The court does not readily assume, therefore, that property introduced by a partner thereby becomes partnership property.

This is illustrated by the leading case of *Miles v Clarke* [1953] 1 All ER 779. Clarke carried on a photographic business in premises of which he owned the lease. He and Miles went into partnership and for a time the business was successful. However, eventually a petition for dissolution was presented as the partners were unable to agree. The question arose as to which assets were partnership property and which belonged to the partners individually. Harman J held that in the absence of express agreement he would hold property to be partnership property to the extent necessary to give business efficacy to the agreement. Therefore, the lease of the business premises belonged on dissolution to Clarke alone, each partner was entitled to his own business connections which he had brought into the firm and only the stock in trade (unused films, chemicals, etc.) could be regarded as partnership property.

online resource centre

Interactive online exercises (Student Learning Activities) which complement the topics covered in this chapter are available at www.oxfordtextbooks.co.uk/orc/business09_10/.

Liability of partners to outsiders

This chapter covers the following topics:

3.1 Introduction

In the course of carrying on the partnership's business, the partners will incur debts and other obligations. In this chapter, we look at the nature of the partners' liabilities in these circumstances as well as the extent to which an individual partner can bind the partnership as a whole. We will then go on to look at whether it is possible for individuals who are not partners at the time the debt or obligation was incurred (whether because they have been held out as partners or because they are admitted to the partnership subsequently) to be liable for that debt or obligation.

3.2 Nature of liability

Partners are liable for the debts and obligations of the partnership without limit (s. 9 PA 1890). Their liability is joint in the case of contractual obligations and joint and several in the case of tortious obligations (see **3.6**). The significance of this distinction was much reduced by the Civil Liability (Contribution) Act 1978 which allows proceedings to be brought successively against persons jointly liable despite an earlier judgment against others.

Where a partnership is unable to pay its debts out of partnership property, the creditor is entitled to obtain payment from the private estates of the partners. Special rules apply in such cases, so as to attempt to do justice both to the creditors of the firm and to the creditors of the individual partners. It is not our intention to deal with these rules in detail. However, they may be summarised as follows:

(a) In the first instance, the partnership property is used to pay partnership creditors in priority to private creditors and the private property of each partner is used to pay his private creditors in priority to partnership creditors.

(b) If the private creditors of a particular partner are paid in full from private property, then partnership creditors may resort to the balance of that partner's private property.

(c) If the partnership creditors are paid in full from partnership property then the private creditors of a partner may resort to the balance of his share of the partnership assets.

3.3 Partnership and agency

3.3.1 Introduction

The relationship between partnership law and agency is very close. Indeed, most of the rules regulating the relationship between a partnership and the outside world can be explained purely in terms of particular applications of agency principles.

3.3.2 Types of authority of a partner

The partnership as a whole is bound by a partner acting within the scope of his authority. The authority of a partner may arise in three ways:

(a) First, the authority of the partners (or of a particular partner) may be specifically agreed upon by the partners—authority of this type is called 'express actual' authority.

(b) Secondly, authority may be implied either from a course of dealings between the partners (which amounts to an actual agreement) or because the authority is a natural consequence of an authority actually given to the partner—this is normally called 'implied actual' authority.

(c) Thirdly, authority may arise from the fact that a person dealing with a partner is, in certain circumstances, entitled to assume that the partner has authority to bind the firm—this type of authority is generally called 'apparent' or 'ostensible' authority, although terminology in agency law is far from consistent.

3.3.3 Express and implied actual authority

The scope of express and implied actual authority depends on the agreement between the parties. The partnership agreement may specify what powers the partners individually are to have and may specify that some are to have greater powers than others. The extent of actual authority, whether express or implied, is not, in practical terms, of great significance to a person dealing with a partner. This is because, whether or not there is actual authority, he will be able to rely on apparent authority in most circumstances in relation to most normal types of transaction. The outsider need only rely on actual authority where the partner has done something which the law does not consider to be within the apparent authority of a partner.

A partnership is bound by decisions and actions of its employees acting within the scope of their authority. An outsider seeking to rely on a decision or action of an employee would have to show that the employee had actual authority, had been held out (by the partners) as having actual authority or had been held out (by the partners) to be a partner. An individual partner cannot delegate authority to the employees (this is an application of the well known maxim of agency law *delegatus non potest delegare*).

The Partnership Act 1890 has little to say about a partner's actual authority. However, s. 6 recognises that the firm is bound by 'the acts or instruments' entered into with the authority of the firm.

3.3.4   Apparent authority

3.3.4.1   General principles

The scope of apparent (or ostensible) authority is not always easy to establish or describe. Such authority is sometimes said to result from a type of estoppel whereby the principal (in this case the partnership as a whole) represents, by words or conduct, that the agent (that is the partner who is negotiating with the outsider) has authority to bind the firm. Once such a representation is made and acted upon by the outsider the partnership cannot deny the authority of the individual partner to bind the firm. Alternatively, apparent authority may be said to arise simply from the fact that the partner who is negotiating *appears* to have authority to bind the firm and it is, therefore, reasonable for the outsider to assume such authority. In fact nothing really turns on this distinction, since application of either test is likely to produce the same result in most circumstances.

3.3.4.2   Section 5 PA 1890

It is clear that the liability of the firm may result from the actual holding out of an agent (not necessarily a partner) as having a particular authority. However, in most cases the outsider seeks to rely on an apparent authority resulting from the fact that a person is known to be a partner in a firm. The outsider is then entitled to assume that the partner has the usual authority of a partner to bind his firm. This principle is laid down in s. 5 PA 1890 which says:

Every partner is an agent for the firm and his other partners for the purpose of the business of the partnership; and the acts of every partner who does any act for carrying on in the usual way the business of the kind carried on by the firm of which he is a member bind the firm and his partners, unless the partner so acting has in fact no authority to act for the firm in the particular matter, and the person with whom he is dealing either knows that he has no authority, or does not know or believe him to be a partner.

The easiest way to understand the scope of the section (and thus of that part of the partner's authority which derives from the usual authority given to partners generally), is to examine ach of the qualifications on a partner's authority which the section recognises.

(a) *Partner can only bind the firm 'for the purposes of the business of the partnership'*

The first qualification is that the partner can only bind the firm 'for the purposes of the business of the partnership'. The section does not say, therefore, that *anything* which a partner does binds the firm. The partnership agreement may be of some assistance in deciding what is the scope of the partnership business. However, it is not conclusive. In *Mercantile Credit Co. Ltd v Garrod* [1962] 3 All ER 1103,

Mocatta J held that the test as to whether a type of business is within the scope of the partnership depends on what is apparent to the outside world in general. Consequently a sleeping partner in a garage business whose agreement specifically excluded dealing in cars was held liable on a contract for the sale of a car as this was within the scope of what outsiders would expect the business to include.

(b) *Partner must do act 'for carrying on in the usual way the business of the firm'*

The second qualification in s. 5 is that the partnership is only bound if a partner does an act 'for carrying on in the usual way the business of the firm'. This restriction excludes the liability of the firm where the transaction is for the purposes of the business but is itself of an unusual type. For example, in *Niemann v Niemann* (1890) 43 ChD 198, a debt was owed to a partnership; one of the partners intended to accept payment of the debt in the form of shares in a company. This was held not to be binding on the other partner in the absence of a specific agreement. Similarly, *Powell v Brodhurst* [1901] 2 Ch 160 decided that a partner does not have ostensible authority to accept payment of a debt due to another partner personally rather than to the firm.

(c) *No actual authority and outsider knows this or does not know or believe that person is a partner*

The third qualification to s. 5 is that the firm is not bound if the partner has no actual authority and the outsider either knows this or does not know or believe the person with whom he is dealing to be a partner. Clearly in such cases the firm is not bound whether one takes the view that apparent authority depends on estoppel or on appearance of authority. The outsider cannot say that he has relied on any misrepresentation nor can he claim that there appeared to be authority when he knows this to be untrue or does not think he is dealing with an agent at all.

A partner who makes a contract with an outsider without authority will be personally liable to the outsider for breach of warranty of authority where the partnership as a whole is not made liable on the contract. However, where a contract made without authority is ratified by the partnership, it becomes binding on them as well as on the outsider.

Section 8 PA 1890 provides that an outsider is not prejudiced by any restriction placed on the powers of a partner unless he has notice of it.

3.3.5   Examples of apparent authority

The question of what apparent authority a partner has in a particular case is determined by the application of s. 5 to that particular case. This is at least in part a question of fact. However, over the years the courts have decided upon examples of powers which will be assumed to be covered by apparent authority in the case of all partners in the absence of some special circumstance. The court has also recognised certain powers which it will be assumed all partners in a trading partnership have in the absence of some special circumstance. The powers of partners in a trading partnership are more extensive than the powers of partners in general. This is because the court recognises the need of the partners and the persons dealing with them to rely on normal trading practices.

Examples of powers assumed to be available to partners generally include:

(a) power to buy and sell goods (not just stock) used in the business;

(b) power to hire employees;

(c) power to receive payment of debts due to the partnership;

(d) power to pay debts owed by the partnership including a power to draw cheques for this purpose;

(e) power to engage a solicitor to represent the firm.

A partner in a trading partnership will be assumed to have all the above powers and also:

(a) power to grant security for borrowings (this does not, however, include a power to create a legal mortgage);

(b) a wider power than is given to a non-trading partner to deal with cheques and bills of exchange.

3.4 Persons held out as partners

So far we have only considered the liability of actual partners to outsiders. A person who holds himself out as a partner or who 'suffers himself to be represented as a partner' is liable to anyone who 'on the faith of such representation' gives credit to the firm as if he were a partner (s. 14 PA 1890). The commonest example of the application of this rule is where a person allows his name to be used by the partnership (e.g., on notepaper) after he has ceased to be a partner (as to which, see **5.3.3.3(b)**).

A person cannot be held liable under s. 14 unless he has in some way contributed to the mistake made by the person giving credit to the firm, for example by allowing his name to be given as a partner. It is not, however, necessary that he himself should have done anything to inform the person giving credit.

Section 14 only applies where credit is given to the firm. This is construed widely so that, for example, the apparent partner is liable where goods are delivered, as well as where cash is lent, to the firm.

3.5 Liability of new partners

Section 17(1) PA 1890 provides that 'a person who is admitted as a partner into an existing firm does not thereby become liable to the creditors of the firm for anything done before he became a partner'. This provision ensures that an incoming partner is not liable to the existing creditors of the firm merely because he has become a partner.

As between himself and the existing partners the incoming partner may agree to pay a share of debts owed to existing creditors. This does not make him liable to the existing creditors as they are not privy to the contract. The new partner may become liable to existing creditors by a novation (that is, a tripartite contract between the old partners, the new partner and an outsider whereby the existing contract between the old partners and the outsider is discharged and replaced by a contract between the new firm, including the new partner, and the outsider). However, this will not be a regular occurrence.

3.6 Partners' liability in tort

A partner who himself commits a tort is liable according to general principles of the law of tort. The liability of the firm as a whole is governed by s. 10 PA 1890:

Where, by any wrongful act or omission of any partner acting in the ordinary course of the business of the firm, or with the authority of his co-partners, loss or injury is caused to any person . . . the firm is liable . . . to the same extent as the partner so acting or omitting to act.

It should be noted that the firm (as opposed to the actual tortfeasor) is only liable if either the commission of the tort was authorised by the partners or was committed 'in the ordinary course of business'. A partnership is also liable to the same extent as other employers (under common-law principles of vicarious liability) for torts committed by its employees.

3.7 Suing or being sued

A partnership is not a separate legal entity. Nevertheless, the partners may sue or be sued in the firm's name under Ord. 81 of the Rules of the Supreme Court (now contained in Sch. 1 to the Civil Procedure Rules). All the partners at the date when the cause of action accrued are then parties to the action. Where an action is brought against a partnership in the firm's name the writ may be served on any partner, on any person having control or management of the business at the principal place of business or by post to the principal place of business.

A person who has a judgment against a partner for the partner's personal liability may enforce that judgment against the partner's share of partnership property by means of a charging order (s. 23(2) PA 1890). He may not enforce such a judgment against the partnership property by means of execution or garnishee proceedings (s. 23(1)). Where a charging order is made the other partners may discharge it by paying off the judgment debt; if a sale of the property is ordered, they may purchase it. A charging order gives the other partners a right to dissolve the partnership if they wish (s. 33(2)).

 online resource centre

Interactive online exercises (Student Learning Activities) which complement the topics covered in this chapter are available at www.oxfordtextbooks.co.uk/orc/business09_10/.

Partnership disputes

This chapter covers the following topics:

4.1 Introduction

We saw in **Chapter 2** that a decision of the majority of the partners on an 'ordinary matter' is binding on the minority. The wishes of the majority prevail over those of the minority who object. However, partnership law provides some machinery for protecting the partner who is aggrieved by what the other partners have done.

In this chapter we will look at the remedies available to a partner, which include dissolution of the partnership, appointment of a receiver and remedies available under the terms of the partnership agreement itself.

4.2 Dissolution by the court

Dissolution of a partnership may occur automatically (e.g., on the death of a partner) by notice (e.g., any partner can give notice dissolving a partnership at will) or by court order (e.g., in the case of permanent incapacity of a partner). The various circumstances in which dissolution takes place will be considered in **Chapter 5**. In this chapter we intend to consider only those types of dissolution which provide a remedy to a partner against his co-partners under s. 35(c), (d) or (f) PA 1890.

4.2.1 Section 35(c): conduct prejudicial to the business

Section 35(c) provides that a partner may apply to the court for dissolution:

when a partner, other than the partner suing, has been guilty of such conduct as, in the opinion of the court, regard being had to the nature of the business, is calculated to prejudicially affect the carrying on of the business.

This paragraph may be relied upon even though the prejudicial conduct has nothing directly to do with the partnership. A conviction for dishonesty, for example, would be likely to be regarded as prejudicial conduct in the case of many professional partnerships even though the dishonesty did not relate to the practice as such. The test is an objective one so that it need not be shown that the guilty partner *intended* to affect the business (this is so despite the use of the word 'calculated' in s. 35(c)).

4.2.2 Section 35(d): breach of partnership agreement

Section 35(d) provides that a partner may apply to the court for dissolution:

when a partner, other than the partner suing, wilfully or persistently commits a breach of the partnership agreement, or otherwise so conducts himself in matters relating to the partnership business that it is not reasonably practicable for the other partner or partners to carry on business in partnership with him.

This paragraph contemplates that the trust between partners has broken down. If this breakdown results from persistent breaches of the partnership agreement or conduct in relation to the business (although not conduct in relation to other matters), then the court can order dissolution. Many of the cases under this paragraph have revolved around financial irregularities (such as failure to account for money received on behalf of the partnership or payment of private debts from partnership money).

4.2.3 Section 35(f): just and equitable dissolution

Section 35(f) provides that a partner may apply to the court for dissolution 'whenever in any case circumstances have arisen which in the opinion of the court render it just and equitable that the partnership be dissolved'. This provision is the equivalent of s. 122(1)(g) Insolvency Act 1986, which is in essentially similar terms but applies only to companies. The cases decided under s. 122(1)(g) (and its predecessors) are relevant also to s. 35(f), especially where the company which was the subject of the petition was intended to be run as if it were a partnership. Deadlock or other irreconcilable differences between partners are the most likely grounds on which a successful petition could be based. Exclusion of a partner from management (contrary to s. 24(5)) would also be grounds for petition, although this case would also probably be covered by s. 35(d).

4.3 Appointment of a receiver

The court has power to appoint a receiver to run the business of a partnership for the protection of the partners. The receiver's duty is to carry on the business of the partnership for the benefit of the partners generally, not to realise a security, so that his position is quite different from that of a company receiver appointed by a debenture-holder. There is comparatively little authority as to when a receiver will be appointed, but it does seem to be an exceptional step and the court is particularly reluctant to make an appointment in the case of a professional partnership (*Floydd v Cheney* [1970] 2 WLR 314).

4.4 Arbitration

Disputes may be solved by arbitration if the partners agree to this. It is common to make provision for arbitration in the partnership agreement. As in other types of contract an arbitration clause cannot effectively oust the jurisdiction of the court altogether. A clause drawn widely in an attempt to oust the jurisdiction of the court entirely will be held to be void. If an action is commenced despite the presence of an arbitration clause the court has a discretion to stay the proceedings to enable the arbitration to take place.

The court action can continue without there being any question of a stay when, as a matter of construction, the court decides that the dispute which has arisen is not covered by the arbitration clause in the partnership agreement. The clause should expressly state that disputes arising during dissolution may be referred to arbitration and that the clause is binding on assignees of partners.

4.5 Expulsion of a partner

4.5.1 Introduction

We have seen in this chapter that it is possible for a partnership to be dissolved by the court as a way of giving the plaintiff partner a remedy against his co-partners. However, the circumstances of the dispute within the partnership may be such that some partners would prefer to get rid of one or more of their co-partners without fully dissolving the partnership.

4.5.2 Requirement for provision in partnership agreement

This is only possible if an appropriate provision is included in the partnership agreement, as s. 25 PA 1890 provides that 'No majority of the partners can expel any partner unless a power to do so has been confirmed by express agreement between the partners'. The question as to whether expulsion should be provided for, and if so by what majority, is one of the issues which must be considered when a partnership agreement is being drafted (see **Chapter 6**).

4.5.3 Content of expulsion clause

Where an expulsion clause is included in the agreement it will normally state that specific activities (such as fraud) or breaches of certain terms of the partnership agreement (such as that requiring a partner not to compete with the partnership or to devote the whole of his time to the business) will justify expulsion. Bankruptcy of a partner is a ground for the automatic dissolution of the whole partnership (s. 33(2) PA 1890), but in order to avoid the consequences of dissolution it is common for the partnership agreement to provide that a bankruptcy will not cause dissolution, rather that it will justify expulsion.

An expulsion clause will generally deal with the manner in which the expulsion is to be effected. It is normal to provide that written notice must be given to the offending partner and that it is to have immediate effect. The partnership agreement will normally distinguish expulsion and retirement in respect of financial arrangements.

Thus, if annuities are to be paid the agreement would normally provide that an expelled partner should forfeit his rights.

4.5.4 Exercise of expulsion clause

If an expulsion clause is included in the partnership agreement, then the power must be exercised strictly in accordance with the agreement and in a bona fide manner and for the benefit of the partnership as a whole (*Blisset v Daniel* (1853) 10 Hare 493).

 online resource centre   Interactive online exercises (Student Learning Activities) which complement the topics covered in this chapter are available at www.oxfordtextbooks.co.uk/orc/ business09_10/.

Termination of and retirement from a partnership

This chapter covers the following topics:

5.1 Introduction

An individual may cease to be a partner on the happening of one of the following events:

(a) the dissolution of the partnership;

(b) his retirement; or

(c) expulsion from the partnership.

If the partnership is dissolved, the *partnership* will come to an end and its assets and business dealt with accordingly. The situation is different on the retirement or expulsion of a partner. Here, the former partners can carry on the *business*, albeit through the medium of a newly constituted partnership.

In this chapter, we will consider the legal consequences of the occurrence of these events.

The taxation consequences of the events covered in this chapter will be considered in **Chapter 18.**

5.2 Dissolution of partnership

If an event occurs which causes a partnership to be dissolved, the partnership relationship ceases and any partner may demand that the assets of the business are realised. Under the Partnership Act 1890 certain events result in automatic dissolution unless the partnership agreement provides otherwise. Dissolution is such an extreme step that it is common for partners to provide expressly in their partnership agreement that dissolution is *not* to occur automatically on the occurrence of the events specified in the Partnership Act.

5.2.1 The methods of dissolving a partnership

5.2.1.1 Dissolution by notice

Under ss. 26 and 32(c) PA 1890, one or more partners can, at any time, give notice to their fellow partners to dissolve the partnership. This notice takes effect from the date specified in the notice but if the notice is silent on the point, it takes effect from the date when all partners received the notice. Dissolution under ss. 26 and 32(c) can result in an immediate dissolution of the partnership. This could have disastrous consequences for the business.

However, ss. 26 and 32(c) can be overridden if the partnership agreement contains provisions to the contrary. As a result many partnership agreements require a minimum period of notice to be given before the partnership is dissolved.

5.2.1.2 Dissolution by agreement

The partnership agreement can specify circumstances which cause the partnership to be dissolved, such as the occurrence of a particular event. The agreement can also specify the manner in which the partnership will be dissolved.

5.2.1.3 Automatic dissolution

A number of events cause partnerships to dissolve automatically:

(a) *Bankruptcy, death or charge*

The death or bankruptcy of a partner causes the partnership to be automatically dissolved, unless the partnership agreement contains provisions to the contrary (s. 33(1) PA 1890). Since dissolution is a serious matter for the other partners, many partnership agreements provide that, instead of causing automatic dissolution, the death of a partner shall give rise to the same consequences as a retirement (see **5.3**). A bankruptcy is often treated in the same way as an expulsion (see **4.5**). If a partner allows his share of the partnership property to be charged for his personal debts, the other partners have an *option* to dissolve the partnership (s. 33(2) PA 1890).

(b) *Illegality*

Partnerships formed to carry out an illegal activity or which are contrary to public policy are automatically dissolved. A change of circumstances (including a change in the law) can subsequently make illegal a partnership initially formed for a legal purpose. In these circumstances, s. 34 PA 1890 provides that the partnership is dissolved on the happening of the event which makes the business unlawful (for example, the date the change in the law takes effect). A provision to the contrary in the partnership agreement will not override s. 34.

(c) *By expiration*

Under s. 32(a) and (b) PA 1890, a partnership is dissolved:

(i) if it was entered into for a fixed term, upon the expiration of that term;

(ii) if it was entered into for a single adventure or undertaking, upon the completion of that adventure or undertaking.

A provision to the contrary in the partnership agreement overrides s. 32(a) and (b).

If the agreement is silent and the partnership continues despite the occurrence of the events set out above, s. 27 provides that a partnership at will, dissolvable by notice, is brought into existence. Such a partnership is subject to the terms of the original agreement to the extent that these do not conflict with the incidents of a partnership at will.

5.2.1.4   Dissolution by the court

Finally, a partner may apply to the court for dissolution of the partnership provided one of the statutory grounds for dissolution by the court exists. This is only really an option when an easier method of dissolution is not available, either under the Partnership Act or under any partnership agreement.

Under s. 96 of the Mental Health Act (MHA) 1983, the court has power, if satisfied after considering medical evidence that a partner is a mental 'patient', to dissolve or give directions for the dissolution of any partnership of which a 'patient' is a member. A 'patient' is a person incapable, by reason of mental disorder, of managing his own property and affairs.

In addition to s. 96 MHA 1983, s. 35 PA 1890 sets out grounds for dissolution by the court. Those grounds which give the partners a remedy in the event of a dispute (that is to say, s. 35(c), (d) and (f)) have been considered in **4.2**. The full list of s. 35 grounds is as follows:

Section 35(a)
Repealed by the predecessor to the Mental Health Act 1983.

Section 35(b)
When a partner, other than the partner suing, becomes permanently incapable of performing his part of the partnership contract.

Whether or not a partner has become *permanently* incapable is a question of fact. Since there may be difficulties in proving either that the partner is incapable or that his incapacity is permanent, and since there will be difficulties in running a partnership where a partner has a long illness, it is common to include a term in the partnership agreement allowing expulsion or insisting on retirement once a partner has been absent through illness for more than a specified time.

Section 35(c)
When a partner, other than the partner suing, has been guilty of such conduct as, in the opinion of the court, regard being had to the nature of the business, is calculated to affect prejudicially the carrying on of the business (see **4.2**).

Section 35(d)
When a partner, other than the partner suing, wilfully or persistently commits a breach of the partnership agreement, or otherwise so conducts himself in matters relating to the partnership business that it is not reasonably practicable for the other partner or partners to carry on the business in partnership with him (see **4.2**).

Section 35(e)
When the business of the partnership can only be carried on at a loss.

This is arguably one of the most important grounds for dissolution. In order for s. 35(e) to be invoked, the circumstances must be such as to make it a practical impossibility for the partnership to make a profit. If the partners who find themselves in this position cannot agree to bring the partnership to an end, this may be a valuable right if a delay in terminating the partnership will increase the amount of the loss, for which all the partners will be personally liable. It is important to note that a partnership is not necessarily insolvent simply because it is making a loss. It may well have valuable assets which, when sold, will discharge all liabilities and provide a surplus for the partners.

Section 35(f)
Whenever, in the opinion of the court, it is just and equitable that the partnership be dissolved (see **4.2**).

5.2.2   The legal consequences of dissolution

5.2.2.1   Continuing authority of partners for purposes of winding up (s. 38 PA 1890)

The occurrence of one of the events set out in **5.2.1** will cause the partnership to be dissolved but there may be various steps which need to be taken to wind up the affairs of the firm. Section 38 provides that, after the dissolution, the authority of each partner to bind the firm (as well as the other rights and obligations of the partners) continues despite the dissolution but only to the extent necessary to wind up the affairs of the partnership, and to complete transactions begun but unfinished at the time of the dissolution. However, where the dissolution is by order of the court, this authority can be terminated by the appointment of a receiver (who will simply wind up the business) or of a receiver and manager (who will continue running the business but only with a view to the beneficial realisation of the assets by means of, for example, a sale of the business as a going concern). Such appointments are likely to be made where there is a likelihood of dispute if the former partners try to wind up the affairs of the partnership.

5.2.2.2   Realisation of partnership property on dissolution

Once the firm has been dissolved, the value of the assets owned by the partnership will be ascertained, as will the extent of the debts and liabilities owed to creditors. In so far as it is necessary, the assets will be sold to raise the funds to discharge the debts. The partners may merely sell the assets used in the business or they may decide to sell the business as a going concern. If the partners decide to adopt the latter course of action, they may be able to sell the business for more than the aggregate market value of the assets used in the business because the sale price may take into account the 'goodwill' attaching to the business. (It should be borne in mind that the purchasers in this instance may well be some of the partners from the dissolved firm who wish to continue the business under a new guise.)

Goodwill has been defined as 'the whole advantage, whatever it may be, of the reputation and connection of the firm' (*Trego v Hunt* [1896] AC 7). This 'advantage' can arise as a result of various factors. If the partners have considerable expertise in their chosen field, their customers may return repeatedly. This 'goodwill' may, however, be largely personal to the partners with the result that it would disappear if they ceased their involvement in the business. Conversely, if the firm is situated in a prime location (such as the main shopping street in the town), the business may be very successful because of the convenience of access for its customers. In this latter case, the goodwill may attach to the premises rather than the partners, and so may be a very valuable asset of the partnership since it can be passed on to successors.

If the firm has saleable goodwill, a value will be attached to it. The valuation of goodwill is somewhat speculative and any formula for determining its value is inevitably rather artificial. A common formula is to ascertain the net profits of the business for a particular year and then for the parties to agree to multiply the period's profits by an agreed number, often two or three.

Where goodwill is sold, the purchasers will want to protect their investment against the loss of custom arising from the former owners setting up in competition in the same vicinity. Accordingly, the purchaser may wish to include a restrictive covenant in the sale agreement to guard against this possibility. If the purchasers are some of the partners of the dissolved partnership, they too should consider including restrictive covenants to protect their interests.

5.2.2.3 Application of the partnership property on dissolution (ss. 39 and 44 PA 1890)

Once the assets and liabilities have been ascertained, s. 39 entitles each partner to have the property of the partnership applied so that the debts and liabilities of the firm are discharged first. Once these liabilities have been met, any surplus is distributed to the partners (after deducting any sums for which each partner is liable to contribute to the firm, such as contributions to make up losses or deficiencies of capital). In order to ensure that the assets of the partnership are not distributed to the partners personally before the outside creditors are paid off, s. 39 goes on to give each partner the right to apply to the court to wind up the business and affairs of the firm in such a way as to ensure that the s. 39 order for application of assets is observed.

Section 44 provides that once the creditors of the firm have been paid, subject to any contrary agreement, the assets of the firm shall be applied in the following order:

(a) in repaying advances received from partners;

(b) in repaying the amounts shown as standing to the credit of each partner on his capital account; and

(c) any balance being divided between the partners in accordance with the profit–sharing ratio.

If the partnership has made losses (including losses or deficiencies of capital), these shall be met in the following order:

(a) from profits;

(b) from capital;

(c) from contributions made by the partners in the proportion in which profits are divisible.

Both parts of s. 44 are subject to contrary agreement. In particular the partners may agree to share surplus assets and to contribute to capital losses in a ratio different from the normal profit sharing.

5.2.2.4 Notification of the dissolution

Section 38 gives partners continued authority to bind the firm after dissolution for the purpose of winding up the business (see **5.2.2.1**). If a partner exceeds this authority, under s. 36(1) PA 1890 outsiders dealing with the firm after a change in the constitution are entitled to treat all apparent members of the firm as still being members until the outsider has notice of the change (see **5.3.3.3**).

In order to protect themselves from liability for unauthorised debts incurred after the dissolution, the partners in the dissolved firm are entitled publicly to notify the fact of the dissolution (s. 37 PA 1890). To obtain protection from liability on unauthorised debts incurred with *existing* customers, the former partners should give notice personally to the customer.

Notice in the *London Gazette* is sufficient to gain protection from liability on debts with *new* customers (this point is considered in more detail in relation to retirement in **5.3.3.3**).

5.2.3   Problems on dissolution

5.2.3.1   Introduction

When the value of the partnership business is insufficient to pay back all monies owing, problems can arise on a dissolution. Such a shortfall can result in two main outcomes: either the outside creditors can be paid off but there is insufficient cash to pay back partners' capital contributions; or there is not even enough to pay back outside liabilities. Each of these will be looked at in turn.

5.2.3.2   Insufficient to pay back partners' capital

This is best explained by reference to a number of examples.

EXAMPLE 1

A, B and C are in partnership sharing profits equally, each having contributed £50,000 to the partnership. If only £90,000 remains (after paying off creditors), then there is a shortfall (loss) of £60,000, which according to s. 44(a) should be borne equally.

Technically, each partner should pay into the business £20,000 so that each can draw out his £50,000 in full. It is plainly impractical to do this, however, and each partner would simply draw out £30,000.

EXAMPLE 2

Instead suppose that A, B and C are in partnership sharing profits equally, each having contributed £50,000, £40,000 and £10,000 respectively to the partnership. If only £40,000 remains to satisfy partners' contributions, then there is a shortfall (loss) of £60,000, which again should be borne equally. Here it is more crucial that each partner contribute to the loss because of their initial unequal contributions. Note, in particular, that C will have to pay in £20,000 to receive £10,000 back. In reality, however, A and B will pay nothing and C will contribute £10,000. (This figure is reached by setting off C's capital entitlement against the £20,000 contribution.) The resulting £50,000 will then be divided between A and B to give them £30,000 and £20,000 respectively, which amounts to their initial capital contributions less £20,000.

EXAMPLE 3

Suppose in example 2 that C could not, in fact, contribute any further money. According to *Garner v Murray* [1904] 1 Ch 57, A and B would not have to make good this deficiency but simply pay in £20,000 each in the usual way. The resulting £80,000 would then be distributed between A and B according to their ratio of contribution, i.e., 5:4. A would receive £44,444.45 ($\frac{5}{9} \times$ £80,000) and B £35,555.55 ($\frac{4}{9} \times$ £80,000).

It will be noted that there is a curious disparity between examples 2 and 3 in that in example 2, because he can contribute, C is worse off than in example 3. Because of this, it is crucial when advising potential partners in a business to consider whether or not they wish to avoid the effect of s. 44 and agree that the partner who contributes the most should bear the most loss.

5.2.3.3 Insufficiency to meet liability to creditors

In **5.2.3.2** it has been assumed that creditors' and partners' loans have been fully satisfied. If the assets of a partnership prove insufficient to meet these liabilities first, the situation is much the same; any deficiency must be made up by partners according to their profit-sharing ratios (subject to any contrary agreement). Again the problem comes when a partner is unable to contribute. Here the situation is more pressing because the overriding effect of s. 9 means that outside creditors are not concerned with the niceties of s. 44 and the partners who can pay must pay to satisfy these liabilities. If this is not done, then the outside creditors will look to enforce their entitlements by legal means.

The inability of partners to pay off their creditors is a topic in itself—such partners will face potential bankruptcy (see **Chapter 25**). However, since the Insolvent Partnerships Order 1994 (amending the previous Order of 1986), it is possible for creditors to apply to have a partnership wound up as if it were an unregistered company. This procedure is essentially the same as for a registered company. However, for the most part, such an application is unlikely to be of use to a creditor unless it is in conjunction with bankruptcy petitions against the partners in question (see **26.10**).

5.3 Retirement of a partner

5.3.1 Circumstances when 'retirement' occurs

The term 'retirement' is most frequently applied to mean a person retiring from full-time work having reached the statutory age of retirement. However, in the partnership context 'retirement' simply means leaving the partnership voluntarily irrespective of the age of the partner in question.

5.3.2 Retirement under the Partnership Act 1890

Partnership agreements can, and should, contain provisions dealing with retirement by partners. This is because the Partnership Act 1890 does not specifically deal with retirement. Under the 1890 Act, the only option available to a partner is to give notice under s. 26. If a s. 26 notice is given the partnership will be *dissolved* (see **5.2.1.1**); the section does not permit a partner to retire leaving the partnership otherwise unaffected. To avoid this, suitable provisions must be included in the agreement. One common form of wording provides that the partner wishing to retire should give written notice of a specified length (say, six months or one year). On expiry of the notice period, the retiring partner will leave and may be entitled to some financial settlement from his former partners but otherwise the partnership continues unaffected.

Partnership agreements frequently provide that a deceased person is to be treated as having retired. Additional problems relating specifically to death are considered in **5.4**.

5.3.3 The legal consequences of retirement

5.3.3.1 Debts incurred before retirement

The mere fact that a partner retires does not release him from his obligations in respect of debts incurred while he was a partner. Section 17(2) PA 1890 provides that 'a partner who retires from a firm does not thereby cease to be liable for partnership debts or obligations incurred before his retirement'.

To avoid the problems of having to meet such debts after retirement, the retiring partner should, if possible, ensure that the debts are paid before he leaves. Since this may be difficult in many cases, the partner will be concerned to gain protection in other ways. In some cases it may be agreed that he will be indemnified by his former partners or that he will be released from his obligations by the creditor.

5.3.3.2   Debts incurred after retirement

The general rule is that only partners are liable for debts incurred by the partnership and so ceasing to be a partner prevents the *former* partner becoming liable on future debts as the retirement terminates the agency relationship. However, this general rule is subject to ss. 36 and 14 PA 1890. Under these sections a former partner becomes liable for debts incurred *after* he has left the partnership in certain circumstances.

5.3.3.3   Section 36

Section 36(3) provides that the estate of a partner ' . . . who, *not having been known to the person dealing with the firm to be a partner*, retires is not liable for partnership debts contracted after the date of the . . . retirement'.

The date at which knowledge is tested for the purposes of this subsection is the date of retirement. If a creditor does not know at that date of the retiring partner's connection with the firm, the former partner will not be liable; the fact that the creditor may subsequently discover the former membership cannot make the former partner liable.

The subsection was considered in *Tower Cabinet Co. Ltd v Ingram* [1949] 2 KB 397. A and B were in partnership. A retired and B continued the business under the old name. After A's retirement, the business ordered goods from a new supplier and failed to pay. The supplier sought to enforce judgment against A. The only knowledge the supplier had of A's connection with the firm was that A's name appeared on headed notepaper which, contrary to A's express instructions, had not been destroyed. The court found that, as the customer had no knowledge prior to A's retirement that A was a partner in the firm, A was completely protected by s. 36(3). (A further question arose of A's possible liability under s. 14(1)—see below.)

In cases where creditors know of the partner's connection with the firm before the former partner retires, s. 36(3) is of no assistance. Section 36(1) provides that 'where a person deals with a firm after a change in its constitution, he is entitled to treat all apparent members of the old firm as still being members of the firm until he has notice of the change'. It is necessary to consider what constitutes 'notice' for this purpose; and what makes a former partner an 'apparent' member of the continuing firm.

(a) *Notice*

Section 36(2) provides that in respect of persons who had no dealings with the firm before the date of the dissolution or change a notice in the *London Gazette* (where the firm has its principal place of business in England and Wales) will be sufficient notice.

Thus, to protect himself from liability to new customers who knew of his connection with the firm a retiring partner should ensure that a notice is published in the *London Gazette*.

Notice in the *London Gazette* will not be sufficient to relieve the former partner from liability in respect of customers who did have dealings with the firm prior to the dissolution or change. If the retiring partner wishes to be absolutely protected from liability for future debts he should give the customers formal notification.

(b) *Apparent membership*

Where persons dealing with the firm know that a person was a partner, that partner will be liable for new debts so long as he is an apparent member of the firm (and until he gives notice). Persons may be 'apparent members' either because a customer has had dealings with them before or because their names appear on the notepaper or on a sign on the door or because the customer has some indirect information about their being partners.

A retiring partner should ensure that his apparent membership of the firm is terminated. He should give actual notice to existing customers and should publish a notice in the *Gazette* to cover the situation where people have not had dealings with the firm but are aware of the partner's connection with the firm.

5.3.3.4 Section 14

Liability for subsequent debts may also arise under s. 14 PA 1890. It will be recalled from **3.4** that s. 14(1) provides that:

Every one who by words spoken or written or by conduct represents himself, or who knowingly suffers himself to be represented, as a partner in a particular firm, is liable as a partner to any one who has on the faith of any such representation given credit to the firm, whether the representation has or has not been made or communicated to the person so giving credit by or with the knowledge of the apparent partner making the representation or suffering it to be made.

Therefore, even if no liability arises under s. 36, the former partner may be liable to any person (whether they had previous dealings with the firm or not) who has given 'credit' to the firm on the faith of a representation that he is still a partner which is made by the former partner or which he has 'knowingly' allowed to be made.

The word 'apparent' in s. 14(1) has the same meaning as in s. 36(1) so that the decision in the *Tower Cabinet* case (see above) is equally relevant in these circumstances. In the case, it was alleged that the former partner had allowed himself to be held out as a partner. However, since the former partner had not authorised the use of the old notepaper, he had not 'knowingly' allowed himself to be held out as an 'apparent' partner and so no liability under s. 14 arose.

A retiring partner should ensure that his name is removed from any signs and that any notepaper is destroyed in order to prevent an accusation that he knowingly allowed himself to be represented as a partner.

5.3.3.5 Compliance with Business Names Act 1985

After the change in the partnership, the notepaper will normally be changed and care should be taken to ensure that it complies with the requirements of the Business Names Act 1985 (which were considered in **1.8**).

5.3.3.6 Dealing with the finances

Once the partner has retired from the firm, the arrangements for severing, or changing the basis of, the financial connection with the firm will be of considerable importance. These matters are generally covered by the partnership agreement and usually relate to the provision for the partner (and for his dependants) of some form of pension (whether paid by the former partners, under an approved annuity contract, or under a consultancy arrangement). In addition, the arrangements will deal with the former partner's entitlement (if any) to payment for his share in the partnership assets (which may include goodwill).

If there is no agreement, the former partner has a right to receive the net value of his share in the partnership property from his former partners.

5.4 Death

5.4.1 Introduction

As we saw in **5.2.1.3** above, death causes the automatic dissolution of a partnership. In order to avoid inconvenience to the surviving partners it is common to provide in the partnership agreement that instead of causing an automatic dissolution of the partnership, a deceased partner shall be treated as if he had retired.

5.4.2 Right of estate to share in profits and obtain amounts due

Subject to contrary agreement, s. 42(1) PA 1890 provides for the situation where any member of a firm has died (or otherwise ceased to be a partner) and the surviving (or continuing) partners carry on the business of the firm without any final settlement of accounts as between the firm and the outgoing partner or his estate. The outgoing partner or his estate is entitled at the option of himself or his personal representatives to claim:

(a) such share of the profits made since the dissolution as the court may find to be attributable to the use of his share of the partnership assets; or

(b) interest at the rate of 5% p.a. on the amount of his share of the partnership assets.

Any amount due from the surviving partners to the deceased partner's personal representatives in respect of his share is a debt accruing at the date of the death (s. 43).

5.4.3 Treatment in the partnership agreement

Raising a large capital sum to pay to the estate of a deceased partner may strain the resources of a partnership which is continuing after the death of a partner. This issue is normally dealt with by the partners in the partnership agreement as follows:

(a) by taking out insurance cover;

(b) by providing that on death (and/or retirement) capital sums due should be paid by yearly instalments over a specified period—interest being payable on the amount outstanding;

(c) by providing for a method of calculating the amount due;

(d) by providing that the deceased (or retiring) partner is to be entitled to a fixed amount in lieu of a share of profits. This avoids the need to apportion profits to the date of death (or retirement).

5.4.4 Liability for debts

Every partner is jointly liable for debts and obligations of the firm incurred while he is a partner. In addition, s. 9 PA 1890 provides that the estate of a deceased person is severally liable for such debts and obligations so far as they remain unsatisfied *but* subject to the prior payment of the deceased partner's personal debts. A partnership creditor can, therefore, proceed against the estate of a deceased partner in respect of partnership debts (even after obtaining a judgment against the other partners) provided some part of the debt is unsatisfied. However, partnership creditors are postponed to the deceased partner's own creditors.

So far as subsequent debts are concerned, s. 36(3) PA 1890 provides that the deceased partner's estate is not liable for partnership debts contracted after the death. However, if the deceased partner's personal representatives take part in the management of the business they make themselves liable for debts incurred from the time their participation commences.

online resource centre

Interactive online exercises (Student Learning Activities) which complement the topics covered in this chapter are available at www.oxfordtextbooks.co.uk/orc/ business09_10/.

The partnership agreement

This chapter covers the following topics:

6.1 Introduction

In this chapter we will look at the provisions which should be considered for inclusion in a partnership agreement. Much of the contents of a partnership agreement will address issues raised by the provisions of the Partnership Act 1890 which we considered in **Chapters 1** to **5**, or which may be relevant to the tax provisions applicable to partnership which will be considered in **Chapters 17, 18** and **23**. Those detailed provisions should be borne in mind when reading this chapter.

Before we look at the possible contents of a partnership agreement, we will consider whether a formal, written agreement is necessary at all, and at the end of the chapter we have included a section dealing with the points which a prospective new partner might wish to consider before putting his signature to a partnership agreement.

6.2 Is a written partnership agreement necessary?

A written agreement is not required for the formation of a partnership. This contrasts with the position of a company where the memorandum and articles, which have contractual effect under s. 14 CA 1985, must not only be in writing but must also be registered with the Registrar of Companies.

In practice, many partnerships decide that the agreement between the partners, as to how the business is to be regulated, should be in the form of a written agreement. Such an agreement is often called a partnership agreement, a partnership deed or articles of partnership.

The draftsman of a partnership agreement should bear in mind that many provisions of the Partnership Act 1890 apply to regulate the relationship of the partners except to the extent that there is contrary agreement. However well intentioned and however well drafted such legislation is, it is unlikely that it will entirely coincide with the wishes of a particular group of businessmen setting up a partnership.

The draftsman's task in drafting a partnership agreement is more onerous than his task in drafting articles of association for a company. In the case of a company a 'model' set of articles (Table A) is provided, which will suit the needs of most companies with comparatively minor alterations. The provisions of the Partnership Act are both more out of date and less comprehensive than those of Table A. The nature of a partnership agreement must, of course, depend upon the circumstances but we have set out in the next paragraph the most important matters which need to be considered.

6.3   The clauses of the partnership agreement

6.3.1   The parties

The parties to the agreement will be the partners, old and new.

6.3.2   The commencement date and term of the partnership

While most partnerships will be partnerships 'at will' (and so can last indefinitely subject to notice to dissolve the partnership being given), it is possible to specify the length of the partnership's 'life'. Although the date the partnership agreement was entered into can determine the commencement of the partnership (which could be a newly constituted partnership following the retirement or admission of partners), partnership agreements often include a term stating the date on which the partnership commenced.

6.3.3   The nature of the partnership's business

The *ultra vires* rule does not apply to a partnership. The business should, however, be specified so that a partner who objects to what is being done by way of new types of business can insist on the agreement being followed. Unless the partnership agreement provides to the contrary, the clause specifying what business is to be carried on can only be altered with the unanimous agreement of the partners (s. 24(8) PA 1890). This clause may also specify where the partnership is to carry on business.

6.3.4   The partnership name

The business name of the partnership should be specified. The requirements as to approval for and publicity of business names were dealt with in **1.7**.

6.3.5   The income of the partnership

If the partnership agreement is silent on the point, the partners will share the income (and liabilities) of the partnership equally. Even if this is in accord with the partners' wishes, it is best to state specifically the way in which the partnership's profits will be shared. However, in many partnerships, this simple position is not what the partners require. The share of profits between the partners may be unequal to reflect differing levels of contributions of capital, or differing levels of involvement in the partnership's business. Some partnerships may choose to build a mechanism into their partnership agreements for regular reviews of the profit–sharing ratios to take into account the relative achievements of the partners. Other partnerships adopt a 'lock step' arrangement by which a partner's share of the profits may increase by a fixed amount annually over a period of years. If the partners have agreed among themselves that some or all of them should receive 'interest' on capital or 'salary' (see **17.5**), these arrangements should be set out in the partnership agreement. However, care should be taken to ensure if a 'salary' is paid to the partner that the Revenue cannot argue that the recipient was, in reality, an employee rather than a full equity partner (if the latter is what the partners were trying to achieve).

6.3.6 The capital of the partnership

A clause (or group of clauses) should be included dealing with the financial relationships between the partners. This should state what investment each partner is to make in the business, how each partner will satisfy his obligation to contribute capital (for example, whether in cash or assets) and over what period (if the capital contribution is not to be made in full on admission to the partnership). Although it may be difficult to specify the circumstances, it is worth giving thought to the circumstances in which further capital might have to be introduced. The reverse of these provisions is what should happen to the capital when the partnership is dissolved or a partner retires. What are the arrangements for a partner to withdraw capital and how is the goodwill of the business to be dealt with when a partner leaves?

6.3.7 The property of the partnership

The partnership agreement should include provisions specifying which property is to be regarded as partnership property and which is to remain the property of individual partners.

6.3.8 The management of the partnership

Small partnerships of two or three people will usually be run by the partners (perhaps in conjunction with a small number of employees) and each partner will have an equal say in management. In a large partnership (especially a professional partnership where there may be dozens of partners), a more complex management structure may be considered desirable and the structure should be specified. In the absence of contrary agreement all partners have an equal say in management. Among the more mundane, but very vital, matters which should be considered under this heading are questions such as where will the partnership maintain its bank account, who should be entitled to sign cheques for the partnership, who will allocate work to the employees, what authority is each partner to have in relation to buying stock, paying bills and so on? In most cases, the clause dealing with management of the partnership should be stated in general terms. It is better, for example, to say that junior partners are to have such functions as are assigned to them by the managing or senior partners than to list in minute detail what they are to be authorised to do.

6.3.9 The effect of prolonged absence

It is now common to find included in partnership agreement clauses dealing with the consequences for a partner who is absent from the business for a prolonged period. This may be through illness, maternity leave or compassionate leave. The nature of the provisions will be determined by the necessity for the partners to balance the needs of the business with supporting their fellow partner. However, these provisions often mirror corresponding provisions found in employment contracts (so that a partner may be permitted to be away from the partnership's business for six months due to illness before he can be expelled, or the partnership agreement may provide maternity leave provisions similar to the statutory provisions which employees enjoy).

6.3.10   Restrictions

Terms may be included dealing with the partners' obligations to the firm. It is quite common, for example, to provide that the partners are to give their whole time to the business of the firm or to provide that they are only to take up other businesses with the approval of their partners. Consideration should also be given to the inclusion of a clause preventing competition with the firm during the lifetime of the partnership (even if the partners are not full time), although such competition would in any case normally be a breach of the partners' duty of good faith. Similarly, it is often desirable to include a restrictive covenant to prevent competition with the firm by a partner after he has left the firm. Such a term must be reasonable otherwise it may be declared void as being a term in unreasonable restraint of trade. The partners may also decide to place specific restrictions on the activities of particular partners in relation to the running of the business. For example, a partnership agreement could prevent an individual partner from charging or selling any of the partnership's assets.

6.3.11   Partnership disputes

It is sensible to anticipate that problems may arise within the partnership and so provide for how disputes should be resolved. Commonly, clauses dealing with disputes require the partners to refer the dispute (whatever subject matter of the dispute may be) to an independent arbitrator. This approach may lead to the resolution of the dispute and thus avoid the dissolution of the partnership.

6.3.12   Dissolution, death, retirement and admission of partners

It is sensible to set out the circumstances in which the partnership will be dissolved or in which a partner can be expelled from the partnership. If the partnership comes to an end, tax liabilities can arise (see **Chapter 23**) and the partnership agreement should include a provision as to whether the firm should set aside a proportion of each partner's profit share to provide a fund to discharge any tax liability which might arise. Any outgoing partner, if he is retiring, will be concerned to secure an income during his retirement. While the partner can create a fund from which a pension can be paid during his years as a partner, many partnerships provide annuity or consultancy arrangements for former partners. The terms of such arrangements should be set out in the partnership agreement. Secondly, since the election for assessment on the continuing basis can mean that an incoming partner can be taxed on a share of profits in excess of the amount he actually receives, it is also common for the incoming partner to be indemnified by the existing partners for any extra tax he suffers as a result. The agreement should specify how new partners are to be admitted to the partnership. In the absence of agreement to the contrary, new partners may only be admitted with the unanimous consent of the existing partners (s. 24(7) PA 1890).

6.4 Issues for an incoming partner

We have seen the legal consequences of admission to a partnership in **Chapter 3** and the tax consequences of admission will be considered in **Chapter 23**. However, before accepting the offer of a partnership, a prospective partner needs to consider whether the partnership's business, management and finances are such as to justify the risk of taking on unlimited liability with his future fellow partners.

The partnership agreement will be a useful source of information about the way the partnership's affairs are handled but the agreement will be, by no means, the only document the prospective partner will want to examine. Other documents will include previous years' signed accounts, as well as previous years' budgets and management accounts (which will show whether the business has suffered an unexpected shortfall in income or cost overruns which will need to be explained). The prospective partner should try to anticipate any future financial problems the partnership may face by investigating whether there are any contingent liabilities, whether the firm's insurance cover is adequate, and what steps the firm is taking to make provision for bad debts. Perhaps the most significant protection against problems in the future would be if the firm has a carefully thought out, effective business strategy and the prospective partner will need to satisfy himself that he considers the strategy to be appropriate given the firm's position in its particular market place.

online resource centre
Interactive online exercises (Student Learning Activities) which complement the topics covered in this chapter are available at www.oxfordtextbooks.co.uk/orc/ business09_10/.

Companies

Limited companies

This chapter covers the following topics:

7.1 Introduction

In this chapter we shall begin to look at the legal position of limited companies. Many businesses are run by limited companies. These range from international conglomerates to companies owned by one person running a small business. Before turning to the detailed legal rules about companies, we need to see how they fit into the complex pattern of institutions which the law has created. We shall also introduce the distinction between private and public companies. Further information about public companies will be found in **Chapter 16**.

7.2 Corporations

A 'company' is in law a corporation, that is, an artificial legal 'person' with rights and obligations distinct from those of its members. Business associations were occasionally made corporations by Royal Charter from about the Sixteenth Century (for example, the East India Company in 1600), but until the Industrial Revolution few businesses were incorporated. With the growth of the canal and railway systems, incorporations were permitted in increasing numbers under Acts of Parliament. Eventually the concept of the company as a medium for any business came into being with the introduction of the Companies Act 1862. Since then, numerous Companies Acts have been introduced during the Nineteenth and Twentieth Centuries. The vast majority of corporations currently in existence are companies formed under the Companies Act 1985. With the advent of the new Companies Act 2006, which supersedes the 1985 Act, companies will be formed under the provisions of that Act. (The new regime for company formation introduced by the 2006 Act will be effective from 1 October 2009.)

7.3 Sources of company law

7.3.1 Company legislation

Until recently, the Companies Act 1985 was the most important source of company law. It consolidated legislation contained in earlier Companies Acts and other pieces of legislation dealing with company law. The 1985 Act had been amended in significant respects by the Insolvency Act 1986, the Companies Act 1989 and a number of statutory instruments made under the Act.

The 1985 Act applied throughout Great Britain although a number of provisions applied only to Scotland or only to England and Wales. Northern Ireland has its own legislation which is substantially the same as the British legislation.

In recent years, proposals came to the fore to reform company law. This was instigated by the Company Law Review, the result of which was a report presented to the Secretary of State in July 2001. A year later, in response to this, the Government published an initial White Paper, 'Modernising Company Law'. In March 2005, a second White Paper was published, 'Company Law Reform' which led to the Companies Bill being published in November 2005. Finally, this Bill became law when the Companies Act 2006 received Royal Assent on 8 November 2006.

The key theme behind the 2006 Act is to reflect the reality of companies in operation today. Much of the previous system was predicated on the basis of large companies being the norm, whereas in fact the vast majority of companies are owner-managed with five or fewer persons involved. Therefore, one of the stated aims of the reform is to simplify the creation and operation of private companies, based around a 'think small first' approach.

The 2006 Act comes fully into force on 1 October 2009, although elements of the 2006 Act have already been introduced on a staggered basis, the main relevant commencement dates being 1 October 2007, 6 April 2008 and 1 October 2008.

Whilst the 2006 Act introduces many reforms, many of the basic concepts of company law remain unchanged and a sizeable percentage of the Companies Act 1985 has been restated within the 2006 Act. The new Act, therefore, both reforms and consolidates elements of company law.

Throughout this text, reference will be made to the 2006 Act only, unless specific reference to the 1985 Act is still thought appropriate.

7.3.2 Judicial decisions

Company law has been an amalgam of increasing statutory regulation and common law, the latter being particularly relevant to the obligations and duties of directors and the rights of minority shareholders. Judicial input has always been significant in assessing the impact of both these branches of company law. One impact of the 2006 Act is to reduce substantially the relevance of the common law, so the weight attached to previous common law decisions may ultimately diminish.

The introduction of any new legislation brings with it possible unanswered questions, so it is anticipated that the role of the courts over the new few years will be crucial in clarifying any doubts which exist in respect of the effect of the 2006 Act.

7.3.3   Tax legislation

The taxation of companies is largely dealt with in the Income and Corporation Taxes Act 1988 as amended by subsequent Finance Acts. Companies' capital gains are largely dealt with in accordance with the Taxation of Chargeable Gains Act 1992, as amended. Again, many decisions of the courts have interpreted the meaning of this legislation. The taxation of companies is examined in detail in **Chapter 19**.

7.3.4   The general law

It is worth pointing out that the general law applies to companies as it applies to individuals, except to the extent that it has been modified by specific rules of company law. The general law of contract, for example, applies to companies with very few modifications, as does the law of tort, competition, and so on. This is really just a consequence of the fact that a company is a corporation and, therefore, in law a 'person' with legal rights and obligations.

7.3.5   The company's own regulations: articles of association

Despite the vast amount of law which applies to companies, a great deal of freedom of choice is given to each individual company as to how it will be administered. This is both desirable and inevitable because of the widely differing circumstances in which each company operates. To provide for its own internal administration each company must have a set of regulations known as *articles of association*. These may be specially prepared for the company by the lawyer who assists with its formation; however, regulation has provided for a model form of articles (Table A) and most of the regulations currently adopted by companies tend to follow that model. The provisions of Table A are contained in a statutory instrument (SI 1985/805) which came into force with the 1985 Act.

With the new 2006 Act will come new Model Articles, which will become effective from 1 October 2009. Obviously for some time to come, the majority of companies in existence will have been formed under the 1985 Act regime, so Table A and variations thereof will still be common forms of articles. Additionally, as an interim measure, Table A itself was modified from 1 October 2007 to remove some inconsistencies with those elements of the 2006 Act then in force (notably those relating to shareholder decisions), so companies formed after that date which adopted Table A (in whole or in part) will be governed by the provisions of that version of Table A. (For further discussion of this area, see **Chapter 14**.)

7.4   Registration

Companies are formed (or incorporated) by a process called *registration*. Until the end of September 2009, the conditions for registration set out in the Companies Act 1985 are relevant. As at 1 October 2009, the conditions in the 2006 Act replace them. The two systems are different in points of detail, but both amount to a process of registration.

Registration involves sending a number of documents and a fee to the Registrar of Companies, the official responsible for registering companies in England and Wales. A company comes into existence on the issue of a *certificate of incorporation* by the Registrar.

The Registrar is also responsible for maintaining records relating to registered companies. These records contain information which companies are required by law to disclose in relation to a wide range of matters. Records are kept at Companies House, which for companies incorporated in England and Wales is in Cardiff. (For companies registered in Scotland, a separate Companies House is based in Edinburgh.) The reader will find the Companies House website a useful reference source—see www.companieshouse.gov.uk.

The process of registration is examined in more detail in **Chapter 8**.

7.5   Types of registered company

7.5.1   Companies limited by shares

Most registered companies are 'limited by shares'. This expression refers to the *liability* of the members (or shareholders—the terms are almost interchangeable) of the company for that company's debts on a liquidation. The effect of a company being limited by shares is that, on a liquidation, the liability of a member is limited to the amount, if any, which remains unpaid on his shares. This is described further below.

When a company issues shares, the person taking the shares must agree to pay the company for them. Usually payment will be made immediately but sometimes shares will be issued 'unpaid' (sometimes expressed as 'nil-paid') or 'partly-paid', in which case payment must be made later. If the company goes into liquidation and is insolvent, any member who has not fully paid for their shares is liable to pay the amount outstanding to the liquidator, who will apply such amount in paying the company's debts. That is the extent of that member's liability for the company's debts. In the case of a member who has paid in full for his shares, he will have no liability (in normal circumstances) for the company's debts.

EXAMPLE

Charles subscribes for 500 £1 shares in Regency Furnishings Limited ('Regency').

If Charles pays £500 for the shares, his shares are said to be fully-paid, so no further liability for Regency's debts can fall on Charles.

Instead, if Charles pays 50p per share, his shares are said to be partly-paid. In effect, £250 remains as an outstanding obligation to Regency. Regency's constitution may contain rules about how and when it can demand the outstanding balance, but, in any event, on any liquidation of Regency, Charles will be obliged to contribute the remaining £250.

The position of a shareholder in a limited company is quite different from the position of a member of a partnership (see **3.2**). If a partnership business fails each of the partners stands to lose not only what he has invested but also any private wealth which he may have. Limited liability can be an enormous advantage to a businessman, although creditors (particularly those who have lent money to the company) may require personal guarantees of the company's debts from shareholders, thus reducing the advantage.

7.5.2   Companies limited by guarantee

A small number of companies are limited by guarantee rather than by shares. This means that each member undertakes to pay a specified amount if the company is wound up (i.e., the guarantee) while he is a member or within a year after he ceases to be a member. Most companies limited by guarantee are charities or other non-trading companies.

7.5.3 Unlimited companies

An unlimited company is one which is registered under the Companies Act but without any limit on the liability of the members. If an unlimited company goes into liquidation the members are liable to contribute the whole of their private wealth (if so much is needed) to the payment of the company's debts. The creditors cannot sue the members direct but must claim in the liquidation. The liquidator then calls for contributions from the members. For this reason, an unlimited company is not a suitable choice for a trading entity or one which will incur substantial obligations.

7.5.4 Public and private companies (see also Chapter 16)

Nearly all company law rules apply equally to all companies. There are, however, a number of rules which distinguish between 'public' companies and 'private' companies. The important issue to note is that public and private companies are creatures of statute and the differences between them are determined by the Companies Act. Any company will be private unless it is specifically incorporated as a public one. Bringing a public company into being is effectively an administrative task. The only substantive matter is that the company's share capital must satisfy certain minimum requirements—the aggregate nominal value of all shares in issue must be at least £50,000 and each share must be at least one quarter paid up. (In other words, the company must have received at least £12,500 from its shareholders for those shares.)

The vast majority of companies in existence are private. Public companies, being more regulated, are less attractive. This difference has been made more acute by the Companies Act 2006, which has sought to provide greater freedom to those who operate private companies. Probably the principal reason for wanting a public company is that only public companies can issue shares or debentures to the public (hence the description 'public company'); a private company is prohibited from so doing. Private companies which want to circumvent the prohibition will have to convert to public status first. (These issues are discussed in more detail in **Chapter 16**.)

7.5.5 Other definitions

All companies are public or private but there are a number of other categories of company to which special rules apply:

(a) *Listed company*

A company is in this category if its shares are listed with the UK Listing Authority and traded on a stock exchange. Because of UK Listing Authority and London Stock Exchange rules only public companies can obtain a listing. Listed companies are subject to a more stringent regulatory regime (see **16.3**). Listed companies may also be referred to as 'quoted' companies and in general parlance the two terms are synonymous. However, the Companies Act 2006 includes within it the use of the defined term 'quoted company', so care should be taken in the use of this term.

(b) *Close company*

This category is relevant only for tax purposes; special tax rules apply to close companies (see **19.5**). Virtually all private companies are close and so are some public companies. A company which is not close is sometimes called an 'open company' but 'non-close company' is more correct.

(c) *Small and medium-sized companies*

These are companies which because of their relatively small size (in financial terms) are exempt from providing certain information in their accounts. In addition, certain categories of small companies are now exempt from the requirement to have an audit of their accounts. Further discussion of this topic can be found in **Chapter 15**.

7.6 Separate legal personality

As we have already seen, a company is a 'body corporate'; that is, it is a legal person distinct from its members and officers (i.e., its directors and secretary). Even if a company is 100% owned and controlled by a shareholder, that company has a completely separate legal personality from that of the shareholder. This is clearly illustrated in the leading case of *Salomon v A. Salomon and Co. Ltd* [1897] AC 22.

A number of consequences flow from this separate legal personality, so that a company:

(a) is able to own property;

(b) is liable for its own debts;

(c) can sue its debtors;

(d) is liable to be sued by its creditors; and

(e) has 'perpetual succession'—this means that the company does not cease to exist just because a member (however many shares he may own) dies or otherwise ceases to be a member.

7.7 'Lifting the veil of incorporation'

There are a number of circumstances in which the court may be willing to ignore the fact that a company is a separate legal person. Legislation also sometimes ignores the distinction between a company and its members. These circumstances are rather fancifully described as 'lifting the veil of incorporation' because the law looks behind the legal 'veil' which separates the company from its members and officers.

The occasions when the veil of incorporation is lifted are hard to classify and limited. It is probably open to the courts to extend the circumstances in the future. However, the case of *Adams v Cape Industries* [1990] Ch 433 suggests considerable judicial reluctance to do so. It is, of course, open to Parliament to do so by legislation.

7.7.1 Company legislation

The Companies Act 2006 and the Insolvency Act (IA) 1986 contain a number of rules which depart from the general principle of separate legal personality; for example:

(a) *Fraudulent trading*

Section 213 IA 1986 provides that any person who is or was knowingly a party to fraudulent trading by a company whose business is being carried on with intent to defraud creditors or other persons, may be liable to pay the debts of the company. This liability arises only if the company is being wound up (although criminal penalties may be imposed for fraudulent trading under s. 993 CA 2006 even if the company is not being wound up).

(b) *Wrongful trading*

Section 214 IA 1986 provides that directors of the company may be personally liable in cases of wrongful trading. This arises where a company becomes insolvent and the directors then fail to take steps to protect creditors. This type of liability only arises if the company is being wound up.

Sections 213 and 214 are discussed further in **Chapter 27**.

(c) *Group accounts*

Where companies are members of a group, group accounts must be produced to reflect that the financial transactions of the subsidiaries are in reality activities of the holding company (s. 399 CA 2006).

7.7.2 Decisions of the courts

7.7.2.1 Attempts to avoid legal obligations

The courts have occasionally lifted the veil of incorporation by making orders against companies where the proprietors have used a company as a means of avoiding a personal legal obligation; that is the company in question is being used as a deliberate façade to obscure the reality of the situation. For example in *Jones v Lipman* [1962] 1 WLR 832, the defendant had contracted to sell land to the plaintiff and later conveyed it to a company in an attempt to avoid the possibility of an order of specific performance (an order of specific performance cannot normally be made once a third party has acquired rights in the subject matter of the contract). The company was owned and controlled by the defendant and so an order of specific performance was made against the company as well as the vendor.

7.7.2.2 Agency and trusts

In a few cases the court has held that a company is either an agent for its shareholders or their trustee; however, the exact scope of these decisions is rather unclear and these cases ought to be regarded as providing exceptions rather than general rules. A company will *not* generally be regarded as either an agent for, or trustee of, its members.

7.7.3 Tax legislation

Tax legislation often imposes tax liability on shareholders to reflect the fact that transactions of their company are in reality transactions conducted on their behalf. It is not proposed to deal with all the rules involved but the following examples should be sufficient to indicate their scope:

(a) The companies in a 'group' of companies (i.e., broadly speaking, a holding company and its subsidiaries) are in many ways treated as one company for corporation tax purposes. Thus the rate of tax depends on the size of the group's profits rather than on the size of each company's profits, losses made by one member of a group can generally be set off against profits made by others, and dividend payments within the group may be ignored for tax purposes.

(b) Gifts made by a close company are treated as made by its members for the purpose of inheritance tax.

(c) The sale of a business to a company in return for shares can usually be ignored for capital gains tax purposes.

Formation of a limited company

8

This chapter covers the following topics:

8.1 Introduction

In this chapter, we shall look at the process by which a limited company is formed and the steps required both for and following its formation. We shall also look at shelf companies, as an alternative means of providing a company to a client, and the related changes which can be made to a company's main features.

Whatever the reason for a new company, the process of registering a company is governed by the Companies Act. All company registrations from 1 October 2009 have to comply with the 2006 Act. However, as many of the companies currently in existence will have been registered under the 1985 Act, this chapter considers both regimes, as appropriate. (The processes are fundamentally the same, but 1985 Act companies and 2006 Act companies show a number of differences in their make-up.)

8.2 Promoters

Those who wish to form a company are usually known as the 'promoters' of the company. There is no legal definition of a promoter; whether someone is a promoter is a question of fact. However, it is generally accepted that a promoter owes certain duties to the company which he seeks to create. These include duties of good faith and disclosure. It is important to advise promoters of their potential liability for any contracts which they might enter into on behalf of the proposed company prior to its incorporation (see **8.3**).

For the purposes of this chapter, we have used the term 'promoters' to mean any person or persons wishing to set up a company which will be used as a vehicle for their business.

A solicitor advising a client on the formation of a new business or on changing an existing business into a company, would first discuss the advisability of incorporation, compared to the alternatives of remaining a sole trader or forming a partnership. This requires a detailed knowledge of partnership law, company law and relevant tax considerations. We therefore leave the topic of choice of business medium until **Chapter 32**.

Solicitors may also set up companies for their clients as part of a transaction, for example, a company may be set up to carry out a specific activity within a transaction or trading assets may be hived into a newly-formed company and that company sold on, rather than the assets themselves being sold.

8.3 Pre-incorporation contracts

Difficulties may arise in relation to contracts made by the promoters on behalf of a proposed company. They may wish to make contracts to acquire premises, machinery, stationery and so on, prior to the company becoming incorporated. This may be due to a desire to have things 'up and running', so that trading can commence immediately the company is incorporated. This creates a problem as the company cannot enter into contracts until it has been incorporated as, until such time, it is not a legal person. The promoters cannot act as its agents, since the principal does not exist.

Should the promoters purport to enter into a contract *on behalf of* the unformed company, s. 51 CA 2006 will apply. This provides that:

A contract that purports to be made by or on behalf of a company at a time when the company has not been formed has effect, subject to any agreement to the contrary, as one made with the person purporting to act for the company or as agent for it, and he is personally liable on the contract accordingly.

The threat of personal liability means that the safest course is to enter into contracts only after incorporation, when they can be entered into by the company. If this is not possible, then the following may be considered:

(a) preparing a draft contract which will be entered into by the company following incorporation;

(b) entering into a binding contract under which the promoters are personally liable until incorporation, at which time the contract is novated, i.e., a new contract on the same terms is entered into between the company and the third party (note that the third party's consent to novation will be required); or

(c) entering into a binding contract under which the promoters are personally liable until incorporation, at which time the promoters transfer the benefit of the contract to the company in return for the company's agreement to indemnify them in respect of their liability to the third party.

8.4 Methods of providing the client with a company

There are two main methods by which a client can be provided with a company. The solicitor may form a new company *from scratch*. In doing so, he can ensure that the company meets the client's particular requirements in every way: the company is effectively 'tailor-made' and brought into existence for the client.

Alternatively, the solicitor can arrange for the client to acquire a 'shelf' company. This type of company *has already been incorporated*, either by law stationers or, sometimes, by the firm of solicitors itself. Since the company already exists, it must be transferred over to the client.

These methods are compared later in **8.11**. For the moment, we shall look at the steps required for the incorporation of a company from scratch.

8.5 Steps leading to incorporation

8.5.1 Introduction

Whilst all new companies are set up under the provisions of the Companies Act 2006, lawyers still need to be aware of the way in which companies were set up under the Companies Act 1985 for two main reasons:

(i)   The differences in the constitutions between 1985 Act companies and those of 2006 Act companies result in some important consequences for each type of company, to which lawyers must be sensitive;

(ii) Company searches in respect of 1985 Act companies will reveal registered information which was required under the 1985 Act.

Also, as the 2006 regime is designed to be a simplified version of the one it replaces, the historical context is useful to make sense of the new regime.

In this section, therefore, we will deal with both regimes and draw appropriate comparisons between them.

(In this chapter we will consider the formation of private limited companies only. For the formation of public companies, please refer to **Chapter 16**.)

8.5.2 Incorporation under the Companies Act 1985

For a company to be registered under the Companies Act 1985, the promoters or their solicitor had to deliver to Companies House the following:

(a) a memorandum of association;

(b) articles of association;

(c) Form 10, setting out details of the registered office, the directors and secretary (if one was to be appointed) of the company;

(d) Form 12, a statutory declaration of compliance with the requirements of the Companies Act 1985 for registration.

Of the above documents, the most important were the company's memorandum and articles. As we shall see, for companies now set up under the 2006 Act, whilst the articles continue to be very significant, the memorandum has decreased considerably in importance.

8.5.3 Incorporation under the Companies Act 2006

The new Act has made some substantial changes to both the process of incorporation and the constitution of a company. The main relevant provisions are to be found in Parts 2 and 3 of the 2006 Act.

Perhaps the main difference is that much of the information which was provided through submission of the memorandum of association is, instead, provided in the application for registration (s. 9 CA 2006), although a simplified memorandum is still required to be submitted—see below.

The application for registration must state:

(a) The proposed name of the company.

(b) The proposed situation of the company's registered office, e.g., England, Wales, Scotland or Northern Ireland.

(c) Whether or not the liability of the members is to be limited (either by shares or guarantee), which will normally be the case.

(d) Whether or not the company is to be public or private.

Additionally, the application must also contain:

(a) A statement of share capital and initial shareholdings.

(b) A statement of the company's proposed officers.

(c) A statement of the intended address of the company's registered office.

It will no longer be necessary to complete a statutory declaration, as was the case with the previous Form 12. Instead, s. 13 CA 2006 requires a statement of compliance to be submitted with the application.

If particular articles of association are required, they should be submitted with the application for registration (s. 9(5)(b)). If this is not done, the relevant Model Articles will be deemed to be the articles of the company by default (s. 20 CA 2006). (See further discussion below at **8.6.8.**)

All these documents must be sent to the Registrar of Companies together with the fee of £20. This will result in the application being processed within five to six days. If the new company is required urgently, it is possible to pay a fee of £50, which guarantees same-day incorporation.

Electronic incorporation is also possible, although special software is required. The fees are then reduced to £15 and £30 respectively for the same type of service.

8.6 Issues to be considered on registration

8.6.1 Introduction

We shall now consider the specific issues which the process of registration raises. There are a number of features of a company which need to be confirmed by a lawyer to ensure that the proposed company meets the client's requirements.

8.6.2. Memorandum of association

Every company must have a memorandum. Historically its principal function was to set out the *raison d'être* of the company and to regulate its dealings with outsiders. Five compulsory clauses had to be included in the memorandum. These related to:

(a) the name of the company;

(b) the *situs* of the registered office;

(c) the objects of the company, that is, what its purpose was;

(d) the liability of the members, that is, whether or not it was limited;

(e) the authorised share capital of the company, that is, the initial pool of shares out of which shares could be allotted by the company to prospective shareholders.

Together with the articles, the memorandum formed the constitution of a company.

The position under the 2006 Act is much different; the significance of the memorandum has been substantially reduced for newly-registered companies and it is now only relevant to the application for registration (s. 9(1)). Effectively, it will be of historical interest only once a company has been registered and no longer forms part of the constitution. It is in a much different form to the previous 1985 Act version, needing to contain only two clauses (s. 8 CA 2006):

(a) a statement of intent of the subscribers to form a company;

(b) a statement by the subscribers that they agree to become members of the company and to take at least one share each. (In the case of a single member company, there will obviously only be one subscriber.)

As a result of these changes, for companies set up under the 1985 Act, the contents of their memoranda which are no longer required for inclusion in a valid memorandum will be deemed to be included within the articles (s. 28 CA 2006). For this reason, it is not possible to ignore the contents of the memorandum of a 1985 Act company.

8.6.3 The name of a company

8.6.3.1 Choice of name

Generally, the promoters have freedom of choice as far as the company's name is concerned. The purpose of a company's name is to differentiate the company from all other registered companies. The Companies Act 2006, therefore, prohibits the Registrar from registering a company with a name which:

(a) does not end with the word 'limited' (or its Welsh equivalent 'cyfyngedig' if appropriate) if the company is a private limited company (s. 59 CA 2006);

(b) is the same as that of an existing registered company (s. 66(1) CA 2006); or

(c) in the opinion of the Secretary of State constitutes a criminal offence, or is offensive (s. 53 CA 2006).

In addition, the approval of the Secretary of State is necessary for the registration of a company under a name which suggests a connection with the Government or a local or public authority (s. 54 CA 2006). Furthermore, the inclusion in a company's name of particular words specified in regulations made under s. 55 CA 2006 (so-called 'sensitive' words) will also require the approval of the Secretary of State. In either instance, consultation with the relevant government department or institution specified in the regulations is sometimes required before the Registrar gives its approval.

If a name is rejected by the Registrar, a certain amount of expense and delay is bound to occur as the promoters or solicitor will have to submit a further set of documents applying for formation with a new name. Therefore, to minimise the risk of a name being rejected the promoters or solicitor should consult the index of company names kept by the Registrar of Companies shortly before the application for registration. If the name is already in use a new name should be chosen. If the name is not in use then the application should progress quickly as there is no procedure for reserving a name.

8.6.3.2 Power of Secretary of State to order change of name

The Secretary of State has power to direct a company to change its name in the following circumstances:

(a) within 12 months of registration, if the name is the same as or, in the opinion of the Secretary of State, too like a name appearing in the index of names at the time of registration, or is the same as a name which should have been in the index at that time (ss. 67 and 68 CA 2006);

(b) within five years of registration, if misleading information was given at the time of registration for the purposes of a company's registration by a particular name (s. 75 CA 2006); and

(c) at any time, if the name gives 'so misleading an indication of the nature of the company's activities as to be likely to cause harm to the public' (s. 76 CA 2006).

8.6.3.3 Passing-off

Registration of a company with a particular name does not give the company any protection against a passing-off action if an existing business trades under a similar name and its business is likely to be affected by the similarity.

Additionally, third parties are able to object to a company's registered name on the basis that they already have goodwill in the same or a similar name (s. 69 CA 2006). Such an objection will have to be made to a company names adjudicator, which is a new office created by the 2006 Act (s. 70 CA 2006).

8.6.3.4 Trade marks

If a company registered a name which included a registered trade mark of another business, it would be open to an action for infringement of such trade mark. It may therefore be prudent for the promoters or their solicitor to inspect the trade marks register before applying for registration, should there be any concern in this regard.

8.6.4 Registered office

A company's registered office determines the jurisdiction under which it is formed. Under the 1985 Act, the memorandum had to state that the company's registered office would be situated in England (which includes Wales for this purpose) or Wales (to the exclusion of England) or Scotland (for a Scottish registered company), as appropriate. The function of this clause was therefore to determine the company's domicile. The specific address of a company's registered office was included in the details provided in Form 10, as part of the registration process.

This requirement has now been replaced by the need to state both the intended situation of the company's registered office and its actual address in the application for registration (ss. 9(2)(b) and 9(5)(a) CA 2006), hence the fact that a registered office clause is no longer necessary in the memorandum.

8.6.5   A company's objects and the *ultra vires* doctrine

Because a company is an artificial person, there exists the concept of a company's objects, or purposes, and the powers it is to have. The wording and location of a company's objects can differ from company to company, due to the historical development of this concept. It is, therefore, important to analyse it chronologically.

For well over a century, until the advent of the CA 2006, the objects had to be stated in the memorandum. Originally any contracts made, or acts done, by a company not within its stated objects, or reasonably incidental thereto, used to be void on the basis that they were *ultra vires*. Because of this rule, objects clauses were traditionally drafted very widely. In particular, it is usual to find in older memoranda many sub-clauses which seek to list all the businesses and activities which the company could conceivably wish to undertake at any time. These would also be followed by a statement that each sub-clause should be construed as independent of each other.

Certain decisions of the courts sought to temper the impact of the *ultra vires* rule for companies; however, it remained problematic and lawyers continued to draft wide, and very long, objects clauses.

The introduction of s. 35 CA 1985 all but abolished the rule in relation to transactions between *a company and an outsider*. (This provision is carried over into s. 39 CA 2006.) Despite this, many companies still submitted a long form of objects clause when they registered.

An alternative, short form objects clause was possible under s. 3A CA 1985 which provided:

Where the company's memorandum states that the object of the company is to carry on business as a general commercial company—

(a) the object of the company is to carry on any trade or business whatsoever, and

(b) the company has power to do all such things as are incidental or conducive to the carrying on of any trade or business by it.

Where a company adopted this simple form of objects clause, the powers of the company would include the power to carry on any trade or business. The intention behind this statutory 'short-hand' was to allow companies to replace their extensive objects clauses with a single sentence.

However, due to uncertainty about the ambit of the phrase 'trade or business' many companies adopted a 'belt and braces' approach and had both the new form of clause and a traditional long-form objects clause following it.

The position has now been reversed under the CA 2006; the objects of any company now registered will be completely unrestricted, unless a specific provision to the contrary is included in a company's articles (s. 31 CA 2006). For this reason, the revised form of memorandum no longer has to contain an objects clause.

It is expected that most companies will want to take advantage of this situation and rely upon the statutory implication. However, it may be in certain situations (for example, where a company is being created with a definite objective in mind) that those setting up a company will require or deem it necessary to delineate a company's objects in the articles.

For existing companies, the importation of the objects clause from the memorandum into the articles (s. 28 CA 2006) will have the effect of continuing to impose limits on the company's objects. Therefore, such companies may wish to alter their articles to remove any such restriction and take advantage of the approach offered by the new Act. (See further discussion at **8.13**.)

Overall, the significance of a company's objects is now somewhat minimal, especially for those registered under the 2006 Act with unrestricted objects. However, directors are under a duty to observe a company's constitution (s. 171 CA 2006), so, in relevant circumstances, lawyers must continue to determine whether or not a company's constitution restricts its activities in any way.

8.6.6   Limited liability

There exists the possibility of both limited and unlimited companies (see **7.5**). As such, it is necessary to determine the status of a company's shareholders at the time of registration. (For most purposes, shareholders will want the benefit of limited liability.) It is necessary, therefore, to make a statement to this effect in the application for registration (s. 9(2)(c) CA 2006).

Previously, under the 1985 Act (and before), the same outcome was achieved by a limited liability clause being included in the memorandum of association which was submitted for registration purposes. This clause is no longer necessary in memoranda under the 2006 Act.

8.6.7   Initial shareholders and share capital

Most companies will be created with a share capital. In turn, this means that those companies must be created with shareholders, although it is possible to set up a company with only one shareholder (s. 7(1) CA 2006). A company's initial shareholders will be the subscribers to the memorandum, who must agree to take a minimum of one share each (s. 8(1)(b) CA 2006).

Specific details of the subscribers' shareholdings must be set out in the statement of capital and initial shareholdings. This statement will provide details of:

(i)   The total number of shares taken on formation by the subscribers;

(ii)   The aggregate nominal value of those shares;

(iii) The rights attaching to those shares;

(iv) The number, nominal value and class of shares taken by each subscriber and the amount paid up on each share.

Specific discussion of a company's share capital is contained in **Chapter 11**. For these purposes, it is sufficient to recognise that all shares must have a nominal, financial value attributed to them, normally denominated in Pounds Sterling. In turn, the relevant shareholder will normally agree to pay the company an amount at least equivalent to the nominal value of the shares subscribed for.

EXAMPLE

Charles and William set up a company by subscribing to the memorandum. They each agree to take 50 shares fully-paid with a nominal value each of £1. As a consequence:

(i) The total nominal value of shares taken by Charles and William is £100.

(ii) Each of Charles and William will have a shareholding with a nominal value of £50 and will, accordingly, each have to pay to the company £50.

8.6.8   The articles of association

This important topic has already been considered briefly at **7.3.5** and a fuller discussion can be found in **Chapter 14**, to which the reader should refer. This section, therefore, simply introduces some of the main issues relevant on incorporation.

The articles are the main constitutional document of a company (s. 17 CA 2006). These regulate the company's internal affairs and contain provisions dealing with such matters as directors' powers, proceedings at members' meetings, conduct at board meetings and so on. By statutory implication, a company and all its members are bound into the provisions of the articles (s. 33(1) CA 2006). When preparing to incorporate a company, one of the most important matters to discuss with the promoters is the contents of the articles and their effect.

A company is able to choose the type of articles it thinks appropriate, but standard form articles have been provided by statutory instrument for companies for many years to assist with the process. The latest versions of these are referred to as the Model Articles and are set out in the Companies (Model Articles) Regulations 2008.

Effectively, a company has four choices:

(a) It can have prepared specially drafted articles from scratch. (This is likely to be a rare occurrence and will be expensive.)

(b) It can adopt standard articles supplied by its legal advisers with or without amendment. (Many law firms will have these as a standard precedent, which they can recommend to clients.)

(c) It can adopt the Model Articles wholesale, with no amendments.

(d) It can adopt the Model Articles, but with bespoke amendments.

With the exception of choice (c), a company must register its chosen articles as part of its application for registration. A failure to do so will mean that the Model Articles will apply to the company by default (s. 20 CA 2006).

8.7 The certificate of incorporation

Upon receipt of an application for registration of a company, Companies House will examine the registration documents and, provided they are in order and the chosen name is still available, will sign a certificate of incorporation stating that the company is incorporated on a particular date and that it is limited (if appropriate). The Registrar of Companies specifies the company's unique registered number on the certificate and this must be quoted on all official documents and business letters.

From the date of incorporation the company becomes a legal entity (s. 16(3) CA 2006). At the same time as the Registrar issues the certificate, he must (under s. 1064 CA 2006) 'officially notify' the fact of issue. This means he must place a notice to this effect in the Government's official newspaper (in England and Wales, the *London Gazette*).

8.8 Steps necessary after incorporation

Once the certificate of incorporation has been issued the company's existence begins. One of the first things which is likely to happen is for the board of directors to conduct its first meeting. The agenda for this will include such matters as:

(a) The approval and execution of any service contracts for board members.

(b) The allotment of any shares over and above those allocated to the subscribers to the memorandum.

(c) The appointment of auditors to the company (if thought necessary).

(d) The appointment of bankers to the company.

(e) Instructions to make the necessary entries in the relevant registers of the company, e.g., the registers of members and the registers of directors.

(f) Alteration of the company's automatically designated accounting reference date (if thought necessary).

In turn items (a) and (b) may require reference to the shareholders, so a general meeting would also have to be called to coincide with the board meeting.

8.9 Publication of a company's name

There are a number of statutory provisions concerning publication of a company's name. Note, however, that whilst the 2006 Act imposes the obligation to make disclosures, the detailed provisions are contained within the Companies (Trading Disclosures) Regulations 2008.

8.9.1 Disclosure of registered name

A company is required to:

(a) display its registered name at its registered office and any other place of business in which its business is carried on, in a position which can be seen by any visitor to such places and in letters which can be read by the naked eye;

(b) ensure that its name appears on business letters, correspondence and documentation, notices, official publications, cheques, orders for money or goods, invoices and websites.

8.9.2. Additional disclosures

A company's business letters, order forms and website should also contain the following information:

(a) the place (i.e., country) of registration of the company;

(b) its registered number;

(c) the address of its registered office.

There is no need to include the names of directors on a company's stationery, but if the name of *any* director appears on a business letter (other than in the text or as a signatory) on which the company's name appears, then the names of *all* the directors who are individuals and the corporate names of all the corporate directors must appear in legible characters.

8.9.3. Penalties for default

Failure to comply with any of the above disclosure requirements without reasonable excuse makes the company and every officer authorising the issue of a letter, etc., liable to a fine.

8.10 Statutory registers

8.10.1 The registers

Companies are required by the Companies Act 2006 to keep certain registers—often referred to as the company's 'books'.

There is no required format for registers and they may be kept in hard copy or electronic format (s. 1135 CA 2006), so the term 'books' is somewhat of a misnomer.

As far as a private limited company is concerned, the two most important registers it must keep at its registered office are:

(a) A *register of members* (s. 113 CA 2006) containing each member's name, address, dates of entry on the register and cessation of membership together with details of the shares held. (Note that s. 115 CA 2006 requires an index of members to be kept if a company has more than 50 members and the register is not already kept in the form of an index.)

(b) A *register of directors* (s. 162 CA 2006) setting out in respect of each director their name, service address, country of residence, nationality and date of birth. A separate register of directors' residential addresses must also be maintained (s. 165 CA 2006). Failure to maintain either of these registers is an offence by both the company and any officer in default and is punishable by a fine.

8.10.2 Inspection of company books

Both the register of members and register of directors must be kept available for inspection by members and the general public at the registered office. (They may also be kept at a place other than the registered office provided the Registrar is notified.) Inspection of registers by members is free; all other persons must pay a prescribed fee. It is also possible for either members or outsiders to request a copy of the register of members on payment of a fee. (The rights for outsiders to see the register of members is of particular use in takeover situations, when the company is a possible target for a bid and the bidder wishes to find out more about that company's shareholders.)

In recent years there has been some sensitivity about the availability of directors' home addresses to the public through the right to inspect a company's registers. For this reason, the 2006 Act only requires that the register of directors includes a service address, which can obviously be different from a home one. The separate register of residential addresses is not available for public inspection.

8.10.3 Other documents to be kept by a company

Other documents which should be kept at the registered office include:

(a) Directors' service contracts (s. 228 CA 2006), which can be inspected by members free of charge. Members can also, on payment of a fee, ask to be supplied with a copy of any service contract;

(b) records of shareholder resolutions of the company (passed at general meetings or otherwise) for a period of 10 years (s. 358 CA 2006), which can be inspected by members free of charge.

Companies are also obliged to record and maintain minutes of all directors' meetings for 10 years (s. 248 CA 2006). However the Act does not require these to be maintained at the registered office for inspection.

8.11   Comparison of 'tailor-made' with 'shelf' company

8.11.1   The tailor-made company

This is a company formed following the procedure outlined above. The documentation will be tailored to the promoters' requirements, with the memorandum and articles including provisions appropriate to the particular circumstances of the case. The promoters will most likely be the subscribers to the memorandum (the company's first members) and may also be the company's first directors and secretary.

This method can be relatively expensive, as every application for registration will be unique to the client. In addition, there will be the time involved in waiting for Companies House to process the application, which can take around five days (although an expedited, same-day, incorporation service is available for £50).

8.11.2   The shelf company

This is a company which has already been incorporated—normally by a company formation specialist, law stationers or a firm of solicitors—from whom it is then purchased by the promoters. In other words, the promoters do not seek to register their own company from scratch; they simply take over a company which has already been formed, but which will have carried on no commercial functions.

Shelf companies are invariably set up according to a standard formula, such that they are relatively inexpensive to create and 'bulk' applications can be made. (A law stationers, for example, may set up thousands of companies in this way each year.)

These companies are, however, no different to any other company, in that they must fulfil all the requirements for registration. A shelf company will, therefore, have directors, shareholders, a registered office, a name and a memorandum and articles. Most or all of these aspects of the shelf company will have to be altered to suit the needs of the relevant promoters and ownership of the company be transferred to the promoters.

In the remainder of this section, we will consider the issues surrounding the necessary conversion of each of the elements of a shelf company. This process of conversion normally involves decisions of both the directors and shareholders of the shelf company, but, as these decisions are very often a standard requirement, supporting pro forma documentation will ensure that the process is effectively an administrative one.

8.11.2.1   Memorandum of Association

As a company's memorandum ceases to have any relevance beyond its initial registration, that of the shelf company will be of no consequence to those taking it over.

8.11.2.2   Company name

Shelf companies are generally created with wholly imaginary and often unusual names. (This is to avoid any application being rejected on the basis that a company is already registered with the same name.) As a result, the name of the chosen shelf company will have no connection with the promoters or their business. If the name of their company is unimportant to the promoters, this will cause no problems; however, if they wish their company to trade under their own names or a chosen name, it will have to be changed. (See **8.12** for further discussion of the process of changing a company's name.)

8.11.2.3 Articles of association

As regards the articles, the shelf company is likely to have been incorporated with either Model Articles or with standard amended articles. Great care must be taken to ensure that the articles are suitable for the promoters' wishes. If they are not, they will have to be amended in accordance with the Companies Act, which requires the members to pass a special resolution approving the change (see **Chapter 14** for further discussion of this area).

8.11.2.4 Directors and shareholders

Representatives of the entity which formed the shelf company will have signed the memorandum as subscribers, and will have been named in the registration documentation as officers of the company. This means that they become the first members, directors and secretary (if any) of the company, and their names should appear in the company's books as such. (It is likely that there will be only one or two subscribers and/or directors of the shelf company.)

In order for ownership and control of the shelf company to be passed to the promoters, it is necessary that:

(a) the first members *transfer* their shares to the promoters;

(b) the first directors and secretary (if any) *resign* their positions; and

(c) the promoters are appointed as new directors and secretary (if one is required).

An alternative means by which ownership and control can be vested in the promoters is for a 'letter of renunciation' to be supplied with the shelf company. This letter contains a renunciation of rights as shareholders and company officers in favour of the promoters, which avoids the need for formal transfer of the shares and resignation of the existing directors.

8.11.2.5 Accounting reference date

The date of registration of the shelf company will determine its accounting reference date, that is, the date on which its accounting year ends. If this is not suitable, it will have to be changed to meet the promoters' needs. (See **8.14** for further discussion of this issue.)

8.11.2.6 Registered office

As part of the process of registration of the shelf company, details of the company's first registered office will have been supplied (normally the address of the law stationers or the solicitors' firm which has set up the company). If this is not suitable, it will have to be changed to meet the promoters' needs. (See **8.15** for further discussion of this issue.)

8.11.3 Advantages and disadvantages

The greatest advantage of utilising a shelf company is generally considered to be speed and certainty. The promoters may obtain a company immediately, often for a comparatively low price.

A tailor-made company will inevitably take longer to form (even using the same-day service) due to the need to take instructions and complete documentation. The cost of the latter will almost certainly be greater than the initial cost of a shelf company. However, it is possible to set up a company from scratch using relatively standard documentation, after which discussions can take place with the client about the particular suitability of, say, the articles which can be amended subsequently. Also, the promoters may prefer a company set up from scratch, as it has no prior history.

There are no hard and fast rules as to when a tailor-made or shelf company should be used. The advantages and disadvantages above should be considered in conjunction with the circumstances of the particular case, including any time or budget limitations of the promoters.

8.12 Change of name

8.12.1 Introduction

As seen above, it may be that the name of a shelf company has to be changed to suit a client's purposes. By contrast, if a company is tailor-made for a client, it is unlikely that it will want to change its name for the foreseeable future. However, at some future date, it may be thought desirable to make such a change.

8.12.2 Choice of name

As on incorporation, a company has general freedom to choose whatever name it likes, but this is subject to the same restrictions which apply on incorporation and the powers of the Secretary of State to direct a change of name (detailed in **8.6.3**).

8.12.3 Procedure under the Companies Act 2006

Section 77 CA 2006 allows two methods by which a company may change its name: either by special resolution or by any alternative method stipulated in a company's articles. Such a method could be simpler or more difficult than by special resolution, so could include, for example, either a majority or unanimous decision of the directors or the shareholders.

Note that the Model Articles do not contain any specific provision dealing with change of name. In addition, companies which were set up prior to s. 77 coming into effect (that is, companies incorporated prior to 1 October 2009) are unlikely to include any such provision, as it was not possible to do so under the 1985 Act. In default of any positive action, therefore, it may be the case that many companies will have to change their names by special resolution.

Any change of name must be notified to the Registrar of Companies. The method of notification will depend upon the method by which the company's name was changed. If a special resolution is used, both notice of the change to the name and a copy of the resolution must be sent to the Registrar (s. 78 CA 2006). Where the change is effected by a method in the articles, the company must give notice that this is the case and notice of the change itself (s. 79 CA 2006). A fee of £10 is also payable, in either circumstance. (Note that Companies House offers a same-day change of name service on payment of a fee of £50.)

If the change is satisfactory in the opinion of the Registrar, a certificate of incorporation on change of name will be issued (s. 80 CA 2006), at which point the change of name is effective (s. 81(a) CA 2006). It is important, therefore, to recognise that the change does not take effect at the time the decision is made.

Once the name has been changed, it must be used on the company's notepaper and other documents in accordance with the disclosure requirements discussed at **8.9**.

8.12.4 Use of business name

For some companies, the registered name is somewhat of a statutory formality, as they may choose to trade under a business name for the purposes of their public image. (Effectively, this will be a trade mark of the business. There are many examples on the High Street, for example, of business names.) To avoid companies defeating the restrictions on corporate names through the use of business names, they are regulated by Part 41 CA 2006 (and related regulations), which impose the same restrictions on the use of business names, as for corporate names.

The advantage of a business name is that any change to it is not regulated by the Companies Act, so it can be changed at any time by board resolution. Additionally, the change does not have to be registered at Companies House. (Although, if the business name is also a registered trade mark, a new registration would have to be made to the Trade Marks Registry.)

8.13 Change of objects

8.13.1 Introduction

Companies set up under the 2006 Act are likely to have unrestricted objects, unless a contrary statement appears in the articles (s. 31(1) CA 2006). Companies set up under the 1985 Act regime will automatically have the objects clause in their current memoranda deemed to be included in their articles on the basis of s. 28 CA 2006. In this way, the objects of those companies will continue to have relevance.

8.13.2 Procedure under the Companies Act 2006

To impose, change or remove any restriction on its objects, a company will have to change its articles by special resolution (s. 21(1) CA 2006). In turn, the company will be obliged to send to the Registrar of Companies an amended copy of the articles (s. 26(1) CA 2006), together with a copy of the special resolution (s. 30(1) CA 2006). Section 31(2) CA 2006 also imposes a separate obligation to notify the Registrar of any such change; the change will not be effective until it is registered.

8.14 Change of accounting reference date

8.14.1 Introduction

A company's accounting reference period is the period for which a company must produce annual accounts, as required by the Companies Act 2006. The accounting reference period of a company is determined according to its accounting reference date (ARD).

8.14.2 Accounting reference date of a company

A company's ARD is determined by its date of incorporation (s. 391 CA 2006). The situation is somewhat complicated, because the date of incorporation can result in different rules being applied. However, for our purposes, the most important of these rules is that for any company incorporated after 1 April 1996 (either under the provisions of the 1985 Act or those of the 2006 Act) its ARD will be the last day of the month in which the anniversary of its incorporation falls. Therefore, a relevant company incorporated on 14 July would have 31 July as its ARD and its first set of accounts would have to reflect the period from incorporation until the following 31 July. Thereafter, each set of accounts would represent the period from 1 August to the following 31 July.

8.14.3 Altering the accounting reference date

8.14.3.1 Reasons

A company may wish to alter its ARD for various reasons. Many companies wish to have their accounting period end at the end of the calendar or financial years. Others may be or become part of a group of companies where it makes administrative sense for each company in the group to have the same ARD and hence the same accounting period.

8.14.3.2 Method

A company may alter its ARD by giving notice to the Registrar of Companies pursuant to s. 392 CA 2006. The decision to alter a company's ARD will usually be taken by its board of directors.

Any alteration to the ARD will result either in a shortening or lengthening of the current accounting period. There are two important rules to bear in mind:

(a) If any alteration is to affect a company's initial accounting reference period, this should neither be shortened to less than six months nor lengthened to more than 18 months from the date of its incorporation.

(b) Any alteration to a subsequent accounting reference period must not lengthen it by more than 18 months.

EXAMPLE

Quartz Limited is incorporated on 13 October 2008. Its ARD is, therefore, determined as 31 October. Its first accounts will have to be made up to 31 October 2009. If this is unsuitable, Quartz must notify Companies House of the desired change.

If the preferred date for its ARD is 30 April, Quartz must notify of this change and apply to have its first accounting reference period end on 30 April 2009, i.e., shorten the relevant period. (The alternative would result in an accounting reference period in excess of 18 months.)

Instead, if the preferred date for its ARD is 31 December, Quartz must notify of this change and apply to have its first accounting reference period end on 31 December 2009, i.e., lengthen the relevant period. (The alternative would result in an accounting reference period shorter than six months.)

8.15 Change of registered office

A company's registered office may be changed by giving relevant notice to the Registrar, pursuant to s. 87 CA 2006. (Effectively this is a decision for the board of directors.)

The change is effective in relation to service of documents when registered by the Registrar, although service of documents at the old registered office remains valid for a further 14 days after registration.

 online resource centre   Interactive online exercises (Student Learning Activities) which complement the topics covered in this chapter are available at www.oxfordtextbooks.co.uk/orc/business09_10/.

Directors and secretary

This chapter covers the following topics:

9.1   Introduction

In this chapter, we shall look at the law relating to a company's officers. This is a combination of statute, common law and regulations under a company's articles of association. In respect of this last limb, we will consider both Table A and the Model Articles for Private Companies, as both are likely to be encountered in practice.

9.2   Division of powers within a company

The power to take decisions on behalf of a company is divided between the directors and members. There are a number of powers which are exercisable only by the members under various provisions of the Companies Act, for example, the power to change the articles. Furthermore, the directors may have to seek authorisation from shareholders prior to committing the company to a transaction, for example, a buy-back of shares. However, in most instances, the directors will be able to conduct the business of and manage the company without reference to the shareholders. This is because there will be a general delegation of such authority from the company to the directors through the articles of association (see **9.6.1** below for further discussion).

9.3 Appointment of directors

9.3.1 Introduction

The first directors of a company are the people who are named as such and whose details are provided to the Registrar as part of the process of registration; they automatically become directors on the company's incorporation. Section 154 CA 2006 provides that a private company must have at least one director and that a public company must have at least two directors. For both private and public companies at least one director is required to be a 'natural person', that is, not a company or corporation (s. 155 CA 2006). (It has previously been possible for a private company to exist which simply has one corporate director and for a public company to exist with two such directors. Any companies already set up in this way will have to consider the appointment of a 'human' director either to replace or in addition to a corporate one. However, there is a proposed grace period until October 2010 for relevant companies in existence at the time the 2006 Act was granted Royal Assent, i.e., 8 November 2006.)

From time to time, it will be necessary to appoint further directors, either because one of the directors has ceased to hold office or because it is decided to increase the size of the board. Apart from a few statutory restrictions (dealt with below), the company is free to make whatever provision it wishes in its articles as to the appointment of directors. In particular, there is no general requirement that the directors should be shareholders, nor that they should be chosen by the shareholders. Provision for appointment in a company's articles will be considered first and then some other possibilities.

9.3.2 Provision for appointment in a company's articles

Statute makes no special provision for the method of appointing directors. It is, therefore, a matter for the articles. Companies may adopt various methods to deal with this issue. What follows, therefore, is a general summary of the more common approaches.

Normally the main power to appoint directors is given to the members. This provides for appointment by ordinary resolution (that is, by a simple majority of the members).

Appointments to fill vacancies on the board and appointments of additional directors may also normally be made by the board itself. The articles may specify that persons co-opted in this way hold office until the following annual general meeting, at which point their appointment should be confirmed by ordinary resolution.

Article 17 of the Model Articles for Private Companies allows appointment to be made by ordinary resolution of the members or by a decision of the directors.

It should be noted that neither the previous Table A nor the Model Articles require a director to be a shareholder. If the company wants to restrict membership of the board to shareholders, an article to that effect must be adopted on formation or by later amendment.

9.3.3 Service contracts

It is common for managing directors (see **9.9** below) and other executive directors to enter into service contracts (see **9.8.2.1**) with a company on their appointment to the board. Notwithstanding that both events will usually occur within very close proximity to each other, it is important to understand the distinction between a person:

(a) being *appointed* to the *office* of director; and

(b) *entering* into a *service contract.*

On being appointed to the office of director, the director's conduct is defined primarily by the company's memorandum and articles, common law and legislation. He may receive a *fee* for holding office. On entering into a service contract to carry out an executive role, the director has various rights and obligations defined primarily by the terms of the contract as negotiated with the company. (The director will also be entitled to those rights which the law affords all employees.) One of the main rights under the service contract will be that of receiving a *salary* and related remuneration in return for carrying out the defined obligations.

The distinction is of particular importance should a director be removed from office (see **9.5.1.3** below).

9.4 Retirement of directors

9.4.1 Retirement by notice

The most straightforward way in which a director may vacate office is to retire by giving notice to the company. Usually this takes the form of a letter to the board.

9.4.2 Retirement by rotation

If Table A or similar provisions apply, all the directors may be required to retire from office at the first annual general meeting and one third of them at each subsequent AGM (arts 73–74). The retiring directors are eligible for re-election and are automatically re-elected unless someone else is appointed, or the company resolves not to re-elect them or to fill the vacancy (art. 75).

In the case of a private company, provisions for retirement by rotation are unnecessarily cumbersome and are often not included so that, once appointed, directors hold office permanently until death, voluntary retirement, disqualification or removal from office under s. 168 CA 2006 (see **9.5.1**). The Model Articles for Private Companies recognise this and do not contain any provision for retirement by rotation.

It should be noted that the articles may, however, state that managing directors and directors holding any other executive office are not subject to retirement by rotation in any event.

9.5 Removal of directors from office

9.5.1 Removal of directors under s. 168 CA 2006

9.5.1.1 Power to remove by ordinary resolution

Section 168 CA 2006 provides for removal of directors by ordinary resolution (i.e., by a majority vote of the shareholders). (This provision mirrors its predecessor, s. 303 CA 1985.) The power given by the section overrides anything in the company's articles (even, for example, an article naming a life director) or in an agreement with the director. Section 168 provides the most effective means by which majority shareholders who object to the way in which their company is being run can keep control of the company. Where the directors themselves are the majority shareholders, as they very frequently will be in the case of a private company, the other (minority) shareholders, therefore, have limited rights to object to the way the board is running the company.

9.5.1.2 Procedure

No resolution purporting to remove a director from office is valid unless special notice has first been given to the company of an intention to remove a particular director. This usually emanates from the shareholder or shareholders who wish to remove the director. In effect this gives the company a minimum period of 28 days' 'grace' before any steps are taken by the shareholders in question to remove the director (s. 312(1) CA 2006, superseding the similar provision in s. 379 CA 1985). On receipt of the notice, a company is obliged to send a copy to the director whose removal is proposed.

However, special notice is not sufficient to cause a meeting to be held at which the necessary resolution can be proposed or to have such a resolution included on the agenda of any forthcoming meeting (see *Pedley v Inland Waterways Association* [1977] 1 All ER 209). In most circumstances the shareholders concerned must either invoke their right under s. 303 CA 2006, or any special right they may have under the company's articles of association to cause the directors to call a general meeting for the purpose of considering the director's removal.

9.5.1.3 Director's right to compensation and damages on removal

The shareholders have an absolute right to remove a director. However, this does not deprive the director of any rights to compensation or damages he may have (s. 168(5) CA 2006). When considering these rights, it is important to maintain a distinction between the right to a payment for loss of office and the right to claim damages where there is a service contract between the director and the company.

Should the director be removed from office, then the only compensation for such loss of office he may receive is a payment approved by the company under s. 217 CA 2006. However, removal from office will almost certainly terminate any service contract as it will be impossible for the director to fulfil his obligations. Depending on the terms of the director's remuneration under the contract, damages could be extensive. It is therefore important for the shareholders to consider the financial cost of removing a director.

9.5.1.4 Special voting rights on resolution to remove director

The articles may validly give special voting rights to some of the shareholders either generally or in particular circumstances. In the case of *Bushell v Faith* [1970] AC 1099, the articles provided that:

in the event of a resolution being proposed at any general meeting of the company for the removal from office of any director, any shares held by that director shall on a poll in respect of such resolution carry the right to three votes per share . . .

The director whose removal was proposed owned one third of the shares and so could not be removed. Nevertheless, the article was held to be valid, since all that the Act lays down is that an ordinary resolution may be used to remove a director and an ordinary resolution is one requiring a simple majority of votes. A clause of this type does not, therefore, prevent a resolution from being an ordinary resolution but effectively makes it impossible to remove the director without his consent.

The decision in *Bushell v Faith* has been criticised, but there are some circumstances where it may be appropriate to include in the articles a regulation which makes it impossible for the majority shareholders to get rid of a director who owns a minority of the shares. Such a regulation should be considered, for example, where a small number of people wish to run a company as a 'quasi-partnership'—that is, where they all intend to have a continuing right to take part in management. In other circumstances it may be appropriate to give the shareholders wider powers to remove directors than are given by s. 168 so that, for example, removal by ordinary resolution *without* special notice may be considered appropriate.

9.5.2 Disqualification

9.5.2.1 Company Directors Disqualification Act 1986

Companies legislation contains a number of provisions under which directors are disqualified either automatically or by court order. The most important of these are contained in the Company Directors Disqualification Act (CDDA) 1986. This Act provides for disqualification from acting as a director, liquidator, receiver, or manager of a company and from being concerned with the management of a company for up to 15 years (five years if the order is made by a magistrates' court). Disqualification can be imposed following:

(a) conviction for an indictable offence in connection with the management of a company;

(b) a finding that an offence involving fraud has been committed in the course of winding up a company;

(c) persistent default in filing returns with the Registrar (persistent default is conclusively presumed following three convictions for failure to file returns within five years); the maximum period of disqualification in this case is five years even if the penalty is imposed by a court other than a magistrates' court;

(d) a finding that a person is 'unfit' to be concerned in the management of a company. The order may only be made against a person who is or has been a director of a company which has become insolvent while or after he was a director. For these purposes a company is insolvent if it goes into insolvent liquidation, an administration order is made against it or an administrative receiver is appointed. Where an order is made on the ground of unfitness, the disqualification period must be for a minimum of two years and a maximum of 15.

The CDDA 1986 also contains a provision allowing directors to give an undertaking to the Secretary of State for Trade and Industry not to be involved in the management of a company for a specified period of time. This process of 'fast track' disqualification avoids the need for court proceedings and is intended to increase efficiency in dealing with errant directors.

9.5.2.2 Disqualification under the articles

The articles of a company may make provision for disqualification or automatic retirement in circumstances other than those specified in the Act, for example, if a director:

(a) becomes bankrupt;

(b) is or may be suffering from mental disorder and is admitted to hospital under the Mental Health Act or a court order is made against him on matters concerning mental disorder;

(c) is absent from directors' meetings (without the board's permission) for at least six months and the directors resolve that the office be vacated.

The articles also normally provide for the resignation of directors by their giving written notice to the company. No particular period of notice is required. If the director has a service contract, as, for example, in the case of most full-time directors, there is an implied obligation to give reasonable notice but for the sake of certainty it is better to include a specific period in the contract. Similar provisions to those described above are contained in the Model Articles.

Neither Table A nor the Model Articles contain any express power for the directors to remove one of their kind. However, it is possible for articles of association to reserve such a power either by a majority decision of the board or by a written request from all other directors, for example, a provision stating that a person will cease to be a director if that person receives notice signed by all the other directors stating that that person should cease to be a director. There is judicial authority for the fact that such a power is fiduciary and must be exercised in the best interests of the company (see *Samuel Tak Lee v Chou Wen Hsien* [1984] 1 WLR 1202). On this basis, it is expected that the statutory duties of directors under the 2006 Act (see **9.8**) would also apply to the exercise of this power.

9.6   Powers of directors

9.6.1   Defining directors' powers

The powers of the directors are delegated to them through the articles. For instance, Table A, art. 70 gives the directors wide powers, including in particular power to manage the business of the company. Article 70 is in the following terms:

Subject to the provisions of the Act, the memorandum and the articles and to any directions given by special resolution, the business of the company shall be managed by the directors who may exercise all the powers of the company. No alteration of the memorandum or articles and no such direction shall invalidate any prior act of the directors which would have been valid if that alteration had not been made or that direction had not been given. The powers given by this regulation shall not be limited by any special power given to the directors by the articles and a meeting of directors at which a quorum is present may exercise all powers exercisable by the directors.

Article 3 of the Model Articles for Private Companies contains a more concise definition:

Subject to the articles, the directors are responsible for the management of the company's business, for which purpose they may exercise all the powers of the company.

As with Table A, however, the directors of any company with the Model Articles must still observe an instruction given to them by special resolution (see art. 4).

9.6.2   Exercise of powers

9.6.2.1   Introduction

Decisions of the directors must normally be taken either at a board meeting at which a quorum is present or by unanimous written agreement. This is, however, subject to the directors' power to delegate (e.g., to a managing director, committee of directors or appointed agent—see **9.9** and **9.12**).

9.6.2.2 Calling a board meeting

Article 88, Table A provides that any director may call a board meeting or require the company secretary to do so at any time. No particular period of notice is required, so that a meeting will be validly held if reasonable notice is given. Notice need not be given to a director or alternate director who is absent from the UK (arts 88 and 66).

Similar provisions are contained in the Model Articles, although they do provide for a more specific approach to the contents of the actual notice of any board meeting. (Whether or not this is an attractive development, which will be adopted by many companies, remains to be seen.)

9.6.2.3 What constitutes a meeting?

At face value, a meeting will require the presence of directors in the same venue. However, this can be restrictive and can result in practical difficulties for the board. It also does not allow the use of modern communication methods. A company's articles may, therefore, recognise a wider concept of what a board meeting may be. For example, art. 10 of the Model Articles for Private Companies treats any director as participating in a board meeting if they can communicate to other directors any information or opinions they have on the business being discussed. Furthermore, any method of communication is acceptable and the location of any director is irrelevant as to whether or not he is participating in the meeting.

9.6.2.4 Decisions at board meetings

Decisions at board meetings are taken by majority vote; if there is an equality of votes, the chairman may be given a casting vote. The chairman is chosen by the directors from among themselves. The chairman's casting vote prevents deadlock (without it a resolution fails if there is an equality of votes), but it also means that the director who is the chairman has considerably more power than the others.

Both Table A and the Model Articles allow the chairman to have a casting vote.

9.6.2.5 Prohibition on director voting on resolution in which he is interested

Article 94 of Table A prohibits a director from voting on any resolution concerning a matter in which he has an interest or duty which is material and conflicts or may conflict with the interests of the company. However, this prohibition does not apply to:

(a) a resolution concerning any guarantee, security or indemnity to be given to the director in respect of money lent to the company, or an obligation incurred by the director for the benefit of the company;

(b) an arrangement whereby the company gives a guarantee, security or indemnity to a third party in respect of an obligation of the company guaranteed or indemnified by the director;

(c) an interest arising from his buying any shares or other securities from the company; or

(d) a resolution relating to a retirement benefits scheme.

Article 94 can cause problems where a company has, for example, only two directors, one or both of whom are interested in specific resolutions. Prima facie, the relevant board meeting will be inquorate and the resolution will not be able to be passed validly.

However, art. 96 allows a company to suspend or relax art. 94 by ordinary resolution. Alternatively, if it is thought that the problem will recur, art. 94 could be removed by special resolution or not adopted at the outset.

The Model Articles contain a similar provision (art. 14) and exclude a director who is interested in a particular transaction from counting in the decision-making process for voting and quorum purposes. However, if no conflict of interest arises or if one arises from a permitted cause (as defined—these are quite similar to the ones contained in art. 94, Table A), the exclusion will not apply. A provision is also included which allows the exclusion to be disapplied by an ordinary resolution of the company.

9.6.2.6   Decision by way of written resolution

The articles may allow the directors to pass valid resolutions without holding a board meeting. For example, art. 93 of Table A provides that if *all* the directors entitled to receive notice of meetings (including alternate directors) sign a written resolution, this decision is valid and effective as if it had been passed at a board meeting. Article 8 of the Model Articles also recognises the similar use of a written resolution, but also treats as valid a decision where 'all eligible directors indicate to each other by any means that they share a common view on a matter'. Such informality does have practical benefits, but for evidential purposes, a written record of any such decision would still be appropriate.

9.7   Directors' duties

9.7.1   Statutory duties under CA 2006

9.7.1.1   Introduction

One of the most potentially significant changes introduced in the Companies Act 2006 is the statutory statement of the duties owed by directors to a company. Previously, the majority of directors' duties were founded on common law rules and equitable principles. The statutory duties have been based on these principles and are stated, in s. 170(3) CA 2006 to 'have effect in place of those rules and principles as regards the duties owed to a company by a director'. The common law rules and equitable principles will continue to have relevance: s. 170(4) CA 2006 states that the statutory duties 'shall be interpreted and applied in the same way as the common law rules or equitable principles, and regard shall be had to the corresponding common law rules and equitable principles in interpreting and applying the . . . duties'. In addition, whilst the statutory duties are said to take effect in place of the common law rules and equitable principles, the Act falls short of stating that no common law rules will continue to apply. For these reasons, an outline is provided below (see **9.7.2**) of some of the major fiduciary duties owed by directors to a company. First, however, we shall consider the statutory duties under CA 2006. Each will be considered separately but to summarise them, they are:

(a) to act within the company's constitution and to exercise their powers for proper purposes;

(b) to promote the success of the company;

(c) to exercise independent judgement;

(d) to exercise reasonable care, skill, and diligence;

(e) to avoid conflicts of interest;

(f) not to accept benefits from third parties;

(g) to declare interests in existing and proposed transactions or arrangements.

9.7.1.2   Duty to act within powers

Section 171 CA 2006 requires that a director must:

(a) act in accordance with the company's constitution; and

(b) only exercise powers for the purposes for which they were conferred.

This provision is based on a common law principle illustrated in the case of *Hogg v Cramphorn Ltd* [1967] Ch 254 (see **9.7.2.2**).

9.7.1.3   Duty to promote the success of the company

Under s. 172 CA 2006, a director must act in the way in which he considers, in good faith, would be most likely to promote the success of the company for the benefit of the members as a whole. In doing so, he should have regard (amongst other matters) to:

(a) the likely long-term consequences of any decision;

(b) the interests of the employees;

(c) the need to foster relationships with suppliers, customers, and others;

(d) the impact of operations on the community and the environment;

(e) the need to maintain a reputation for high standards of business conduct;

(f) the need to act fairly as between members of the company.

These requirements appear to be wider than the duties under the previous regime. These were, predominantly, to act in the best interests of the company (being the members, present and future) and, under s. 309 CA 1985, to have regard to the interests of the company's employees. One of the main intentions behind the new regime is the development of a principle of 'enlightened shareholder value'. This is designed to result in companies taking account of a wide range of stakeholders who are potentially affected by their business activities. What remains to be seen is the extent to which directors are going to feel the need to be seen to be complying with the new regime. That is, will board minutes of decisions expressly refer to the fact that each of the above matters was considered? The business community is not in favour of this, as it will increase bureaucracy and costs. Two points are likely to support a lower key approach. First, the fact that the overriding duty under s. 172 remains that of acting for the benefit of the members as a whole, as under the previous regime. Secondly, guidance provided by the DTI has stated that, subject to good faith, the decision as to what will promote success is to remain one for a company's directors, not the courts.

9.7.1.4   Duty to exercise independent judgement

This duty is set out in s. 173 CA 2006. The duty will not be infringed by a director where he acts in accordance with an agreement duly entered into by the company or in accordance with the company's constitution.

9.7.1.5   Duty to exercise reasonable care, skill and diligence

This duty, required by s. 174 CA 2006, is to be judged by reference to the care, skill and diligence that would be exercised by a reasonably diligent person with:

(a) the general knowledge, skill and experience that may reasonably be expected of a person carrying out the functions carried out by the director in relation to the company; and

(b) the general knowledge, skill and experience that the director has.

This test, which combines objective and subjective views, is similar to that applied in judging conduct in relation to wrongful trading under s. 214 Insolvency Act 1986.

9.7.1.6   Duty to avoid conflicts of interest

A director is required, by s. 175 CA 2006, to avoid a situation where he has, or can have, a direct or indirect interest that conflicts, or possibly may conflict, with the interests of the company. The section makes specific reference to situations involving the exploitation of any property, information or opportunity, whether or not the company could itself take advantage of such situation. It is important to note, however, that the section is of no relevance to situations involving contracts with the company itself (s. 175(3) CA 2006). Moreover, if the situation in question is one which cannot reasonably be regarded as likely to give rise to a conflict of interest, the duty is not infringed.

Any potential conflict of interest can, however, be authorised by a quorum of non-conflicted directors (the director with the conflict is not to be counted in the quorum). This provision is currently commonly included in private companies' articles but under the 2006 Act the right is given to private companies by statute, provided that their articles do not contain more restrictive provisions. The right is also available to public companies, but only if their constitutions expressly provide for such right.

9.7.1.7   Duty not to accept benefits from third parties

A director of a company is prohibited, by s. 176 CA 2006, from accepting a benefit from a third party conferred by reason of his being a director or his doing (or not doing) anything as a director. There is an exception to this prohibition if the acceptance of the benefit cannot reasonably be regarded as likely to give rise to a conflict of interest. This duty is a statutory version of the previous common law duty not to make a secret profit (see **9.7.2.1**).

9.7.1.8   Duty to declare interest in proposed or existing transactions or arrangements

A director is obliged to declare the nature and extent of his interest in any proposed transaction or arrangement with the company before the company enters into this arrangement (s. 177 CA 2006). (This deals with the apparent gap in s. 175, excluding such contracts from the ambit of that section.) The declaration may be made at a board meeting or by notice in writing to all directors (s. 177(2) CA 2006). A general notice may also be given by a director, under s. 185 CA 2006, to the effect that he is connected with a particular company or specified person, and should therefore be regarded as interested in any transaction or arrangement that may, after the date of the general notice, be made with that company or person.

The obligation is, however, waived if:

(a) The director's interest cannot reasonably be regarded as likely to give rise to a conflict of interest.

(b) The other directors are already aware of the interest or, at least, ought reasonably to be aware of it.

(c) The interest arises out of the terms of the director's service contract with the company, which have been or are to be considered by the board.

It is believed that where the making of a declaration is effectively of neutral consequence, a director is likely to make it, rather than rely upon the above exceptions. However, where a director (possibly for reasons of an obligation of confidentiality) would prefer not to make a declaration, these exceptions and their ambit are much more significant. Finally, in those instances where directors are simply unaware of their obligation or neglect to fulfil it, these exceptions may be relied upon as a defence in any action for breach of duty.

The s. 177 declaration should be contrasted with the alternative declaration to be made pursuant to s. 182 CA 2006 in relation to pre-existing arrangements entered into by the company, in which a director is interested. (This obligation is particularly relevant at the moment a director is appointed.) Whilst the method for making this declaration and the exceptions to doing so are very similar to those under s. 177, this is not technically a duty, and so, the consequences of failing to comply with s. 182 are different. Instead of this being a breach of duty, it is a criminal offence punishable by a fine (s. 183 CA 2006).

9.7.1.9   Breach of directors' duties

The consequences of a breach (or threatened breach) of the above statutory duties are the same as if the corresponding common law rule or equitable principle applied. Hence, the duties are enforceable in the same way as any other fiduciary duty owed to a company by its directors. Members will therefore be able, with court approval, to commence derivative actions (see **10.7**). Where a director has breached a duty or trust, or has conducted himself in a negligent manner, this conduct may be ratified by an ordinary resolution of the members of the company (s. 239 CA 2006).

9.7.2   Fiduciary duties under the common law

The new statutory duties of directors (see **9.7.1**) are, under s. 170 CA 2006, to have effect in place of common rules and equitable principles. However, s. 170(4) states that regard should be had to such rules and principles in interpreting and applying the general statutory duties. It therefore appears that it will remain important to understand the fiduciary duties owed by directors to a company. In this section we will, therefore, briefly consider the previous common law position.

Directors do not hold the property of their company on trust since the company is a separate legal entity and therefore is able to own property directly. However, directors do owe fiduciary duties to their company. That is, they are in the same position in respect of their powers as trustees or agents with respect to the company. Under the common law, the two main duties for directors to observe were the duty not to make any secret profit from their position and the duty to exercise the powers given to them bona fide for the benefit of the company.

The liability of directors for breach of duty is personal. However, the advice they receive may be relevant to whether they are in breach of duty. In *Norman v Theodore Goddard* [1992] BCC 14 it was held that a director was not liable for breach of fiduciary duty when he reasonably relied on advice given to him by a partner in a firm of solicitors.

9.7.2.1   Secret profit

Profit from position as director
The concept of secret profit is a rather intangible one; it does not, of course, prevent directors from receiving remuneration for their services. A profit is a secret profit if it comes to the director because of his position as a director:

In *Cook v Deeks* [1916] 1 AC 554, two directors of a company negotiated a construction contract with the Canadian Pacific Railroad on behalf of their company. At a late stage in the negotiations they decided to take the contract in their own names. The Privy Council held that they were accountable to their company for the profit; it was only through their position as directors of the company (which had previously contracted with the Canadian Pacific) that they were able to make the profit.

'Secret' means failure to obtain permission

Although the fiduciary duty is to hand over what are described as secret profits, it seems that secrecy in this context means failure to obtain permission rather than actual secrecy:

In *Regal (Hastings) Ltd v Gulliver* [1967] 2 AC 134, the plaintiff company owned a cinema and wished to buy two others in the same town with a view to selling all three together. The company could not raise sufficient money to buy the other cinemas and so another company was set up partly owned by Regal (Hastings) Ltd and partly by some of the directors of Regal (Hastings) Ltd who had money of their own to invest. The new company then purchased the other two cinemas. The purchasers who wished to acquire all three cinemas then purchased all the shares in Regal (Hastings) Ltd and in the new company, thus acquiring control of the companies. The new board of directors then instituted proceedings on behalf of Regal (Hastings) Ltd against its former directors. It was held by the House of Lords that a secret profit had been made since the opportunity to invest in the new company only came to the defendants because they were directors of Regal (Hastings) Ltd. This profit was ordered to be paid to Regal (Hastings) Ltd even though that company had been unable to raise all the money needed for the purchase itself and even though, realistically, the consequences of the order was that the purchaser who had negotiated the purchase of the shares at a fair price got some of the purchase price repaid to their own company.

Secret profit to be paid to company

A secret profit must be paid over to the company even if the company itself could not have made the profit:

In *Boston Deep Sea Fishing Co. v Ansell* (1888) 39 ChD 339, the defendant was a director of the plaintiff company and negotiated a contract on its behalf for the supply of ice to a fleet of fishing smacks owned by the company. The defendant was a shareholder in the ice-making company which had a policy of paying 'bonuses' to any of its shareholders who introduced work to it. The court held that the defendant was liable to the company for the bonuses even though the company itself could not have obtained them since it was not a shareholder in the ice-making company.

9.7.2.2   Exercise of powers bona fide in the interests of the company as a whole

The second requirement of directors' fiduciary duties is that the directors must exercise their powers bona fide in the interests of the company as a whole. This involves two separate restrictions on directors' powers:

(a) Directors must not exercise their powers other than for the purpose for which they were given; if they exercise their powers for some other reason, their decisions may be challenged.

In *Hogg v Cramphorn Ltd* [1967] Ch 254, directors issued shares to trustees for the benefit of employees. The purpose of the directors in issuing the shares was found to be the prevention of a takeover of the company. It was held that the issue could be challenged (even though the directors believed it to be in the interests of the company as a whole), since the purpose of giving directors the power to issue shares is to enable them to raise capital.

(b) Directors must not exercise their powers for motives of personal gain (this often overlaps with the rule against directors making secret profits).

In *Piercy v S. Mills & Co. Ltd* [1920] 1 Ch 77, shares were issued, at a time when capital was not needed, purely for the purpose of strengthening and maintaining the directors' control of the company. The issue was held to be invalid.

(Many of the cases on this type of breach of duty have been concerned with the issue of shares by directors, which power is now much restricted by legislation—see **Chapter 11**.)

9.7.3   Duty to make returns

The duty to make returns to the Registrar of Companies will normally be performed on behalf of a company by its secretary, but directors are in some circumstances also liable to a fine if returns are not made and persistent default can lead to disqualification. The directors are also under a duty to keep minutes of their own meetings and to deliver accounts.

9.7.4   Directors' duties to third parties

A director does not generally owe any direct duty to a person dealing with his company, notwithstanding the requirement under s. 172 CA 2006 to have regard to various third parties' interests. (The duty to have regard to these interests is in fact owed to the company's members.) However, a director can make himself liable to a third party in a particular case if he claims an authority to bind his company which he does not have. The action resulting from such a liability is called an action for breach of warranty of authority (see **9.12**).

9.8   Statutory controls on directors

Because of the very high degree of control which directors are able to exercise over their companies, a number of statutory provisions have been enacted in the Companies Acts for the protection of shareholders and the public generally. These are all now to be found in the 2006 Act.

9.8.1   Disclosure of information

9.8.1.1   Register of directors

Section 162 CA 2006 requires every company to keep at its registered office a register of directors. In respect of each director (including any shadow director) the following information must be given:

(a) present forename(s) and surname, and any former name;

(b) a service address;

(c) the country or state (or part of the UK) in which he is usually resident;

(d) nationality;

(e) business occupation (if any);

(f) date of birth.

The same information must also be sent to the Registrar of Companies. Section 12 CA 2006 requires notification of particulars of the first directors. Where there is any change in directors or directors' particulars (whether because a director is appointed or ceases to hold office, or because of changes in the particulars of the continuing directors), notice must be given to the Registrar within 14 days of any such change. This duty arises under s. 167 CA 2006.

9.8.1.2   Service contracts

Copies of directors' service contracts must be available for inspection by the members (s. 228 CA 2006). If a director does not have a written service contract, then a written memorandum of his terms of service must be kept instead.

9.8.2 Restrictions on freedom of contract

9.8.2.1 Directors' service contracts

The terms of directors' service contracts will usually be determined by the board although members are entitled to information about the terms of such contracts. Section 188 CA 2006 requires the approval of the members by ordinary resolution of any provision in a director's service contract which provides for a guaranteed term exceeding two years. Approval is also required where an existing contract is extended if the aggregate term exceeds two years.

EXAMPLE

D's service contract is for a fixed period of four years and contains no provision for early termination by the company. This contract would require shareholder approval.

D's service contract is for an indefinite period, terminable at any time by the company on six months' notice. This contract would not require shareholder approval.

Alternatively, D's service contract is for an indefinite period, terminable at any time by the company on three years' notice. This contract would require shareholder approval.

If a company agrees to a provision in contravention of s. 188, the provision is void to the extent of the contravention and the company is deemed to be able to terminate the contract by reasonable notice.

9.8.2.2 Substantial property transactions

Section 190 CA 2006 controls arrangements whereby:

(a) a director of a company (or its holding company), or a person connected with that director, is to acquire from the company a substantial non-cash asset; or

(b) the company is to acquire a substantial non-cash asset from one of its directors (or a director of its holding company) or a person connected with that director.

EXAMPLE

The main situations s. 190 is concerned with are:

(a) Co A buys from or sells to X, a director of Co A.

(b) Co A buys from or sells to T, a person connected with a director of Co A.

(c) Co A buys from or sells to Y, a director of the holding company of Co A.

(d) Co A buys from or sells to F, a person connected with a director of the holding company of Co A.

For the purposes of s. 190 a connected person includes (among others) a director's spouse, child or step-child (ss. 252 and 253 CA 2006). Additionally, there are complicated rules for determining the extent to which a company is connected with a director. Put simply, if a director owns at least 20% of the share capital of a company, that company is connected with him (s. 254(2) CA 2006).

A substantial non-cash asset is defined by s. 191 CA 2006 as an asset which has a value which, at the time of the relevant arrangement:

(a) exceeds 10% of the company's asset value and is more than £5,000; or

(b) exceeds £100,000.

A company's asset value will normally be determined by reference to the company's most recent statutory accounts.

The value to be attributed to the asset in question raises two interesting issues. The first is that this value must be the market value of the asset, otherwise directors could manipulate the price paid to fall outside the ambit of the section. Secondly, should the market value be adjudged by reference to any special value which the asset may have to the relevant director? In *Micro Leisure Ltd v County Properties and Developments* [2000] TLR 12, this question was answered in the affirmative. Lord Hamilton put forward the example of a ransom strip of land which, when purchased by a director, would substantially increase the development potential of the director's existing land. It is submitted, however, that situations where the objective market value and the 'director-specific' value are different will be rare.

Any arrangement to which s. 190 does apply must be approved by the company's members by ordinary resolution in advance or must be made on the basis that such approval will subsequently be given. (This requirement does not apply, however, where the company in question is a wholly-owned subsidiary (s. 190(4)(b) CA 2006).)

Additionally, if the relevant director or person connected with that director is:

(a) a director of the company's holding company; or

(b) a person connected with a director of the company's holding company;

an ordinary resolution of the members of that holding company must also be obtained or the transaction must be made on the basis that such approval will subsequently be given.

EXAMPLE

B Limited is a wholly-owned subsidiary of A Limited. Zahid is a director of both companies.

If B Limited were to sell a substantial asset to Zahid, an ordinary resolution of A Limited would be necessary, but not one of the shareholders of B Limited itself (as it is 100% owned). (Although the board of B Limited would have to resolve to sell the asset, in any event.)

S Limited is an 80% subsidiary of T Limited. Cecil is a director of T Limited only.

If S Limited were to sell a substantial asset to Cecil, an ordinary resolution of both T Limited and S Limited would be necessary—the sale is to a director of S Limited's holding company and S Limited is not wholly-owned. (As in the above example, the board of S Limited would have to resolve to sell the asset, in any event.)

Any contract made in contravention of the above requirements is voidable by the company unless:

(a) the contract is subsequently affirmed within a reasonable time by ordinary resolution of the members of the company and any holding company, as necessary;

(b) restitution of the money paid or the relevant asset is no longer possible;

(c) the company has been indemnified by any other persons for the loss or damage suffered by it; or

(d) third party rights (acquired for value without notice) would be affected by avoidance.

In respect of any transaction which contravenes s. 190, the following are potentially liable to account to the company which entered into the transaction for any gain that they made and to indemnify that company for any loss which it suffered as a result of the transaction:

(a) any director of the company or its holding company who was a party to the transaction;

(b) any person with whom the company entered into the arrangement who is connected with a director of the company or its holding company;

(c) the director of the company or holding company with whom any such person is connected; and

(d) any other director of the company who authorised the transaction.

Liability may be avoided by a director where the transaction was with a person connected with a director of a company or its holding company and the director shows he took all reasonable steps to secure the company's compliance with s. 190. In addition, the parties detailed at (b) and (d) above will not be liable if, at the time of the transaction, they were unaware of the circumstances constituting the contravention of s. 190.

The main purpose of s. 190 is to prevent directors from making substantial profits in transactions with their companies and so reinforces the rules about conflicts of interest. One fairly common type of contract which is subject to its provisions is a contract under which a director receives shares in return for assets: for example, if a director who owns business premises (of the requisite value) wishes to transfer them to the company in return for shares, the approval of the members in general meeting must first be obtained.

9.8.2.3 Loans to directors

The Companies Act 2006 has removed some of the restrictions on companies making loans to directors, whilst preserving controls on such transactions. The provisions relating to loans and similar indirect transactions (quasi-loans and credit transactions) are contained in ss. 197–214 CA 2006.

Any company may not make a loan to a director of the company or its holding company nor may it guarantee or provide security in connection with a loan made by any person to such a director, unless the transaction has been approved by ordinary resolution (s. 197(1) CA 2006). (This requirement does not apply, however, where the company in question is a wholly-owned subsidiary (s. 197(5)(b) CA 2006).)

In addition, in those instances where the relevant director is a director of the company's holding company, an ordinary resolution of that company's shareholders is required.

EXAMPLE

Carrington Limited lends money to a director—an ordinary resolution of the shareholders of Carrington is required.

Carrington Limited guarantees a loan made by Credit Bank to a director—an ordinary resolution of the shareholders of Carrington is required.

Carrington Limited lends money to a director of its holding company—an ordinary resolution of the shareholders of the holding company is required. Whether or not the shareholders of Carrington must also approve the loan will depend upon whether or not it is a wholly-owned subsidiary.

Public companies are subject to greater regulation in a number of ways. First they must seek shareholder approval for:

(a) any loan made to a person connected with a director or with a director of any holding company; or

(b) any guarantee or security provided in connection with a loan made by any person to such a connected person.

Secondly, they must also seek shareholder approval before entering into any arrangement with a director or with a director of its holding company or with any person connected with either of those persons which amounts to a quasi-loan. The same is true for any guarantee or security provided by the company in respect of a quasi-loan made by any person to any of those such persons.

Quasi-loans (as defined by s. 199 CA 2006) are effectively situations where a director incurs a payment obligation and the company agrees to meet that obligation on the director's behalf or agrees to reimburse the relevant amount to the director, on the understanding that the director will repay the sum in question to the company.

Thirdly, public companies must also seek shareholder approval before entering into any arrangement with a director or with a director of its holding company or with any person connected with either of those persons which amounts to a credit transaction. The same is true for any guarantee or security provided by the company in respect of a credit transaction entered into by any person for the benefit of any of those such persons.

Credit transactions (as defined by s. 202 CA 2006) are effectively situations where the company (or a third party) sells or leases an asset to the director in return for payment by the director in instalments or on the basis that payment is to be deferred.

EXAMPLE

Partington plc agrees to guarantee a loan made by Credit Bank to the husband of one of its directors. In contrast to a private company, where shareholder approval would not be necessary for the guarantee of a loan made to a connected person, an ordinary resolution would be necessary here.

If Partington plc were to enter into a credit transaction with any of:

(a) a director;

(b) a director of its holding company;

(c) a person connected with a director of its holding company;

shareholder approval would be necessary as follows:

(i) in respect of example (a), an ordinary resolution of Partington's shareholders, unless Partington was a wholly-owned subsidiary;

(ii) in respect of example (b), an ordinary resolution of the shareholders of the holding company and of Partington's shareholders, unless Partington was a wholly-owned subsidiary;

(iii) in respect of example (c), an ordinary resolution of the shareholders of the holding company and of Partington's shareholders, unless Partington was a wholly-owned subsidiary.

In all instances where shareholder approval is required, a memorandum setting out prescribed details of the relevant transaction must be made available to the members in advance of the resolution being passed.

There are a number of exceptions to the above, most notably:

(a) Any company may, without member approval, provide a director (or a director of its holding company) with funds to meet expenditure incurred or to be incurred by him for the purposes of the company or for the purpose of enabling him properly to perform his duties, provided that the aggregate value of any such transactions with a director does not exceed £50,000 (s. 204).

(b) Companies need not seek shareholder approval for any loan, guarantee, security or quasi-loan if the value of that transaction, together with any other similar transactions, does not exceed £10,000 (s. 207(1)).

(c) Companies need not seek shareholder approval for any credit transaction or guarantee or security related to a credit transaction, if the value of that transaction, together with any other similar transactions, does not exceed £15,000 (s. 207(2)).

(d) Any company may, without member approval, provide a director (or a director of its holding company) with funds to meet expenditure incurred or to be incurred by him for the purposes of defending (or avoiding) criminal or civil proceedings which arise out of any alleged negligence or breach of duty or trust of that director in relation to the company (s. 205). (Note that there are a number of detailed conditions which must be fulfilled for the loan to fall within this exception.)

The consequences of failing to obtain the necessary shareholders' approval for a loan, quasi-loan or credit transaction are similar to those in respect of substantial property transactions, namely:

(a) The transaction or arrangement is voidable at the company's instance (subject to issues of impossibility or third-party rights acquired in good faith) (s. 213(2)).

(b) The relevant director of the company or its holding company and any other director of the company who authorised the transaction is liable to account to the company which entered into the transaction for any gain that they made and to indemnity that company for any loss which it suffered as a result of the transaction (s. 213(3) and (4)). (This provision extends to relevant connected persons in respect of loans, quasi-loans and credit transactions or related guarantees or security made or granted by public companies.)

As with substantial property transactions, subsequent affirmation by ordinary resolution is also possible (s. 214).

9.9 Managing directors

9.9.1 Appointment and powers

It is very common for one of the directors of a company to be appointed managing director. The functions actually performed by the managing director vary from company to company, but in practice he will usually be either the most senior director in the company's hierarchy or second in command to the chairman. A managing director cannot be appointed unless the articles so provide. Table A, art. 84 does so provide and additionally art. 72 provides that: '[the directors] may . . . delegate to any managing director . . . such of their powers as they consider desirable to be exercised by him'. The Model Articles contain wider powers of delegation, allowing directors to delegate 'to such persons . . . to such an extent . . . as they think fit' (art. 5).

9.9.2 Service contract

The managing director will usually have a service contract. The terms of the contract will be negotiated by the managing director and the board; the members' approval will be required if he is given security of tenure for longer than two years (s. 188 CA 2006—see **9.8.2.1**). The managing director is both a director and an employee of the company; like other employees he has certain statutory rights against the company if he is unfairly dismissed or made redundant. Since he automatically ceases to be managing director if he ceases to be a director, the members can remove him from both offices by passing an ordinary resolution (s. 168 CA 2006), but this may result in heavy damages being payable by the company for breach of the service contract (see **9.5.1.3** above).

9.10 Alternate directors

The articles can give a director power to appoint (subject to the approval of the board) an alternate director. Once appointed, the alternate director has all the powers of the appointing director until he is removed by the appointing director or the appointing director ceases to be a director. However, the alternate director is not entitled to receive remuneration from the company for his services.

The Model Articles for Private Companies do not contain provision for alternate directors, as it is thought unlikely that directors of private companies would wish to appoint alternates. The equivalent articles for public companies do contain such a provision, which could be adopted by private companies, if the need arose.

9.11 Shadow directors

A 'shadow director' is defined by s. 251(1) CA 2006 as 'any person in accordance with whose directions or instructions the directors of a company are accustomed to act'. However, a person who gives advice in a professional capacity to the directors is not to be taken to be a shadow director. Similar provisions are contained in s. 251 Insolvency Act 1986.

Under a number of provisions of the 2006 Act, shadow directors are treated as directors of the company. Examples of the provisions which apply to shadow directors are:

(a) the general duties of directors (see **9.7.1**);

(b) the statutory restrictions on substantial property transactions and loans (see **9.8.2.2** and **9.8.2.3**);

(c) the requirement to disclose interests in contracts with the company to the board (see **9.7.1.8**); and

(d) the provisions relating to service contracts (see **9.8.2.1**).

In addition, and perhaps more significantly, shadow directors are deemed to be directors for the purpose of wrongful trading under s. 214 Insolvency Act 1986 (see **27.1**), by which they may become personally liable for the debts of an insolvent company. Under the Company Directors Disqualification Act 1986, shadow directors may also be disqualified from holding office or being concerned in the management of a company, as if they were directors.

9.12 The directors and protection of outsiders

9.12.1 Introduction

A company is not a natural person and so can only exercise its powers through agents. Usually contracts will be made on behalf of the company either by the directors or by more junior officials acting on the directors' authority. If a contract is made in accordance with the articles of the company it will be binding on the company, so that the 'outsider' with whom the company is dealing can sue the company if it fails to perform the contract. Where, however, a contract is made by the wrong people (e.g., the directors exercise a power which is vested in the shareholders, or an employee acts without the authority of the directors), or in the wrong way (e.g., a meeting is held but it has not been properly convened), the whole transaction is, prima facie, void. Contracts and other transactions decided upon without proper authority (or without a proper exercise of authority) are described as 'irregular'.

In dealing with irregular contracts the law is faced with a dilemma. If the contract is declared irregular and void, the outsider will not be able to enforce it against the company, even though he may be unaware of the irregularity. On the other hand, if the company is held to be bound by irregular contracts, the directors will, in effect, be able to ignore the requirements of the company's constitution to the possible detriment of the shareholders. The law deals with this dilemma by providing that irregular contracts, though prima facie void, are often binding on the company in certain circumstances. These circumstances result partly from statute and partly from the general law of agency.

9.12.2 Statutory protection

Section 40 (1) CA 2006 provides:

In favour of a person dealing with a company in good faith, the power of the board of directors to bind the company, or to authorise others to do so, shall be deemed free of any limitation under the company's constitution.

(The reference to the company's constitution (for this purpose) includes a resolution of the company and agreements between the company and its members as well as the articles.)

The sphere of directors' actions can be limited by a company's constitution in two main ways:

(a) Any restrictions on a company's objects contained within the articles, which directors have a duty to observe (see **9.7.1.2**); and

(b) Any regulations governing directors' activities contained within its articles, such as a requirement for the board to seek shareholder approval for certain transactions or for it to act in accordance with instructions provided by special resolution.

In respect of the first issue, the following should be borne in mind:

(a) Companies which are set up under the 2006 regime will no longer have any objects clause in their memoranda; their objects will be unrestricted, unless any contrary statement appears in the articles. On the basis that few companies will want to restrict their objects, the possibility of directors committing those companies to an action outside its objects will not be an issue.

(b) The objects clauses of companies set up under the 1985 Act will be deemed to be absorbed into the articles. Directors of those companies will still, therefore, have to consider the ambit of the objects clause, unless their company chooses to re-move the objects clause altogether from the articles.

The effect of s. 40 CA 2006 is that:

(a) where an unconnected third party;

(b) acting in good faith;

(c) enters into a contract with a company;

(d) which contract has been decided on or authorised by the board of that company then, notwithstanding any restrictions on the board's powers under the company's constitution (and whether or not the third party is aware of any such restriction), the contract will be valid. However, the directors may be liable to the company for any loss caused on the basis that they have breached their duty to the company.

It should be noted that under s. 40(2)(a), a person dealing with the company is not under an obligation to enquire as to any limitation that the directors may be subject to.

Requirements of good faith

The protection of s. 40 is given only to persons who act in good faith. However, good faith is presumed unless the contrary is proved (s. 40(2)(b)(ii)) and knowledge that the directors are acting beyond their powers is not of itself sufficient proof of bad faith (s. 40(2)(b)(iii)).

Transaction with connected party

Section 41 CA 2006 makes a limited exception to s. 40. This applies where the board of a company exceed their powers in a transaction with a director or a person connected with a director. In such cases the transaction is voidable by the company. Whether or not it is avoided, the director or connected person and any director who authorised the transaction is liable to account to the company for any gain he makes and to indemnify the company against any loss. Where a transaction is irregular and is made between the company, a director and one or more third parties the court has a wide discretion which enables it to protect any innocent third party.

The company's right to avoid a contract under s. 41 is lost if:

(a) restitution becomes impossible;

(b) a third party who has acquired rights bona fide for value would be affected;

(c) the transaction is affirmed by the shareholders; or

(d) the company has been fully compensated by an indemnity against any loss or damage.

9.12.3   Agency

9.12.3.1   General position

A company can only act through agents; the authority of agents to act for a company depends on the general law of agency. The actions of an agent are binding on a principal if the agent has actual authority or authority arising from estoppel. The agent may also be personally liable to the third party (i.e., to the outsider) if the principal (i.e., the company) is not liable.

9.12.3.2   Actual authority

The scope of the actual authority of a company's agents depends upon the constitution of the company. The board of directors, acting collectively, usually has very wide powers to act on behalf of the company. The articles will usually permit delegation to committees of directors and to a managing director (or to other directors exercising similar executive functions).

Of fundamental concern, therefore, is the status of the agent director. Section 161 CA 2006 provides that the acts of a director are valid notwithstanding that it is afterwards discovered:

(a) that there was a defect in his appointment;

(b) that he was disqualified from holding office;

(c) that he had ceased to hold office;

(d) that he was not entitled to vote on the matter in question.

This section protects an outsider dealing with a company and means that it does not have to be concerned with certain procedural or legal irregularities which may have occurred and which it may not have been alive to or been able to discover when dealing with the director.

9.12.3.3 Agency by estoppel

A company may be bound by the acts of a person acting on its behalf when it is estopped from denying that person's authority. The estoppel may prevent the company from denying that the alleged agent is its agent or that he has power to bind the company in a particular way.

Agency by estoppel may result either from 'holding out' (that is, a representation that the agent has authority, even if no actual authority existed) or from a representation that the agent is a member of a particular class of agent which is recognised to have certain powers to bind its principals.

'Apparent authority'

Directors do not generally have authority to act alone, so a company is prima facie not bound by the actions of a single director, unless the board has conferred upon him actual authority by formal delegation of that authority in accordance with the articles. However, directors may conduct company business in all manner of contexts, either as a board or individually. Contracting third parties need the comfort of knowing that whenever they deal with a director, the director's actions can be relied upon. Effectively, apparent authority serves this purpose and ensures that the company is still bound, irrespective of the existence or otherwise of actual authority.

The main requirement is that the board has represented to the third party that the director has authority in the particular transaction. The representation does not need to be formal or active; often it will simply be the fact that the director is allowed to conduct himself in a particular way.

Possibly the leading case on this is *Freeman and Lockyer v Buckhurst Park Properties* [1964] 1 All ER 630, where a director was often left in overall charge of the company, due to the absence overseas of the other main board member. The director in question had engaged the services of a firm of surveyors, without reference to his fellow board members, due to the circumstances described. The company in due course refused to pay the surveyors' fees on the basis that the director had engaged the surveyors without actual authority to do so. The Court of Appeal held that the company was so bound, due to the apparent authority of the director.

Usual authority

It is a well-established rule of the law of agency that a principal is estopped from denying that an agent of certain recognised classes has the authority normally associated with that class (unless, of course, he tells the third party that there is a restriction on the power of the agent). In relation to companies, this rule has been applied to managing directors. If a company describes one of the directors as a managing director, it is estopped from denying that he is a managing director (even if he has not been appointed) and that he has the authority of a managing director (even if his appointment includes terms restricting his authority). This type of authority is best described as 'usual authority'.

A director may also have an authority because of some other office which he holds. For example in *First Energy (UK) v Hungarian International Bank* [1993] 2 Lloyd's Rep 194, a bank manager was held to have authority (by reason of his office) to make a statement as to a loan agreement which was binding on the bank. The bank manager in question was not a director but his authority would have been the same if he had been.

The company secretary has been held to have usual authority to bind the company to contracts concerning administration.

9.12.3.4   Liability of agent to third party

A person purporting to act as agent for a company will be personally liable to a third party for breach of warranty of authority if it turns out that he had no authority to bind the company.

9.12.3.5   Ratification

If a contract is made by an agent without authority so that the company is not bound by the contract, the company can ratify, and thus retrospectively validate, the contract. Ratification may be effected by the people with actual authority to bind the company (i.e., normally the board, but in some cases the members in general meeting—see s. 239 CA 2006). Ratification will usually be implied where the company has accepted performance of the contract.

9.13   The company secretary

9.13.1   Appointment

As from 6 April 2008, s. 270 CA 2006 has removed the requirement for a private company to have a secretary. Such companies set up prior to this date will already have one appointed. Therefore, they may either keep a secretary in post or bring this appointment to an end. Private companies set up after this date have the option of incorporating with or without an appointed secretary. In the latter instance, a secretary may be appointed at a later date.

It will remain a requirement, under s. 271, for public companies to have a secretary. The appointment and removal of secretaries is a matter for the articles and is normally reserved to the board of directors (see, for example, Table A, art. 99). The New Model Articles for Private (but not public) Companies contain no such provision, in recognition of the impact of s. 270.

9.13.2   Responsibilities and powers

The secretary is responsible for keeping the various records of the company, such as minutes of board and general meetings and the various records which must be kept at the registered office. He is also an officer of the company and so is liable to a fine if the company is in breach of the provisions of the Companies Act which require information to be filed with the Registrar of Companies.

Where a private company has no secretary, the duties of a secretary may be carried out by a director or any person authorised by the directors to carry out such duties.

Many company secretaries are given powers far in excess of those contemplated by the Companies Act. Often the secretary is responsible for the administration of the company and performs the functions of an office manager as well as of a record-keeper. The courts have, therefore, recognised that an outsider is entitled to rely on a decision taken by the secretary which relates to administration even if it turns out that the decision was not authorised by the board (i.e., the secretary has usual authority to make such contracts). Thus in *Panorama (Developments) Guildford Ltd v Fidelis Furnishing Fabrics Ltd* [1971] 2 QB 711, the Court of Appeal held that a company was bound to pay for the use of cars hired by the secretary purportedly on behalf of the company but in fact for his own use.

9.13.3 Register

Companies are required to keep a register of secretaries (where appointed) and to notify the Registrar of Companies within 14 days of any change (ss. 275 and 276 CA 2006 respectively). (Although note that until 1 October 2009, the governing provision will actually be s. 288 CA 1985, which contains similar requirements.)

online resource centre

Interactive online exercises (Student Learning Activities) which complement the topics covered in this chapter are available at www.oxfordtextbooks.co.uk/orc/business09_10/.

Shareholders

This chapter covers the following topics:

10.1   Introduction

This chapter will deal with the position of shareholders in relation to a company. We will look at the following issues:

(a) registration of membership;

(b) the powers of shareholders in relation to their company;

(c) the legal protection given to shareholders by the rules of equity and by the Companies Act;

(d) the payment of dividends to shareholders.

You will find references to shareholders throughout this Guide so that this chapter is intended to deal with their position in the company in general terms. Bear this in mind as you progress through your studies—it is always dangerous to pigeonhole things too much. You cannot understand the position of shareholders fully until you understand the position of directors (and vice versa).

10.1.1   The right to membership

It has already been explained (see **Chapters 7** and **8**) that all private companies must have at least one 'member'. Section 112 CA 2006 provides that:

(1) The subscribers of a company's memorandum are deemed to have agreed to become members of the company, and on its registration become members and must be entered as such in its register of members.

(2) Every other person who agrees to become a member of a company, and whose name is entered in its register of members, is a member of the company.

This means that membership begins either:

(a) When a company is registered, in respect of the subscribers to the memorandum; or

(b) When the shareholder's name is entered in the register of members, in any other instance.

In respect of this second instance, the *right* to become a member may result from a contract between the company and the purchaser of new shares (this is called an allotment or issue of shares; see **Chapter 11**). The right may also arise because an existing shareholder transfers shares to someone else by sale or gift. It may also arise when a member dies or becomes bankrupt. At that time the shares are automatically transmitted to the personal representative or trustee in bankruptcy. From this we can see that it is the ownership of shares which entitles the shareholder to become a member of a company, but a company must formally register that person as a member for their membership to take effect. (This is particularly important in the area of buying and selling shares; see **Chapter 12** for further details.) Hence, the terms 'member' and 'shareholder' mean almost the same thing, but there is a technical difference.

When someone becomes a shareholder and is registered as a member that person normally acquires some influence over the company's activities, as well as ownership of a percentage of the company.

10.1.2 Protection of shareholders

In most companies, it is the directors who actually run the company (see **Chapter 9**). As there may be a conflict between the interests of the directors and the shareholders, the law steps in to provide a measure of protection to the shareholders. When giving advice on these matters, it is vital to distinguish between shareholders in various categories. As we have already seen (see **9.5**), a shareholder with a majority of the votes has the power to remove the directors from office. When this power is available to a shareholder it is likely to be the most effective way in which he can control the company. Bear in mind, however, that with owner-managed companies, the directors and shareholders will be the same people, so they will have rights in both capacities. (These matters are dealt with more fully in **10.3** below.)

10.2 Registration of membership

10.2.1 Contents of the register

Every company must keep a register of its members and their shareholdings (s. 113 CA 2006). The following information must be recorded:

(a) the names and addresses of the members;

(b) the number of shares held and, where the company has more than one class of issued shares, the number of each class held by each member;

(c) the amount paid or agreed to be considered as paid on the shares of each member;

(d) the date at which each member was entered in the register;

(e) the date at which each member ceased to be a member.

Additionally, pursuant to s. 123 CA 2006, if the company has only one member, the register must also contain:

(a) a statement to that effect and of the date when this occurred;

(b) if the company formerly had only one member, a statement that the number has increased to two or more and the date when this occurred.

The register must normally be kept at the registered office of the company and, if kept elsewhere, the Registrar of Companies must be notified (s. 114 CA 2006). The register of members itself is not sent to the Registrar but the annual return made by a company contains details of the membership.

No particular form of register is required, but under s. 115 CA 2006 an index is required if the register is not kept in the form of an index and there are more than 50 members. (This provision is of little relevance to private companies since very few of them have more than 50 members.)

10.2.2 Trusts

In certain instances, the legal and beneficial title to shares is split by the beneficial owner appointing a nominee to hold the legal title in the shares on their behalf, normally for reasons of anonymity or convenience. Section 126 CA 2006 provides that 'no notice of any trust . . . shall be entered on the register of members . . . ' The effect of this is that the company need only deal with the nominee, as the legal owner of shares, even if it knows that they are held on trust. The company must, therefore, pay dividends to the trustee and allow the trustee to exercise any voting powers attached to the shares. Accordingly, the beneficial owner is technically disenfranchised. (Although, this situation does not, of course, affect the position as between the nominee and the true owner. The nominee must, therefore, hand over to the beneficial owner any dividend he receives and vote in accordance with the owner's wishes.)

The 2006 Act has introduced a new concept whereby a shareholder (i.e., the nominee) may appoint another person to enjoy or exercise their rights, that is, the beneficial owner, if the articles so permit (Part 9 CA 2006). It is not expected that many closely-held, private companies will want to take advantage of this possibility, but it may have more relevance to listed companies, where a number of their investors may hold their shareholdings through nominees.

Additionally, shareholders in listed companies will automatically enjoy the ability to nominate another to enjoy 'information rights', that is, to receive copies of all communications from the company to its shareholders. In this way, a beneficial owner can be kept informed of relevant activity within the company.

10.3 Powers and duties of shareholders

10.3.1 Sources of shareholders' powers

The powers of the shareholders are not easy to define succinctly. As we saw in **Chapter 9**, most of the decisions of a company are taken by the board of directors, but certain powers are specifically given to the members by the Companies Act and these cannot be taken away by the memorandum or articles. In addition to these powers which are guaranteed by law, certain powers are also given to members by the articles. Thus, if Table A applies, the members have power to elect new directors and to declare dividends. It should be noted that the powers given to members are given collectively; therefore, a shareholder (or group of shareholders) who controls the majority of the votes at a company meeting is obviously in a far stronger position than a 'minority' shareholder.

10.3.2   Powers of control

In practical terms, a majority shareholder has extensive powers of control, exercisable ultimately by removing or threatening to remove the directors from office. A minority shareholder often has no real power (unless he is a director and/or can persuade the majority to agree with him), but his position is protected by a number of rights, mostly statutory, some of the most important of which are discussed later in this chapter.

The powers and rights given to members depend in many cases on the holding of a particular proportion of the company's shares (or votes). For example, a number of types of decision require a special resolution (75% majority)—a shareholder who controls 75% of the votes is, therefore, able to exercise powers which a shareholder with a simple majority (that is, over 50%) could not exercise alone. Conversely, a shareholder with more than 25% of the votes can block a special resolution even though he does not have enough votes to be in control of the company. (This is sometimes called negative control.)

10.3.3   Duties of shareholders

Just as the powers and rights of members largely depend on the proportion of votes that they control, so the duties of members differ depending on whether or not they are in control of the company. The basic rule is that members (whether or not in control) can exercise their right to vote as they wish, so that they can take account of their own interests to the exclusion of conflicting interest of other shareholders. However, this does not mean that shareholders are *entirely* free to vote as they please; as we shall see in the sections which follow, acting purely out of naked self-interest may entitle those affected by such actions to bring an action in the courts.

The powers of shareholders to control their companies are normally exercised by passing a resolution by the required majority at a general meeting called by the appropriate notice at which a quorum is present. Members who are absent do not count in the voting unless they have validly appointed a proxy to represent them. Alternatively, a written resolution may be used (unless the company is public).

(Company meetings and resolutions are dealt with in **Chapter 13**.)

10.4   Internal disputes—introduction

The courts are very reluctant to get involved in disputes within a company. In particular, they are not willing to do anything which might amount to interference with business decisions. Internal disputes must therefore usually be resolved under the terms of the company's articles. For example, if there are disputes about business policy, the view of the majority of the board will prevail. In the case of an equal division on the board, the deadlock can be resolved by the chairman's casting vote if the articles so provide.

The power of the shareholders is rather limited. In this section, we will look at the procedures which are available to shareholders for their protection. At the outset of this discussion, it is important to recognise that there are two main methods of shareholder protection: either a shareholder will be relying upon their contractual rights which derive from the company's constitution or they will be seeking a statutory remedy.

10.5 The constitution as a contract

10.5.1 Contract between members and company

Section 33 CA 2006 states that:

The provisions of a company's constitution bind the company and its members to the same extent as if there were covenants on the part of the company and of each member to observe those provisions.

In turn, s. 17 defines the constitution as including the articles and any special resolutions of the shareholders. (Note that for companies incorporated under the 1985 Act regime, the influence of the memorandum will continue to be felt through the impact of s. 28 CA 2006, which will deem relevant provisions of the memorandum as part of the articles.)

The effect of this important section is that the constitution forms an agreement which contractually binds:

(a) a company to each of its members; and

(b) the members of the company to each other.

Thus, if specific provisions are not observed, an action may be taken to enforce the obligations imposed by the company's constitution. The extent to which obligations are enforceable is considered further below.

10.5.2 Membership rights

An obligation imposed by the constitution on a member or on the company for the benefit of a member is only enforceable if it relates to membership rights. The most obvious examples of membership rights which have been enforced as a result of actions based on the section include:

(a) the right to a dividend once lawfully declared (*Wood v Odessa Waterworks Co.* (1889) 42 ChD 636);

(b) the right to share in surplus capital on a winding up (*Griffith v Paget* (1877) 5 ChD 894); and

(c) the right to vote at meetings (*Pender v Lushington* (1877) 6 ChD 70).

The most obvious obligation of a member which may be enforced by a company is the obligation to pay for shares issued by it.

It should be noted that a company's articles are a contract complete in themselves. The court will not normally, therefore, imply any additional terms into the articles. A good example of this rule is found in *Bratton Seymour Service Co. v Oxborough* [1992] BCC 471, where the rule worked in favour of the members, as the company, which was set up to manage a development of flats, claimed unsuccessfully that the members had an obligation to contribute to the upkeep of certain communal areas related to the flats.

10.5.3 Other rights

Obligations imposed by the constitution which do not relate to membership rights are not enforceable under s. 33. A member may, therefore, be left without any remedy, even though the company has failed to observe an article which would have benefited him. This is illustrated by the case of *Eley v Positive Government Security Life Assurance Co.* (1876) 1 ExD 88. When the company was formed a provision was included in the articles naming the plaintiff as solicitor of the company. He was never, in fact, appointed to the office but did become a member of the company. It was held that he could not sue the company (under the provisions of earlier corresponding legislation) because the right to be appointed as solicitor was not a *membership right* of the plaintiff.

Similarly, in *Beattie v E. and F. Beattie Ltd* [1938] Ch 708, a dispute arose between a company and one of its directors concerning the repayment of sums improperly paid to the director. The director wished to refer the matter to arbitration in accordance with an article requiring arbitration of disputes with members, but was held not entitled to insist on arbitration since the dispute was between the company and the plaintiff in his capacity as *director,* not in his capacity as shareholder.

10.5.4 Implied contracts

The terms laid down in the constitution may be impliedly incorporated into a contract made with the company. For example, in *Re New British Iron Company, ex parte P. Beckwith* [1898] 1 Ch 324, there was no express agreement between the directors and the company regarding their remuneration. However, the articles stated that the board was to receive an annual sum of £1,000. This was held to be a binding obligation on the company, even though the directors were not claiming in their capacity as members.

10.5.5 Shareholders' agreements

Shareholders may wish to regulate their dealings with each other outside the articles (or as a supplement to them). For example, they may wish to stipulate that there must be unanimity between them regarding the appointment of a new director, irrespective of the mechanism for appointment of directors in the articles. Such provisions can be enshrined in a shareholders' agreement, rather than the articles. The important thing to note is that such an agreement will only bind those shareholders who are parties to it. The constitution binds all shareholders at any time in the life of the company. (Further discussion of this topic is found in **Chapter 29**.)

10.6 Actions by shareholders

10.6.1 Personal or representative action

When a member sues to enforce the memorandum or articles under s. 33 CA 2006, he may be seeking a remedy for himself *or* for himself and a large number of other members whose rights have also been infringed. Paragraph 19.6 of the Civil Procedure Rules 1998 makes provision for a representative action 'where more than one person has the same interest in a claim'. The plaintiff shareholder then represents the interests of all the shareholders (except the wrongdoers) and the judgment is normally binding on, and enforceable by, them.

10.6.2   Derivative action

10.6.2.1   History of the derivative action

A shareholder is not usually permitted to sue where a wrong is done to the company of which he is a member. This rule was known as the rule in *Foss v Harbottle* (1843) 2 Hare 461, and there were two justifications for it. First, since a company is a separate legal person distinct from its members, the company is the proper plaintiff in an action where a wrong has been done to the company. Secondly, the decision whether or not to sue can be taken either by the directors or by the members in general meeting, and the court is unwilling to interfere with this decision by imposing its own views on the company. At the same time, however, the courts did recognise that in some exceptional circumstances it was appropriate to allow a shareholder to sue on behalf of the company, since otherwise justice could not be done, for example, where the majority shareholders were using their position of power within the company to obtain a direct personal advantage or where the actions of the board had produced a result which was injurious to the interests of the company or the members as a whole. Therefore, a number of exceptions to the rule in *Foss v Harbottle* developed on a case by case basis, under which a shareholder could bring an action if the company would not. This type of action was normally described as a 'derivative action' because the right of the member to sue was not personal to him but derived from the right to sue which the company had failed to exercise.

These exceptional cases should be contrasted with cases where the personal rights of a shareholder are affected. In such cases, the shareholder does not need to rely upon an exception to *Foss v Harbottle* at all, but can sue because of the contractual rights which he has under s. 33 (*Pender v Lushington* (1877) 6 ChD 70). It was not always easy to decide whether or not a shareholder had a right of action under the exceptions to *Foss v Harbottle* or under s. 33. The distinction was crucial, however, as a shareholder always has *locus standi* to enforce its own personal rights, but only a very limited right to sue on behalf of the company. Secondly, wrongs done to a company could be ratifiable by the majority and a court would bow to the wishes of the majority in such situations. (Although occasionally, ratification itself could amount to wrongdoing, justifying a derivative action (*Cook v Deeks* [1916] 1 AC 554).)

10.6.2.2   Impact of the Companies Act 2006

The Companies Act 2006 has now codified derivative actions (Chapter 1, Part 11 CA 2006) and all derivative actions will henceforth have to brought under the statutory provisions. (The relevant sections came into force on 1 October 2007.)

Section 260(3) states that a derivative action must be brought in respect of a cause of action arising from an actual or proposed act or omission involving negligence, default, breach of duty, or breach of trust by a director. The common view of this is that it expands the opportunities for derivative actions. (Although the possibility to complain specifically about the actions of the majority shareholders has been removed, on the basis that the more appropriate claim is for unfair prejudice; see **10.7**.) Under the common law any misfeasance by a director which was ratifiable by the majority was not sufficient grounds to found an action (on the basis that the majority should be allowed to determine the issue). The distinction between ratifiable and non-ratifiable actions is no longer an issue; all default and breaches by directors are arguably grounds to bring an action. Secondly, it was previously very difficult to bring a derivative action for directors' negligence (*Pavlides v Jensen* [1956] 2 All ER 518). Moreover, the Act does not stipulate the need to prove, for example, wrongdoer control or fraud on the minority (that is, the exercise of power for dubious or personal ends). At first glance, therefore, it would appear that in all instances of breach or default by a director, any shareholder would automatically have the ability to launch a derivative action. However, s. 261 imposes a 'screening process', under which such a shareholder must apply to the court for permission to pursue a claim and must demonstrate a prima facie case for such permission to be granted. In making its decision, a court must take into account the matters set out in s. 263, which include:

(a) whether or not a person acting to promote the interests of the company would or would not continue the claim;

(b) the good faith of the shareholder bringing the claim;

(c) any prior authorisation or ratification of the act or the possibility of subsequent ratification;

(d) in particular, the views of shareholders with no interest, direct or indirect, in the matter.

Most of these concepts are new and it remains to be seen how far the existing jurisprudence regarding derivative actions will be considered relevant or influential in determining them. It is suggested that the applications for permission to prosecute a claim may in themselves end up as significant as the trial of the substantive issue itself.

Finally, any shareholder bringing a derivative action must consider three practical points:

(a) If the action is successful, the judgment will give a remedy to the company (which has been wronged) rather than to the claimant.

(b) Any internal dispute in a company can deflect the attention and energies of those involved away from the proper business of running the company.

(c) Professional costs will be incurred by all parties, including the shareholder.

Under the previous regime, it was generally accepted that any reasonable claim brought in good faith would entitle the shareholder to an indemnity for costs from the company. However, irrespective of this issue, if the company does end up meeting some or all of the costs of the action, this may simply erode the benefit of the action brought.

10.7 Unfair prejudice

10.7.1 Introduction

In addition to the derivative action, statute has afforded shareholders the possibility to complain about conduct of others within a company since the introduction of s. 210 CA 1948. This became (in revised form) s. 75 CA 1980 and this, in turn, became s. 459 CA 1985. The latest statement of this right is found in s. 994 CA 2006, which provides that:

A member of a company may apply to the court by petition for an order . . . on the ground (a) that the company's affairs are being or have been conducted in a manner that is unfairly prejudicial to the interests of the members generally or of some part of its members (including at least himself) or (b) that an actual or proposed act or omission of the company (including an act or omission on its behalf) is or would be so prejudicial.

Section 994 is effectively the same as the previous s. 459, so cases decided under the previous section are likely to be valid in interpreting its effect.

10.7.1.1 Grounds

A shareholder may petition under s. 994 if he can show that he has suffered unfair prejudice. As will be seen from the wording of the section, the prejudice must have arisen from the way in which the affairs of the company were being conducted or from an actual or proposed act or omission by the company. The prejudice must have affected the interests of at least some of the members of the company (but it can affect them all equally). If these things can be shown then the court will have to consider what remedy would be appropriate.

10.7.1.2 Rights as shareholder must have been prejudiced

If the petitioner is to succeed he must show that his rights as a shareholder have been prejudiced. In *Re Postgate and Denby* [1987] BCLC 8, it was held that such rights include all rights given under the company's memorandum and articles, statutory rights, and also rights arising out of agreements and understandings between members. The Law Commission reviewed shareholder remedies in 1997 (Law Com No. 246, para. 1.9). In this report a number of guiding principles were iterated, one of which was:

A member is taken to have agreed to the terms of the memorandum and articles of association when he became a member, whether or not he appreciated what they meant at the time. The law should continue to treat him as so bound unless he shows that the parties have come to some other agreement or understanding which is not reflected in the articles or memorandum. Failure to do so will create unacceptable commercial uncertainty. The corollary of this is that the best protection for a shareholder is appropriate protection in the articles themselves.

(It is likely that this viewpoint was influential on the House of Lords' decision in *O'Neill v Phillips*, discussed below.)

Thus, in *Re A Company (No. 004377 of 1986)* [1987] 1 WLR 102, the petition failed as the articles of the company laid down exactly what was to happen if the quasi-partnership ended for any reason. This included a right for a majority shareholder to buy the shares of the minority. The minority shareholder might indeed be prejudiced by such a provision but he could not claim that the prejudice was unfair as he had (by joining the company) agreed to this in advance.

10.7.1.3 Test for unfair prejudice

The test as to what amounts to unfair prejudice is primarily objective. In the leading case in this area, *O'Neill v Phillips* [1999] 2 All ER 961 (a case on s. 459), Lord Hoffmann explained that '. . . a balance has to be struck between the breadth of the discretion given to the court and the principle of legal certainty . . . It is highly desirable that lawyers should be able to advise their clients whether or not a petition is likely to succeed'. Moreover, he was opposed to the application of a 'wholly indefinite notion of fairness'. In order to provide objectivity in the concept, his Lordship relied upon the fact that 'the manner in which the affairs of the company may be conducted is closely regulated by rules to which the shareholders have agreed' (effectively the company's constitution, but also formal and informal agreements or understandings between members). On this basis, he came to two conclusions about unfair prejudice:

(a) A member will not ordinarily be entitled to complain of unfairness unless there has been some breach of the terms on which he agreed that the affairs of the company should be conducted.

(b) There will, however, be cases in which equitable considerations make it unfair for those conducting the affairs of the company to rely upon their strict legal powers.

For these reasons, Mr O'Neill's claim failed. He may have had a legitimate expectation that Mr Phillips, the majority shareholder, would confer various benefits upon him (such as an increased share in profits and more shares in the company), but he had no formal grounds upon which to base a claim. It is submitted, therefore, that Lord Hoffmann's approach has narrowed the scope of a claim under s. 994 for the simple reason that one must, in fact, establish the specific terms upon which it was agreed that the company's affairs be conducted (which may well be outside the company's articles of association). Furthermore, one must prove an actual breach of such terms or show that they were being used in a way which offends against equitable considerations.

10.7.2   Powers of court

10.7.2.1   Orders

If a petition under s. 994 is successful the court 'may make such order as it thinks fit for giving relief in respect of the matters complained of' (s. 996(1)). Section 996(2) lists particular types of order which may be made but is expressly stated to be without prejudice to the general power given by s. 996(1). The powers listed in s. 996(2) are to:

(a) regulate the conduct of the company's affairs in the future;

(b) require the company to refrain from doing or continuing an act complained of by the petitioner or to do an act which the petitioner has complained it has omitted to do;

(c) authorise civil proceedings to be brought in the name and on behalf of the company by such person or persons and on such terms as the court may direct;

(d) require the company not to alter its articles without leave of the court;

(e) provide for the purchase of the shares of any members of the company by other members or by the company itself and, in the case of a purchase by the company itself, the reduction of the company's capital accordingly.

10.7.2.2   Power to authorise civil proceedings

The power to authorise civil proceedings subject to terms may prove particularly useful. A shareholder may be deterred from bringing a derivative action, by the prospect of heavy costs. It may, therefore, be attractive to petition under s. 994 in the hope of obtaining an order for the action to be pursued by the company. The court will ensure that such a petition can be dealt with (in suitable cases) without the substantive issue being tried in the s. 994 proceedings.

10.7.2.3   Purchase of petitioner's shares

In practice, the most common remedy awarded to a successful petitioner is that his shares should be purchased by the wrongdoers who have caused the unfair prejudice. The question of valuation causes considerable problems in such cases. The courts have held that the shares should be valued as at whatever date is fair to the petitioner. This usually means that the shares are valued at the date when the prejudice to the petitioner began. If a different date is chosen the court will usually order that the valuer should value the shares as if the prejudice had not taken place.

10.8 Just and equitable winding up

Companies may be wound up on a number of grounds. Winding up is the process by which a company's existence is brought to an end; it usually results from the insolvency of the company. However, one type of winding up is available as a remedy to shareholders of solvent companies—this is winding up under s. 122(1)(g) Insolvency Act 1986, which provides for winding up where 'the court is of the opinion that it is just and equitable that the company should be wound up'. Winding up is a rather drastic solution to problems arising within a company and is now much less important, due to the remedy for shareholders available for cases of unfair prejudice.

10.9 Shareholders and profits

Basically there are four ways in which a company can deal with its profits:

(a) retain them in the business;

(b) use them to pay interest on debentures and other borrowings;

(c) pay directors' fees (and bonuses);

(d) pay them as dividends to the shareholders.

If profits are retained in the business the shareholders ought to benefit in the long run, since the capital value of the company (and thus of the shares in it) will increase. A payment of interest on borrowings will often be a payment to an outsider, which reduces profits available to the shareholders. However, most such payments are tax-deductible, so can contribute towards the reduction of a company's taxation liabilities. Directors' fees are expenses of the business which an accountant would regard as reducing the profit available to shareholders, but in the case of many small, private companies the directors and shareholders are the same people; thus a payment of directors' fees can be, in a commercial sense, equivalent to a payment of profit to the shareholders. However, the tax consequences are quite different. In simple terms, dividends are paid out of after-tax profits in the company's hands and will be taxed again as an income receipt in the hands of the recipient shareholder. The payment of a bonus or increased salary will be treated as an income expense of the company, which can be set against its taxable profits, but will again be taxed as an income receipt in the hands of the recipient director. The tax-deductible nature of salaries/bonuses can make them more attractive than payment of a dividend.

A company is, in any event, not entirely free to choose between the four different uses of profits for the following reasons:

(a) It will often be contractually bound to make payments of interest and directors' fees.

(b) There are company law rules which prevent the company from paying dividends except to the extent of 'profits available for the purpose'. (The reason for this is that the original investment made in the company by shareholders may not be returned to them, except in limited circumstances, until the company is wound up.)

(c) It will often be commercially unwise for the company to pay out all its profits, since some will be required to provide for future contingencies or for the expansion of the business.

10.10 Declaration and payment of dividends

A dividend is a payment to the shareholders of the company which provides them with a return on their investment. It is not a payment of interest on the money invested, since the shareholder does not have an automatic right to the dividend—as we shall see, it becomes payable only if 'declared' by the company (or otherwise authorised under the articles) and only if the Companies Act permits payment in the circumstances (see **10.11**).

The method of declaration of a dividend is essentially an internal matter for a company determined by its articles. By way of example, therefore, we shall focus on the method set out in Table A. (The procedure set out in art. 30 of the Model Articles for Private Companies is very similar.) However, in all circumstances the articles of the relevant company should be referred to.

10.10.1 Procedure

10.10.1.1 Table A

The provisions of Table A in respect of dividend payments provide for the following procedure:

(a) After the accounts have been prepared the directors will consider what dividend, if any, ought to be declared, and will make a recommendation of that amount.

(b) A meeting of the shareholders will be held at which the question of declaring a dividend will be considered. The members may reject the directors' recommendation or declare a dividend smaller than that recommended, but art. 102 prevents them exceeding the amount recommended by the directors. Any dividend must be formally declared by ordinary resolution.

Once the dividend has been declared, the members will be paid the dividend by the company. The amount of dividend paid to each member depends on the nominal value of the shares held, no account being taken of any premium paid on the shares.

The reason why the members cannot declare a dividend in excess of the directors' recommendation is that the directors are the managers of the company's business, and so are in a better position than the members to assess the economic ability of the company to pay dividends; it is therefore probably a sensible provision to include in the articles. If members with a majority of the votes object to the dividend policy of the directors they can exercise their right to remove the directors from office under s. 168 CA 2006.

Traditionally, the declaration of a dividend was a standing item on the agenda of the AGM, although Table A does not prevent consideration of dividends at other general meetings (art. 105). (For private companies, a dividend could also be declared by a written resolution, if the company does not choose to hold a general meeting.)

The demise of the AGM for private companies (see **13.1**) may alter practice in this area and may result in a greater opportunity or need for the board to declare dividends independently of the members, normally as interim dividends (see below).

10.10.1.2 Interim dividends

During the course of an accounting period (i.e., a 12-month period in respect of which the company's accounts are prepared), the directors may decide to pay an interim dividend (Table A, art. 103). However, the directors may only pay an interim dividend if it appears to them to be 'justified by the profits of the company available for distribution'. It is not necessary for such dividends to be formally declared by ordinary resolution of the shareholders. (Article 30(1) of the Model Articles for Private Companies also permits interim dividends.)

10.10.1.3 Other possible arrangements

The articles of the company may validly provide that directors are to declare all dividends without holding a general meeting. It is also possible (although undesirable), for the articles to require payment of all the company's profits as dividends (subject to the legal restriction referred to below).

10.10.2 Classes of share

If there are different classes of shares they may have different rights to dividends. Thus, if there are preference shares, the ordinary shareholders will usually not be entitled to any dividend until the preference shareholders have received their dividend (which will be expressed as a fixed amount per share or a fixed percentage).

EXAMPLE

A company has 2,000 £1 shares of which 1,000 are ordinary shares and 1,000 are 10% preference shares; the company declares a dividend of £150. The preference shareholders are entitled to their 10% (i.e., £100) and the ordinary shareholders get the balance (i.e., £50 or 5p per share).

10.10.3 Legal entitlement to dividend

Once declared by the members in general meeting, a dividend is a debt due to the members from the company. The member is, therefore, entitled to sue the company if the dividend is not paid. An interim dividend is not, however, a debt due from the company, so that the members have no right to it until it is actually paid.

10.11 Restrictions on sources of dividends

10.11.1 The basic rule

So as to ensure that money invested by shareholders is not returned to them before the company is wound up, there have always been rules based on judicial decisions preventing the payment of dividends other than out of profits. Statute now lays down clear rules as to what funds are available for the payment of dividends. These rules, which were first introduced in 1980, are designed to implement the European Communities' Second Directive on Company Law and differ somewhat from the rules previously established by the courts—the statutory rules (now contained in the Companies Act 2006) are generally more restrictive.

Section 830(1) CA 2006 provides that: 'A company shall not make a distribution except out of profits available for the purpose.' The term 'distribution' is defined by s. 829 and includes all distributions of assets to members except:

(a) the issue of bonus shares;

(b) the redemption or purchase of its own shares by the company (see **12.4**);

(c) reduction of capital (see **11.2.9**); or

(d) a distribution on winding up.

Most dividends are paid in cash and are included in the definition of 'distributions', since cash is just as much an asset as other types of property.

10.11.2 'Profits available'

10.11.2.1 Definition

'Profits available for the purpose' of paying dividends are defined by s. 830(2) as 'accumulated, realised profits, so far as not previously utilised by distribution . . . less . . . accumulated, realised losses . . .'. This means that each year it is necessary to calculate the company's trading profit and any capital profits that have been made on the disposal of fixed assets. These are the 'realised profits' from which must be deducted any realised losses, that is, any trading loss or loss made on the disposal of a fixed asset. However, a dividend is only payable if there are *accumulated* realised profits in excess of *accumulated* realised losses. This means that the balance of realised profits can be carried forward from year to year. It is not, therefore, necessary to make a profit every year in order to pay a dividend—all that is required is that there should be a balance of profits taking this year and previous years together.

EXAMPLE

	Realised profit/(loss)	Dividend	Balance to carry forward
Year 1	4,000	1,000	3,000
Year 2	2,000	1,000	4,000
Year 3	(3,000)	1,000	nil

The dividend in year 3 is lawful because in year 1 the realised profits were £4,000 and the dividend only £1,000, so that £3,000 worth of profits could be carried forward. In year 2, the realised profits were £2,000 and the dividend £1,000, so that a further £1,000 could be carried forward. In year 3, there was a realised loss of £3,000 which had to be deducted from the accumulated profits of £4,000, thus leaving £1,000 for a dividend.

Just as realised profits not used to pay dividends may be carried forward to later years and used to pay dividends in those later years, so realised losses which are not balanced by realised profits accumulated from previous years must be carried forward to later years and set off against realised profits before a dividend can be paid. Thus (continuing the example above):

	Realised profit/(loss)	Dividend	Balance to carry forward
Year 4	(2,000)	nil	(2,000)
Year 5	1,000	nil	(1,000)
Year 6	2,000	1,000	nil

In year 4, there was a loss, and since no accumulated profits were available from years 1 to 3, no dividend could be paid. In year 5, a profit of £1,000 was made but this could not be used to pay a dividend since the accumulated realised loss (£2,000 from year 4) was more than the realised profit. In year 6, the £1,000 dividend was the maximum which could be paid because £1,000 of the loss from year 4 had to be set off against the profit.

10.11.2.2   Unrealised losses

It should be noted that, although realised losses must be made good out of realised profits before a dividend can be paid, there is no requirement that *unrealised* losses must be made good. For example, if a company owns land which it knows to be declining in value, it can still go on paying dividends out of realised profits, since the loss on the land is only realised when the land is sold. Similarly an unrealised profit cannot be used to pay a dividend. A company which is making small realised losses cannot, therefore, pay a dividend even if it knows its land is increasing in value by more than the losses.

10.11.2.3   Calculation of profits and losses

Section 830 does not lay down particular rules as to how profits and losses are to be calculated; normal accountancy practice must be applied in deciding whether a profit or loss has been realised.

10.11.3   Justification of distribution by reference to the 'relevant accounts'

10.11.3.1   The 'relevant accounts'

Whether a company has got any profits available for distribution can only be judged by reference to properly drawn up accounts. Section 836 CA 2006 lays down rules as to which accounts are to be used at any particular time for deciding whether there are profits available. Usually the company must rely on the last set of accounts prepared in accordance with the duty imposed on the company under Chapter 4, Part 15 CA 2006 and circulated to members pursuant to s. 423 CA 2006.

In *Bairstow v Queen's Moat Houses plc* [2001] 2 BCLC 531, the Court of Appeal emphasised the fact that failure to comply with this requirement would render any distribution unlawful, even if there existed available profits in reality.

10.11.3.2   Interim and initial accounts

If the company wants to pay a dividend which is not justified by its last accounts it can prepare 'interim' accounts specially for the purpose of showing that profits are available for distribution (s. 836(2)(a)). This might be done, for example, if the company had made a loss and so could not pay a dividend but has now started to make profits again and does not want to wait until the next full set of accounts are produced. Similarly, if a company wishes to pay a dividend before it has prepared *any* accounts (i.e., broadly speaking, during its first year after incorporation) it can prepare 'initial' accounts to justify the dividend payment (s. 836(2)(b)).

Interim and initial accounts must be prepared in much the same way as the normal final accounts of the company. Also, these accounts must enable a reasonable judgement to be made as to the amount of profits, losses, assets and liabilities of the company at the time (ss. 838(1) and 839(1) CA 2006). Because of the expense involved in preparing such accounts, it will usually be better to wait until accounts are produced in the normal way before paying the dividend.

10.11.4 Consequences of unlawful distributions

Section 847(2) CA 2006 requires any member to repay a distribution which he 'knows or has reasonable grounds for believing' to be unlawful. Additionally, if a dividend is paid unlawfully, the directors will normally be personally liable to the company, since they will have recommended and paid (or permitted payment of) the dividend in breach of their duty as trustees of the company's assets. (See, for example, *Bairstow v Queen's Moat Houses plc* [2001] 2 BCLC 531.)

11

Company finance

This chapter covers the following topics:

11.1 Introduction

Once a company is formed it will need to spend money to get its business going. It may need to buy stock, buy or rent premises, pay wages, advertise and pay the general expenses involved in running a business. The money that the company needs to start its business is often called capital. Technically, however, 'capital' is the liability of the company to the people who have provided it with money on a long-term basis, effectively the shareholders.

A company can raise money either in the form of an investment by shareholders or in the form of borrowing. Once the business is established, profits may be retained in the business, thus producing a third source of finance. (Retained profits may be paid out to shareholders in the form of dividends. As such, they need to be represented as part of the capital of the company in the accounts.)

This chapter will look at how companies raise money through share allotments and borrowing. It is important to note that an important source of information as to how a company is capitalised is the balance sheet, which will provide both details of debt and share funding.

EXAMPLE

A Limited is funded in the following manner:

Share capital	£1,000
Retained profits	£25,000
Borrowings	£10,000

A total, therefore, of £36,000 has gone into the company, but there is also a corresponding liability to pay back the borrowings. In very simple terms, the assets would be represented as follows in A Limited's balance sheet:

ASSETS	
Cash	£36,000
Liabilities	£10,000
Net Assets	£26,000
CAPITAL	
Share capital	£1,000
Retained profit	£25,000
Total	£26,000

Note how the assets match the capital, hence the fact that the figures 'balance'. (It is recommended that **15.7**, which looks at the balance sheet in more detail, is read in conjunction with this chapter.)

11.2 Issue of shares

11.2.1 Legal nature of shares

A share in a company is a chose in action. Its value to the shareholder depends on the particular contractual rights which he obtains from owning the share. These contractual rights are obtained when the shares are issued to him by the company, if he is the original owner, or when they are transferred or transmitted to him. This section is concerned with the issue of shares by a company; transfer and transmission are dealt with in **Chapter 12**.

11.2.2 Rights attaching to shares

The rights attached to shares vary from company to company and a company may issue different classes of shares with different rights attached to them. It is, therefore, difficult to generalise about the exact nature of a share, but the following points may be of assistance:

(a) Nearly all shares give the shareholder a *right to a dividend* (i.e., a share in profits), but a dividend is only payable if the company has made profits and it is decided to declare a dividend (see **Chapter 10**).

(b) Most, but not all, shares give the shareholder a *right to vote* at general meetings of the company.

(c) If the company is wound up the shareholder will have a *right to repayment* of his investment (in the comparatively unlikely event that the company is then solvent) and in most cases a *right to participate* in any undistributed profit.

(d) The Stock Transfer Act 1963 lays down a procedure for the transfer of shares but does not guarantee the shareholder a *right to transfer*.

(e) Shareholders are given certain *rights as a matter of law* by the Companies Act. Many of these rights are, however, only given to shareholders who have a right to vote at company meetings (e.g., the rights to remove directors and to appoint and remove auditors referred to in **Chapter 9**).

In the case of a private company the voting rights will often be as important as the financial rights. This is especially so in the case of a shareholding which gives voting control, since it effectively carries with it the right to control many major decisions of the company.

11.2.3 The value of shares

The value of shares clearly depends to some extent on the rights attached to them but it also depends on other factors—particularly the profitability of the company and its asset worth.

All shares must have a 'nominal value' (also called 'par value'). (For most English registered companies, the nominal value chosen is normally £1, for obvious reasons.) This figure says little about the true value of the shares, since shares can be issued for more (but not less) than nominal value and, once issued, their true value will fluctuate either upwards or downwards as the company is more or less successful.

EXAMPLE

Control Systems Limited has 1,000 ordinary shares of £1 each in issue. Accordingly, these shares have a nominal value of £1 each. However, if Control Systems, as a business entity, is worth £2,000,000, to buy all the shares in this company and, thus, assume total control over it, would cost this amount. Therefore, each share has an actual worth of £2,000.

11.2.4 Procedure for the issue of shares

When new shares are created by a company they are said to be 'issued' or 'allotted' by the company to the people who have contracted to buy them. Any proposed issue of shares is likely to raise a number of complex legal matters. These will be now considered in turn.

11.2.4.1 *Limit on the size of the allotment*

The relevant share capital of a company (its issued or allotted share capital—s. 546 CA 2006) will be increased automatically every time an allotment of shares is made by the size of the fresh allotment (s. 617(2)(a) CA 2006). The 'default position', therefore, is that companies are free to make allotments of any size at any time.

However, companies incorporated under the 1985 Act are still be bound by the limit imposed by the authorised share capital clause contained in their memoranda, which is deemed to be incorporated into the articles. If this clause would prohibit any subsequent allotment, the solution will be for a company to alter its articles to remove this restriction or to amend upwards the limit imposed. Although this is technically a change to the articles, it can be achieved by ordinary, rather than special, resolution.

EXAMPLE

Cranwell Limited was formed under the Companies Act 1985. Accordingly, it has a memorandum which complies with that Act, including a share capital clause which states that: 'The share capital of the company is £1,000 divided into 1,000 shares of £1 each.'

Cranwell has 800 shares in issue and wishes to allot a further 400 shares. The above clause, therefore, prevents this; the balance of share capital from which to make the allotment stands at 200 shares. The two solutions, therefore, are either:

(a) Amend the clause to increase the amount stated to at least 1,200 shares (or such higher amount as is desirable); or

(b) Delete the clause entirely to remove the restriction totally.

11.2.4.2 *Directors' authorisation*

For private companies with only one class of share in issue, directors are free to allot further shares of the same class without prior reference to the shareholders, subject to any restriction imposed upon them in the articles (s. 550 CA 2006). However, where the company is public or where there are different classes of shares in issue or the proposed allotment will result in such a situation, the advance consent of shareholders by ordinary resolution or authority from the articles will be required (s. 551 CA 2006).

There is, however, one caveat to the general applicability of s. 550. It only applies automatically to companies formed on or after 1 October 2009. For all other private companies it will be necessary for the shareholders to pass an ordinary resolution allowing the directors to take advantage of the section; effectively as a one-off 'trigger' event.

Any necessary authorisation to allow an allotment may be given either for a particular exercise of the directors' power or generally, and may be unconditional or subject to conditions. Whether the authorisation is given by ordinary resolution of the members in general meeting or by the articles, it must state the maximum amount of shares which the directors may issue and the date when the authority will expire. The authority cannot be given for more than five years from formation of the company or the passing of the resolution (as the case may be) and can be revoked or varied by the company in general meeting at any time. Once given, the authority can be extended by up to five years by a further resolution of the company.

Resolutions under s. 551 are passed as ordinary resolutions (so that a simple majority is sufficient). The resolution must be registered with the Registrar of Companies within 15 days of its being passed (s. 551(9)).

If the directors issue shares without authority they commit an offence (s. 549(4)) (and presumably would be liable to the company for breach of duty) but the issue of shares remains valid (s. 549(5)).

Some companies may have in their articles pre-existing authority to allot shares up to a specified amount, which will have been granted under the predecessor to s. 551, namely s. 80 CA 1985. If this authority has not expired, it will continue to be valid authority for the directors, but they will still have to comply with the limits specified therein. If this would be problematic, the company can either change its articles by special resolution or vary the authority (or grant fresh authority) by ordinary resolution.

11.2.4.3 *Rights of pre-emption*

Under s. 561 CA 2006, if it is proposed to issue shares to any person, they must first be offered to the existing shareholders, in proportion to their existing holdings, on terms at least as favourable as those proposed for the issue to that person. Section 562 stipulates the manner in which offers under s. 561 must be made; in particular, the members must be given at least 21 days to accept the offer or reject it (s. 562(4) and (5)).

This right of pre-emption does not apply if the shares are to be issued wholly or partly for non-cash consideration (s. 565).

Furthermore, s. 561 will only apply if the shares to be allotted are 'equity shares', as defined by s. 560. What constitutes an equity share depends upon the rights which the share does or does not enjoy, and, therefore, understanding the concept first requires a sound knowledge of such potential rights. However, put simply, shares which enjoy only fixed entitlements in respect of both dividends and a return of capital are not equity shares and are not subject to s. 561. (See **11.2.2** and **11.5** for more specific discussion of rights which shares may enjoy.)

A failure to comply with either s. 561 or s. 562 will result in any director who knowingly authorised or permitted such failure being liable to compensate any shareholder to whom an offer should have been made for any loss, damage costs or expenses.

Section 567 allows private companies the possibility of excluding the effect of ss. 561 and 562 either wholly or partially through a provision in the articles. Additionally, all companies can disapply the effect of s. 561 in respect of specific allotments, either through a special resolution or provision in the articles, although it is important to distinguish between allotments where the directors do and do not require shareholders' authority and the extent and nature of that authority (contrast ss. 569, 570 and 571).

(Note that the articles of some companies may have taken advantage of the similar regime which existed under the Companies Act 1985 to disapply the pre-emption rights previously imposed by s. 89 CA 1985—see ss. 89–95 CA 1985.)

Section 561 gives shareholders a useful degree of protection in cases where the effect of issuing shares would be to water down their influence within the company and their entitlement to dividends. A higher degree of protection still can be given if the articles provide for pre-emption rights on *any* issue of shares, so that the company will not be able to offer shares for a non-cash consideration unless the members are willing to give up their rights.

It should be noted that s. 561 is only concerned with the *issue* of shares. It should not be confused with any provision in a company's articles which provides for pre-emption rights where an existing shareholder wants to *transfer* his shares (see **Chapter 12**).

11.2.4.4 *Directors' fiduciary duties*

The directors may not issue shares in breach of their fiduciary duty, so that the approval of the members is required if the motive behind the issue is anything other than the raising of further investment in the company.

Very often the courts have, in such circumstances, been prepared to declare such allotments unlawful (see **9.7.2.2**). It is a moot point as to whether or not, if a s. 551 authority is obtained, a separate approval of the shareholders is required to cover this point. It is submitted that it is not. However, there may be circumstances where such a rule does not hold true; for example, if the s. 551 authority is obtained by deception, or if it was granted some time before the actual allotment takes place and the company's circumstances have changed to such an extent that, if asked again, the shareholders may not grant such an authority.

11.2.5 **Payment for shares**

11.2.5.1 Consideration

A contract for the issue of shares may provide for payment in cash or for some other consideration. If the full nominal amount is paid at the time of the allotment, the shares are said to be 'fully paid up'. If not, they are 'partly-paid'. In this case, the outstanding amount can be asked for by the company making a 'call'. (The details of such a device will normally be specific to the company's articles.) Additionally, if the company goes into liquidation, the shareholder is obliged to contribute the outstanding sum to the company. (See **7.5.1** for further discussion of this area.) Payment in full on issue of the shares is usually required, so that partly-paid shares are rather uncommon.

Companies may not issue shares at a discount to their nominal value. This is prohibited by s. 580 CA 2006, which makes the allottee liable to the company for the shortfall. As such, it is impossible to pay less than the nominal value of a share and for that share to be treated as fully paid up by the company.

EXAMPLE

Sage Pharmacies Limited purports to allot to Constance 2,000 £1 ordinary shares as fully-paid. Constance only pays 60 pence per share. As such, Constance still owes 40 pence per share.

11.2.5.2 Premium

Shares can be issued at a premium, that is, for more than their nominal value. (For the consequences of this, see **11.3.2**.)

11.2.6 Registration of allotments

Section 555(2) CA 2006 requires a return of allotment to be made to the Registrar of Companies within one month of the issue of shares. This return effectively details the allotment which has taken place. The return must also be accompanied by a statement of capital, giving details of the company's share capital at that time (s. 555(4)).

Section 554 imposes on companies an obligation to register any allotment in the internal register of members within two months of its occurrence. Further, s. 769 requires a company within the same time period to have share certificates ready for delivery to the relevant shareholders.

11.2.7 Issue of shares to the public

Section 755 CA 2006 prohibits a private company from offering shares (or debentures) to the public or from issuing them with a view to an offer for sale to the public. Any action in contravention of this prohibition can result in a court ordering that the company in question re-register as a public company (ss. 757 and 758). (An application to the court in this instance can be made by either a member or creditor of the company or the Secretary of State.)

11.3 Share capital

11.3.1 Introduction

Once shares have been issued they are said to form part of the 'capital' of the company. Issued capital is measured by reference to the nominal value of shares in question.

EXAMPLE

If 500 shares each with a nominal value of £1 have been issued, the issued capital is £500. If those shares have been issued at nominal or par value, the issued share capital will be matched by £500 cash received for the shares and this fact will be represented in the balance sheet. Whilst a massive over-simplification of what a balance sheet actually looks like, the accounting treatment would be as follows:

ASSETS
Current Assets   £500

CAPITAL
Share capital   £500

If, in fact, those shares were issued for more than their nominal value, for example, shareholders have paid £10 each for their shares (that is, at a premium of £9 per share), this will not affect the issued share capital figure. However, the company will have received a total of £5,000 for the is-sued shares.

To ensure that there is a matching correlation between the company's assets and the way the shareholders have contributed to those assets, the total amount of the premium (that is, £4,500) will have to be recorded in the balance sheet of the company to reflect this additional contribution by the shareholders. The issued share capital figure plus the share premium will then represent the £5,000 received. Again, by way of simple example, the accounting treatment would be as follows:

ASSETS
Current Assets   £5,000

CAPITAL
Share capital   £500
Share Premium   £4,500
                   £5,000

(See 11.3.4 below for further discussion of the share premium account.)

(Issued) share capital is really a liability of a company to its shareholders, since the company will one day be liable to repay the shareholders' investment (usually, in fact, only when the company is wound up).

11.3.2   Alteration to share capital

Most instances of an alteration to a company's share capital under s. 617 will be brought about by an allotment of shares. However, it is also possible under that section to alter share capital in the following ways:

(a) By consolidation;

(b) By subdivision;

(c) By reduction.

Shares are consolidated if they are consolidated into a smaller number of shares of a larger nominal amount (e.g., 1,000 £1 shares become 100 £10 shares); subdivision is the opposite (1,000 £1 shares become 10,000 10p shares). Any consolidation or subdivision of share capital can be achieved by ordinary resolution of the shareholders, unless the company's articles prohibit or restrict such alteration.

Since the change brought about by any consolidation or subdivision is really only a nominal one, there will seldom be any advantage in making it, unless the value of each share is either extremely large or extremely small, in which case subdivision or consolidation may be of some cosmetic value.

Under ss. 641–653 CA 2006, companies may reduce their share capital. The reasons for wanting to do this vary and are often quite technical. For example, public companies are only permitted to pay dividends if their net assets exceed their share capital (s. 831 CA 2006). If this is not the case, one solution is to reduce the share capital. (For public companies listed on the Stock Exchange, a failure to pay out a dividend can be prejudicial to the share price of the company.)

It is beyond the scope of this book to deal with this issue in any detail. However, in order to have a basic understanding, the following important issues should be borne in mind:

(a) the shareholders must approve the reduction by special resolution;

(b) the reduction must be sanctioned by the court;

(c) in a number of circumstances, creditors have a right to object to the reduction;

(d) should the reduction affect separate classes of shareholders differently, there may be a class rights issue under s. 630 CA 2006.

This process is available to any company (s. 641(1)(b)). However, an alternative process is also available for private companies, which involves, instead, a special resolution to authorise the reduction, together with statements of solvency about the company from each relevant director (s. 641(1)(a)). This process was specifically introduced by the 2006 Act to make it simpler and cheaper for private companies, removing the need for an application to the court.

11.3.3 Maintenance of capital

For the protection of people dealing with the company, share capital has to be 'maintained' by the company. This does not mean that the money invested has to be deposited or set aside as a fund to guarantee the company's creditors. The money is available to be used by the company as 'working' capital, to pay for the expenses of its business. What maintaining capital means is that it must not, normally, be returned to the members in any way while the company is a going concern.

Two major consequences of this rule are:

(a) that dividends may only be paid out of profits (see **10.11**);

(b) that capital invested cannot be returned to the members except:

(i) by a properly approved reduction in capital; or

(ii) where the company redeems or purchases its own shares (see below and **Chapter 12**).

11.3.4 Share premium account

As has already been explained, it is common for shares to be issued for more than their nominal value. The excess is not strictly speaking share capital, but is required by s. 610(1) CA 2006 to be credited to a 'share premium account' (i.e., an account showing the company to be liable to the members for the amount of the premium). The share premium account has to be maintained in the same way as share capital; thus assets representing it cannot be returned to members. (The specimen balance sheet at **15.7** contains an example of the accounting treatment of a share premium.)

11.3.5 Company as member of itself and purchase of own shares

11.3.5.1 The company as its own shareholder

A company may not be registered as its own shareholder. However, shares can be transferred to a trustee or nominee for the company. In addition, a subsidiary is prohibited from owning shares in its holding company.

11.3.5.2 Original prohibition on purchase of own shares

The traditional position was that it was illegal for a company to buy its own shares (*Trevor v Whitworth* (1887) 12 App Cas 409). This is because use of its money by a company to purchase its own shares is in effect a return to the shareholder of his investment and so is a reduction of capital. Statute has since intervened to modify this restriction, by the recognition of both redeemable shares and buy-back of shares in defined circumstances.

11.3.5.3 Redeemable shares

Section 684 CA 2006 gives companies power to issue redeemable shares; that is, shares which can be bought back by the company at the option of the company or the shareholder. In the case of a private company, its articles may exclude or restrict this possibility; a public company, by contrast, must be authorised by its articles to issue redeemable shares. The terms of redemption must be set out in the articles or can be left to the directors to determine, so long as they do so prior to the allotment (s. 685). No share can be redeemed unless it is fully-paid (s. 686).

Any redemption has to be notified to the Registrar of Companies within 28 days of its happening (s. 689). A statement of capital must also be sent, which sets out details of the company's share capital after the redemption.

11.3.5.4 Buy-back of shares

It was thought to be desirable for companies, particularly small family companies, to have the power to purchase their own shares as this would provide an additional market for the shares. Section 690 CA 2006, therefore, gives companies power to purchase their own shares, unless this is displaced or restricted by a provision in its articles.

Examples of cases where the power is useful include buying out dissident shareholders and the provision of funds to the estate of a deceased shareholder to assist in the payment of inheritance tax. In fact, all companies have the possibility of buying back some of their shares and it is not uncommon to read in the financial press of major public companies doing so. To reflect the diversity of companies which may effect buy-backs, the legislation distinguishes between 'off-market' and 'market' purchases (s. 693). The specifics of this distinction are beyond the scope of this Guide. However, only a small number of companies whose shares are traded on an investment exchange, e.g., the London Stock Exchange, will have the option of undertaking a market purchase. What follows, therefore, is an explanation of the mechanics of an off-market purchase.

First, as with redeemable shares, no share can be bought back unless it is fully-paid (s. 691(1)). The contract for purchase must be approved by special resolution before the company enters into it (s. 694(1)). The members whose shares are to be purchased must not use the votes given to them by the shares which are to be purchased on that resolution (s. 695). The resolution will be invalid unless:

(a) where a general meeting has been called, a copy of the contract (or a memorandum of its terms) is made available for inspection by the members at the company's registered office for a period of at least 15 days ending with the date of the meeting and also at the meeting itself;

(b) where a written resolution is being used, a copy of the contract (or a memorandum of its terms) is sent to every eligible member at the same time as the written resolution (s. 696).

Once the shares have been purchased by the company they are treated as cancelled and the company's issued share capital is reduced accordingly (s. 706). (The reader should note the very limited exception to this rule contained in s. 724 CA 2006 allowing certain shares traded on an investment exchange to be held in treasury by the purchasing company for subsequent re-allotment. However, as explained in the previous paragraph, buy-backs involving listed companies are beyond the scope of this Guide.)

Within 28 days after the shares have been purchased a return must be made to the Registrar of Companies stating the number and nominal value of the shares purchased and the date of purchase (s. 707). This return will have to bear stamp duty at the rate of ½% of the consideration paid. In addition, s. 708 requires notice of cancellation of any shares, which will always be the case for private companies, together with a statement of capital, which sets out details of the company's share capital after the cancellation.

11.3.5.5 Financing buy-back or redemption

When shares are redeemed or purchased by the company the money used to pay for them (including any payment representing a premium over the nominal value) must generally come out of distributable profits or the proceeds of a fresh issue of shares. Where the shares are purchased or redeemed with assets representing profits the legislation requires the capital of the company to be maintained. Thus, s. 733 CA 2006 requires the company to open a 'capital redemption reserve' equal to the reduction in the share capital. This reserve is treated in the same way as share capital or the share premium account; that is, it is shown in the balance sheet as a liability due to shareholders which has to be maintained until the company goes into liquidation.

EXAMPLE

BALANCE SHEET OF JCT LIMITED

FIXED ASSETS

Premises		200,000
Fixtures		20,000
		220,000

CURRENT ASSETS

Stock	30,000	
Debtors	40,000	
Cash	70,000	
	140,000	

CURRENT LIABILITIES

Creditors	40,000	
		100,000
		320,000

CAPITAL

Share capital		250,000
Share premium		10,000
Profit & loss		60,000
		320,000

JCT buys back 10,000 ordinary shares of £1 each at a price of £20,000. The purchase is made wholly out of profits. The amendments to the balance sheet are:

(a) reduce cash by £20,000;

(b) reduce share capital by £10,000 (i.e., the nominal value of the shares);

(c) reduce profit and loss by £20,000 (to reflect the use of profits to buy back the shares);

(d) create capital redemption reserve of £10,000 (equivalent to the reduction in capital).

BALANCE SHEET OF JCT LIMITED FOLLOWING BUY-BACK

FIXED ASSETS		
Premises		200,000
Fixtures		20,000
		220,000
CURRENT ASSETS		
Stock	30,000	
Debtors	40,000	
Cash	50,000	
	120,000	
CURRENT LIABILITIES		
Creditors	40,000	
		80,000
		300,000
CAPITAL		
Share capital	240,000	
Share premium	10,000	
Capital redemption reserve	10,000	
Profit and loss	40,000	
	300,000	

In the case of a *private* company, payment out of assets representing capital is permitted both in respect of a buy-back and a redemption (s. 709). The use of capital in this way (the 'permissible capital payment') is only possible once distributable profits and the proceeds of any fresh issue of shares made for the purpose have been used up (s. 710). In order to protect the interests of members and creditors the following detailed procedural requirements must be satisfied:

(a) The articles must not expressly restrict or prohibit the use of capital assets for this purpose.

(b) The directors must make a statement that the company will remain solvent and will, in their view, be able to carry on business as a going concern for at least a year (s. 714). The directors' certificate must be supported by an auditors' report in which the auditors certify that they are not aware of anything which would indicate that the directors' view of the situation is unreasonable. (The directors will commit a criminal offence if they have no reasonable grounds for the opinion expressed in their statement (s. 715).)

(c) Not later than one week after the date of the directors' statement, a special resolution approving the payment must be passed. The members whose shares are to be purchased may not use the votes on those shares on this resolution. In addition, both a copy of the statement and the auditors' report must be made available at any general meeting held for the purpose or must be sent out with any written resolution (s. 718).

(d) Within a week of the above resolution, the company must have published details of the proposed buy-back in the *London Gazette*. It should also notify its creditors directly or through a notice in a national newspaper (s. 719). This is to put all interested creditors on notice, as they have the right to object to the use of capital, by applying to court for an order cancelling the resolution (s. 721). (Dissenting members also have this right.)

(e) The payment for the shares must be made by the company not less than five nor more than seven weeks after the date on which the resolution is passed (s. 723). This period is laid down so that members or creditors who object to the purchase have time to challenge the purchase in court.

In addition, where a payment is made out of capital, the company's accounts must reflect this. Under s. 734 CA 2006, where the permissible capital payment is less than the nominal value of the shares redeemed, the amount of the difference must be transferred to a capital redemption reserve. Where the permissible capital payment is greater than the nominal value of the shares redeemed, the situation is different. The company may then reduce the amount of any capital redemption reserve, share premium account, fully-paid share capital or unrealised profits of the company standing in any reserve by a sum not exceeding the amount by which the permissible capital payment exceeds the nominal amount of the shares. There are also accounting requirements where a company uses the proceeds of a fresh issue of shares to buy back shares.

EXAMPLE

BALANCE SHEET OF BHW LIMITED

FIXED ASSETS		
Premises		100,000
Fixtures		20,000
		120,000
CURRENT ASSETS		
Stock	30,000	
Debtors	40,000	
Cash	70,000	
	140,000	
CURRENT LIABILITIES		
Creditors	40,000	
		100,000
		220,000
CAPITAL		
Share capital		150,000
Share premium		50,000
Profit and loss		20,000
		220,000

BHW buys back 20,000 ordinary shares of £1 each at a price of £30,000. The purchase is made from a combination of available profits (£20,000) and a permissible capital payment of £10,000. The amendments to the balance sheet are:

(a) reduce cash by £30,000;

(b) reduce share capital by £20,000 (i.e., the nominal value of the shares);

(c) reduce profit and loss by £20,000 (to reflect the use of profits to buy back the shares);

(d) create capital redemption reserve of £10,000 (equivalent to the amount by which the permissible capital payment is less than the nominal value of shares redeemed).

BALANCE SHEET OF BHW LIMITED FOLLOWING BUY-BACK
(Permissible capital payment is less than nominal value of shares redeemed)

FIXED ASSETS

Premises			100,000
Fixtures			20,000
			120,000

CURRENT ASSETS

Stock	30,000		
Debtors	40,000		
Cash	40,000		
	110,000		

CURRENT LIABILITIES

Creditors	40,000		
			70,000
			190,000

CAPITAL

Share capital			130,000
Share premium			50,000
Capital redemption reserve			10,000
Profit and loss			
			190,000

If BHW had bought the 20,000 ordinary shares of £1 each at a price of £50,000, then the accounting treatment would be different. In this case, the purchase was made from a combination of available profits (£20,000) and a permissible capital payment of £30,000. The amendments to the balance sheet are:

(a) reduce cash by £50,000;

(b) reduce share capital by £20,000 (i.e., the nominal value of the shares);

(c) reduce profit and loss by £20,000 (to reflect the use of profits to buy back the shares);

(d) reduce share premium account by £10,000 (equivalent to the amount by which the permissible capital payment exceeds the nominal value of shares redeemed).

BALANCE SHEET OF BHW LIMITED FOLLOWING BUY-BACK
(Permissible capital payment exceeds the nominal value of shares redeemed)

FIXED ASSETS

Premises			100,000
Fixtures			20,000
			120,000

CURRENT ASSETS

Stock	30,000		
Debtors	40,000		
Cash	20,000		
	90,000		

CURRENT LIABILITIES

Creditors	40,000		
			50,000
			170,000

CAPITAL

Share capital			130,000
Share premium			40,000
Profit and loss			
			170,000

11.4 Financial assistance by company for purchase of shares

Section 678 CA 1985 makes it illegal for any public company to give financial assistance directly or indirectly to assist someone to purchase shares in that company (or its holding company). (This issue in discussed in greater detail in **Chapter 12**.)

11.5 Classes of shares

11.5.1 Introduction

In most companies, all the shares issued have the same rights attached to them. It is possible, however, for a company to issue shares with different rights. The reasons for this are many, but the main driver will be that shares can be considered as both a mechanism for control (because of the possible voting rights they may carry) and investment (either because of dividends which are paid out by the company or the fact that they increase in value as the company increases in value). Some shareholders will be more concerned with the latter than the former, and vice versa. Therefore, more than one type of share will be necessary to satisfy this demand. The shares are then said to belong to different classes. For example, a company may issue preference shares, that is, shares which have a better right to receive a dividend than ordinary shares. It is also possible to give some shareholders a greater measure of control over the affairs of the company either by creating voting and non-voting shares or by providing that all shares are to carry a right to vote but that some will have more votes than others.

It is not intended to provide an exhaustive explanation of all possible share rights. However, it is important to distinguish between the two most common types of share in issue—ordinary and preference shares.

11.5.2 Ordinary shares

By far the most common type of share in issue is the ordinary share. Ordinary shares entitle the holder to dividends, should such be declared (see **10.10** and **10.11**). They also normally entitle the holder to voting rights.

11.5.3 Preference shares

Preference shares are a more sophisticated investment mechanism than ordinary shares. They may be 'preferred' in two particular ways.

First, they may carry the automatic right to a fixed, annual dividend, normally calculated as a percentage of the nominal value of the shares. This right may, in addition, be cumulative, which means that should funds not be available to satisfy a dividend payment in a particular year, the preferred shareholder's entitlement is carried forward until funds are available.

Secondly, on a winding up, they may stand ahead of other shareholders in having their capital contribution to the company repaid to them.

(Each of these rights is independent of the other, so some preference shares may carry one but not both entitlements.)

Thus, preference shares appear to have clear advantages over ordinary shares. However, they tend not to carry voting rights, and the preferred rights themselves are normally restricted to a fixed amount. This can mean, for example, that in certain situations ordinary shareholders may receive better dividends than preferred shareholders. As a way of redressing the balance, preference shares may also carry with them rights of participation, which effectively means that as well as enjoying preferred rights, they may also enjoy the rights which ordinary shares carry.

Rights of participation are not compulsory and must be negotiated between the company and the potential shareholder, along with all other preferential rights.

EXAMPLE

Dividend

Tony has 50 ordinary shares of £1 each and Nick has 100 5% preference shares of £1 each in Lineout Limited. Should Lineout have £5 with which it can pay out a dividend, Nick will be paid first, which will use up the full amount, so none will go to Tony. However, should Lineout have £50 with which it can pay out a dividend, Nick will be paid first, but will still only receive £5, allowing Tony to receive £45.

If, however, all Nick's shares were participating, the balance of £45 would have to be divided between Nick and Tony, resulting in Nick receiving two-thirds of this amount and Tony one third.

Winding up

If Nick's shares also carry preferential rights on a winding up and the amount available for distribution to shareholders is £100, Nick will have his capital contribution returned first, resulting in nothing being available for Tony. However, should the amount left be £1,000, Nick will still receive his £100 first, but Tony will receive both his capital contribution, plus the remainder, that is, the full £900.

Instead, if Nick also had rights of participation on a winding up, the order of pay-out would be:

1. Nick £100;
2. Balance of £900, split one third Tony; two-thirds Nick.

11.5.4 Rights of redemption

Redeemable shares have already been mentioned earlier in this Chapter. Strictly speaking they are not a class of shares separate from ordinary or preference shares; instead, rights of redemption can be attached to either of these types of shares. (It is suggested, however, that redeemable preference shares are more likely to be created than redeemable ordinary shares, on the basis that redeemable preferred shares are a way of providing for a finite and certain investment in a company.)

11.6 Finance through borrowing

11.6.1 Express and implied power

A trading company has an implied power to borrow for the purpose of its trade. This is because the trade will be authorised by its objects and the borrowing will be reasonably incidental to the power to carry on the trade.

A company with power to borrow also has an implied power to give security for the loan. It is preferable to include express powers if a full objects clause is adopted rather than to rely on implied ones. In practice, banks (and other professional lenders) would probably continue to check the company's express powers despite the abolition of the consequences of the *ultra vires* rule referred to in **11.6.2**.

11.6.2 *Ultra vires* borrowing

Section 39 CA 2006 provides that 'the validity of an act done by a company shall not be called into question on the ground of lack of capacity by reason of anything in the company's constitution'. At face value, therefore, a prospective lender need not concern itself with any limitations on a company's activities. However, there is still an ancillary issue in respect of the requirement for directors to observe any restrictions which the articles may place on the powers of a company. Any lender which is aware of such a situation or which deliberately ignores such an issue may find the validity of the loan and, more particularly, any supporting security, open to challenge. This is a powerful incentive, therefore, for banks to satisfy themselves of the *vires* of a company before lending to it.

11.6.3 Exercise of borrowing powers

The power to borrow must be exercised in accordance with the company's articles of association. If the company has adopted Table A or similar, the directors will have power to borrow in circumstances where the loan is to be used for the purposes of the business (art. 70). (See also art. 3 of the Model Articles for Private Companies.)

11.7 Secured loans

11.7.1 Types of security

A prudent lender will usually require security for a loan made to a company. Any assets of the company may be charged by way of security. Usually security will be in the form of a mortgage, a fixed charge, a floating charge or all three. The essential benefit of such security is that it allows the lender the possibility of selling the assets of the borrower should the borrower default on repayments of the loan. The proceeds of sale can then be used by the lender to recoup some or all of the outstanding loan. Therefore, a key issue for any lender taking security is that the company in question actually owns the assets which will be charged. Also a lender will want to know if there are other charges already attaching to such assets. Such investigations are commonly referred to as 'due diligence' and one of the key responsibilities of a lawyer acting for a lender will be to carry out due diligence on the client's behalf. (See further **11.13** for some of the usual investigations made.)

In addition to charges over the assets of the company, a lender may frequently require personal guarantees from the directors. Where a personal guarantee is given by a director who is also a shareholder, the benefit of limited liability is effectively lost to the extent of the guarantee.

When companies borrow money, they will more often than not enter into a 'debenture' with the lender. (For a discussion of the contents of this document, see

Chapter 28.) Unfortunately, the term 'debenture' covers a variety of loan instruments and has no one specific usage. In its simplest form, it means a document issued by a company acknowledging debt of that company. This will clearly cover unsecured loan agreements. However, in commercial circles the term very often implies that the debt is backed up by some form of security. (In fact, such documentation may be called a 'mortgage debenture'.) It is quite common to find a debenture document providing a lender with a variety of different security rights and interests, backing up a loan made to a company. The loan itself will usually be the subject of a separate legal document, in which will be set out the terms of lending and repayment.

To complicate matters further, companies may issue 'loan stock' or 'debenture stock' which consists of transferable *securities* in a company, carrying with them a contractual right to interest and repayment of the sum paid for them. These can also be classed as debentures (s. 738 CA 2006). Therefore, care should always be exercised in both the use and interpretation of the term and the actual documentation in question should be inspected to establish the nature of a company's indebtedness.

Finally it is equally important to distinguish between the terms 'security' and 'securities'. The former is a generic term for charges over property; the latter covers all forms of transferable instruments in a company, most commonly shares and loan stock.

11.7.2 Mortgages and fixed charges

A lender may take security in the form of a mortgage or a fixed charge. The essential difference between the two is that a mortgage requires the formal transfer of title in the asset to the mortgagee, subject to an automatic right for title to be transferred back to the mortgagor once the debt is repaid—the so-called 'equity of redemption'. There are no such formalities required to create a fixed charge, merely an intention by the parties that the asset in question can be appropriated by the charge-holder and sold by it. However, in most security documentation, it will be clear from the wording that a fixed charge is intended. Both types of security must attach to specific, identifiable assets or assets which can be ascertained and defined.

In the case of a mortgage, the mortgagee actually owns title to the asset and can, thus, sell it without reference to the mortgagor, provided that the mortgagor is in default under the loan. In the case of a fixed charge, title remains with the chargor, but the chargor is not entitled to sell the asset without the consent of the charge-holder.

Mortgages can either be equitable or legal. Legal mortgages require specific formalities to be fulfilled, in particular the transfer of title in the property according to the law. An equitable mortgage is created where there is evidence of a desire to create a mortgage without fulfilling all such formalities.

It is important to note that mortgages specifically of freehold and leasehold property are somewhat different and are governed, inter alia, by Part III of the Law of Property Act (LPA) 1925. In particular, the creation of a mortgage over land is not possible by the transfer of the legal estate (s. 85 LPA 1925). Instead it must be created by way of a charge by deed expressed to be by way of legal mortgage.

An equitable mortgage is weaker than a legal one, in that a bona fide purchaser for value without notice of the equitable mortgage takes the property free from it. However, there are in place specific registration requirements which make it more difficult for such a purchaser to claim ignorance of such a fact, particularly in relation to registered and unregistered land. Also, the circumstances of the equitable mortgage may mean that the owner cannot sell the property in any event. For example, if A gives B possession of a share certificate as security for a loan made by B to A, this may constitute an equitable mortgage. (It cannot constitute a legal mortgage as no effective transfer of title in the shares from A to B has taken place; see **12.2.3.**) Without possession of the share certificate, A cannot effectively transfer title in the shares to anybody else.

All fixed charges are equitable. Confusingly, they may sometimes be referred to as equitable mortgages. In fact, commentators and judges often use the terminology loosely. Rather than worry about specific labels, the main distinction mentioned above should be borne in mind; that is, a mortgage either grants or purports to grant a proprietary interest in property, whereas a fixed charge grants an immediate right over property which can be exercised in certain situations.

A further important distinction is that between fixed and floating charges, which is discussed next.

11.7.3   Floating charges

A floating charge is an equitable charge over assets of a particular description owned by the company from time to time. A floating charge can be given over assets which are repeatedly dealt with by the company. Perhaps stock-in-trade is the clearest example. A company cannot give a fixed charge over its stock since to do so would prevent it from selling that stock without first obtaining the consent of the mortgagee. This would obviously hinder the ability of the company to carry on its business. However, if it gives a floating charge over the stock, the charge will 'float' over whatever stock the company owns from time to time—it can therefore sell the stock free from the charge and buy new stock to which the charge will automatically attach.

The nature of a floating charge was defined by Romer LJ in *Re Yorkshire Woolcombers' Association Ltd* [1903] 2 Ch 284, in the following way:

. . . if a charge has the three characteristics I am about to mention it is a floating charge:

> (a) if it is a charge on a class of assets of a company present and future;
>
> (b) if that class is one which, in the ordinary course of business of the company, would be changing from time to time; and
>
> (c) if you find that by the charge it is contemplated that, until some future step is taken by or on behalf of those interested in the charge, the company may carry on its business in the ordinary way as far as concerns the particular class of asset I am dealing with.

In the case of *Re Spectrum Plus Ltd* [2005] 2 BCLC 269, the House of Lords considered this dictum once again and provided fresh insight into its significance. Lord Scott proffered an analysis of the history of the case law surrounding this issue. As part of this analysis, he pointed out two key things:

1. that Romer LJ's dictum was never intended to be definitive, nor would a charge always have to demonstrate all three characteristics to be classed a floating charge;

2. that the first two characteristics were not, in any event, distinctive of a floating charge, albeit they may be quite typical. It was the third characteristic which distinguished a floating charge from a fixed.

As regards this second point, Lord Scott expressed a view that ' . . . if a security has Romer LJ's third characteristic . . . it qualifies as a floating charge, and cannot be a fixed charge, whatever may be its other characteristics.' For this reason he held that:

. . . the essential characteristic of a floating charge, the characteristic which distinguishes it from a fixed charge, is that the asset subject to the charge is not finally appropriated as a security for the payment of the debt until the occurrence of some future event.

At first sight a floating charge would seem to give no security at all to the lender since the company can continue to deal with the assets which are charged. However, a floating charge 'fixes' on the charged assets owned by the company at the time when the charge 'crystallises'. A floating charge crystallises when:

(a) The winding up of the company commences (in the case of a winding up by the court this is usually when the winding-up petition is presented (s. 129(2) Insolvency Act 1986); in the case of voluntary winding up it is when the winding-up resolution is passed (s. 86 IA 1986)).

(b) A receiver is appointed by the court.

(c) A receiver is appointed by the lender under a power given by the debenture.

(d) Any other event occurs which the debenture specifies will cause crystallisation.

Due to some very technical issues arising out of the Bills of Sales Act, individuals and partnerships are effectively prevented from creating floating charges, only companies. By analogy, it is believed that limited liability partnerships can also grant these charges, on the basis that they are a legal personality akin to a company. (See **Chapter 31** for discussion of limited liability partnerships.)

11.7.4 Advantages and disadvantages of floating charges

As far as the borrowing company is concerned a floating charge has one great advantage over a fixed charge; that is, until crystallisation, it can deal freely with the charged assets without the permission of the lender.

From the lender's point of view a floating charge suffers from a number of disadvantages when compared with a fixed charge. In particular:

(a) Its value as a security is uncertain until crystallisation.

(b) It is postponed to execution and distress for rent completed before crystallisation.

(c) It is postponed to preferential creditors on the liquidation of the borrowing company (see **26.8.4** and **26.8.5**).

(d) It is postponed to later fixed charges in certain cases (see **11.9.1**).

(e) A percentage of monies realised under the floating charge must be set aside for the benefit of unsecured creditors in a liquidation (see **26.8.5**).

(f) It may be invalid as a security if the company goes into liquidation within a year (see **27.4**).

Historically, the great advantage of a floating charge over the whole of the assets and undertaking of a company was that it allowed the chargee the ability to take control of the company in certain circumstances by appointing an administrative receiver, who would then realise the charged assets of the company on the chargee's behalf. This possibility was removed in all but a few well-defined circumstances by the changes which the Enterprise Act 2002 made to the Insolvency Act 1986. However, it may, instead, be possible for a floating charge-holder to appoint an administrator over such a company. (See **26.4** for further discussion.)

11.8   Registration of charges

11.8.1   Introduction

Many types of security granted by companies must be registered at Companies House. In this way, they are said to be 'perfected', that is, they are effective against third parties. The current relevant provisions are contained within Part 25 CA 2006.

11.8.2   Section 860 CA 2006

11.8.2.1   Requirement to register charges

Section 860 requires registration with the Registrar of Companies of most types of charge and mortgage created by a company. Registration is required of all floating charges and other charges over the company's land, goodwill, book debts and many other types of property. A complete list is beyond the scope of this Guide. Certain types of charge are not covered by s. 860 so that a charge over shares in another company owned by the borrowing company is not registrable, nor is an unpaid vendor's lien or any other charge arising by operation of law. For the purposes of this section (**11.8**), the term 'charge' is used to include mortgages and fixed and floating charges, unless specific reference is made.

11.8.2.2   Method of registration

Registration must be made by delivering to the Registrar the instrument creating the charge (which is returned after registration), prescribed particulars of the charge and a fee of £13 within 21 days. This means within 21 days of the execution of the instrument creating the charge (which may be longer than 21 days after the indebtedness secured by the charge is incurred by the company). The duty to register is imposed on the company and if it fails to register in time it, and every officer of the company in default, is liable to a fine. However, any person interested in the charge may register it instead. (As we shall see below, it is very much in the interests of the lender to make sure that the charge is registered.) A charge is not registered in time if particulars of it are submitted for registration within 21 days but incorrectly completed (*R v Registrar of Companies, ex parte Esal (Commodities) Ltd* [1985] 2 All ER 79).

11.8.2.3   Register of charges at Companies House

The Registrar keeps a register of the charges created by each company (s. 869(1) CA 2006) from which the following information can be discovered:

(a) the date of creation of the charge;

(b) the amount secured by the charge;

(c) short particulars of the property charged;

(d) the persons entitled to the charge.

This register is open to public inspection along with the other information on the company's file at Companies House on payment of the Registrar's fee (currently £1).

11.8.2.4   Certificate of registration

Once he has registered the charges, the Registrar gives a certificate of registration, which is conclusive evidence that the requirements of the Act as to registration have been complied with. Registration gives constructive notice of the charge to anyone dealing with the company and since the Registrar's certificate is conclusive evidence of *proper* registration, a later chargee cannot complain that the registered particulars are inaccurate. (For example, in *National Provincial and Union Bank of England v Charnley* [1924] 1 KB 431, the registered particulars understated the amount of the loan and yet a later creditor was held to have constructive notice of the proper registration and therefore could not object to full payment of the earlier charge in priority to his charge.) Although the registered particulars will seldom be inaccurate (since the Registrar checks them against the charge before issuing his certificate), a prudent lender should check the instruments creating any prior charges so as to be certain of the amount secured and the extent of the property given as security (this can be done by searching at the company's own registered office; see **11.8.4**).

11.8.2.5 Extension of time limit for registration

If the charge is not registered within 21 days the court may extend the time limit, provided that it is satisfied that the failure to register was:

> . . . accidental, or due to inadvertence or to some other sufficient cause, or is not of a nature to prejudice the position of creditors or shareholders of the company, or that on other grounds it is just and equitable to grant relief . . .

The court may impose terms and will, in practice, always impose a condition that the registration is not to prejudice rights acquired by other persons before registration finally takes place.

11.8.3 Effect of non-registration

Section 874(1) provides that failure to register a registrable charge shall result in the relevant security being void against a liquidator, an administrator and any creditor of the company. The importance of this provision is that if the company goes into liquidation before the loan has been repaid, the unregistered chargee loses his security. This is so even if a later secured creditor had actual notice of the charge when he took his security (*Re Monolithic Building Co.* [1915] 1 Ch 643). It should be noted that non-registration makes the security void against the liquidator or creditor but not against the company. The lender is, therefore, entitled to enforce his security against the company up to the time when winding up commences (but not after that time, since the security is then void against the liquidator).

Furthermore, s. 874 (1) is stated to be:

> . . . without prejudice to any contract or obligation for repayment of the money secured . . . and when a charge becomes void under this section, the money secured by it immediately becomes payable.

The chargee can, therefore, demand payment immediately if the charge is not registered even if the instrument creating the charge provided for repayment at a later date.

The practical problem is that, although the secured debt is not extinguished by non-registration of the charge, the chargee will only rank as an ordinary creditor in a liquidation of the company. This means that the chargee will have to wait until those with valid, registered fixed and floating charges (and preferential creditors) have been paid out of the company's assets. The chargee ranks with all the other ordinary creditors and, if there are insufficient assets to pay all the ordinary creditors, may only receive a fraction (or none) of the money due to it (see **26.8** for a more detailed discussion of the order of entitlement to assets on a liquidation).

11.8.4   Company's register of charges

Section 876 requires the company to keep a register of all the charges affecting its property at its registered office. The register must contain a description of the charged property, the amount of the charge and the name of the chargee. Failure to comply with the requirement may result in a fine but does not make the security of the charge invalid.

Section 875 also requires the company to keep *copies* of all charges registered under s. 860 at its registered office where they are open to inspection by members and creditors. A person lending money to the company should check these copies carefully so that he can see what charges, if any, the company has created over the property which is to be charged to him.

The Companies Act does not require a company to keep a register of debenture-holders. Some public companies do keep such a register in respect of loan stock (i.e., long-term loans freely transferable from holder to holder), so that they have a record of the person currently entitled to the interest. A private company, which cannot issue debentures to the public, will not need such a register.

11.8.5   Other types of registration: charges over land

In addition to registration under the Companies Act, mortgages of, and charges on, land by a company may have to be registered at HM Land Registry or at the Land Charges Department (depending on whether the land is registered or unregistered, respectively).

11.9   Priority of charges

11.9.1   Fixed charges

A company which creates a floating charge retains the right to deal with its assets. As we have already seen, this means that the value of the security may be reduced by the sale of the assets over which the charge floats. Furthermore, unless it contractually agrees not to do so (see below), the company is free to deal with the assets by charging them. As a result, a floating charge, even though properly registered, is normally postponed to a later fixed charge.

The floating charge will usually only have priority over later fixed charges if:

(a) the instrument creating the charge prohibits the creation of later fixed charges ranking in priority to or *pari passu* (i.e., equal) with the floating charge (such a provision is usually in the form of a 'negative pledge'); *and*

(b) the later fixed chargee has *notice of this prohibition* at the time when he takes his charge.

11.9.2   Floating charges

As between several floating charges, the *first in time* will have priority provided that it is properly registered. However, a later floating charge over some particular type of asset will probably take priority over an earlier floating charge over the whole of a company's property (*English and Scottish Mercantile Investment Co. v Brunton* [1892] 2 QB 700).

11.9.3 Avoidance of charges

In certain circumstances charges may be avoided, other than for non-registration, if made within a short period before the commencement of insolvency proceedings. This topic is dealt with in **Chapter 27**.

11.10 Remedies of debenture-holders

11.10.1 Express and implied powers

If the company fails to pay interest or principal money (i.e., the debt itself) the lender may sue as a creditor or petition for winding up. In addition, the debenture may contain an express power of sale and a power to appoint a receiver (see below). The debenture will state the circumstances in which these powers are to arise. It may, for example, give such powers to the lender when his interest is in arrears for a specified period, when the company breaks any term of the debenture, when any other creditor of the company appoints a receiver and when the company suffers execution by a judgment creditor.

Section 101 LPA 1925 gives the lender implied power to sell and to appoint a receiver if the debenture is made under seal and interest is two months in arrears or principal money has not been paid three months after it becomes due. In drafting a debenture, express powers should be given since they can be made wider than the implied powers; if the debenture is not executed as a deed, express powers are essential.

11.10.2 Application to the court

In the absence of express powers an application may be made to the court for sale or appointment of a receiver or manager if:

(a) liquidation of the company has commenced; or

(b) the company is in arrears with payment of principal or interest; or

(c) the lender's security is in jeopardy.

If the court orders sale the chargee will be paid the principal money and interest and any balance will be paid to the company. The assets will be treated as disposed of by the company so that a chargeable gain or allowable loss may result—thus affecting the company's corporation tax position (see **Chapter 19**).

11.11 Receivers

A receiver is appointed to realise the security of a debenture-holder. His position is, therefore, different from that of a liquidator, whose function is to wind up the company entirely. Once the receiver has paid the debenture-holder he will return any surplus to the company, which may then continue to trade. In fact, very often the appointment of a receiver by a debenture-holder will lead to the liquidation of the company, for example, because, after his appointment, the receiver finds that he can only obtain payment by winding up the company or because other creditors petition for winding up.

It is important to distinguish between a receiver and an administrative receiver. For the effect of an appointment of an administrative receiver see **Chapter 26**. Note, however, that the possibility of appointment of an administrative receiver is now considerably reduced.

11.12 Position of lenders and debenture-holders

Many debentures are short-term loans to a company (typically by a bank) on which interest will be paid by the company at a fixed or variable rate. The lender will consider the interest part of his general profits rather than as a source of investment income.

Some types of debenture are issued to people who have lent money to the company on a long-term basis and who may, therefore, be regarded as investors in the business. The nature of their investment is quite different from the investment made by shareholders. As we shall see in **Chapter 21**, the tax treatment of debenture interest is usually different from the treatment of dividends paid to shareholders. There are a number of other important differences between the two types of investment, which may be summarised as follows:

(a) Debenture-holders are not members and so do not have the right usually given to the members of voting at meetings.

(b) Debenture interest is payable out of capital if the company fails to make profits, so that a debenture is a safer investment (although if the company makes large profits the debenture-holders will not usually benefit).

(c) Debenture-holders are creditors on a winding up and will usually have a charge over some or all of the company's assets, whereas shareholders are repaid their investment only if the company is solvent.

(d) Debenture-holders, unlike shareholders, may be repaid while the company is a going concern (usually at a fixed date or at the option of the company). Shareholders may only be repaid where capital is reduced or where the company redeems or purchases its own shares.

11.13 Steps to be taken by a lender to a company

A person who wishes to lend money to a company should take the following steps either personally or through his advisers. Some of them are dictated by common sense, others by legal requirements:

(a) Investigate the financial standing and management of the company.

(b) Search at the Companies' Registry to see the company's last few sets of accounts and of what charge particulars have been registered.

(c) Search at the company's registered office—inspect copies of charges and obtain evidence of discharge of any registered charges.

(d) Search at the Land Registry or Land Charges Department (as appropriate) if a charge is to be taken over land.

(e) If there are any floating charges, make sure that they have not crystallised. (Until regulations requiring registration of crystallisation are made there is no machinery for ensuring this, but the directors of the company should be asked to certify that no events leading to crystallisation have occurred and, if possible, confirmation should be obtained from the chargees.)

(f) Include in the debenture power to appoint a receiver and a power of sale. If the charge is a floating charge, provide for its crystallisation.

(g) Ensure that the charge is registered within 21 days.

online resource centre

Interactive online exercises (Student Learning Activities) which complement the topics covered in this chapter are available at www.oxfordtextbooks.co.uk/orc/ business09_10/.

Disposal of shares

This chapter covers the following topics:

12.1 Introduction

In this chapter we shall consider the various ways in which a shareholder in a company may dispose of his interest in the company either during his lifetime or on death.

On disposal of shares tax will often become payable, although there are a number of reliefs available; this topic is dealt with in **Chapter 18**.

A disposal of shares by a substantial shareholder will alter the control of the company and possibly affect the rights of the remaining shareholders. The interests of the incoming shareholder and the remaining shareholders have to be balanced against each other. Arrangements for achieving a balance between those interests have to be anticipated and made in advance (usually by drafting suitable articles when the company is formed). It is, therefore, essential that potential problems should be foreseen and suitable arrangements made for the particular circumstances of each company.

We shall also consider financial involvement by a company in providing financial assistance for the purchase of its own shares or those of a holding company.

12.2 Transfer of shares

12.2.1 Introduction

A transfer of shares may be made by means of a sale or a gift *inter vivos*. The death or bankruptcy of a shareholder gives rise to an automatic transmission of shares (which will be followed by a transfer) and the special rules for transmission are dealt with later in the chapter.

A transfer of shares is likely to involve consideration of each of the Companies Act 2006, the Stock Transfer Act 1963 and the relevant company's articles of association.

12.2.2   Contract for sale

A shareholder who wishes to sell his shares may make a contract in any form that he wishes. The contract for sale is sufficient to give the purchaser an equitable interest in the shares. As between vendor and purchaser, the vendor will be liable to account to the purchaser for any dividends received and to vote as directed by the purchaser. However, *membership of the company* does not begin until the purchaser is registered as a member in the register of members which the company is required to keep. An entry cannot be made in the register of members until the company has received a 'proper instrument of transfer' (s. 770(1) CA 2006): this will take the form of a stock transfer form.

12.2.3   Procedure for transfer

Section 1 Stock Transfer Act 1963 provides that a transfer of fully paid shares may be made on a stock transfer form signed by the transferor and specifying:

(a) particulars of the consideration;

(b) description of the number or amount of the shares;

(c) particulars of the person by whom the transfer is made; and

(d) the full name and address of the transferee.

Once the sale of the shares has been agreed the vendor should execute a stock transfer form and send it together with the share certificate to the purchaser, who pays the stamp duty (see **12.2.4** below). The purchaser will apply to the company for registration by sending the stamped transfer and share certificate to the company. The transfer must be registered within two months of the application (s. 771(1) CA 2006) (unless refused; see below) and the company must send the purchaser a share certificate within the same period (s. 776(1) CA 2006). The procedure explained above applies on a gift of shares as well as on a sale (save that no stamp duty is payable).

The process of registration is effectively controlled by the board and the way in which it can and should respond to any proposed transfer will be determined by the articles. (See **12.2.5** for more detailed discussion.) However, any potential transferee should recognise that registration may not always be an automatic right and may in some circumstances be refused.

Section 771(1)(b) CA 2006 requires that any notice of refusal to register must be sent to the transferee within two months of the application, accompanied by reasons for the same. Section 771(2) also permits the transferee to request information on the reasons for refusal in addition to that supplied by the company in the first instance. However, the Act provides no guidance about these issues, especially the extent or the detail of the information in question. This may, therefore, prove to be an area which is ripe for dispute in the future.

(It should be noted that shares of publicly quoted companies may be transferred electronically under the CREST system. Such shares are said to exist in uncertificated form. The details of this system are beyond the scope of this Guide. Useful information on CREST can be found on its website www.crestco.co.uk.)

12.2.4   Stamp duty on transfer of shares

Stamp duty on a transfer of shares is charged at a rate of 0.5% of the consideration payable with the resulting figure being rounded up to the nearest £5. In any circumstances where the amount of stamp duty is calculated at £5, that is, where the consideration is £1,000 or less, no actual duty is payable.

EXAMPLE

Consideration payable	Stamp duty charged
£1	£nil*
£70	£nil*
£830	£nil*
£1,620	£10
£45,763	£230
	• In each instance, the stamp duty calculation results in an amount of £5, hence the fact that no duty is payable.

Certain transfers of shares are exempt from stamp duty. One of the most common types is a gift of shares, i.e., a transfer for no consideration in money or money's worth. The purchaser of the shares pays the relevant amount of duty.

12.2.5 Restrictions on right to transfer

Unless the articles provide to the contrary, every shareholder has a *right* to transfer his shares (which in effect means that the transferee has a right to be registered). However, the articles of the company can impose a restriction on the right to transfer shares. In the case of private companies a restriction is extremely common. A restriction is often thought to be desirable since it enables the company (usually through the directors) to refuse to allow unsuitable outsiders to join the company. An example is art. 24 of Table A which provides as follows:

The directors may refuse to register the transfer of a share which is not fully paid to a person of whom they do not approve and they may refuse to register the transfer of a share on which the company has a lien. They may also refuse to register a transfer unless:

(a) it is lodged at the registered office or at such other place as the directors may appoint and is accompanied by the certificate for the shares to which it relates and such other evidence as the directors may reasonably require to show the right of the transferor to make the transfer;

(b) it is in respect of only one class of shares; and

(c) it is in favour of not more than four transferees.

Thus, the directors can refuse to register a transfer of shares in the following circumstances:

(a) where the transfer is of partly paid shares;

(b) where the transfer is of fully paid shares over which the company has a lien (where Table A applies unamended, there is only a lien for calls on partly paid shares); or

(c) where the transfer is of fully paid shares (whether or not the company has a lien) and the requirements set out in (a), (b) and (c) of art. 24 are not complied with.

The person responsible for drafting the articles of a company should consult their clients to see what alternative or further restrictions, if any, they require.

Where there are restrictions on the right to transfer shares, the company must decide within two months of application for registration, whether or not to permit the transfer. If within that time the company has not given notice of refusal of registration to the transferee together with its reasons, the company and its officers who are in default are liable to a fine (s. 771(3) and (4) CA 2006) and the transferee becomes *entitled* to be registered.

It is not possible to consider all the possible types of restriction on the right to register but some of the more common restrictions will now be considered.

12.2.5.1 'The directors may in their absolute discretion decline to register any transfer of any share, whether or not it is a fully paid share'

At one time a company could not be a private company unless there was a restriction in its articles on the right to transfer shares. (This requirement was removed by CA 1980, which was consolidated into CA 1985.) Whilst the historical premise for this particular restriction has disappeared, it may still be regarded as a useful restriction on transfer. As with most restrictions on transfer, it is the directors who have power to refuse registration. The power is a negative one, that is, the directors have power to *refuse* registration—their positive approval is not required. This may seem an unimportant distinction but it means that a resolution of the directors is required to refuse registration, and since a resolution requires a majority in favour, an equality of votes will not be sufficient (unless, of course, the chairman has a casting vote and is against registration). This should be borne in mind in the case of 'two-man' companies, since either director will be able to ensure a transfer of his own shares merely by voting *against* the resolution to refuse registration. The directors' power to refuse registration must be exercised in good faith but it is very difficult to prove bad faith. The directors do not need to give reasons for refusal even if the article does not specifically excuse them from doing so.

It should be noted that this restriction is a restriction on the right to *transfer* shares, it is not a restriction on the right to *sell* them. If shares are sold but the purchaser is not registered, the vendor will hold the shares on trust for the purchaser. The purchaser will not be able to sue the vendor for damages (or his money back) unless the vendor guaranteed that registration would take place.

12.2.5.2 'The directors may decline to register a transfer of any share in favour of a person of whom they disapprove or of a share over which the company has a lien'

This restriction gives the directors two grounds for refusing registration. One is clearly subjective, whilst the other is objective. A company may wish to restrict the transfer of a share over which it has a lien as a way of protecting its security over the asset. In terms of an 'undesirable' shareholder, the provisions of s. 771 CA 2006, which require the company to give reasons for any refusal, will be particularly relevant. Moreover, the transferee is entitled to ask for further reasonable information about the reasons for the refusal (s. 771(2)). This could be fertile grounds for dispute.

12.2.5.3 'The directors may decline to register a transfer of any share except a transfer to [a member of the company or to a member of the family of the transferor]'

This type of restriction may be appropriate to restrict a shareholder in his right to bring in outsiders against the wishes of other members of the company; it leaves him free to transfer to insiders (i.e., the existing members of the company) or his own family. The words in square brackets could be adapted to include various other groups of permitted transferees, e.g., named persons or employees of the company. The term 'family' must, of course, be defined by the articles.

12.2.5.4 'The directors may refuse to register the transfer of a share, and if they do so, the instrument of transfer must be returned to the transferee with notice of refusal unless they suspect that the proposed transfer may be fraudulent'

This wording is found in art. 26(5) of the Model Articles for Private Companies. It is not dissimilar to some of the provisions already discussed. Note that it expressly recognises the obligation to provide the transferee with a notice of refusal to register.

12.2.6 Pre-emption rights

The object of restrictions on the right to transfer shares is to keep a private company private. However, the restrictions referred to above are not entirely sufficient for that purpose since they are merely restrictions on *transfer* and do not prevent sale or gift of the equitable title to the shares. If it is decided that the company should be kept completely private, the articles should include pre-emption rights. The usual provision is that a member who wishes to transfer shares must first offer them to the existing members of the company. In drafting an article providing for pre-emption rights the following points should be considered:

(a) Should the transferring member be free to transfer to *any* existing member of the company or should he be obliged to offer his shares to *all* the existing members in proportion to their present holdings?

(b) Should the transferring member be obliged to transfer part of his holding to the existing members if they do not wish to take all the shares which he proposes to transfer?

(c) Should any exceptions be made to the pre-emption rights? For example, the articles may provide that the pre-emption rights do not apply on a transfer to a member's family as defined by the article.

(d) How is the price payable to be fixed? It is quite common for the price to be fixed by agreement or by the auditors if no price can be agreed between vendor and purchaser.

(e) How long are the other members to be given to make up their minds? A period should be specified for the avoidance of doubt.

(f) How is the transferring member to give notice of his intention to sell? It is quite common for the article to require notice to be given to the company. The secretary will then inform the other members of the offer.

A pre-emption right is a right given to the other members of the company. It is also possible for the articles to provide that a member who wishes to transfer shares shall have a right to *require* the other members to buy his shares.

It is always important to preserve the distinction between pre-emption rights on transfer and those on allotment (see **11.2.4**). The former are not compulsory and can only be imposed by inclusion in the articles; the latter are and are imposed by statute.

12.3 Transmission by operation of law

When a member of a company dies, his shares vest automatically in his personal representative, who is entitled to any dividend paid by the company but may not vote at general meetings. The personal representative does not, however, automatically become a member of the company since membership begins only with an entry in the register of members. A personal representative will have to prove his title to the shares, by production of the grant of representation. Having done so, he has two courses of action open to him:

(a) The personal representative can apply, by means of a letter of request, for registration by the company as a member (the entry in the register of members will not refer to his representative capacity). The articles of the company will usually contain a provision (such as Table A, art. 30 or art. 27 of the Model Articles) permitting the personal representative to be registered as a member. If he is registered as a member, a subsequent transfer to a beneficiary will require a stock transfer form to be completed.

(b) Alternatively, if the personal representative wishes to sell the shares so as to raise cash for the purposes of the deceased's estate or when he wishes to vest the shares in the deceased's beneficiary, he can do so without himself being registered, by means of a stock transfer form.

A restriction on the right to transfer shares does not apply to a transmission on death unless the articles specifically so provide.

12.4 Buy-back and redemption by a company

As we have already seen (**11.3.4**), a company can issue redeemable shares or buy its own shares in certain circumstances. Effectively, this is a form of transfer, which allows a shareholder a method of exit from the company (or, at least, a reduction in their shareholding). In contrast to other forms of transfer, however, the shares bought back or redeemed are cancelled.

12.5 Financial assistance

12.5.1 Introduction and rationale

One of the fundamental principles of company law is the concept of maintenance of capital. That is, the capital of a company, as represented by its assets, should be maintained for the benefit of the company, its shareholders and its creditors. Companies should not generally return capital invested by shareholders, save on a winding up. Any derogation from this principle should be regulated to prevent abuse. This principle lies at the core of the regulation of financial assistance for the purchase of shares.

The general prohibition on financial assistance (see **12.5.2**) is designed, therefore, to maintain the capital of a company. In practical terms, it aims to prevent individuals acquiring a company's shares where that company's assets are used or put at risk by helping to finance the acquisition.

Until recently, the statutory prohibition on financial assistance has been fairly extensive in its scope. Given the consequences of breaching this prohibition, there has been great sensitivity in practice about its application, such that the spectre of financial assistance arises in many transactions, along with all its concomitant complications. This led to a belief that the provisions on financial assistance may result in greater inconvenience and cost than the harm they are designed to prevent. As such, the Companies Act 2006 has introduced a substantially altered   regime, which is only of relevance to public companies.

12.5.2   General prohibitions on financial assistance

Unlawful financial assistance can occur in four defined situations:

(a) Where a *public* company gives financial assistance directly or indirectly to any person for the purchase of its shares or any subsidiary thereof (either public or private) does the same (s. 678(1) CA 2006).

(b) Where a public company subsidiary gives financial assistance directly or indirectly to any person for the purchase of shares in its private parent company (s. 679(1) CA 2006).

(c) Where a public company (or any subsidiary thereof) gives financial assistance directly or indirectly for the purpose of reducing or discharging any liability incurred by a person in buying shares in that public company (s. 678(3) CA 2006).

(d) Where a public company subsidiary gives financial assistance directly or indirectly for the purpose of reducing or discharging any liability incurred by a person in buying shares in that company's private parent company (s. 679(3) CA 2006).

Hence, assistance can be given before, at the same time as, or following, the time of the acquisition of the shares in question and may be given directly or indirectly. It should be noted that the prohibition is also operative not only where a person is acquiring shares in a company but also where such person is proposing to acquire shares.

12.5.3   Types of financial assistance

These are defined in s. 677 and examples are provided below. The examples are by no means exhaustive and lawyers need to consider the full financial ramifications of the acts of relevant companies before, during and after acquisitions of shares in such companies or any of their parent companies.

12.5.3.1   Financial assistance by way of gift

A simple example would be the provision by a company of funds to an individual to buy shares in that company or any parent company. Another example would be a sale or transfer at an undervalue. Note that this could be a sale or transfer of the shares themselves, or a sale by a company to an individual of an asset at an undervalue, which the individual then sold at full value in order to apply the realised funds in buying shares in the company.

12.5.3.2   Financial assistance given by way of guarantee, security or indemnity

These are forms of financial assistance which are provided indirectly. An example of each form is set out below.

Guarantee
A Limited gives a guarantee to a bank in respect of the obligations of C, who has borrowed from the bank in order to buy shares in B plc, the parent company of A Limited.

Security
E Limited is acquiring F plc, a subsidiary of G Limited. To finance the purchase, E Limited is borrowing from a bank. The bank requires security for the loan in the form of charges over the assets of both E and F plc. The latter is therefore providing financial assistance by way of security for the purchase of its shares by E Limited.

Indemnity

H plc offers its shares as consideration to buy the shares in T plc which H plc wishes to take over. It offers to the shareholders of T plc, in return for their agreement to sell their shares to H plc, an indemnity against any losses suffered as a result of their receipt of shares in H plc (due to, for example, fluctuations in their market value). Here, H plc is providing financial assistance by way of indemnity for the purchase of its shares by the shareholders of T plc.

12.5.3.3   Financial assistance given by way of loan

A public company providing a loan to one of its directors to allow him to buy shares in that company or its parent company is a simple example of this form of financial assistance. (Note also that the provisions of ss. 197 CA 2006 et seq. would also have to be considered.) However, s. 677(c)(i) also refers to assistance:

> by way of any . . . agreement under which any obligations of the person giving the assistance are to be fulfilled at a time when in accordance with the agreement any obligation of another party to the agreement remains unfulfilled.

This part of the section exists to extend its ambit beyond loans to other types of credit or deferred payment transactions. An example of this would be where K plc sells assets to M Limited and allows deferred payment for those assets, in the knowledge that M Limited is about to buy shares in K plc. By deferring payment, K plc has provided assistance to M Limited for the purchase of shares in K plc.

12.5.3.4   Financial assistance reducing to a material extent a company's net assets

This provision covers any form of financial assistance, other than those described in **12.5.3.1** to **12.5.3.3**, where the effect of providing the assistance is to reduce to a material extent a company's net assets. The latter are taken as being the aggregate of the company's assets less the aggregate of its liabilities, using the actual market value of the assets (as opposed to the book value) at the time of the provision of the assistance. There is no definition in the Companies Act of what is a material reduction: it is a matter to be assessed by reference to the individual circumstances of each case.

An example of this form of financial assistance is where a private company subsidiary pays the professional fees of those involved in the purchase of shares in its public parent company, provided that the purpose of this was to assist the acquisition of the company's shares, and the amount involved reduced the subsidiary company's net assets to a material extent.

12.5.4   Consequences of providing unlawful financial assistance

A company which provides unlawful financial assistance is liable to a fine and directors may be liable to imprisonment or a fine, or both. Any contract to provide financial assistance is illegal and therefore the obligations of the providing company cannot be enforced.

12.5.5   General exceptions

12.5.5.1 Principal and larger purpose exceptions

A number of exceptions exist to the general prohibitions described above, viz:

(a) if the company's principal purpose in giving the assistance is not to give it for the purpose of any such acquisition, or the giving of assistance for that purpose is but an incidental part of some larger purpose of the company and in either instance the assistance is given in good faith in the interests of the company (ss. 678(2) and 679(2) CA 2006).

(b) if the company's principal purpose in giving the assistance is not to reduce or discharge any liability incurred by a person for the purpose of the acquisition of shares in the company or its holding company, or the reduction or discharge of any such liability is but an incidental part of some larger purpose of the company and in either instance the assistance is given in good faith in the interests of the company (ss. 678(4) and 679(4) CA 2006).

Whether or not the principal or larger purpose exceptions can be relied upon will depend on the facts of each case. The burden of proof is on the company providing the assistance to convince the court that an exception applies.

The leading case on this matter is *Brady v Brady* [1989] AC 755, which considered s. 153 CA 1985, the forerunner to the above provisions. The financial assistance given in this case was part of a scheme to assist some shareholders in buying out others to resolve a management deadlock. The court drew a distinction between the purpose of providing financial assistance and the reason for so doing. The former was held as being to allow shareholders to acquire shares in the company, whilst the latter was held as being the resolution of the deadlock. The court found, on the facts, that there was no evidence of any principal purpose to which the assistance was subsidiary or any larger purpose.

The result of *Brady v Brady* is that 'purpose' has a narrow interpretation. For a company to rely on the exceptions in s. 153, there had to be clear evidence of either:

(a) a principal purpose other than the acquisition of shares for which financial assistance is given to an individual; or

(b) a larger purpose for the company (as opposed to individual shareholders, directors or prospective purchasers of shares) in providing financial assistance to an individual other than the acquisition of shares.

In addition, the company had to satisfy the court that it acted in good faith in the interests of the company. Given the narrow interpretation that was given to the exceptions in s. 153, and the requirement of good faith, it is difficult to be confident as to the circumstances in which the equivalent exceptions in the 2006 Act can be relied on.

12.5.5.2 Other exceptions

Section 681 provides that certain events will not amount to financial assistance. These include:

(a) a distribution by way of dividend or in the course of a company's winding up;

(b) an allotment of bonus shares;

(c) a reduction of capital;

(d) a redemption or buy-back of shares; and

(e) anything done under an order sanctioning a compromise or arrangement with members or creditors of the company.

Given that the exceptions described above are specific events, these may be relied on with more confidence than the exceptions in **12.5.5.1**.

Finally, there are some very specialised exceptions in s. 682 which relate mainly to issues concerning the provision of assistance to employees to partake in employee share schemes. The details of these are beyond the scope of this book.

12.5.6   Private companies and financial assistance

The new 2006 Act regime obviously benefits many transactions involving private companies. However, it is suggested that even where the prohibitions in ss. 678 and 679 are irrelevant, an instance of financial assistance may still need careful legal analysis, particularly from the perspective of directors' duties. An ill-conceived or irresponsible method of financial assistance which results in subsequent financial harm to the company providing it could leave directors exposed to claims that they neither promoted the success of the company nor acted with reasonable care and diligence. The practice may develop, therefore, of seeking prior approval of shareholders and directors may be well served to obtain appropriate accountancy advice about the financial repercussions of any proposed financial assistance, in any event.

 online resource centre   Interactive online exercises (Student Learning Activities) which complement the topics covered in this chapter are available at www.oxfordtextbooks.co.uk/orc/business09_10/.

Company meetings and resolutions

This chapter covers the following topics:

13.1 Types of general meeting

In this chapter, we shall look at meetings of shareholders and the resolutions which are passed at such meetings. In **Chapter 10**, we saw that there are certain powers which can only be exercised within a company by the shareholders. In this chapter, we are concerned with how those powers are exercised. The rules about these matters are sometimes quite technical but their importance cannot be overestimated. A solicitor advising a company or shareholder may often be called upon to see that the correct procedures are adopted. Moreover, those procedures will have to be reflected in correctly drafted documentation, such as notices of meetings or minutes of meetings, which the solicitor will normally produce on behalf of the client.

It is important to recognise that these meeting procedures will be governed by a combination of statute and the relevant company's articles. In some instances, statute will be prescriptive; in others its effect can be displaced or modified by the articles.

We are not concerned in this chapter with directors' meetings (which were dealt with in **Chapter 9**); we are only concerned with meetings of shareholders. Shareholders' meetings are also called 'company meetings' or 'general meetings'. Company meetings are of two types: annual general meetings and general meetings.

13.1.1 Main changes under the Companies Act 2006

The position under the Companies Act 1985 was relatively complicated. Much of what the 2006 Act has attempted to do is to streamline the governance of shareholders' meetings, particularly for private companies, which is in line with the Government's 'think small first' policy. The main contrasts between the new system and the one it replaced are:

(a) Under the 1985 Act, there were four possible resolutions which shareholders might pass: ordinary; special; extraordinary and elective (the last being in respect of private companies only). Under the 2006 Act, only two shareholders' resolutions are recognised: ordinary and special.

(b) Under the previous regime, the type of resolution to be proposed at a shareholders' meeting determined the length of notice required, which was either 14 or 21 days. The 2006 Act only requires 14 days' notice in every circumstance except the annual general meeting of a public company, where 21 days' notice is required. (A company's articles may, however, require longer notice in certain situations; see discussion at **13.4.2**.)

(c) Previously all companies were required to hold an annual general meeting, although the shareholders of a private company could dispense with this requirement through an elective resolution passed to this effect. (Elective resolutions generally were a way of allowing private companies a limited form of deregulation from the requirements of the 1985 Act, if shareholders so wished.) Under the new regime, only public companies must hold annual general meetings.

(d) The 1985 Act recognised the concept of a written resolution of the shareholders of a company as an alternative to a formal meeting and vote. However, the consent of all shareholders of a company to a resolution in such form was required for it to be passed. (This is in contrast to a resolution passed at an actual meeting where the votes of only those shareholders present are relevant for determining whether or not a resolution is passed.) This meant that written resolutions could only effectively be used where there was unanimity amongst all the shareholders of a company. The 2006 Act has liberalised somewhat the use of written resolutions by allowing them to be passed by the same majority as is required in a general meeting.

13.1.2   Annual general meetings

Only public companies are now required to hold annual general meetings (AGMs) (s. 336 CA 2006). An AGM must be held in each period of six months beginning with the day following the company's accounting reference date. Normally companies use the AGM as an opportunity to fulfil certain statutory or regulatory requirements, for example, that they lay before the company in general meeting copies of their annual accounts. (This requirement used to apply to all companies, public or private (s. 241 CA 1985). As from 6 April 2008, only public companies are obliged to present accounts to a general meeting (s. 437 CA 2006).)

13.1.3   General meetings

Any meeting which is not an AGM is a general meeting (GM). As a consequence, both public and private companies may hold GMs. A GM is held as and when necessary.

Previously, this type of meeting was often referred to as an Extraordinary General Meeting and the articles of some companies would state this fact explicitly. It is arguable, therefore, that if a company's articles insist on the use of such terminology, then it is necessary to use the epithet 'Extraordinary'.

The procedure for calling GMs will be considered shortly, but first it is necessary to consider the types of resolution needed to transact business at general meetings.

13.2 Resolutions

A company in general meeting can only transact business by passing the appropriate type of resolution. There are two types of shareholder resolution: ordinary and special.

13.2.1 Ordinary resolutions

An ordinary resolution is one which requires a simple majority of votes in favour if it is to be passed (a simple majority means more votes in favour than against—an equality of votes is not sufficient—s. 282(1) CA 2006). Where there is equality an ordinary resolution may, however, be passed on the chairman's casting vote if the articles so provide. In the case of a small company, the decision as to whether to allow an article giving a casting vote may be crucial. The presence of a casting vote resolves the problem of deadlock but may in some cases be considered to give the chairman too much power. An ordinary resolution is sufficient to transact any business at a general meeting save in those cases where the Companies Act requires a special resolution or where the articles require a special resolution or unanimity of the members.

13.2.2 Special resolutions

A special resolution requires a 75% majority—that is, at least three votes must be cast in favour of the resolution for every one cast against it (s. 283(1) CA 2006).

13.2.3 Which type of resolution is required?

The Companies Act sets out a number of circumstances in which shareholders' resolutions are required, either to cause something to happen or, more commonly, to allow the directors to commit the company to a course of action. A company's articles may also impose further requirements for a decision of the shareholders, however, instances of these tend to be relatively rare.

As a basic rule, special resolutions are required where the deemed prejudice to shareholders could be considerable. Therefore, a proposed change to the articles requires such a resolution to bring it into effect (s. 21 CA 2006). By contrast, ordinary resolutions normally act as shareholder permission for a transaction. For example, a proposed substantial property transaction between a director and a company needs the prior consent of the shareholders by ordinary resolution (s. 190 CA 2006), but the directors must still decide to commit the company to the transaction.

It is not the intention of this chapter to set out all possible instances of special and ordinary resolutions. Reference to the necessary resolution is made, as appropriate, in the other chapters dealing with company law issues.

13.3 Calling a general meeting

As we saw in **Chapter 9**, directors' meetings can be called quite informally at the request of any one of the directors. The position in relation to general meetings is more complicated. As with so many aspects of company law, the rules are partly statutory and partly depend on the provisions of the company's own articles. Most of the statutory rules are designed to protect the shareholders, whose voting rights would be worthless if they were not backed up by rights to be notified of meetings or to call meetings themselves.

13.3.1 Call by directors

Section 302 CA 2006 gives the directors power to call general meetings of a company. This power is actually a statutory restatement of a regular practice, which has in the past been governed by the articles. The articles of nearly, if not all, companies set up prior to the 2006 regime are likely to contain a provision granting directors the authority to call shareholders' meetings. In most instances, therefore, general meetings of a company will be called by the directors.

13.3.2 Shareholders' right to requisition meeting

13.3.2.1 Requisition to directors

Section 303(1) CA 2006 permits a specified percentage of shareholders to request the directors to call a meeting. This can be a valuable right in circumstances where the shareholders disagree with the approach of the board and want to air their views in a formal environment.

Such a request can be in paper or electronic form (s. 303(6)) and must state the general nature of the business the shareholders want dealing with at the proposed meeting. It can include the text of any specific resolution to be proposed to the meeting (s. 303(4)).

The specified percentage is sufficient members of the company to represent at least 10% of the paid-up share capital of the company as carries the right to vote at general meetings (s. 303(2) and (3)).

Once such a requirement is made of the directors, they must call a meeting within 21 days, which must be held on not more than 28 days' notice (s. 304(1)). Such notice must include a copy of any proposed resolution received from the requisitionists (s. 304(2)) and if that resolution is actually a special resolution, the specific requirements for special resolutions contained within s. 283 of the Act must be complied with in the notice, otherwise the directors are deemed not to have fulfilled their obligation under this section (s. 304(4)).

13.3.2.2 Power of shareholders to call meeting in default

If the directors of a company fail to comply properly with a s. 303 request, s. 305 CA 2006 permits the requisitionists (or any of them representing more than one half of the total voting rights of all of them) to call a meeting instead. In doing so, the meeting must be called as much as possible in the same manner as that in which meetings are required to be called by the directors (s. 305(4)) (presumably under both the Act and the articles, as is relevant). The date of such a meeting must be no later than three months from the date on which the directors' obligation under s. 304 arose (s. 305(3)).

13.3.2.3 Court power to order meeting

Section 306(1) CA 2006 gives the court power to order meetings if for any reason it is impracticable either:

(a) to call a meeting of a company in any manner in which meetings of that company may be called; or

(b) to conduct a meeting in the manner prescribed either by the Act or by the company's articles.

An application to court for such an order can be made by either a director or shareholder (s. 306(2)). The predecessor to this section, s. 371 CA 1985, was often used to get round either practical problems to do with calling meetings or to resolve issues of deadlock in 'two-man' companies, where a dissenting shareholder refused to attend a general meeting, thus rendering it inquorate. See, for example, *Re Opera Phonographic Ltd* [1989]. (See discussion of quorum issues below at **13.5.1**.)

13.4   Notice of meetings

13.4.1   Service of notice

Section 301 CA 2006 makes it a pre-condition of the validity of any resolution of the shareholders that notice of the meeting and the resolution is given in accordance with the Act and the company's articles. Subject to any provision in the articles, every member and every director of a company must receive notice of a general meeting (s. 310).

The following explanation will look at the statutory requirements which will have universal application. It will also be important to consider in every instance the articles to ascertain any specific further requirements which must be fulfilled.

Section 308 CA 2006 permits a notice of a general meeting to be given either:

(a) in hard copy form; or

(b) in electronic form (most commonly by e-mail or possibly by text message); or

(c) via a website; or

(d) by a combination of any or all of the above.

Schedule 5 to the 2006 Act sets out rules for any communications sent out by a company, including those in electronic form or via a website. Communication in either of these two forms requires the prior consent of a shareholder.

Additionally, in respect of website communications:

(a) Shareholders must still be notified of the presence of the information or notification on the website and that it is in respect of a general meeting, stating the time, date, and place of the meeting (s. 309).

(b) As an alternative to seeking the consent of every member in every circumstance, a company may by a provision in its articles or by a shareholder resolution provide for website communication, after which shareholders must be asked to agree to the supply of information via a website and will be deemed to do so unless they specifically object within 28 days of such a request.

In respect of closely-held companies, the use of a website is probably academic, because e-mail or paper notification is likely to be the most appropriate method. However, the website method may have more attraction to companies with a large number of shareholders.

13.4.2   Length of notice

13.4.2.1   Full notice

The length of notice required depends on the nature of the meeting and the company. For private companies all general meetings must be called on at least 14 days' notice

(s. 307(1) CA 2006). For public companies all general meetings must be held on at least 14 days' notice, except AGMs where 21 days' notice is required (s. 307(2) CA 2006).

The calculation of what the notice period should be is always something which should be treated with care. Section 360 of the 2006 Act clarifies the issue by excluding from the notice period both the day of giving the notice and the day of the meeting itself.

The above notice periods are minima, laid down by the Companies Act. Each company must decide upon the notice periods it wants and state them in its articles of association. Clearly most companies will elect to follow the Companies Act, but companies can provide for different notice periods, provided that they do not fall below the statutory minima. Note that it is quite common for articles to provide for 'clear days' of notice, that is, *exclusive* of the date of service and the date of the meeting, which echoes the effect of s. 360 above. Moreover the articles may also deem a date of receipt of any notice, so this needs to be factored into the calculation of the necessary notice period. The golden rule is always to err on the side of caution.

13.4.2.2   Short notice procedure

For many companies, it is often unnecessarily burdensome to wait for full notice periods to elapse. The Companies Act, therefore, provides a mechanism for 'short-circuiting' the process by allowing for shorter notice than already mentioned.

For private companies, s. 307(5) provides that shorter notice than that normally required may validly be given in respect of all general meetings of such a company if a majority in number of members owning not less than 90% of the shares, which carry an entitlement to attend and vote at the meeting, agree to such shorter notice. Note that a private company may demand a higher percentage than 90%, but this must not exceed 95% (s. 307(6)(a)). It is quite unlikely for a company to avail itself of such a possibility and in the case of a company with small numbers of shareholders and relatively similar-sized shareholdings, the difference between 90% and 95% acceptances is usually academic, as agreement of most, if not all, shareholders will be needed to meet this threshold.

EXAMPLE

Scenario one
Random Limited has three shareholders, A, B and C, who each own 30%, 30% and 40% of the voting share capital in the company. Consent to short notice of a general meeting of Random Limited can only effectively be given by all the members of the company.

Scenario two
Colston Limited has four shareholders, A, B, C and D, who each own 45%, 45%, 5% and 5% of the voting share capital in the company

   (a) If A and B only consent to short notice, this is not effective consent, as they do not constitute a majority in number, despite owning between them 90% of the voting share capital.

   (b) If A, C and D only consent to short notice, this is not effective consent, as, whilst they constitute a majority in number, they only own between them 55% of the voting share capital.

   (c) If A, B and either C or D consent, this is effective consent.

Therefore, it does not matter if the required percentage is 90% or set at 95% in Colston's articles; shareholders owning at least 95% of the voting capital must consent in any event.

For *public* companies shorter notice than that normally required may validly be given if:

(a) in the case of an AGM all the members entitled to attend and vote at the meeting agree to short notice (ss. 307(7) and 337(2)); and

(b) in the case of any other general meeting a majority in number of members owning not less than 95% of the voting shares and entitled to attend and vote at the meeting agree to short notice.

For many private companies (especially family companies or companies where the members are all directors), the possibility of short notice allows a meeting to be held at very short notice—normally by informally gathering together all the relevant shareholders and then obtaining their consent to formal notice of the general meeting. However, for companies with large numbers of shareholders, it is not normally a practical alternative to the giving of proper notice.

13.4.3   Contents of notice

The notice of a meeting must state the date, time and place of meeting (s. 311(1) CA 2006). It must also describe the business which is to be transacted sufficiently for members to be able to decide whether they wish to attend (s. 311(2) CA 2006). If a special resolution is to be proposed, its wording must be set out verbatim in the notice and must be expressed to be proposed as a special resolution (s. 283(6) CA 2006).

It is a question of judgement in each case how much detail of the business needs to be stated. However, in drawing up a notice it is better to err on the side of inclusion rather than exclusion. A company's articles can demand fuller information than that required by s. 311(2), in any event. For both of these reasons, there is normally no distinction drawn between ordinary and special resolutions and full wording of either type of resolution will usually be set out in the notice.

Section 325 CA 2006 requires that any notice of a general meeting should always tell a member of their right under s. 324 to send a proxy (who need not be a member) to attend and speak and vote on their behalf. If any additional rights in this regard are afforded by the company's articles, these rights should also be stated.

13.5   Proceedings at meetings

13.5.1   Quorum

A meeting cannot consider business unless a quorum is present at the time when the meeting proceeds to business. Unless the articles otherwise provide or the company has only one member, two members personally present or their proxies or their representatives (in the case of a corporate shareholder) are a quorum (s. 318).

The appointment of a representative of a corporate shareholder is governed by s. 323 CA 2006 and ss. 324 to 331 contain provisions about proxies. (A company may, if it chooses, provide for further rights for proxies over and above those provided by the Act—s. 323.)

13.5.2 Voting

13.5.2.1 Show of hands

A vote on a resolution will normally be decided on a show of hands, that is, one shareholder, one vote (s. 284(2) CA 2006). However, the inequities of this when there are diverse shareholdings are obvious. Therefore, a vote may, instead, be taken on a poll, that is, one vote per share (s. 284(3)).

13.5.2.2 Poll

A poll must be demanded at the relevant meeting and a company's articles will make provision for how this is done. The only stipulation the Companies Act 2006 makes is that a provision in the articles is void if it renders ineffective a call from a poll from either at least five members or members holding more than 10% of the voting rights or any member or members with 10% of the paid-up capital with a right to vote (s. 321(2)).

It is quite normal for articles to provide for more extensive rights by allowing any two members (instead of five) or the chairman to call for a poll as well.

Proxies have the same right to call for a poll as the member or members they represent.

The following examples demonstrate the difference between voting on a show of hands and voting on a poll.

EXAMPLE

Cotton Limited has four shareholders, A, B, C and D, who each own respectively 45%, 40%, 10% and 5% of the voting share capital in the company.

Assume that in each of the scenarios which follow all of the shareholders in Cotton attend the meeting in question and that there are no abstentions.

Scenario one—ordinary resolution: vote on a show of hands
At least three of the four shareholders must vote in favour for the resolution to be passed.

Scenario two—ordinary resolution: vote on a poll
Any permutation of at least three shareholders voting in favour will be sufficient for the resolution to be passed.

If only two shareholders vote in favour, it must either be A and B or A and C. (Neither A and D nor B and C, for example, constitute a majority.)

Scenario three—special resolution: vote on a show of hands
Any permutation of at least three shareholders voting in favour will be sufficient for the resolution to be passed.

Scenario four—special resolution: vote on a poll
Irrespective of how C and D vote, A and B must vote in favour.

13.6 Minutes and returns

Minutes must be kept of all decisions taken at general meetings and must be available for inspection by the members at the registered office (ss. 355 and 358 CA 2006). Copies of special resolutions must be sent to the Registrar of Companies within 15 days of being passed (s. 30 CA 2006), as must any resolution authorising directors.

13.7 Written resolutions

13.7.1 Validity

A *private* company may pass resolutions in writing under s. 288 CA 2006, without a meeting or any previous notice being given. Such a company may pass any type of resolution—ordinary or special—using this procedure, save for two exceptions. These are the removal of a director under s. 168 CA 2006 or removal of an auditor under s. 510 CA 2006. (There were similar provisions in the 1985 Act.)

For a written resolution to be effective, a required majority of the members of the company entitled to vote on the resolution must consent to it as follows:

(a) For ordinary resolutions, members representing a simple majority of the *total* voting rights of the members entitled to vote on the resolution (s. 282(2)).

(b) For special resolutions, members representing at least 75% of the *total* voting rights of the members entitled to vote on the resolution (s. 283(2)).

Section 284C(1) stipulates that in respect of a written resolution each member has one vote in respect of each share held.

Therefore, whilst the validity of resolutions at general meetings is based on a count of the votes cast by the members actually present, by contrast, the effectiveness of a written resolution is based upon all the votes which could be cast.

The date of any written resolution is determined by the time at which the required majority has signified its agreement to it (s. 296(4)). A member signifies his agreement when the company receives from him, either in hard copy or electronic form, an authenticated document indicating his agreement to the resolution (s. 296(1)).

EXAMPLE

Random Limited has three shareholders, A, B and C, who each own 30%, 30% and 40% respectively of the voting share capital in the company.

In respect of a proposed special resolution:

(a) if A and B only attend a general meeting and vote in its favour (either on a show of hands or a poll), this will be a unanimous vote and the resolution will be passed;

(b) instead, if A and B only consent to the resolution in the form of a written resolution, the resolution will not be passed, as A and B only hold 60% of the voting capital in the company, not the minimum of 75% required.

(Note that in respect of (b), the position would be different if an ordinary resolution was proposed.)

Under s. 300 CA 2006, any provision in a private company's articles which prevents it from passing written resolutions using the statutory procedure is void.

For many private companies, written resolutions are quite often a preferred alternative to the holding of a general meeting.

13.7.2 Documentation

As with the calling of general meetings, a request for a written resolution will normally be prompted by the board of a company. In this instance, s. 291 CA 2006 must be complied with, otherwise all officers of the company in default will commit an offence, although such default will not affect the validity of the resolution itself. The requirements of s. 291 are:

(a) The resolution must go out to all members entitled to vote on the resolution.

(b) This may be done either in hard copy, electronic form, or through a website (or a combination of any or all of these methods).

(c) The resolution must be accompanied by a statement explaining how a member may consent to the resolution and the date by which the resolution must be passed. (A written resolution will lapse if not passed by either the period set out in the articles or, if there is none, by the end of the 28th day after the circulation of the resolution—s. 297(1).)

Section 291 envisages either individual copies of the resolution for each member or a single copy to be submitted in turn to each member. Consent to a resolution is normally achieved by a member signing and dating a document which includes the full text of the resolution.

In the same way that members of a company can requisition the board to call a general meeting, so s. 292 of the 2006 Act provides that members representing at least 5% of the total voting rights of all members can require a written resolution to be distributed at their instance. (The articles can provide for a lower percentage.)

In many instances of closely-held companies, if possible, arrangements will be made for all relevant shareholders to be present to receive and agree to the written resolution simultaneously. This will provide certainty that the resolution has been received by all relevant shareholders and that it has been consented to at a particular moment in time. Posting out or e-mailing written resolutions to shareholders and waiting for their responses is much less satisfactory.

13.7.3 Effect on requirements for specific resolutions

There are a number of resolutions which require specific documents to be available for inspection at the registered office in advance of the relevant general meeting and at the meeting itself for the resolution to be effective (normally for the purpose of informing shareholders), for example:

(a) authority for purchase of own shares—the relevant contract for the purchase or a memorandum thereof must be available (required by s. 696 CA 2006);

(b) reduction of share capital by a private company—the supporting solvency statement of the directors must be available (required by s. 642 CA 2006);

(c) approval of the term of a director's service contract—a memorandum of the contract, including details of the relevant term, must be available (required by s. 188 CA 2006);

(d) approval of loans, etc., to directors—a memorandum setting out prescribed details of the loan, etc., must be available (required by ss. 197, 198 or 201 CA 2006, depending upon the particular type of transaction).

If the written resolution method is chosen instead, the above requirement must be varied. The basic, alternative requirement in each case is the supply or disclosure of specific information or documentation to all members at or before the time at which the written resolution is supplied.

13.7.4 Recording

Copies of all written resolutions passed must be maintained in the same way as minutes of a general meeting (s. 355 CA 2006).

The articles of a private company

This chapter covers the following topics:

14.1 Introduction

In this chapter, we will look at the articles of a private company. We saw in **Chapter 8** that all companies are required to have articles of association and that these articles define and regulate the relationships within the company. We also saw that 'standard' articles are made available through regulation and that a company can either adopt these articles wholesale or have articles specifically drafted for it (often based on those standard articles).

In this chapter, we will look at some of the major terms which it may be desirable to include in the articles of a private company. We will also look at the way in which the articles of a company can be altered and any restrictions thereto.

Until recently, Table A (contained in the Companies (Tables A to F) Regulations 1985) was the model set of articles available for adoption by companies. These articles were introduced at the same time as the Companies Act 1985 came into effect and the regime under that Act informed much of the content of Table A. Table A has been amended on a number of occasions since its introduction in 1985, most recently in October 2007, so the date of incorporation of a company will determine which particular version of Table A is relevant to that company (if, indeed, Table A was adopted in whole or in part). In other words, a company which was incorporated in 1992 and which chose Table A as its articles will have articles which differ from a company which was incorporated in 2008 and also adopted Table A.

To put all this into context, many companies in existence will have Table A articles or, at least, articles based on Table A. A particular consequence of this situation is that currently many companies' articles will be premised on the basis of the regime as set out by the Companies Act 1985. For companies (mainly private) to take advantage of the liberalised regime afforded by the 2006 Act, it will be necessary for them to make relevant alterations to their articles. (Generally the 2006 Act does not displace or update any provisions within pre-existing articles.)

As part of the changes to company law effected by the Companies Act 2006, a new set of short-form articles for use by private companies has replaced Table A, as the standard set of 'default' articles for private companies. (Additionally, a standard set of articles for public companies has also been created.) These new Model Articles are effective from 1 October 2009 and reflect the regime under the 2006 Act. (In the same way as for Table A, the new Model Articles are not compulsory for companies, nor do they automatically replace the articles of pre-existing companies.) With the introduction of the Model Articles, it is expected that more and more companies are going to be set up with these Model Articles or variations thereon.

Perhaps one of the most notable features of the Model Articles for private companies is that they are about half the length of Table A. This has been achieved by relying much more on the 2006 Act to regulate matters and by simplifying many procedural matters. In particular, the provisions governing general meetings are considerably less than in Table A, perhaps reflecting the view that the written resolution should be the normal method for achieving shareholders' decisions.

As with Table A, the Model Articles are likely to have their pros and cons in various instances, so it is not expected that lawyers will advise clients to adopt them unquestioningly. Furthermore, many law firms have their own standard articles, which they are likely to consider superior. Indeed, one of the possible criticisms of the Model Articles is that they are not a comprehensive source of guidance for those running companies and reference will often have to be made to the Act itself to fill in the gaps.

In many ways, the articles of a company should be looked on as all other contracts—there are likely to be as many variations as there are similarities. Therefore, it is important never to assume the contents of a company's constitution and any lawyer needs to be satisfied that the articles have been accurately complied with.

We will now consider some of the main issues which a company's articles are likely to address. (Note that all references to the Model Articles are to the version for private limited companies, unless otherwise indicated.)

14.2 Provisions concerning shares and membership

14.2.1 Share capital

The first part of Table A deals with shares and membership of the company. It provides for the creation of different classes of shares (arts 2 and 3). There are also provisions which deal with partly–paid shares and the company's lien for amounts unpaid on shares (i.e., if shares are issued without being paid for in full the company has a lien (a charge) over the shares to secure payment for them). There are relatively few cases where shares are issued by private companies without payment in full at the time of issue, so these provisions are unlikely to be of particular relevance.

The Model Articles contain a similar permission to allot shares of differing rights (art. 22). However, perhaps to reflect the rarity of partly-paid shares in private companies, there is no mention of a lien. (Furthermore, art. 21 specifically requires all shares to be fully paid–up on issue.)

Two specific consequences of art. 22 should be noted:

(a) The rights of any shares issued may be determined by ordinary resolution. This may have some administrative convenience. However, it is quite often the case that specific and detailed share rights will be set out in the articles for reasons of certainty.

(b) Advantage is taken of s. 685 CA 2006 to permit the directors to determine the terms of any redeemable shares, although, again, for reasons of certainty, a company may prefer to set out these rights in the articles.

14.2.2 Issue of shares

Neither Table A nor the Model Articles give directors authority to issue shares. It may be considered desirable to include such power in the articles of a company so that a meeting of members is not needed for the issue of shares when the company is newly-formed and for the foreseeable future. (Remember that the effect of s. 550 CA 2006 is that directors of companies with only one class of shares are able to allot further shares of the same class without the need for authority from the shareholders, so the inclusion of such a provision is likely to anticipate allotments in wider circumstances.)

Any issue of shares wholly for cash has to be offered to the existing members pro rata their shareholdings in accordance with the statutory pre-emption rules set out in s. 561 CA 2006, unless the articles make alternative provision. Those drafting the articles should consider whether this would be appropriate. (Neither Table A nor the Model Articles make any such provision.) A number of amendments are possible and the following, in particular, might be considered:

(a) a provision which excludes or disapplies the statutory pre-emption rights so as to allow shares to be issued to non-shareholders or other than pro rata (provided the directors are authorised to issue shares, if necessary);

(b) in contrast, a provision which imposes pre-emption rights which are more extensive than those provided by statute—statutory pre-emption rights of the existing members only apply when the consideration for the proposed allotment is cash and when the shares are of a specified type. As such, a provision could be inserted providing for pre-emption rights in respect of every possible category of allotment.

14.2.3 Transfer of shares

In the case of many private companies, it is considered appropriate that a shareholder should not be free to transfer their shares to anyone they choose. The reason for this is that if an existing shareholder is free to transfer to anyone he is, in effect, in a position to decide who his fellow shareholders' future associates should be. In Table A transfer of shares is dealt with in arts 23–28. A shareholder is free to transfer his shares to anyone in most cases. The directors have power to refuse only if the shares are not fully paid or the company has a lien on them (the company will only have a lien if the shares have not been fully paid for unless there have been other amendments to Table A).

Article 26(5) of the Model Articles, in contrast, grants the board absolute discretion to refuse the registration of any transfer. This should be read in conjunction with s. 771 which imposes an obligation to give notice to the transferee of any refusal, together with the reason for it, within two months of the transfer being lodged with the company.

Notice that with this type of provision a majority vote of the directors is needed to refuse to register the transfer. If the directors are equally divided and there is no casting vote the transferee will become entitled to be registered.

The power of the directors to refuse to register a transfer does not prevent an existing shareholder from selling his shares or giving them away; it simply prevents the transferee from becoming the legal owner of the shares. If the registration is refused then the existing shareholder holds the shares on trust for the purchaser or donee who becomes the equitable owner of the shares. Quite what the ongoing relationship between the two parties will then be is uncertain. However, this is obviously an undesirable situation for the transferee to be in (especially if a considerable amount of money has been paid for the shares). Therefore, every effort should be made in advance by the solicitor of the transferee to ascertain that there will be no such problems.

The provisions of both Table A and the Model Articles are relatively unsophisticated and a company may wish for a transfer provision which is more directed.

There is a considerable range of possibilities. We will consider a few examples.

14.2.3.1   A requirement that a member who wishes to sell should first offer the shares to the existing members pro rata

This type of right is usually called a pre-emption right. It should not be confused with the statutory pre-emption right which arises on the issue of new shares for a cash consideration (and which was referred to above). The Companies Act 2006 does not impose any pre-emption rights where a shareholder wishes to transfer shares.

In its simplest form a pre-emption right which applies on transfer will provide that if a shareholder wishes to transfer his shares, he must first offer them to some or all of the existing shareholders, either in all circumstances or in some specified circumstances. The details of such clauses vary very considerably. An attempt is usually made to be fair to both the shareholder who wishes to transfer his shares and to those who may wish to buy.

In drafting such a clause, the following are among the matters which should be considered:

(a) Are all the other shareholders to be entitled to buy some of the shares? (The right could be restricted for example, to the directors or to shareholders of the same class.)

(b) Are the shares to be offered to those entitled according to the proportion of shares which they own? (This is by far the most likely arrangement.)

(c) If a shareholder does not wish to buy, then what is to happen to the proportion of the shares which he could have bought? (In such a case the article could provide for a second round of offers to those shareholders who did take up the initial offer, or it could allow the selling shareholder to sell to whoever he chooses once the initial offer has been rejected.)

(d) How is the price to be fixed? (It is important that there should be a mechanism, otherwise the shareholder who wishes to sell to an outsider could circumvent the pre-emption procedure by offering to sell at an excessive price. The article may require an independent valuation by a specially appointed accountant, may provide for valuation by the company's own auditor or may fix the price in some arbitrary way.)

(e) Are there to be time limits? (There should be, otherwise the procedure will be unfair to the shareholder who wishes to sell as the others will be able to cause him delay.)

(f) Are there to be any safeguards in case the selling shareholder refuses to make the offer? (A common provision is to say that the directors are his agents and so can make the offer on his behalf.)

14.2.3.2 Variations on the above approaches

Within the range of absolute refusal of a transfer to pre-emption rights for existing members are many hybrid transfer articles. Some examples are:

(a) complete freedom to transfer, so long as to a family member or another shareholder, otherwise the directors may refuse to register the transfer;

(b) complete freedom to transfer, subject to specifically defined exceptions, such as transferees who are not based in the UK or corporate transferees.

14.3 Provisions concerning meetings of shareholders

14.3.1 Relationship with statute

The original 1985 version of Table A made provision for company meetings in arts 36–63. These regulations were based upon the requirements of the Companies Act 1985. The Companies Act 2006 made a number of changes to the way statute regulates shareholder meetings, particularly those of private companies (see **Chapter 13**). As these revisions do not normally overturn any contrary provisions in a company's articles, companies with this type of Table A articles (or similar) may find themselves complying with internal regulations which are more stringent than the minima now set out in statute.

Furthermore, the changes brought about by the 2006 Act were introduced at a time when Table A was still the effective default articles and before the Model Articles were introduced. In recognition of this issue, as from 1 October 2007 until 30 September 2009, revised versions of Table A (for both public and private companies) were in existence. (See the Companies (Tables A to F) (Amendment) Regulations 2007 and the Companies (Tables A to F) (Amendment) (No 2) Regulations 2007 for Private Companies Limited by Shares and the Companies (Tables A to F) (Amendment) (No 2) Regulations 2007 for Public Companies Limited by Shares.) Therefore, companies which were incorporated between those dates and which adopted Table A (in whole or in part) will have articles the provisions of which regarding general meetings do dovetail with the 2006 Act.

What follows is an explanation of those provisions which commonly need specific consideration. Where appropriate, a contrast will be made between the 1985 version of Table A and the 2007 version. (For ease of reference, we shall refer to these as Table A 1985 and Table A 2007.)

14.3.2 Notice of general meetings

Article 38 of Table A 1985 stipulates that 21 clear days' notice must be given of:

(a) An annual general meeting;

(b) A general meeting at which a special resolution is to be considered; and

(c) A general meeting at which a resolution to appoint a director is to be considered.

These requirements are now possibly excessive, as s. 307 CA 2006 only requires a minimum of 14 days' notice for all general meetings of a private company. Companies which are subject to this requirement may want to make the necessary change to their articles.

By contrast, Article 38 of Table A 2007 stipulates 14 days' notice for all types of resolution, in line with the 2006 Act. There is no equivalent provision included in the Model Articles, as the 2006 Act is relied upon.

14.3.3   Consent to short notice

Table A 1985 effectively repeated the statutory provisions in the Companies Act 1985 regarding consent to short notice. In particular, the requisite percentage of consenting shareholders must be 95%. Section 307 CA 2006 allows for a lesser minimum percentage of 90% and a maximum of 95%. Therefore, whilst Table A 1985 still dovetails with statute, there may be some administrative convenience to be found in choosing the lesser percentage by an alteration to the articles. Table A 2007 follows the 2006 Act and stipulates the lower percentage of 90%. There is no equivalent provision included in the Model Articles, as the 2006 Act is relied upon.

14.3.4   Quorum

Unsurprisingly, the quorum for a general meeting is often set at two shareholders (or their representatives). Both versions of Table A stipulate a quorum of two, but the 2007 version also makes provision for a quorum of one in the case of a single shareholder.

Article 38 of the Model Articles stipulates that a quorum is necessary for valid business to be transacted at a general meeting, but relies upon the provisions of s. 318 CA 2006 to determine the number, which is two members present or their proxies or representatives (in the case of corporate shareholders), unless the company has a single member, in which case this figure is reduced to one.

Section 318 is subject to contrary provision in the articles, so companies may wish to include alternative quorum requirements. For example, whilst a quorum of two will be appropriate in many instances, an alternative to this may be that all current members must be present to form a quorum; this may be appropriate where the shareholders are few in number and each wants equal influence in the company. Another requirement may be that specifically identified shareholders have to be present; again this would be to reflect the respective power and influence of certain shareholders.

14.3.5   Chairman's casting vote

The chairman's casting vote contained within art. 50 of Table A 1985 could be a useful mechanism for overcoming deadlock at shareholder level. However, it could also prove to be an excessively powerful right. Shareholders, therefore, need to consider carefully the continued inclusion of art. 50 (or similar) in the articles, should this provision exist.

This issue has now been superseded to an extent by the 2006 Act, which has effectively nullified the concept of a casting vote at general meetings through the requirements of ss. 281 to 283 and any pre-existing provision is now ineffective unless the provision was in existence prior to 1 October 2007. For this reason, neither Table A 2007 nor the Model Articles provide for the possibility of a casting vote.

14.3.6   Voting on a poll and proxy notices

The mechanisms for the above in both versions of Table A are thorough but possibly over-bureaucratic for small, closely-held companies. Simpler procedures may, therefore, be substituted for these.

Also, the rights of proxies have been increased under the 2006 Act to allow them to vote on a show of hands (ss. 284 and 285). The absence of such a statement will not disenfranchise any proxy holder, but it may be appropriate to update the articles to reflect the new position.

The Model Articles (art. 44) regulate the demand for a poll in a simpler way. A poll may be demanded:

(a) In advance of the relevant meeting;

(b) At the meeting itself prior to the matter being put to the vote on a show of hands;

(c) Immediately after the vote on a show of hands.

Whilst there are some technical differences between Table A and the Model Articles, they each provide for the following persons to demand a poll:

(a) The chairman of the meeting;

(b) Two or more shareholders having the right to vote at the meeting;

(c) One or more shareholders holding at least one-tenth of the total voting rights.

In terms of the appointment of a proxy, the Model Articles (arts 45 and 46) are somewhat less prescriptive than the provisions in Table A and grant a company greater flexibility in terms of the form and delivery of a proxy notice.

14.3.7 Written resolutions

Table A 1985 reflects the fact that, at the time of its introduction, there was no statutorily endorsed method of making shareholder decisions by written resolution. As such, art. 53 provided for this. Since that time, written resolutions have been formalised in statute and the procedures in the 2006 Act can now be regarded as the only possible method of passing effective written resolutions.

As such, neither Table A 2007 nor the Model Articles contain any mention of written resolutions and companies with articles which do so may wish to delete art. 53 or similar for reasons of clarity.

14.4 Provisions concerning directors

14.4.1 Introduction

The commentary at **14.3.1** is equally applicable here. Both Table A 2007 for private companies and the Model Articles have removed some of the more complex and undesirable provisions concerning directors, mainly because they were tied into a company's AGM, which for private companies is no longer a legal requirement.

More generally, however, legislation governing directors' proceedings is minimal, so there is not the same option for the Model Articles to rely upon the 2006 Act, as is the case with general meetings.

14.4.2 Number of directors

Both versions of Table A stipulate a minimum number of two directors (art. 64), but no maximum. This is subject to any contrary stipulation by ordinary resolution. As the minimum number of directors is determined by statute (one for private and two for public) and as a company is unlikely to find any material benefit in a ceiling limit on the number of directors, this provision is somewhat otiose and could be removed. The Model Articles do not contain any equivalent provision.

14.4.3   Retirement by rotation

Table A 1985 (arts 73 et seq.) makes elaborate provision for directors to retire by rotation (one-third of the board retires each year in most circumstances and is presented for re-election at the relevant AGM). Such provisions are unnecessary in the case of a private company and it is desirable to remove them, especially now that the need for private companies to hold annual general meetings has disappeared. Note, however, that art. 84 tended to ameliorate the position, by excluding the managing director and any other executive director from the need to retire by rotation.

Neither Table A 2007 for private companies (but not for public companies) nor the Model Articles contain provision for retirement by rotation.

14.4.4   Appointment of directors

Both versions of Table A contain two methods for appointing directors; either by ordinary resolution or by a board decision (regs. 76–79). Whilst the former results in a permanent appointment (subject to retirement by rotation in the 1985 version), the latter is temporary under Table A 1985, requiring confirmation by the shareholders at the next available AGM. In a closely-held company, such reference of a board decision to the shareholders is inappropriate.

Moreover, there is no longer a requirement on private companies to hold an AGM, so the mechanism for confirmation has become inappropriate. (This is reflected in the 2007 version of Table A, where any appointment by directors is permanent.)

Finally, there are complex notice provisions contained in all versions of Table A which relate to these methods of appointment. Generally the worth of these notice provisions must be questioned in a closely-held company.

The position under the Model Articles is considerably more straightforward; a director may be permanently appointed either by ordinary resolution or a decision of the directors (art. 17). Also, there are no concomitant notice provisions.

14.4.5   Removal of directors

The members of the company have power to remove a director from office by ordinary resolution (see s. 168 CA 2006.) It may be considered appropriate to include in the articles a *Bushell v Faith* clause, which will grant a director who is a shareholder weighted voting rights which effectively give him the power to defeat the resolution for his removal.

Whilst a *Bushell v Faith* clause is acceptable to protect a director, any attempt to deprive the shareholders of their rights under s. 168 is not, so any attempts to provide the shareholders with 'alternative' methods of removal in the articles must be treated with caution. However, it is also acceptable to allow the board to decide on the removal of a director. The mechanism commonly employed is to state that a director must resign if requested by all other directors to do so.

14.4.6   Directors' decision-making

Regulation 88 of both versions of Table A governs directors' proceedings in the following ways:

(a) Any director may call a board meeting, as may any secretary at the request of a director. There are no specific requirements about the form or content of any notice. Also, the common law implication is that any notice must be reasonable in length.

(b) It is not necessary to notify any director who is absent from the UK of a board meeting.

(c) All board decisions can be taken by a majority of votes.

This, and other related provisions of Table A, assume that the board meeting is the appropriate forum for decisions of the directors. However, reg. 93 alternatively permits decisions to be made by a unanimous written resolution of the directors.

The Model Articles restate much of the above, but some important differences should be noted.

First, there exists the possibility for the directors to make decisions unanimously outside the forum of the board meeting if they all indicate to each other *by any means* that they share a common view on a matter (art. 8(1)). One possible method of doing so is by a written resolution of all directors, which reflects the similar possibility under Table A. However, other possibilities might be e-mail exchange or simply informal discussions outside a specific board meeting.

Whilst such concepts may mirror practice in some small, closely-held companies, it is suggested that possible dangers lurk with such practice being seen as generally appropriate. First, there are evidential problems with recording such decisions. Secondly, and related to the first issue, in those instances where the directors' duty to promote the success of the company is germane, the absence of a properly recorded discussion and decision in a board meeting may make it harder for the board to defend its position at a future date.

Secondly, art. 9 regarding the calling of board meetings is more detailed and prescriptive than Table A. Whilst this extra information is only likely to reflect what has to happen in any event to call a board meeting effectively, there is a requirement that the content of the notice must indicate how it is proposed that the directors should communicate with each other, if they are not to be in the same place during the meeting. This reflects and supports the possibility anticipated by art. 10 that directors need not be in the same place to hold a board meeting, so long as they can each communicate to each other any relevant information or opinions.

14.4.7   Quorum

Both versions of Table A allow the board to determine the quorum, but the default provision is two directors. Additionally, if the number of directors falls below the number required for a quorum, those directors or director may only act either to fill the vacancies in the board or to call a general meeting. Article 11 of the Model Articles is couched in similar terms, except that it states explicitly that the quorum must never be less than two.

As with the quorum provision for general meetings, the suitability of this provision needs to be considered. First, the discretion for setting the quorum could be removed altogether and any change could be left to the shareholders by a change to the articles. Alternatively, in a company with several directors, a stipulated quorum of only two may be regarded as too few. Also, the presence of particular directors may be regarded as essential to the quorum, so these persons could be specified as a necessary part of the quorum.

Conversely, a minimum quorum of two directors effectively excludes the possibility of a private company only having a single director appointed.

14.4.8   Chairman's casting vote

Both versions of Table A provide the chairman of the board of directors with a casting vote. This is unaffected by the recent changes brought about by the 2006 Act. As such, the Model Articles also contain a casting vote provision (art. 13).

The inclusion of such a provision needs careful consideration to ensure that one director is not given disproportionate power at board level.

14.4.9   Restrictions on voting

Both versions of Table A contain a provision (reg. 94) which prevents directors from voting at board meetings on any matter in which they have a material interest (either direct or indirect) if that interest conflicts or may conflict with the interests of the company. If a director is so prevented, he also cannot count in the quorum (reg. 95).

It is usual to remove this provision in the case of a company with only a small board. If this provision is not amended or removed, then it may be difficult to transact business in certain cases as there may not be enough directors qualified to vote who can constitute a quorum at the meeting.

Note, however, that there are specific exclusions to reg. 94 in Table A and reg. 96 allows the shareholders by ordinary resolution to suspend or relax the prohibition in reg. 94.

A similar prohibition can be found in art. 14 of the Model Articles, but its scope is defined differently in the following ways:

(a) The board decision must be in respect of an actual or proposed transaction or arrangement with the company.

(b) The director simply has to be interested in the relevant transaction.

(c) If, however, that interest cannot reasonably be regarded as likely to give rise to a conflict of interest, the prohibition does not apply.

(d) Alternatively, if the interest falls within the stated categories of permitted causes the prohibition does not apply.

Irrespective of which of the above prohibitions applies, if any, it should always be remembered that, independently of the articles, a director is obliged by s. 177 CA 2006 to make a declaration of any interest he may have in a transaction with the company.

14.4.10   Secretary

Private companies are no longer required to have a secretary, but may continue to appoint somebody to this role (s. 270 CA 2006). Both versions of Table A allow for this event, by authorising the board to make any such appointment on such terms as it thinks fit. The Model Articles contain no such mechanism, but it is presumed that any desired appointment will fall to the directors to confirm, in any event.

14.5 Single member companies

Much of the previous discussion assumes that companies will have at least two directors and/or shareholders. It is possible to create a private company with only one director and one shareholder. This situation will normally arise when either a sole trader is looking for the benefit of limited liability or where a company is a wholly-owned subsidiary of another.

Table A (or similar) will possibly be inappropriate in a number of ways, as it is premised on the basis of at least two directors and shareholders, and specific thought needs to be given to articles which reflect the reality of the situation, particularly in relation to meetings of both the board and shareholders. It will be equally important to remember that such specific articles will need amendment if the number of directors or shareholders increases above one. If there is a high possibility of this at some time in the future, the articles should perhaps anticipate this change in circumstances.

14.6 Alteration of articles

14.6.1 Power to alter

Section 21 CA 2006 gives a company power to alter its articles by special resolution.

The articles of a company may not be made unalterable. A clause in the articles which purports to prevent the shareholders from altering the articles is invalid. However, a contract between shareholders as to how they will vote on a resolution to alter the articles is not void (*Russell v Northern Bank Development Corporation* [1992] 1 WLR 588). In addition, s. 22 CA 2006 will provide for the entrenchment of specified provisions of the articles if the relevant provision is included in the articles on the formation of the company or is included subsequently with the approval of all the members of the company. The method for entrenchment can be any mechanism for amendment or removal of the specified provisions which is more restrictive than the passing of a special resolution. (This entitlement is effective from 1 October 2009.) It is important to recognise that entrenchment does not mean that the specified provisions can never be altered, but the mechanism chosen may make the possibility of any subsequent change extremely remote.

14.6.2 Registration

Once the special resolution altering the articles has been passed, the resolution and a printed copy of the amended articles must be sent to the Registrar within 15 days. The Registrar officially notifies his receipt of these documents and the company cannot rely on the changes as against other persons who did not know of such changes until he has done so under the same rules as for change of name and alteration of objects. The company must ensure that copies of the altered articles are available, so that the directors and secretary may consult them and in case any member exercises his statutory right to a copy of the articles (s. 32 CA 2006).

14.6.3 Alteration to be for the benefit of the company

14.6.3.1 Shareholders may decide for themselves

There are no provisions in the Companies Act giving shareholders, or any particular proportion of the shareholders, power to challenge the validity of an alteration to the articles. However, the courts have held that an alteration is invalid if it is not 'bona fide in the interests of the company as a whole' (per Lord Lindley MR in *Allen v Gold Reefs of West Africa Ltd* [1900] 1 Ch 656). The test is very much easier to state than to apply to the facts of particular cases. As we have already seen in relation to derivative actions (see **10.6**), the court is very reluctant to interfere with decisions made by the majority in a company.

The court will normally regard an alteration as being in the interests of the company if the majority of the shareholders are in favour of the alteration (as they must be since a special resolution will have been passed before any question as to the validity of the alteration can arise). Thus in *Allen v Gold Reefs of West Africa Ltd* the articles contained a provision imposing a lien on partly-paid shares. One shareholder owed money to the company and the articles were altered to impose a lien on fully-paid shares as well as on partly-paid shares. The court regarded the fact that one (and only one) shareholder was indebted to the company at the time of alteration as something exciting suspicion as to the bona fides of the company, but nevertheless came to the conclusion that the alteration was in the interests of the company as a whole. Clearly it is in the interests of a company that it should have security for money due to it and no discrimination against particular members was expressed in the altered articles.

Shuttleworth v Cox Brothers and Co. (Maidenhead) Ltd [1927] 2 KB 9, is perhaps a stronger illustration. The majority of the directors suspected that one of the board had been guilty of misconduct but they had insufficient proof of any grounds giving a right to dismiss him. They therefore altered the articles to say that any director would cease to hold office if requested to resign by the majority of the directors. The test applied by the court was whether any reasonable man could come to the conclusion that the alteration was in the interests of the company. If it was open to a reasonable man to come to that conclusion, the alteration would only be invalid on proof of actual bad faith. The court was satisfied that a reasonable man could come to the conclusion that the alteration was in the interests of the company and so, since the plaintiff could not prove actual bad faith, the alteration was held to be valid.

14.6.3.2 Discrimination

The courts have recognised that an alteration to the articles cannot be in the interests of the company as a whole if it discriminates against some members, however few. At first sight this seems strange in view of the two cases mentioned above, both of which appear to involve actual discrimination against a particular shareholder. However, on closer analysis neither of those cases involved any discrimination. In *Allen v Gold Reefs of West Africa*, the lien applied, potentially, to all the fully-paid shares whoever owned them, so that it might apply to any shareholder at some time. Similarly in *Shuttleworth v Cox*, the new article potentially applied to any shareholder who became a director and who fell into disfavour with the rest of the board. A good illustration of the type of case where an alteration *is* discriminatory and so void is given by the Australian case, *Australian Fixed Trust Proprietary Ltd v Clyde Industries Ltd* (1959) SR (NSW) 33. In that case the articles were altered so as to require shareholders who were unit trust managers to obtain the approval of the majority of their unit-holders before exercising the voting rights attached to their shares. This clearly discriminated against shareholders who happened to be unit trust managers and so was void.

The narrowness of the distinction between cases which are, and cases which are not, discriminatory is well illustrated by the cases of *Sidebottom v Kershaw, Leese and Co. Ltd* [1920] 1 Ch 154, and *Brown v Abrasive Wheel Co.* [1919] 1 Ch 290. In *Sidebottom v Kershaw, Leese*, the articles were altered so as to give the directors power to direct a shareholder who was concerned with a competing business to transfer his shares. This was held to be a valid alteration. The company could properly come to the conclusion that it was in its interests that competitors be excluded from membership and there was no discrimination based on the number of shares owned. In *Brown v Abrasive Wheel Co.*, the articles were altered to give 90% of the shareholders power to require the minority shareholders to sell their shares. In fact, the majority shareholders (who owned 98% of the shares) had good commercial reasons for wanting the alteration, but nevertheless the court held that the alteration was invalid. Although it was bona fide in the interests of 98% of the present shareholders it was not in the interests of the other 2%, nor was it necessarily in the interests of future shareholders and so it was discriminatory.

14.6.3.3   Conclusion in the common law

The two basic rules which seem to have evolved from the cases are:

(a) The members may generally decide themselves whether an alteration is bona fide in the interests of the company as a whole.

(b) The court will interfere with their decision where the members could not properly come to that decision because it discriminates between groups of members.

14.6.3.4   Section 994 CA 2006

It should be noted that much of the usefulness of the common law has been superseded by the above section (formerly s. 459 CA 1985). The alteration of articles to the prejudice of some part of the members will be good grounds under which to bring an action under s. 994. However, if the alteration affects directors as opposed to shareholders (as in the *Shuttleworth* case), the common law is still of relevance. (See **10.7** for further discussion of unfair prejudice.)

14.6.3.5   Class rights

Section 630 CA 2006 deals with class rights, i.e., different rights attaching to different shares. The basic rule is that any proposed amendment to any class rights must be approved either:

(a) in writing by three-quarters of the shareholders in the relevant class; or

(b) by a resolution passed by three-quarters of the shareholders in the relevant class at a separate meeting of the class of shareholders in question.

Alternatively, the articles themselves may set out rules covering this issue which may require a greater or lower level of consent than above.

Any proposed amendment to the articles which affects any class rights must first receive such approval as well as be approved itself by special resolution of the company as a whole.

online resource centre   Interactive online exercises (Student Learning Activities) which complement the topics covered in this chapter are available at www.oxfordtextbooks.co.uk/orc/business09_10/.

Disclosure obligations of companies and company accounts

This chapter covers the following topics:

15.1   Introduction

One of the core concepts of company law is that information about a company, its 'constitution' and financial status should be made available to the public. (This is one of the 'trade-offs' for limited liability.) The purpose of this policy of 'openness' is to enable anyone interested in the affairs of a company (whether they are current or prospective shareholders in the company or its creditors) to have access to the information they need to make an informed judgement on the company's financial affairs and the abilities of the company's management. They will also be able to determine whether the company and its directors have the necessary authority and powers to enter into the transaction which, for example, a third-party creditor may be considering. In any transaction involving a company, it is prudent to carry out relevant searches to obtain all necessary information *and* to obtain confirmation from the company that such information is up to date and correct.

Information is made available by the company:

(a) keeping at its registered office records and registers available for inspection by its members and the public (see **8.10**);

(b) disclosing financial information to its members through the annual directors' report and annual audited accounts;

(c) delivering to the Registrar of Companies documents which the Registrar in turn makes available to the public for inspection; and

(d) the publication of certain information about the company in the *London Gazette*.

In this chapter, we will look at the information about companies which is publicly available, paying particular attention to the rules with which the company must comply in relation to its accounts, as well as giving some guidance on how to interpret the published accounts of a company.

Currently this area is governed by elements of either the 1985 Act or the 2006 Act and companies' disclosure responsibilities will continue to be governed by the two Acts until 1 October 2009.

15.2 Company searches

15.2.1 General

While information about a company can be obtained from advertisements placed by the Registrar of Companies in the *London Gazette* or from inspecting the records and registers maintained by the company at its registered office, the most common method of acquiring information on a company is by making a search at the Companies' Registry. The Registrar of Companies keeps copies of the information supplied to him by the company and this is available for public inspection. In this section of the chapter, we will look at the information which a company must supply to the Registrar and then look at the procedure for making a company search.

15.2.2 The information available for inspection

The information available for inspection at the Companies' Registry includes the following:

(a) the company's memorandum and articles of association;

(b) particulars of directors and secretary (giving details both of the original directors and secretary as well as subsequent changes);

(c) particulars of the issue of shares;

(d) particulars of (most) charges;

(e) particulars of all special resolutions (and any elective and extraordinary resolutions passed under the 1985 Act regime);

(f) notice of the accounting reference date;

(g) notice of any increase of capital;

(h) particulars of resolutions granting directors authority to allot shares;

(i) particulars of the address of the registered office (both the first address and subsequent changes);

(j) the annual return; and

(k) the accounts.

Of this list, the last two items merit further consideration (see **15.3** for the rules relating to the accounts which the company must file). So far as the 'annual return' is concerned, currently s. 363 CA 1985 requires every company to make an annual return to the Registrar on Form 363 once in every year (a fee of £15 is payable for electronic filings; £30 for paper ones). (Section 854 CA 2006 will replace s. 363 as at 1 October 2009.) The company is required to file returns signed by a director or the secretary made up to the company's return date which must be within 12 months of the date of the previous return or, in the case of a new company, of the date of incorporation. The return must be filed with the Registrar within 28 days of the return date.

The contents of the return are determined by statute/regulation. The details which it will contain are:

(a) the address of the registered office of the company;

(b) the company's principal business activities;

(c) the location of the register of members if it is not kept at the registered office;

(d) the location of the company's register of debenture holders if it is not kept at the company's registered office;

(e) the company's type (that is to say, public limited company, private company limited by shares, or whatever);

(f) details of the company secretary (if any);

(g) details of every director plus nationality, date of birth, business occupation and the particulars required for the register of directors;

(h) details of the company's issued share capital;

(i) details of the members of the company on the date on which the return is made up plus the persons who have ceased to be members since the last return;

(j) details of the shares held by members.

15.2.3 Failure to file annual returns

In addition to accounts, the annual return is one filing which Companies House expects to receive every year from a company. As such, policing default is very easy. Failure to submit an annual return in the due time period is a criminal offence and both the company and all officers thereof are liable to a fine (s. 363(3) and (4) CA 1985). (This sanction will be maintained by s. 858 CA 2006.) Additionally, persistent failure to comply with filing obligations can be grounds for a disqualification order being made against a director (s. 3 Company Directors Disqualification Act 1986).

15.2.4 The procedure for making a company search

The wide range of information which companies are required to file with the Registrar of Companies is filed by the Registrar by reference to each company's unique company number. With the company's current name or registration number (and on payment of the relevant fee), it is possible to obtain a copy of the company's file. To do this, a company search can be carried out in person, by post, telephone or via Companies House Direct, a web-based on-line service. Full details of the latter, together with information on all Companies House services, can be obtained at www.companieshouse.gov.uk. The on-line service provides free access to certain general company information, including an index of all registered companies. More specific information and company documents can be downloaded on payment of the relevant fees. Companies House can also supply copies of company documentation on request by post, fax or e-mail. Company information up to 31 December 2002 can be supplied via a set of microfiches.

15.3 The duty to submit accounts

15.3.1 What is meant by 'accounts'?

As a general rule (although see discussion at **15.4** below) limited companies are required by the Companies Act 2006 to prepare a set of 'individual accounts' for each financial year of the company (s. 394 CA 2006). These consist of a profit and loss account and a balance sheet (s. 396 CA 2006). Any accounts prepared must give a true and fair view of the financial status of the company (s. 393 CA 2006). They must also comply with specific rules on format and content (see both The Small Companies and Groups (Accounts and Directors' Report) Regulations 2008 and The Large and Medium-sized Companies and Groups (Accounts and Reports) Regulations 2008).

Where a company is a parent company (and is not a 'small' company; see **15.4** below) it must also prepare group accounts (s. 399 CA 2006), which must comprise a consolidated balance sheet and a consolidated profit and loss account setting out financial details of the parent and all its subsidiaries (s. 404 CA 2006).

Additionally, a directors' report must accompany the accounts (s. 415 CA 2006). This report must contain details of all directors during the relevant financial year, the principal activities of the company throughout the year and the amount of any dividend recommended by the directors. Also, unless the company is 'small' (see discussion below at **15.4**), this report should contain a 'business review', which effectively is an analysis of the company's performance and the risks it may be facing (s. 417 CA 2006). This review is designed to give shareholders the opportunity to assess how well directors have fulfilled their duty to promote the success of the company.

Subject to certain exceptions, there is a duty for all accounts to be audited (s. 475 CA 2006). As a consequence, companies must normally appoint auditors annually, who are required to produce a report on the accounts. This report effectively benchmarks the contents of the accounts against certain established accounting standards. (In reality, auditors prepare both the accounts and their report—it is unlikely that a company will prepare accounts independently of the auditors and then submit them for audit.)

15.3.2 Provision of accounts to members

Annual accounts must be approved by the board and signed off on its behalf. Once this has been done, the company must send copies of the accounts to the shareholders (s. 423 CA 2006). For private companies this must be no later than the deadline for submission of the accounts to Companies House, which is nine months from the end of the relevant accounting period.

For public companies, there is a different procedure, which allows shareholders greater influence. Once they have been prepared, the final accounts must be laid before the company in general meeting (s. 437(1) CA 2006). This meeting is called the accounts meeting (s. 437(3) CA 2006) and in most circumstances this will be the annual general meeting of the company. The relevant accounts must be sent out to shareholders no later than 21 days before the accounts meeting (s. 424(3) CA 2006).

15.3.3 Filing of accounts

Subject to what is said below about small and medium-sized companies, all companies must send copies of their accounts to the Registrar of Companies. In the case of private companies, this must be no later than nine months after the end of the relevant accounting period (s. 442(2)(a) CA 2006) and for public companies this must be no later than six months after the end of the relevant accounting period (s. 442(2)(b) CA 2006). These accounts are then a matter of public record and anyone who pays to do a company search will be able to get a copy of the accounts of most companies.

Failure to deliver accounts on time has a number of consequences, namely:

(a) Automatic civil penalties on a scale which is linked to the length of the delay (s. 453 CA 2006). (Note that the penalties are higher for public than private companies.)

(b) Criminal penalties (by way of fine) for every relevant director.

(c) The failure may amount to grounds for disqualification proceedings against the directors concerned under the Company Directors Disqualification Act 1986.

15.4 Small and medium-sized companies

15.4.1 Small companies

If a private company comes within the definition of a small company for a particular financial year, its duty to deliver accounts to the Registrar of Companies is modified by ss. 444 and 444A CA 2006. (Note that public companies can never be small for these purposes.) Effectively this means that it can submit fewer elements of its accounts/reports than normal and, if it prefers, abbreviated accounts, instead of the ones actually prepared for statutory purposes. Additionally, certain information can be omitted from the accounts and reports. The combined effect of these provisions is that a small company can maintain a greater degree of privacy about its financial status. (There is an additional exemption for small groups of companies from the duty to produce consolidated accounts. The detail of this is not considered.)

A private company is small if at least two of the following criteria are satisfied:

(a) the company's turnover does not exceed £6.5 million;

(b) its balance sheet total does not exceed £3.26 million;

(c) the average number of employees does not exceed 50 people.

In the above definitions 'turnover' effectively means the sums earned by the company in selling goods or services before deducting expenses. The balance sheet total is, broadly speaking, the value of the company's assets without deducting any liabilities. The number of employees should be calculated as an average over the relevant financial year.

The status of a small company is not permanent, nor is it safe to assume that a company will benefit from the regime simply because it fulfils the conditions for a small company in a particular financial year. Put simply, a company must either acquire small company status at the outset of its existence and then lose that status by ceasing to be a small company for two consecutive years or, if it does not start out as small, it must acquire small company status by being small for at least two consecutive years. This rather confusing rule is best explained by an example.

EXAMPLE

Scenario A
Assume that Lazlo Limited is a small company for its first financial year. If Lazlo ceases to fulfil the relevant conditions in its second financial year, it will still be a small company for that financial

year. However, if this situation continues for the third financial year after incorporation, it will at this point lose its small company status.

Scenario B
Assume that Lazlo Limited is not a small company for its first financial year, but that it fulfils the relevant conditions in its second financial year. It will still not be a small company for this second year. However, if it fulfils the relevant conditions in its third financial year after incorporation, it will at this point acquire small company status.

Scenario C
Assume that Lazlo Limited has fulfilled the relevant conditions for small company status for the previous two financial years. For the most recent financial year, however, it does not fulfil those conditions. Nevertheless, it will continue to be a small company for the purposes of the current financial year.

In addition to revised filing requirements, small companies may benefit from an exemption from audit (s. 477 CA 2006). The benefit of this is that audit is a relatively expensive process, so the exemption can result in a cost saving for a company. However, even if the board of directors decide to dispense with an audit, members holding at least 10% in nominal value of the company's issued share capital have the right to demand an audit (s. 476 CA 2006).

As well as being a small company for the financial year in question, a company must also have a turnover which is not more than £6.5 million and a balance sheet total which is not more than £3.26 million. (As we have seen, companies may qualify as small in respect of their status for the previous financial year, so this rule ensures that companies are actually small for the financial year in question.)

15.4.2   Medium-sized companies

The exemptions from reporting and filing available to small companies are available to a lesser degree for medium-sized companies, although medium-sized companies can never benefit from the exemption from audit. (As with small companies, medium-sized companies are not exempt from the requirement to produce full accounts nor from the requirement to provide accounts to their own shareholders.)

A medium-sized company is one which satisfies at least two of the following criteria:

(a) its turnover does not exceed £25.9 million;

(b) its balance sheet total does not exceed £12.9 million;

(c) the average number of employees does not exceed 250.

These conditions should be applied in the same way as for the calculation for small companies. Additionally, medium-sized company status is acquired and lost in the same way as for small companies.

15.5   Appointment of auditors

Where auditors are required, their appointment is regulated by the Companies Act 2006. Both the board of directors and the shareholders (by ordinary resolution) have the power to appoint auditors in defined circumstances (s. 485 for private companies and s. 489 for public companies). In simple terms, the very first appointment of auditors is made by the board and thereafter the shareholders make the appointment. The appointment of auditors should happen annually. For public companies, therefore, the annual accounts meeting, i.e., the AGM, is the most appropriate forum; for private companies, a specific general meeting could be called for this purpose or it could be effected by written resolution. However, to reduce the administrative burden on private companies, s. 487(2) provides for automatic reappointment of incumbent auditors (appointed by the shareholders), unless:

(a) The company's articles require annual appointment;

(b) The shareholders have either resolved by ordinary resolution to block the reappointment or an objection to the reappointment has been received by the company from at least 5% of the shareholders who would be entitled to vote on such a resolution;

(c) The board has resolved that an audit is unnecessary for the financial year in question.

15.6 Profit and loss account

A profit and loss account is an account which shows what income the company has received in a particular period of time and what expenses have been incurred by the company in producing that income. Once the expenses are deducted from the income the resulting figure is a profit (or a loss if the expenses are more than the income). The profit and loss account is strictly speaking only designed to show income profits. If a company makes a capital profit (for example, if it sells its factory for a profit) this may be shown as an addition to the profit and loss account. It will then usually be labelled as an 'exceptional item' as opposed to the ordinary income profit.

Profit and loss accounts are almost always prepared for 12-month periods (the company may wish to produce forecasts or full accounts for its own internal purposes on a more regular basis). The period covered by the accounts ends with the accounting reference date which the company can choose for itself (see **8.14**). Companies are not required to prepare accounts for a calendar year (although some companies do choose 31 December as their accounting reference date, in which case the accounts will be for a calendar year).

A very simple traditional profit and loss account might look like the following:

EXAMPLE

XYZ Ltd
Profit and loss account
Year ending 31 March 2000

	£	£
INCOME		
Sales		200,000
Opening stock	80,000	
Purchases	90,000	
	170,000	
Less closing stock	70,000	
		100,000
Gross profit from sales		100,000
Interest received		8,000
		108,000

EXPENDITURE		
Wages	55,000	
Miscellaneous	10,000	
		65,000
PROFIT BEFORE TAX		43,000
DEDUCT TAX		12,000
TRANSFERRED TO RESERVE		31,000

Notice the following points in relation to it:

(a) The account is divided into three parts. The first shows the income of the business. The second shows the expenditure which is incurred in earning that income and the third shows what has happened to the income. (This third part is strictly speaking the appropriation section rather than part of the profit and loss account itself. If any dividends were paid they would be shown as a deduction in this section.)

(b) In the income section the opening and closing stock are shown. Unless stock is taken into account it is impossible to work out the profit. If a company has a storeroom full of goods left over from last year which it sells this year, it cannot calculate its profit unless it takes into account the fact that it paid for that stock.

(c) The figure which is labelled transferred to reserve is what is left of the profit after the tax has been paid. It is in effect profit which has been retained in the business. An explanation of the term 'reserve' in this context is given in 15.7.

15.7 Balance sheet

A balance sheet shows the assets and liabilities of the company. An asset is something of value or potential value. The factory which a company owns is an asset, so is any money which it has in the bank. Sometimes the balance sheet will also show much more intangible things such as goodwill. Goodwill is the difference between the real assets of a company and its overall value to a purchaser. For example, a company running a business in a shop might own the following assets:

	£
The shop	100,000
Fixtures (shelves, etc.)	10,000
Stock (the goods for sale)	5,000
Cash	2,000

If the company decided to sell the business it would be likely to want more than £117,000 for it. The real value of the business includes the fact that it has a loyal group of customers, or it is situated in a good location for running this type of business (or both). The difference between the assets value and what the shop could be sold for is the goodwill of the business.

The liabilities part of the balance sheet includes liabilities due to outsiders (such as bills owed by the shop), money owed to the bank or other lenders. The money which would be paid to the shareholders if the company were wound up is also shown as a liability because, at least in theory, it will be paid out to the shareholders one day.

A simple traditional balance sheet might look like this:

EXAMPLE

Balance sheet of XYZ Ltd
31 March 2000

	£	£
FIXED ASSETS		
Premises		400,000
Fixtures		10,000
		410,000
CURRENT ASSETS		
Stock (goods for sale and/or materials)	5,000	
Cash	2,000	
	7,000	
LESS CURRENT LIABILITIES		
Electricity bill	4,500	
		2,500
		412,500
CAPITAL		
Share capital		200,000
Share premium account		160,000
Bank loan		10,000
Reserves		42,500
		412,500

Notice the following points in relation to it:

(a) The totals balance, i.e., the net assets of the company equal its capital. This happens because of the 'double entry' system used to record transactions in the company's books. A simple example of this is where share capital is contributed to a company. If someone buys shares for £100 at par value, this would be represented in a balance sheet by two entries. The company would have £100 in cash, a current asset; and it would have capital of £100 (a liability to the shareholder). Extrapolating this, a company's net assets will always reflect its capital, as is seen here. They can effectively be seen as the way in which a company has employed its capital in its business.

(b) A distinction is made between fixed assets and current assets. Fixed assets are assets which are likely to be held by the company for a considerable period of time. Current assets are those which are likely to be used up by the company in the course of its business.

(c) Current liabilities (that is sums owed by the company which are likely to be paid within a year) are shown as a deduction from current assets. They are accordingly not in the same part of the account as the long-term liabilities.

(d) The second half of the balance sheet is labelled 'capital'. Although in common parlance the word capital often means money or wealth, to an accountant it is a liability which is owed to someone with a proprietary or other long-term interest in the business. The money owed to the bank is included in capital on the assumption that it is a long-term loan and so is something like an investment in the business. If the same money was owed to the bank on an overdraft it would be shown as a short-term liability like the electricity bill.

(e) The other sums shown under the heading of capital are all sums due to the shareholders of the company. The share capital is the liability which arises from the fact that the shareholders paid the nominal value of their shares to the company at some time in the past. The share premium is the liability which arises from the fact that when the shares were issued the shareholders paid more than the nominal value for them. The difference between these two sums is theoretical only. Remember that a company cannot generally return the sums invested by the shareholders until the company is wound up.

(f) The item referred to as reserves is in a way a balancing item. If the company was wound up its assets would realise £417,000. This would be used to pay the bank and the outstanding bill. This would then leave £402,500 for the shareholders. They would be repaid their original investment of £360,000 (shown in share capital and share premium). This would then leave £42,500. The reserve is in effect a liability owed to shareholders which results from the fact that the company has made profits over the years.

(g) The balance sheet is dated 31 March. Businesses constantly acquire and dispose of assets, pay bills and incur new liabilities. A balance sheet is, therefore, always relevant to a particular moment in time, not to the whole of a period of time (in which respect contrast the profit and loss account).

(h) The company has a surplus of short-term assets over short-term liabilities. The resulting surplus is called net current assets (confusingly it is also often called 'working capital' even though it is an asset). This figure is particularly important as it is a strong indication of the solvency of the company.

15.8 Format of accounts

Formats for both profit and loss accounts and balance sheets are set out in Regulation (see **15.3.1**). These are templates which all companies must choose from in presenting their accounts for each financial year. They set out the order in which all the different items in the accounts must appear. For the purposes of illustration we have not adhered exactly to any of the formats in the very brief examples given above.

Companies' published accounts are often difficult for beginners to follow because much of the information is given in the form of notes. Indeed the published profit and loss account is likely to contain very little information about the company's income and expenditure unless close attention is paid to the notes as well as to the account itself.

15.9 Interpretation of accounts

15.9.1 Introduction

In this section, we will look at some ideas about interpretation of accounts. Interpretation is a process whereby information is extracted from the accounts for two main purposes:

(a) to assess the company's present financial position in relation to profitability and solvency;

(b) to predict the future prospects of the company.

Neither of these processes is an exact science. Interpretation of accounts will not always produce a 'right answer' but rather an opinion about the company.

15.9.2   Reasons for interpretation and sources of information

Interpretation of accounts is likely to be undertaken by or for a variety of people for a variety of reasons. In particular the management of the company may wish to know how efficient the business is. Investors or potential investors in a quoted company will want to know whether the company is over- or undervalued (in their opinion) at the present price of the shares. Creditors will be particularly concerned to investigate the company's solvency.

The most obvious source of information about the accounts of the company is the published accounts of the company. It should be noted, however, that these accounts will not provide as much information as the interpreter might ideally like. The management of the company will have more detailed accounts than the published accounts in the form of what are usually called management accounts. These are not available to the public (not even to the shareholders) as a matter of right, but sometimes the management may be willing to show them to others such as potential lenders or purchasers of the business.

If the information which is available to the particular investigator is limited to published accounts, then he will usually do well to look at the accounts for several years. In interpreting the performance of a business the trend over a period of time is very important. Past results are not necessarily a guide to the future, but nevertheless they may give some indication of the likely progress of the company in the future. An investor, for example, is likely to be more interested in a company which shows a long record of growth than one which has been merely holding its own.

15.9.3   What are the limits inherent in accounts?

The most obvious limit is the possibility of outright fraud. If the accounts are a work of fiction they will tell you nothing useful. The process of auditing accounts ensures that fraud is unusual.

Published accounts are produced once a year and, as we have seen, may be submitted to the Registrar up to six months after the end of the accounting period (nine months if the company is private). This means that the accounts may be quite considerably out of date. The balance sheet date should be checked both to see how out of date the accounts are and also to see how typical that date might be. The balance sheet of a resort hotel business may tell a very different story if it is drawn up just after the end of the season (when there will be an unusually large amount of cash or an unusually small overdraft), than if it is produced at the end of the winter.

The notes to the accounts should be examined carefully to see what the company's policy is in relation to valuation of assets. In particular, have the fixed assets been re-valued recently so that the figures approximate to market value? If not, then the fixed assets may be shown at historic cost (i.e., what was paid for them) in which case they, and so the company, may be worth much more than shown.

Another important factor to look for is how debtors have been dealt with in the accounts. The figure described as debtors shows the amount of money owed to the company. Almost all businesses suffer some degree of bad debts. That is, some of the people who owe them money cannot or will not pay what they owe to the company. Bad debts and an estimate of potential bad debts ('provision for bad debts') should be deducted in computing the profits, and from the current assets of the company, otherwise the accounts will be misleading.

Often the accounts will include some special feature which is relevant to the accounts in a particular year only. These are usually called exceptional items. For example, in a particular year a company may have sold a fixed asset or issued shares. In both of these cases it will have received a large amount of cash. If it has not yet spent the cash then the net current assets figure may be unusually high. Will the company still have enough cash to pay its creditors if it replaces the fixed asset which it sold?

15.10 Solvency

A company is solvent if it is able to pay its debts as they fall due. It is important to realise that solvency is not the same thing as profitability. A company may make profits and yet be insolvent. For example, the profits may arise from the fact that the company has supplied goods or services for which it has not yet been paid. This company will be insolvent if it has to pay its own creditors before it collects from its debtors. Similarly a company may be unprofitable and yet solvent for a very long time. For example, a company may be making losses and yet can keep itself going by selling fixed assets.

In judging the solvency of a company it is desirable to work out certain solvency ratios. These are calculations made from the information given in the accounts.

The first of the ratios is the 'current ratio': this is a test of the company's liquidity. Liquidity is the ability of a company to pay its debts in the short term. The current ratio is the ratio of current assets to current liabilities. In the example in **15.7**, the current assets were £7,000 and the current liabilities were £4,500. This gives a ratio of 7:4.5 or 1.55:1. This would generally be regarded as a satisfactory figure as it means that for every pound which the company will have to pay in the short term, it has, or will soon receive, £1.55. However, this does assume that the stock will be easy to sell at the value shown in the balance sheet (in the case of stock the value will normally be the lower of purchase price or current value).

Because stock cannot always be sold in a hurry the liquidity ratio (also known as the acid test) is often preferred to the current ratio. This compares liquid assets (i.e., cash and things as good as cash) with current liabilities. Applying this ratio to our figures we get a ratio of 2:4.5 or .44:1. This is much less satisfactory. It means that for every pound that the company will have to pay, it only has ready access to 44p. This is not necessarily as dangerous as it may seem at first sight, however. If the company can rely on selling a lot of stock quickly it will be able to pay the electricity bill. Similarly the company may have an arrangement with its bank for an overdraft which will see it through the temporary crisis of the payment of the electricity bill.

A company which is in the position of the one illustrated here is in danger of overtrading. This occurs where the company has insufficient working capital (i.e., net current assets). As it pays its bills it may be unable to replace its stock which obviously means that it cannot continue to be profitable and solvent in the future. The solution to this problem may be for the company to acquire more working capital, either by retaining more profits in the business, by acquiring further investment or by increasing the size of its long-term borrowing (the last of these is likely to be a real possibility in view of the large amount of fixed assets and the small amount of borrowing). The fact that not all companies can in practice do any of these things is the reason for a very high proportion of business failures.

15.11 Profitability

The bottom line profit figure is found in the profit and loss account. In our example, the profit is £43,000 before tax and £31,000 after. The proprietor of the business will want to know whether this figure is satisfactory or not. There is no simple answer to this, not least because different people have different expectations and so are more or less easily satisfied. The most important step to take may be to compare with previous years and to compare with other similar business (this is more easily done with large companies as the published accounts of small and medium-sized companies give much less information). However, ratios can help here as with solvency.

15.11.1 Investment

An investor or potential investor will be interested in the whole of the company's financial situation. He will be particularly interested in what return on capital he can expect (i.e., in how much income will be generated by his investment). One simple calculation which may assist in judging this is the 'return on capital employed'. This is the net profit (before tax, dividends and any interest paid) expressed as a percentage of the company capital (including debentures and other long-term loans); in our example this is $43,000/412,500 \times 100 = 10.42\%$. This figure should be judged against previous years' profits and is possible against other similar companies. If the shareholders are also directors of the company, they might wish to treat any directors' fees as part of the return on capital if they exceed what the directors regard as a fair return for their labour.

An alternative to the return on capital calculation is to calculate earnings per share. In our example assume that there are 10,000 shares, the earnings per share would then be $31,000/10,000 = £3.1$ per share (it is usual to deduct tax in this calculation). This information is often given in relation to companies quoted on the stock exchange. Similarly in relation to such companies a price/earnings (or P/E) ratio can be calculated. This compares the market price of the share (on the Stock Exchange) with the earnings per share. A high P/E ratio shows that the stock market has confidence in the company as its shares are valuable despite low earnings. It is not possible to calculate a P/E ratio for a private or unquoted public company as there is no market price for their shares.

15.11.2 Efficiency ratios

These are ratios which are mainly calculated so that the management of the company and other interested parties can calculate how efficient the profit-making process of the company is. The return on capital employed (see **15.11.1**) is a good indicator of the company's general efficiency in making money.

Another useful ratio is the net profit percentage. This expresses trading profit (before deduction of tax and interest payments) as a percentage of sales. In our example this is $43,000/200,000 \times 100 = 21.5\%$. This should be compared with other businesses and with previous years. Whether 21.5% is a good profit margin depends on the nature of the business in question.

online resource centre

Interactive online exercises (Student Learning Activities) which complement the topics covered in this chapter are available at www.oxfordtextbooks.co.uk/orc/business09_10/.

Public companies

16

This chapter covers the following topics:

16.1 Introduction

As you will have seen from **Chapter 7**, it is possible to create three different types of company:

(a) a company limited by shares;

(b) a company limited by guarantee; and

(c) an unlimited company.

We considered the key elements of these three different types of company in Chapter 7. It is possible to incorporate all three types of company as a 'private company' but only companies limited by shares can be 'public companies'.

The differences between the two types of company are important and we will consider them briefly in this chapter.

In addition, we will look briefly at the rules for re-registering a private company as a public company and vice versa, as well as the procedures by which a public company can have its shares listed with the United Kingdom Listing Authority (UKLA) and have its shares admitted to trading on the Stock Exchange. The latter two procedures, whilst separate, are usually referred to together in practice as 'listing'. Similarly, a company which has been successful in gaining a listing and has been admitted to trading is referred to in practice as a 'listed company'.

Although the most well-known companies in the country will (with a few exceptions) be public listed companies they represent a tiny minority of the total number of private and public companies registered at the Companies' Registry. In very simple terms, there are over 2.5 million companies registered in Great Britain, of which around 12,000 are public. Also, being a public company does not automatically mean the company is listed: this is a common misconception.

Until 1 October 2009, all public companies had to be set up or re-registered under the Companies Act 1985. Subject to a few major exceptions, the process under the Companies Act 2006 repeats much of that regime.

16.2   The distinguishing features of a public company

16.2.1   Definition

A public company is defined by s. 4(2) CA 2006 as a company whose certificate of incorporation states that it is public (see **16.2.2.2** below for further discussion).

16.2.2   The differences between public and private companies

The following is a non-exhaustive list of some of the differences between public and private companies.

16.2.2.1   Name

The name of a public company must end with the words 'Public Limited Company' or its equivalent. Equivalent for this purpose includes 'PLC' (although there is no requirement that these letters be capitalised) and, for Welsh companies, Cwmni Cyfyngedig Cyhoeddus (or CCC). The company will be a Welsh company if the company states in its memorandum that its registered office is to be in Wales.

16.2.2.2   The company's memorandum

As the memorandum is simply a registration document, expressing the wish of those setting up the company to be formed as one (s. 8 CA 2006), there is no difference between the memorandum of a public and private company. Instead, the registration document submitted pursuant to s. 9 will have to include a statement that the company should be public. If registration is successful, the fact that the certificate of incorporation states that the company is public will be sufficient evidence of the fact (s. 4(2) CA 2006). (This is in contrast to the situation under the 1985 Act, where the memorandum had to include an additional clause stating that the company was to be a public company.)

16.2.2.3   The nominal value of the share capital

The nominal value of the public company's issued share capital must not be less than the 'authorised minimum' which is currently £50,000 (s. 763(1) CA 2006). When a public company allots shares, it is under an obligation to ensure that at least 25% of the nominal value of each of the shares issued (plus the whole amount of any premium on the shares) is paid on allotment (s. 586 CA 2006). It will be recalled from **7.6.2** that a private company can issue shares without requiring any immediate payment for them (i.e., they can be issued 'nil paid').

16.2.2.4   Number of members and officers

The 2006 Act permits single-member public companies (s. 7(1) CA 2006). (Previously, under the 1985 Act, all public companies had to have a minimum of two members.) However, in contrast to private companies, pubic companies must appoint at least two directors (s. 154(2) CA 2006). Also, public companies must have a suitably qualified secretary appointed (ss. 271 and 273 CA 2006).

16.2.2.5   The issue of shares or debentures

The principal advantage which a public company has over a private company is its ability to raise capital by offering shares or debentures to the public for cash or other consideration; private companies are prohibited from doing so (s. 755 CA 2006). Therefore, if a private company is proposing to make an offer to the public, a shareholder, creditor or the Secretary of State may apply to the court for an order restraining it from such action (s. 757 CA 2006). However, if the offer has already been made, a shareholder, creditor or the Secretary of State may apply to the court for an order that the company be re-registered as a plc or, if this would be impractical, that the company be wound up (s. 758 CA 2006). Alternatively, the court may make a remedial order, which may involve the directors or the company (or both) having to buy-back the shares issued (s. 759 CA 2006).

(Note that offers of shares to the public are governed by Part VI of the Financial Services and Markets Act 2000 and the Prospectus Regulations 2005 (SI 2005/1433). These require the publication of a prospectus approved by the Financial Services Authority in any case where shares are to be 'offered to the public' within the terms of the legislation.)

16.2.2.6   Registration requirements

The procedure to be followed and the documents required to register a public company from scratch are the same as for a private company. Once the Registrar of Companies is satisfied that the documents comply with the registration requirements, a certificate of incorporation will be issued.

However, before the public company can do business or borrow money, the company must obtain from the Registrar a further certificate which will only be issued if the Registrar is satisfied that the company's share capital is adequate (a 'trading certificate') (s. 761 CA 2006). The procedure which the company must go through to get this trading certificate involves a director or the company secretary filing a statement of compliance with the Registrar. The declaration will state that the nominal value of the company's allotted share capital is at least equal to the authorised minimum (of £50,000). The company must also supply details of:

(a) the amount paid up on the allotted share capital;

(b) the amount of the preliminary expenses and details of who will meet them; and

(c) any amount or benefit paid to the company's promoters.

A company which does not obtain a trading certificate before it commences business can face some severe consequences (s. 767 CA 2006). If the company fails to meet its obligations in connection with a transaction entered into at a time when it does not have the additional certificate, the directors will be jointly and severally liable to indemnify the other parties to the transaction for any loss. Furthermore, both the company and its officers will be liable to a fine and if the company fails to obtain this certificate within one year of its registration, the court can wind the company up (s. 122 Insolvency Act 1986).

16.2.3   Special rules applicable to public companies

We saw in **16.2.2.5** that a public company can raise capital by offering shares to the public. This can give the company a much wider source of potential investors than is the case with the private company. The price of this is that to protect the public, public companies are subject to a number of restrictions which do not apply to private companies.

16.2.3.1   Payment for share capital

(a) The original subscribers to a public company's memorandum are required to pay cash for their shares.

(b) At least 25% of the nominal value and the whole of any premium on shares in a public company must be paid on allotment.

(c) A public company cannot accept an undertaking to do work or perform services as consideration for the allotment of shares. (In any event, it is unusual for a private company to seek such consideration for any allotment it may make.)

(d) A public company can accept the transfer of assets to the company as full or part payment for the allotment of shares but any undertaking to transfer those assets to the company must be performed within five years of the allotment. In addition, the company must take steps to satisfy itself that the value of the assets transferred to the company is accurate by obtaining an expert's valuation and report.

(All of the above requirements are contained within both the 1985 and the 2006 Acts.)

16.2.3.2   Pre-emption rights on the allotment of shares

A public company, unlike a private company, cannot make a general exclusion of the statutory pre-emption rights set out in s. 561 CA 2006 by a provision in its articles. However, in respect of specified allotments where the directors are authorised to make those allotments, a public company (like a private company) can disapply these pre-emption rights by passing a special resolution or through a provision in its articles (ss. 570 and 571 CA 2006).

16.2.3.3   Serious loss of capital

The directors of a public company are under an obligation to convene an extraordinary general meeting (EGM) if the company's net assets are 50% or less of its called-up share capital. The meeting must be convened within 28 days of one of the directors becoming aware of this fact and it must be held within 56 days. Obviously, the purpose of the meeting is for the problem to be considered, but the governing provision (s. 656 CA 2006) does not require the directors to take any definite steps to remedy the position.

16.2.3.4   Purchase by a public company of its own shares

Public companies, like private companies, can buy back their own shares and issue redeemable shares. However, only private companies can use capital to purchase or redeem shares (s. 709 CA 2006).

(In addition, the tax rules which allow a shareholder whose shares have been bought by the company to treat the purchase as a disposal for capital gains tax purposes, rather than the receipt of a distribution attracting income tax, only apply to the shares in unquoted companies. It should, however, be remembered that a public company will not necessarily have a listing on the Stock Exchange.)

16.2.3.5   Financial assistance for the acquisition of shares and loans to directors

The rules prohibiting companies from providing financial assistance for the purchase of their own shares now only apply to public companies (s. 678 CA 2006). As has been the case in the past, if this situation could impede a proposed transaction, the answer may be to re-register the company as private to avoid the prohibition (see **16.2.4**).

16.2.3.6   Loans to directors

Whilst loans to directors by all types of company will require shareholders' approval by ordinary resolution (subject to a number of exceptions), only quasi-loans to and credit transactions with directors of public companies need similar shareholders' approval (ss. 197–214 CA 2006).

16.2.3.7   Distribution of profits

In addition to the general rules restricting the funds from which companies can make distributions, s. 831 CA 2006 imposes an extra condition on a public company before it can make a distribution as follows:

(a) Its net assets must not be less than the aggregate of its called-up share capital and undistributable reserves.

(b) The distribution itself must not reduce the net assets to less than the above aggregate.

The undistributable reserves are:

(a) Its share premium account (which will reflect any premium paid to the company by shareholders for their shares).

(b) Its capital redemption reserve (which will have been created if any buy-back of shares has occurred).

(c) The amount by which its accumulated, unrealised profits exceed its accumulated, unrealised losses (on the basis that only realised sums are relevant in the context of distributions).

(d) Any other reserve it is prevented from distributing, either by statute or its articles.

If this prohibition applies and the company wishes to continue to make a distribution, the usual approach is to reduce the share capital, such that the aggregate is then less than the net assets. (See **11.2.10** for further discussion.)

16.2.3.8   Accounting requirements

The provisions which permit 'small' and 'medium-sized' companies to prepare and file less detailed accounts with the Registrar of Companies do not apply to public companies. (See **Chapter 15** for further details.)

16.2.3.9   Written resolutions

The ability for the members of private companies to take decisions by written resolutions rather than passing resolutions at general meetings, does not extend to public companies (s. 288 CA 2006).

16.2.3.10   Annual general meetings

In contrast to private companies, the Companies Act 2006 continues to require public companies to hold AGMs (s. 336 CA 2006) and public companies are likely to continue to use these as an opportunity to fulfil their statutory obligations to lay audited accounts before a general meeting (s. 437 CA 2006) and to re-appoint auditors annually (s. 489 CA 2006).

16.2.4   Re-registration of a private company to a public company and vice versa

Given the various special rules to which public companies are subject, promoters of a company are unlikely to want to incorporate their company as a public company, unless they intend to issue securities in the company to the public within the foreseeable future. However, many companies start life as private companies and are then converted into public companies so that they can be listed and have their shares traded on the Stock Exchange. The reasons why a company might do this are explained in **16.3.2**. Equally, although perhaps less frequently, the shareholders and/or directors of a public company may decide to convert the company into a private company. They may do so for a variety of reasons, for example:

(a) To avoid the prohibition on financial assistance by public companies.

(b) Where the board has decided that the company's securities should no longer be in public hands. (Normally because of the wish to assume a greater control over the company, without reference to external investors. Often referred to as a 'public to private' deal.)

(c) After a successful takeover, where the purchaser of the shares in the takeover target wants the target to continue to operate as a wholly-owned private subsidiary.

16.2.4.1   Re-registration of a private company to a public company

The procedure which the private company will have to go through in order to re-register as a public company is set out in ss. 90–96 CA 2006. The company cannot be re-registered unless it satisfies the various requirements in relation to share capital to which public companies are subject (as explained above).

Provided the requirements with regard to share capital are satisfied, the company must pass a special resolution which:

(a) states that the company should be re-registered as a public company;

and

(b) alters the company's articles to meet the company's new circumstances (by, for example, removing restrictions on transferability).

Once the resolution has been passed an application for re-registration has to be submitted to the Registrar of Companies with:

(a) a printed copy of the company's articles in their altered form;

(b) a copy of the special resolution;

(c) a copy of a statement in writing by the company's auditors confirming that the company's net assets are not less than the combined total of its called-up share capital and distributable reserves (this written statement should relate to a balance sheet prepared for a date not more than seven months before the date the company has made its application for re-registration);

(d) a copy of the balance sheet on which the auditors based their written statement referred to in (c) above together with an unqualified report on the balance sheet by the company's auditors;

(e) certain reports and statutory declarations where shares have been allotted for non-cash consideration since the date of the balance sheet;

(f) confirmation of the details of the proposed secretary where the company does not have a secretary at the time (s. 94(1)(b) CA 2006);

and

(g) a fee of £20 (or £50 if same-day registration is required).

Once the Registrar of Companies is satisfied with these papers, a certificate will be issued confirming that the company has been re-registered as a public limited company

(s. 96 CA 2006). The change to the company's articles and name also take effect as a result.

16.2.4.2   Re-registration of a public company as a private company

It is easier for a public company to be re-registered as a private company than the other way round for the reason that there are no specific criteria for private companies to fulfil (with the exception of having at least one director and one shareholder). Section 97 CA 2006 stipulates that a company must pass a special resolution by which it:

(a) resolves to re-register as a private company;

(b) removes the words 'public limited company' (or their equivalent) from its name and replaces them with 'limited'; and

(c) makes any other alterations to the articles of the company to suit its new circumstances.

An application to re-register pursuant to s. 100 CA 2006 must be delivered to the Registrar, together with the special resolution and a printed copy of the altered articles.

Once the Registrar of Companies is satisfied with these papers, a certificate will be issued confirming that the company has been re-registered as a private limited company (s. 101 CA 2006). The change to the company's articles and name also take effect as a result.

One consequence of a public company re-registering as a private company is that its securities may be less easily transferred. Therefore, protection is given to minority shareholders by s. 98 in case they object to this change in the status of the company. Minority shareholders have the right to apply to the court within 28 days of the special resolution being passed to have the resolution cancelled. Such an application for cancellation can only be made by:

(a) shareholders holding not less than 5% of the nominal value of the company's issued share capital (or for any class of the share capital, if there is more than one); or

(b) not less than 50 of the company's members.

The application for cancellation can only be made by a person who has not consented to or voted in favour of the resolution and the court can make an order either cancelling or confirming the resolution on such terms and conditions as it thinks fit (which could, for example, include ordering that the company should buy the shares of the dissentient member or members).

Re-registering a private company as a public company is always a voluntary act. However, in two circumstances, a public company can be compulsorily re-registered as a private company:

(a) If the court makes an order confirming a reduction of capital of a public company which results in the nominal value of the company's allotted share capital falling below the authorised minimum the company ceases to be a public company. In these circumstances, the court can make an order to the effect that the company will be re-registered as a private company (making consequential amendments to the memorandum and articles of the company) which will avoid the necessity for the company to pass a special resolution to re-register.

(b) The cancellation by a public company of shares (in very specific circumstances) will lead to the company having to apply to be re-registered as a private company, if the cancellation reduces the company's allotted share capital below the authorised minimum.

16.3 Seeking and maintaining a listing

16.3.1 Introduction

In this section, we will look very briefly at the advantages and disadvantages of obtaining a listing and the requirements for seeking and maintaining that listing. It is not our intention to go into this area in detail, but merely to outline the key issues. We have used the expression 'a listing' as a generic expression for obtaining a listing of a company with the UK Listing Authority (UKLA) and having its shares admitted to trading on the Stock Exchange. When its shares have been admitted to the Stock Exchange, which is an international market for buying and selling shares, those who trade shares ('brokers') will quote prices at which they will buy and sell shares of that company. Thus, a listed company may also be referred to as a 'quoted' company, i.e., it is 'quoted' on the Stock Exchange. Also, 'quoted company' has a specific meaning for the purposes of the 2006 Act; see s. 385.

16.3.2 The advantages and disadvantages of a listing

It will take a great deal of time by the officers of the company (and their advisers) to seek and maintain a listing which is, therefore, an expensive exercise. While there may be a number of advantages to the company in being listed, the company will have to accept the imposition of restrictions over and above those imposed on it by the Companies Acts and other legislation which affects every company. The key to understanding the need for these restrictions to be imposed is to appreciate that the principal advantage to a company of being listed is that its shares are more easily marketed and that it therefore has greater access to capital, part of which usually involves an increase in the number of shareholders. Therefore, the company has the obligation to make public information relating to its current performance and future prospects. This is to give the company's current and potential future shareholders adequate information on which to base their decisions on how to deal in the company's shares.

While improved marketability (in the sense that all the shares, including minority holdings, will be freely tradable on a market which is open to a wide range of potential investors) is the principal advantage of the company being listed, it is not the only advantage. The mere fact of being a listed company may improve the status of the company within the market in which it operates. Having its shares quoted on the Stock Exchange may provide a company with a future source of finance as it can issue new shares to raise additional funds rather than borrow money from a bank. Should the company wish to grow by means of acquisitions, it may find that its ability to offer its quoted shares as full or part payment of the purchase price for the company it is acquiring is an attractive and cost-efficient alternative to borrowing money or using its own cash reserves.

While a listing can be attractive to an acquisitive company, it can also create problems for a company which could be the target of a take-over itself. Such a company could find that a potential bidder is able to acquire a stake in it through the open market, although there are a number of mechanisms in place to ensure that a company is aware if it is the target for a potential bid. Another potential disadvantage, particularly if the company seeking the listing has traditionally been run by a small group of directors/shareholders, is that they will find their activities become the subject of much closer scrutiny by both their shareholders and other interested parties (both potential investors and the press) following the listing. Since the price of a company's shares will depend on the market's view of their value, the price can fluctuate, sometimes dramatically, in response to both good and bad news about the company. To prevent people with inside information about the company's activities taking advantage of that knowledge, there are various prohibitions in place to prevent 'insiders' using information for their own benefit which is not freely available.

16.3.3 Regulations governing an application for a listing

When a company wishes to seek a listing, it must follow an application procedure and satisfy admission requirements set out in the Listing Rules. These Rules are published by the Financial Services Authority (acting as the UKLA). The Listing Rules set out the conditions which a company must meet if it is to be considered for listing. They also require the publication of a prospectus, which document must comply with the Prospectus Rules (see **16.3.5.3**). In parallel with this process, the company also has to seek admission for its shares to be admitted to trading on the London Stock Exchange, and must comply with the latter's Admission and Disclosure Standards. If the company is able to satisfy all these requirements, it can be admitted to the Senior Equity Market in London, which is known as the Official List.

(There is a secondary market, open to smaller companies, called the Alternative Investment Market. We shall not look further at the rules relating to companies quoted on this market.)

The lead role in assisting a company to obtain a listing is undertaken by a party required to be appointed under the Listing Rules: an independent approved sponsor who must satisfy certain conditions. The 'approved sponsor' must:

(a) be either an approved person under the Financial Services and Markets Act 2000 or an authorised credit institution;

(b) satisfy the UKLA that it has sufficient experience and standing to discharge the responsibilities of a sponsor;

(c) undertake to the UKLA to discharge the responsibilities of a sponsor as contained in the Listing Rules; and

(d) be entered on the UKLA's register of sponsors.

This role will almost certainly be filled by an investment bank, stockbroker, corporate finance house or firm of accountants. They will have overall responsibility for arranging the issue for the company and will liaise with other professional advisers acting for the company.

To be admitted to listing, the company must be registered as a public company and, normally, it must intend to place on the market shares which are expected to have a market value of £700,000 or more. The company will not be admitted (save in exceptional circumstances) if it has not published or filed accounts covering the three years preceding the application for listing, and the company must have produced by independent accountants a report covering the three preceding years.

As the intention behind a listing is to create a market in shares in the company, any restrictions on transfer which are contained within the company's articles must be removed.

The directors must obviously consider that the company is financially viable and therefore a further condition for admission is that they must be satisfied that the company's working capital is sufficient. This admission requirement is satisfied by the sponsor sending a letter to the UKLA stating that the directors have made careful enquiries to satisfy themselves and the sponsor that the working capital is indeed adequate. The final principal admission requirement is that it must be intended that at least 25% of any class of shares will be in the hands of the public as defined by the Listing Rules.

The Prospectus Rules require a range of information to be published in a prospectus which is made available to potential investors. The purpose of this document is to provide potential investors with comprehensive information on the company seeking to be listed, to allow them to make an informed decision on whether or not to invest. Should information in the prospectus prove to be misleading, false or deceptive, both civil and criminal liability can arise under the Financial Services and Markets Act 2000, as well as liability in contract and tort. The detail of this liability is beyond the scope of this book.

16.3.4 Methods of listing

If the securities do not need to be marketed to new investors (i.e., the company's shares are already sufficiently within the hands of the public (see **16.3.3**) and it does not want, as part of the listing, to issue new shares to new investors), the company can become listed by way of an 'introduction'. Effectively, its existing share capital is 'introduced' to the market by the sponsor. However, if the shares need to be marketed, admission can be achieved by any of the methods set out below.

(a) An *offer for sale* under which securities already in issue or allotted are offered to the public at large. This will entail making application forms available to the public who will complete and return them, paying the specified fixed price for the shares. It is, however, possible for the offer merely to fix a minimum price and require the applicants of the shares to tender a higher price, with the shares going to the highest bidder.

(b) An *offer for subscription* under which securities not yet in issue or allotted are offered to the public at large. The same procedures as in (a) will be followed.

(c) A *placing*. In this case, the company's shares will not be offered to the public generally; rather they will be offered to clients of the sponsor.

(d) An *intermediaries offer*. This involves securities being allocated to 'intermediaries' (for example, Stock Exchange member firms) who will in turn allocate the securities to their own clients.

16.3.5 Continuing obligations after a listing has been achieved

A company, once listed, is subject to a range of continuing obligations. The purpose of these is to maintain a flow of relevant and up-to-date information to shareholders and the market. This is intended to ensure a fair and orderly market in the listed company's shares.

Companies considering a listing should recognise that after the listing there will be a far greater flow of information about the company into the public domain. In turn, the company must set up systems to enable it to meet its continuing obligations. Finally, it may find itself consulting its professional advisers on a regular basis about what it should do to meet these obligations.

Continuing obligations are imposed on listed companies primarily by the Listing Rules and the Disclosure and Transparency Rules.

16.3.5.1 Listing Rules

The Listing Rules require a company to meet a number of continuing obligations. Two of these are requirements to comply with the Disclosure and Transparency Rules (see **16.3.5.2**) and the Model Code. The latter is appended to the Listing Rules and sets out to control dealings in a company's shares by directors and certain employees. In addition, the Listing Rules contain a range of specific continuing obligations, which require:

(a) disclosure of certain information to company shareholders to assist them in the exercise of their shareholder rights, such information to be provided equally to all shareholders;

(b) notifying, and in certain cases seeking approval from, shareholders in relation to specific transactions which the company intends to undertake;

(c) various notifications to be made to the public through the FSA or an RIS (see **16.3.5.2**); and

(d) publication of financial information on interim and annual bases.

Again, the detail of these obligations is beyond the scope of this Guide; however, from the description above you can see how these specific requirements of the Listing Rules are intended to achieve the general objective of continuing obligations.

16.3.5.2 Disclosure and Transparency Rules

These rules implement the EU Market Abuse Directive and the EU Transparency Directive (both of which are beyond the scope of this Guide) and also provide a general requirement of disclosure of information by a listed company. This information, as described below, must be made available to a Recognised Information Service (RIS), which body must be recognised by the FSA. The general disclosure requirement is that a company must make known to the market as soon as possible any 'inside information'. This amounts to any information which is:

(a) precise;

(b) not generally available;

(c) relates to the listed company or its shares; and

(d) which, if generally available, would be likely to have a significant effect on the price of the shares.

Failure to comply with the Disclosure and Transparency Rules may result in:

(a) Private or public censure by the FSA.

(b) The imposition of a fine by the FSA.

(c) Suspension of listing or trading in the company's shares.

Taxation

Taxation of income profits and losses of sole traders and partnerships

This chapter covers the following topics:

17.1 Introduction

This chapter covers the way in which the income profits and losses of unincorporated businesses—essentially, sole traders and partnerships—are determined and assessed. We will look first at the rules that apply to any unincorporated business and then at the specific rules relevant to partnerships.

17.2 Taxable profits

17.2.1 Introduction

The owner(s) of an unincorporated business will be taxed on the profits which the business generates. There is no formal separation between the profit-making apparatus of the business and those involved in it, therefore money earned by the business is treated as money earned by the relevant sole trader or partners. For this reason, unincorporated businesses are often classed as 'transparent' for tax purposes. (Contrast this with a company, where the company is a taxable person in its own right. See **Chapter 19** for more details.)

Taxable profits are determined by calculating the income generated from trading activities, then deducting from that amount the deductible expenditure incurred by the business plus any other sums deductible under tax legislation. An example of the latter is a capital allowance, which operates as deemed depreciation on items of plant and machinery bought by the business. (These are discussed in more detail at **Chapter 22**.)

EXAMPLE

Keystone Bathrooms' income and expenditure for the tax year 2008/09 was as follows:

Income receipts   £375,000
Deductible expenditure   £220,000

It also had capital allowances of £15,000.

Its taxable profits for the tax year in question were therefore: £375,000 – (£220,000 + £15,000) = £140,000.

Where total deductions exceed income receipts, this will result in a loss for tax purposes (see **17.4**).

EXAMPLE

Mansett Financial Services' income and expenditure for the tax year 2008/09 was as follows:

Income receipts   £128,000
Deductible expenditure   £163,000

Its loss for the tax year in question was therefore: £128,000 – £163,000 = (£35,000).

17.2.2 Definition of income receipts

Income receipts must usually be recurrent or capable of recurrence. Income receipts must also be distinguished from capital receipts. In most cases this does not present a problem. Receipts from the sale of stock-in-trade are income: receipts from the sale of fixed assets are capital. For example, if the business is a bathroom fittings shop, the fittings which are sold are stock, but the shop itself is a fixed, capital asset. Similarly, if the business owns a delivery vehicle, this too will be classed as a capital item. Contrast this with a car dealership, where the cars for sale are its stock-in-trade and money received from their sale will be part of its trading income.

The specific rules by which income is ascertained are contained in the Income Tax (Trading and Other Income) Act (ITTOIA) 2005, whilst the basic provisions of income tax are set out in the Income Tax Act (ITA) 2007. (Note that there also exists the Income Tax (Earnings and Pensions) Act 2003 which is relevant for income tax liability on salaries and pensions. This is considered in **Chapter 20**.)

17.2.3 Deductible expenditure

Expenditure is deductible if it is of an income rather than a capital nature. This distinction is similar to the distinction between income and capital receipts, so that, again, evidence of accountancy practice is valuable.

Section 34 ITTOIA 2005 provides that in calculating the profits or gains to be charged to tax, no sum shall be deducted in respect of any disbursements or expenses which have not been *wholly and exclusively* laid out or expended for the purposes of the business. For expenditure to be deducted, it must therefore be 'wholly' incurred for the purposes of the business. Thus, if a sum of money represents partly a business expense but is excessively large and so also partly represents a gift, it is not deductible. Expenditure must also be 'exclusively' incurred for the purposes of the business, so that if money is spent and the motive is partly connected with the business and partly not so connected (e.g., there is an element of personal enjoyment), then the payment is not deductible.

EXAMPLE

Wolfsons is a retailer of electrical goods, operating as a partnership. From its sales receipts of a particular accounting year, it is entitled to deduct items of expenditure incurred during the same period. These must be of an income nature, and wholly and exclusively for the purposes of the business. Common examples of these items of deductible expenditure would be: rent for leasehold premises; salaries paid to employees; utilities (electricity, gas, telecommunications, etc.); council rates; purchases of stock (i.e., electrical goods for re-sale); business stationery; and advertising costs.

By contrast, if Wolfsons owned freehold premises and sold them in order to move to new premises, any receipts and expenditure arising out of these transactions would be of a capital nature, as they would not be linked to the essential profit-making functions of the business. Any tax liability arising would be considered under the capital gains tax regime. (See **Chapter 18**.)

Certain types of expenditure are not deductible because of the provisions of Part 2, Chapter 4 ITTOIA. Many of these provisions refer to types of expenditure which would be non-deductible anyway because they are not revenue expenditure or not wholly and exclusively incurred for the purposes of the trade. Among other things, there is a prohibition on the deduction of provisions for bad debts (s. 35 ITTOIA); and most business entertainment expenses are non-deductible under the provisions of s. 45 ITTOIA.

As mentioned earlier, capital allowances may also be available to deduct from income receipts. The cost of the purchase of a capital asset is itself not deductible, as it is not expenditure of an income nature. However, a designated percentage of the purchase price will be deductible annually from income receipts. (See **Chapter 22** for further details.)

17.2.4 Accounting bases

When calculating profit, a business must apply a consistent method to determine whether receipts and expenses relate to one accounting period or to a later period. If it fails to do so its accounts are useless to the business for the purposes of comparison; what is more, the business could manipulate its receipts and expenses so as to avoid tax.

Almost all businesses produce final accounts on an annual basis. These show its profits—calculated according to normal accountancy practice—and how they are allocated to the proprietor(s). These accounts may not, however, be wholly suitable for tax purposes, as often there are special tax rules which define what is taxable as income and what is deductible as an expense. (See s. 25 ITTOIA for a statement to this effect.)

For tax purposes accounts have to be agreed with the Inland Revenue and must give a true and fair view of profits. Therefore, whilst accounts do not have to be fully audited, certain fundamentals such as creditors, debtors, work-in-progress, and stock must feature in them.

17.2.5 The need to value stock and work-in-progress

As part of the process of calculating the taxable profits of an accounting period, the value of stocks held at both the beginning and the end of that period must be taken into account. This enables calculation of the cost of goods sold. To calculate this figure, the closing stock (i.e., the value of stock at the end of the year) is deducted from the total of the opening stock figure and the amount spent on stock during the year (which accountants call 'purchases'). The resulting figure is then deducted from the total of sales receipts to calculate the gross profit.

EXAMPLE

	£	£
Sales		50,000
Opening stock	10,000	
Add: Purchases	35,000	
	45,000	
Less: Closing stock	(12,000)	
Costs of goods sold		33,000
Gross profit		17,000

Other deductible expenses such as wages are then deducted from the gross profit to arrive at the net profit, which enters into the tax calculation.

Clearly the amount of profit depends on the value placed on stock—the lower the closing stock figure, the smaller is the profit (and, therefore, the tax on it). Stock is valued according to normal accountancy principles, which allow each item of stock to be valued at the lower of cost or market value. Thus where stock has risen in value, an upward valuation is not required, but where it has fallen in value immediate relief is given by the revaluation. Once a closing stock figure has been arrived at for a period it becomes the opening stock figure for the next period.

A business which only supplies services (e.g., a law firm) does not have trading stock. Instead, it will have work-in-progress (that is, work commenced but not yet billed). The same principles apply as with trading stock in terms of valuation at the end of year for accounting and tax purposes.

17.3 The basis of assessment for income tax

Most businesses work on a 12-month accounting period. The period chosen need not correspond with the tax year (which runs from 6 April to the following 5 April). However, all businesses' liability to tax is calculated by reference to income and expenditure in a *tax year*. Because accounting periods and tax years may not correspond, rules are needed for allocating the profits of accounting periods to tax years. This system is known as the current year basis and is discussed below. (The legislative basis for these rules is found in Part 2, Chapter 15 ITTOIA).

A crucial aspect of this system is the role of the tax return in enabling the Her Majesty's Revenue and Customs (HMRC) to discover a business's income. Taxpayers are obliged to provide HMRC with the relevant details of income and expenditure, etc., and to calculate their total taxable income. (They may also wish to calculate the actual tax due thereon, although this can be left to HMRC.) The taxable profits of a sole trader's business will form part of that individual's taxable income on their tax return. In the case of a partnership, an individual partner's share of profits will form part of his or his taxable income. The individual taxpayer then pays tax on their taxable income for a particular tax year. Taxable income is the total income received in that year less all relevant deductions and reliefs. The most notable of these is the personal allowance which, for the tax year 2009/10, is £6,475.

Tax is payable on taxable income at rates set by the Chancellor of the Exchequer in the annual Budget. For 2009/10, income tax rates are:

Basic—20% (payable on *up to* £37,400 of taxable income)

Higher—40% (payable on amounts *in excess of* £37,400 of taxable income).

From April 2010, a new rate of income tax of 50% will apply to income over £150,000. In addition, the personal allowance for those earning over £100,000 will be reduced by £1 for every £2 earned above £100,000.

17.3.1 Current year basis

17.3.1.1 Current year basis

For the purpose of calculating the tax for a specific tax year, HMRC treats profits of an unincorporated business for the accounting period ending in that specific tax year as the income for that tax year. For example, if an unincorporated business makes its accounts up to 30 April each year, the profits made in the business for the year ended 30 April 2009 would be the profits on which the sole proprietor or partners were assessed in the tax year 2009/10.

The dates for payment of tax under the system are 31 January in the year of assessment, 31 July following the year of assessment and 31 January following the year of assessment. The first two instalments are estimated (in effect, payments on account based on the previous year's tax liability). The third will either be a balancing payment or rebate, depending whether tax had been over- or under-estimated, calculated once full details of actual profits have been received by HMRC.

EXAMPLE

Jones & Co (a partnership) makes up its accounts to 30 September each year. The tax liability of the partners for the tax year 2009/10 will be based on profits to the year-end 30 September 2009. Tax will be payable on 31 January 2010 and 31 July 2010 (estimated according to previous year's profits) and any adjustment will be due on 31 January 2011 once actual profits are known.

17.3.2 Opening and closing year rules

17.3.2.1 Introduction

The general rule expressed above regarding assessment is modified when a business has just begun trading or has ceased to trade. These rules are known as the opening and the closing year rules. They will be looked at in turn.

17.3.2.2 Opening year rules

The opening years rules under the new regime apply to the first two tax years of the unincorporated business's 'life'. They are as follows:

Year of commencement	Profits from date of commencement to following 5 April (i.e., the end of the first tax year of the business's life).
Second year	Profits of first 12 months of trade or the current year basis when an accounting period of at least 12 months ends in the tax year.
Third and subsequent years	Current year basis.

EXAMPLE

X commenced business as an electrician on 1 June 2007, taking 30 September as the accounting year end. The business, therefore, started in the tax year 2007/08, the first tax year for assessment. Consequently, the relevant periods for assessment would have been:

First year (2007/08)	Profits from 1 June 2007 to 5 April 2008
Second year (2008/09)	Current year basis, i.e., profits from 1 October 2007 to 30 September 2008
Third year (2009/10)	Current year basis, i.e., profits from 1 October 2008 to 30 September 2009

Instead, if X had chosen an accounting year end of 30 April, the relevant profit for the second year would have been the first 12 months of trading, i.e., 1 June 2007 to 31 May 2008. This is because the accounting date which falls within the second year of assessment (i.e., 30 April 2008) would have been less than 12 months from the commencement of the business. The relevant periods for assessment would therefore have been:

First year (2007/08)	Profits from 1 June 2007 to 5 April 2008
Second year (2008/09)	First 12 months trading, i.e., profits from 1 June 2007 to 31 May 2008
Third year (2009/10)	Current year basis, i.e., profits from 1 May 2008 to 30 April 2009

It will be noted from the above example that, unless an accounting period corresponds exactly with the tax year, some profits will be assessed twice in the first and second years of assessment. Overlap relief will operate in such circumstances (see ss. 204–207 ITTOIA), providing the business with a credit to take account of such double assessment.

17.3.2.3   Closing year rules

When a business ceases there will be a notional accounting period which runs from the day after the end of the last accounting period to be taxed up to the date of cessation.

EXAMPLE

A business ended on 31 December 2008 (i.e., in the tax year 2008/09). Accounts for the business were made up to 30 April.

The relevant accounting periods for the tax years in question were as follows:

2006/07	1 May 2005–30 April 2006
2007/08	1 May 2006–30 April 2007
2008/09	1 May 2007–31 December 2008

17.4   Losses under the income tax system

If a trader makes a trading loss (i.e., deductible expenses exceed income profits) during an accounting period, the relevant assessment to tax on that sum will amount to a 'nil' liability. In addition, tax relief will be available in respect of the loss in the following ways. (Note that the ITA is the relevant legislation; the ITTOIA does not deal with losses.)

17.4.1 Set-off against same year income

Under s. 64 ITA 2007 the amount of the loss may, if the taxpayer so elects, be deducted from any other income of the taxpayer taxable in the year of assessment during which the loss is made. Where, as is usual, the loss-making period is partly in one tax year and partly in another, the Revenue will, in practice, allow the whole of the loss to be set off against the income of the tax year during which that period ends.

If a loss is not fully relieved either because the other income of the year of the loss was insufficient or because the taxpayer did not elect to take the relief, a similar election may be made in respect of the immediately preceding tax year, provided that the trade is still being carried on by the taxpayer on a commercial basis.

It should be noted that under both subsections the loss may be set off against *any* of the taxpayer's income from whatever source. A claim under s. 64 must be made in writing within 12 months of 31 January immediately following the year of assessment in which the loss arose.

Special rules apply to prevent relief under s. 64 being given where the trade is not being carried on with a view to profit.

Trading losses can, in limited circumstances, be set against the taxpayer's capital gains in the tax year when the loss arises and in one following tax year under ss. 261B and 261C Taxation of Chargeable Gains Act 1992. The relief only applies to such losses as have not been used up following a claim under s. 64.

In the April 2009 Budget, the Chancellor made additional provision for unincorporated businesses and partnerships to carry back and set off trading losses against profits of earlier years. This provision extends the current ability (noted above) to relieve losses against profits made in the preceding year, where such losses cannot otherwise be relieved in the year they were suffered. The ability to carry back will be extended from the current one year to a maximum of three, with losses to be applied against later years first. The amount of trading losses that can be carried back—unlimited in respect of the preceding year—will be limited to a maximum of £50,000 per year and to losses of the same trade. This provision will apply to losses made in each of the tax years 2008/09 and 2009/10.

17.4.2 Set-off against future income

Under s. 83 ITA 2007, a loss may be set against income from the same trade (but not from any other source) in future years (without time limit) to the extent that it has not been completely relieved under s. 64, either because no relief was claimed or because the income was insufficient. Relief is given by means of a deduction from the income of the next tax year in which there are profits and then the year after that and so on until the loss is completely relieved.

The following example demonstrates the operation of ss. 64 and 83.

EXAMPLE

The profits and losses of a trade made during accounting periods ending on 31 December each year are as follows:

2007	£5,000	profit
2008	£20,000	loss
2009	£6,000	profit
2010	£7,000	profit

In addition to his trade, the taxpayer has a part-time employment producing an income of £2,000 per annum throughout the period. If claims for relief under ss. 64 and 83 are made, the income tax position is as follows:

	2007/08	2008/09	2009/10	2010/11
Trading income	5,000	nil	6,000	7,000
Employment income	2,000	2,000	2,000	2,000
	7,000	2,000	8,000	9,000
Loss relief	7,000*	2,000**	6,000***	5,000***
Final income	nil	nil	2,000	4,000
	*s. 64	**s. 64	***s. 83	

Note:

(a) The loss occurred in the tax year 2008/09 which means that it can be set off against other profits being taxed in that year, or against the previous year's profits. As there is still some unrelieved loss once this has been done, the balance can be carried forward.

(b) On these figures full relief is not given until 2010/11 even though the loss was made in 2008.

(c) It would probably have been better not to claim relief for 2008/09 since the income for that year would have been covered by personal reliefs which are tax-free anyway. The loss relief was, therefore, wasted.

(d) The deduction in 2009/10 was only £6,000 because in that year no relief could be given against income from other sources (n.b., s. 83 ITA 2007). After the deduction of £5,000 in 2010/11 full relief has been given for the loss.

17.4.3   Carry back of terminal losses

Under s. 89 ITA 2007 a loss made during the last year of a trade may be deducted from income from the same trade in the three years of assessment before the discontinuance (relief under s. 64 will be available for the year of discontinuance), taking later years before earlier years. It should be noted that the relief only applies where the loss is made in the last year of a trade. If a business makes losses for a number of years before discontinuance there will be no loss relief unless the trader has other sources of income—s. 83 cannot help since there will be no future profits, nor can s. 89, since the loss can only be carried back three years and those years will have had nil assessments because of the earlier losses.

17.4.4   Losses in early years of trade

Under s. 72 ITA 2007 losses made during the first four years of a trade may be set off against income of the three tax years before the loss, taking earlier years before later years. The loss can be deducted from all the income of those years from whatever source and the rules of s. 64 dealing with the order in which relief is given where there is more than one source of income apply to s. 72. The principal effect of s. 72 is to allow a sole trader who starts a trade to set the loss off against income received before the business started and hence provide an increased ability for start-up businesses to set off losses in their early years.

17.4.5 General considerations

As would be expected, all the sections giving relief prevent double relief being claimed in respect of the same sum (for example, if relief is claimed under s. 72 only the unrelieved balance, if any, may be carried forward under s. 83). In many cases relief is given by setting a loss off against income which has already been taxed; where this happens the relief is given by means of repayment of tax.

It should be noted that loss relief is not intended as a subsidy for unsuccessful business; there is no guarantee that just because a loss is made relief will one day be given. Where relief is given the saving is, of course, the amount of the tax on the amount of the relief, so that for the basic rate taxpayer a loss of £100 saves £22 in tax.

17.5 Income tax liability of partnerships

17.5.1 General

A partnership is not a separate legal person. It is a group of individuals, each of whom is taxed on his own share of the partnership profits or losses in the light of his own personal reliefs and other sources of income. For the purposes of *assessment* and *collection* of tax each partner is treated as a notional sole trader. The relevant legislation can be found in Part 9 ITTOIA.

17.5.2 Profit share or business expense?

The taxable profit is calculated by applying normal income tax principles to ascertain taxable receipts and deductible expenses. However, in the case of a partnership, it is necessary to examine any payment made by the business to a partner to determine whether it is a deductible expense or an allocation of the taxable profit amongst the partners. A payment in the latter category *cannot* reduce the taxable profit of the partnership.

The following items merit special attention:

(a) *Salary*

The tax treatment of a 'salary' payable to a 'partner' depends on whether HMRC regards the recipient as a true partner sharing in the profits in a particular, agreed way (the decision to allocate profits in this way is normally taken to ensure that one partner is entitled to an agreed portion of profit in priority to the other partners) or whether the recipient is merely an employee in receipt of a salary who is described as a 'partner'. In making their decision, HMRC will consider all the facts and the terms of the partnership agreement entered into by the parties. The terms of the agreement are not conclusive (*Stekel v Ellice* [1973] 1 WLR 191). Where salary is treated as an allocation of profit, it is not deductible from the firm's taxable profits. Where it is a true salary, it is deductible and will be assessed under the Income Tax (Earnings and Pensions) Act 2003, with tax being deducted at source under the PAYE procedure.

(b) *Interest*

'Interest' payable to a partner will not be a deductible expense if it is payable on a partner's contribution of capital to the firm. Such a payment is regarded as part of the agreed method of allocating profits. However, if a partner makes a loan to the partnership, interest payable on the loan will normally be a deductible expense.

(c) *Rent*

Where a partnership pays rent to a partner for the use of assets owned by the partner the amount of the rent will be a deductible expense (unless it is excessive).

17.5.3 Mechanics of assessment—current year basis

Partners are assessed to tax on an individual basis rather than being jointly liable as with all other partnership liabilities (see **3.2**). As a result, each partner is required to include his share of partnership profits in his own tax return and is liable for the tax on his profit share but not that of any other partner. However, the partnership is required to submit a set of accounts and a tax return in respect of total partnership profits. Once these are agreed with HMRC, the final profit figure will be apportioned amongst the partners according to the profit-sharing ratio in force during the accounting period in question. The deadline for submission of returns depends on whether a paper or electronic return is made. The former have to be submitted by 31 October and the latter by 31 January, following the tax year of assessment. Thus, paper tax returns for the year 2009/10 will have to be submitted by 31 October 2010, with online returns to be submitted by 31 January 2011.

The rules applicable if a partner dies or retires or joins the firm are considered in **Chapter 23**.

17.5.4 Losses of a partnership

When a partnership makes a loss, each partner can choose what type of relief to claim in respect of his share of the loss. For example, some of the partners may prefer to claim relief under s. 64 ITA 2007 immediately; others may prefer to wait and claim relief under s. 83 ITA 1988.

17.5.5 National insurance

Partners, being self-employed, are liable to make Class 2 and Class 4 National Insurance contributions at a rate lower than the rate applicable to employees (but the benefits are correspondingly lower), and they are entitled to deduct one half of their contributions when calculating their income tax liability.

 online resource centre   Interactive online exercises (Student Learning Activities) which complement the topics covered in this chapter are available at www.oxfordtextbooks.co.uk/orc/business09_10/.

Capital gains tax and inheritance tax on business assets

This chapter covers the following topics:

18.1 Introduction

One of the principal motivations for people going into business is to earn a living from the income they derive from the enterprise. For many people an equally important motivation is to create a capital asset which they can either sell or give away (whether during their lifetime or on death). The tax charges which can arise on these events are therefore of importance to business people. In this chapter we will examine the capital gains tax and inheritance tax regimes which apply to individuals in relation to businesses and business assets. The capital gains tax regime was simplified for individuals from 6 April 2008. Companies are also liable to pay tax on capital gains and there is explanation of this in **Chapter 19**. (Note: this chapter has been written on the basis of this new, simplified regime for individuals and does not contain any detailed explanation of taper relief, which applied to pre-6 April 2008 disposals.)

18.2 Capital gains tax

18.2.1 General

Capital gains tax is payable, under the provisions contained in the Taxation of Chargeable Gains Act (TCGA) 1992, when a taxable person makes a disposal of chargeable assets giving rise to a chargeable gain unless an exemption or relief applies. Capital gains tax is charged by reference to gains made during a tax year (as with income tax). What follows in this section **18.2** is an explanation of the various rules which need to be considered to establish a taxpayer's capital gains tax liability on any given disposal.

18.2.2   The requirements for a charge to capital gains tax

For the charge to tax to arise, a *taxable person* must make a *disposal of a chargeable asset*.

A 'taxable person' for CGT purposes is anyone who is resident or ordinarily resident in the UK (including the personal representatives of a deceased person).

A 'disposal' is not exhaustively defined in the Act but includes a sale, gift or part disposal.

A definition of 'assets' for capital gains tax purposes is contained in s. 21(1) TCGA 1992, which widely defines it as including 'all forms of property . . . '.

Only 'chargeable' assets can give rise to a liability to the tax but virtually all 'assets' are chargeable assets subject to a few exceptions (such as motor cars and sterling).

18.2.3   The basic calculation

For the tax to become payable, the disposal of chargeable assets has to give rise to a gain, which will occur if the 'consideration for disposal' exceeds the 'allowable expenditure' permitted by the Act. The 'consideration for disposal' equates to the sale price of the asset. 'Allowable expenditure' consists of:

(a) the initial expenditure (that is, the original purchase price or market value if the asset was acquired by way of gift) plus incidental costs incurred in acquiring the asset;

(b) subsequent expenditure (such as money spent on enhancing the value of the asset); and

(c) incidental costs of disposal.

EXAMPLE

Natalie bought a 15% shareholding in Transit Commercial Vehicle Hire Limited five years ago for £75,000. Legal fees incurred in negotiating the purchase amounted to £3,000.

Natalie has recently sold her entire shareholding for £135,000. Legal fees incurred in negotiating the sale amounted to £5,000.

At its simplest, therefore, Natalie's capital gain is:

Consideration for disposal	£135,000
Less allowable expenditure, being:	
Initial expenditure:	
Purchase price	£75,000
Legal fees	£3,000
Deduct subsequent expenditure:	
N/a	
Deduct incidental costs of disposal:	
Legal fees	£5,000
Capital Gain	£52,000

(Note: the calculation of tax on this gain is shown in the example at 18.2.8.)

Where a disposal is other than at arm's length, i.e., where there is a gift element to the disposal, the market value of the asset at the time of disposal is treated as the consideration received. Any transfer between connected persons is always deemed to be otherwise than at arm's length, resulting in this rule applying. Connected persons are defined by s. 286 TCGA 1992. The basic categories are:

(a) a spouse, direct relatives, and relatives of the spouse of the disponer;

(b) companies under common control;

(c) partners in a business and spouses of partners;

(d) trustees and settlors (and any persons connected with the settlor).

This rule is of particular relevance to sales at an undervalue. Such a sale can be an arm's length, commercial transaction, in which case the actual price paid will be the relevant consideration for CGT purposes. However, any such undervalue transaction between connected persons will result in the market value of the asset being substituted.

EXAMPLE

Jo is selling a plot of land to Sheila. The land is worth £120,000, but Jo needs to raise money quickly and Sheila is currently the only interested party. As such, Jo sells the land for £100,000.

If Jo and Sheila are not connected persons, Jo will be treated as receiving £100,000 for CGT purposes.

If Jo and Sheila are connected persons, Jo will be treated as receiving £120,000 for CGT purposes.

18.2.4 Part disposals

Special rules apply in relation to the allowable deductions if there was a partial disposal of the asset. The effect of these rules is to permit the taxpayer to deduct only a proportion of the 'allowable expenditure'. This proportion is equal to the proportion which the part of the asset disposed of bears to the whole asset.

EXAMPLE

X sells part of a piece of land for £50,000. Total allowable expenditure on the whole plot of land amounts to £30,000. If the remaining land is worth £100,000, X can use a percentage of the allowable expenditure calculated as follows:

£50,000 ÷ (£50,000 + £100,000) = 0.33

0.33 × £30,000 = £10,000 allowable expenditure available.

18.2.5 Creation of losses by allowable expenditure

It may be that the 'allowable expenditure' in respect of a particular asset exceeds the sale price or market value. In those circumstances, the loss arising can be set off against other gains made during the current tax year. The gains in the current year must be reduced to nil. Only the balance of the loss once all other gains have been completely wiped out can be carried forward. Such losses can be carried forward indefinitely until gains arise in future years (although a carried forward loss must be set off against future gains as they arise). In contrast to the position for the year in which the loss initially arises, carried forward losses need only be set against the gains of future years to the extent necessary to bring that year's gains down to the amount of the then current annual exemption (see **18.2.6** below).

EXAMPLE

Alan disposed of an asset in 2008/09 for £60,000. The allowable expenditure for that asset was £75,000. Alan was therefore left with a loss of £15,000 and no CGT is payable.

In 2009/10, Alan disposes of another asset, this time for £50,000. The allowable expenditure for that asset was £30,000. Alan therefore made a gain of £20,000.

Alan can now set off his loss of £15,000 against his gain of £20,000. He will set off £9,900 of this loss against the gain. This reduces the gain to £10,100, which is the CGT annual exemption figure for 2009/10. The result will be that (assuming no other disposals take place in 2009/10) Alan will pay no CGT in 2009/10.

Alan still has £5,100 of CGT losses which he can carry forward indefinitely to be set off against future gains as they arise.

18.2.6 Annual exemption

Aside from the deductions and reliefs mentioned already, every individual has an annual exemption from capital gains tax. For the current tax year of 2009/10, the first £10,100 of capital gains is exempt from liability to tax (s. 3 TCGA 1992).

18.2.7 Rate of tax

For the tax year 2009/10, a flat rate of 18% will be applied to capital gains made by individuals. (See **Chapter 19** for companies.)

18.2.8 The CGT calculation

The following is an example of a simple CGT calculation, continuing the example given at **18.2.3**.

EXAMPLE

Natalie bought a 15% shareholding in Transit Commercial Vehicle Hire Limited five years ago for £75,000. Legal fees incurred in negotiating the purchase amounted to £3,000. Natalie has recently sold her entire shareholding for £135,000. Legal fees incurred in negotiating the sale amounted to £5,000.

Capital Gain	£52,000
Deduct annual exemption	£52,000 – £10,100 = £41,900
Final CGT liability	18% of £41,900 = £7,542

18.2.9 Exemptions for specific assets

The TCGA 1992 contains a variety of exemptions for specific assets, the details of most of which are beyond the scope of this book. They include exemption for:

(a) the taxpayer's only or main residence (s. 222 TCGA 1992);

(b) tangible movable chattels having a predictable useful life not exceeding 50 years, e.g., cars and items of plant and machinery (wasting assets) (s. 45 TCGA 1992); and

(c) non-wasting chattels where the consideration for disposal does not exceed £6,000, e.g., paintings and antiques (s. 262 TCGA 1992).

In the case of wasting assets, the effect is normally that the taxpayer cannot claim any allowable loss, as most such assets rarely appreciate in value. In the case of non-wasting chattels, the rule operates as a *de minimis* threshold—HMRC is simply not concerned with the small gains which may ensue from such disposals.

18.2.10 Deferment of tax

It is possible, in certain circumstances, to postpone or defer the payment of tax, as follows:

(a) If the disposal is by way of a gift, or there is a sale at an undervalue, the donor and donee can elect to 'hold over' any gain arising. This will result in the donee being treated as acquiring the asset at the donor's acquisition value (see **18.2.11**).

(b) In certain circumstances, where the owner of certain types of assets sells them (even at full value), he can elect to 'roll over' the gain arising into replacement assets. The effect will be to reduce the acquisition cost of the new assets by the amount of the 'rolled over' gain (see **18.2.12**).

(c) Gains realised on the disposal of any asset may be deferred into an investment in shares in a private limited company (see **18.2.13**).

Each of these will now be looked at in more detail.

18.2.11 Hold-over relief

Hold-over relief is available in circumstances including:

(a) transfers between spouses (s. 58 TCGA 1992);

(b) gifts or sales at undervalue of business assets (s. 165 TCGA 1992), in which case a joint election can be made by the transferor and transferee and any gain arising will be held over (for these purposes, business assets are those used for the purposes of a trade, profession or vocation carried on by the transferor or his personal company and also include shares in an unquoted company or in the transferor's personal company; 'personal company' means that the donor holds at least 5% of the voting rights).

It should be noted that a claim for hold-over relief will mean that the whole gain in question must be held over and cannot be reduced by the donor's annual exemption.

EXAMPLE

A gifts an asset to C when the asset is worth £20,000. A's base cost for the asset is £8,000. Ignoring any other allowable expenditure, the gain on the disposal is £12,000. If A and C elect to hold-over the gain, C takes over the asset with a base cost of £8,000.

A sale at an undervalue produces different results in that the whole of the actual chargeable gain cannot be held over and is, instead, reduced by the amount actually received by the seller in excess of the base cost of the asset sold.

EXAMPLE

S bought an asset for £10,000. S sells this asset to T for £20,000 when it is worth £25,000. S is deemed to receive £25,000, and so, the whole chargeable gain is £15,000.

If S and T elect to hold over, the chargeable gain must be reduced by the amount received by S in excess of the base cost, i.e., £15,000 is reduced by £10,000, which leaves £5,000, the amount of gain which can be held over. Thus, T will take the asset with a base cost of £20,000 (the market value of £25,000 less the £5,000 held over gain). S will be taxed on £10,000 worth of the gain.

18.2.12 Roll-over relief

There are two main types of roll-over relief:

(a) roll-over on the replacement of certain business assets, pursuant to s. 152 TCGA 1992; and

(b) roll-over of any gain from the disposal of any asset into a qualifying investment in shares.

Details of (b) are given at **18.2.13**. Point (a) is explained below. The conditions which must be fulfilled to benefit from replacement asset roll-over relief are:

(a) The original and the replacement asset must both fall within limited categories. The most common are land, buildings and plant and machinery. Both the original and the replacement asset must be used as business assets throughout their periods of ownership.

(b) The purchase of the replacement asset must take place within the 12-month period before, or the 3-year period after, the disposal of the original asset.

(c) To roll-over the whole gain realised on the original asset, the full proceeds of sale must be used to purchase the replacement asset. If a lesser sum is used, an amount equivalent to that by which the proceeds of sale of the original asset exceed the cost of the replacement asset will become chargeable to tax immediately. This may result in the whole gain becoming chargeable, even though the relief is theoretically available.

It is important to note that this relief is available both to individuals and companies disposing of business assets.

EXAMPLE

Ovid Limited is considering selling its trading premises and buying new ones. The proceeds from the sale are likely to be £155,000. It is considering three potential sites; one at £175,000 (Premises A); one at £145,000 (Premises B); and one at £130,000 (Premises C).

Assuming the gain on any sale of the original premises would be £20,000, the following would result:

Premises A—Total gain rolled over, as whole of proceeds of sale used; base cost of new premises for future CGT calculations = £155,000(£175,000 – £20,000).

Premises B—Percentage of gain rolled over (£10,000); base cost of new premises for future CGT calculations = £135,000(£145,000 – £10,000). Tax payable on £10,000 of gain.

Premises C—No amount of gain rolled over—difference in value between original and replacement asset is greater than amount of gain; base cost of new premises for future CGT calculations = £130,000.

18.2.13 EIS deferral of chargeable gains

As well as being a method of filling the public coffers, the taxation system can also be used to 'engineer' certain types of behaviour. Over the past few years, efforts have been made to encourage high net worth individuals to invest in growing private companies, by affording such investment preferable tax treatment. Up until the March 1998 Budget, there existed two schemes: the Enterprise Investment Scheme and Reinvestment Relief. Very simply, the former resulted in income tax relief for investors on the amount invested and also capital gains tax relief for any gains realised on their investment after five years of ownership of the same. The latter was another system of capital gains deferral, with the gain from any disposal being deferred into an investment of appropriate shares, such gain only being realised on a subsequent disposal of those shares.

The Finance Act 1998 resulted in a merger of these systems. However, it should be noted that the overall effect was left very much the same, merely the detail altered. It is beyond the scope of this chapter to examine the intricacies of the scheme as it applies to income tax, so discussion will be limited to its impact as a capital gains tax deferral mechanism.

Any gain realised upon the disposal of any asset by an individual can benefit from the relief. However, to qualify the investment can only take a specified form; that is it must be:

(a) an allotment of fully-paid ordinary shares, with no rights of redemption or preference in whatever form for three years;

(b) in a company whose shares are unquoted;

(c) in a company which only carries on regular trading activities, e.g., is not an investment, property development, farming or forestry company or the like, mainly in the UK;

(d) which does not have a gross assets value of more than £7 million before nor £8 million after the investment (such value to include the value of assets owned by subsidiaries);

(e) and which is not controlled by another company and which does not have any subsidiaries other than ones which fulfil the requirements in (b) to (d) also.

In addition, the investment must take place at least 3 years before or 12 months after the original disposal.

Because this is a scheme to encourage start-up/development capital for companies, any attempt to use the system solely to achieve a tax benefit or failure to use the funds realised in the trading activities of the company will result in the relief being withdrawn, resulting in an immediate liability to tax on the gain deferred. Also, for the same reason, it is not possible to sell shares in a company and then re-invest in that same company.

The investor will not be liable for tax on the original disposal until such time as the shares are sold. However, should the investor cease to be UK resident before the period of five years has elapsed from the date of investment, the relief will be withdrawn.

It is not necessary to invest all of the proceeds of the original disposal to claim the deferral, an investment of an amount equivalent to the gain will be sufficient to defer the full value of it. Once the shares are sold any increase in their actual value will be subject to capital gains tax. (Although note the commentary after the following example.)

EXAMPLE

Sumiya disposes of an asset in January 2003 and realises a gain ('the original gain') of £40,000. She bought the asset in September 1998. In June 2002 she invests in EIS-qualifying shares worth £85,000. These shares are sold in May 2008, realising a gain of £35,000. Issues to note are:

(a) The deferral takes place within three years of the original gain, so is within the time limits.

(b) The amount of the EIS investment exceeds the original gain, so the full amount of this gain is deferred.

(c) The sale in 2008 results in the original gain being taxed.

(d) The sale in 2008 also results in the gain of £35,000 being taxed.

It is important to note a qualification to the above. As was stated at the outset, the other facet of the EIS system results in income tax relief and a capital gains-free investment. There is no reason why any investment under the deferral arrangements may not also result in these benefits for the taxpayer. Note, however, that such benefits are limited to the first £400,000 of shares acquired and that the conditions which must be fulfilled to achieve these benefits are quite strict, most notably that the shares must be owned for at least three years from subscription and that for a period of two years before subscription and five after the investor must not have been connected with the company in question. Therefore, in the above example, the taxpayer would qualify for capital gains exemption on the sale of the shares because she owned them for just under four years.

Finally, it is possible to make an EIS investment and on the realisation of this make a further EIS investment and defer the gain. In this case, on a disposal of the second investment, taper relief can be claimed for the cumulative period of ownership of EIS shares.

It is possible to combine the deferred EIS relief with entrepreneurs' relief (see **18.2.14** below).

18.2.14   Relief on Disposal of a Business (Entrepreneurs' Relief)

18.2.14.1   Introduction

This relief came into effect from 6 April 2008 and is aimed at providing relief from capital gains tax to qualifying individuals who dispose of all or part of a trading business, assets used in such a business or of shares in a trading company.

18.2.14.2   Availability of relief

The relief is available in respect of gains made on the disposal of:

(a) all or part of a business carried on by an individual, alone or in partnership (including professions and vocations but not property letting businesses, save for furnished holiday lettings); or

(b) assets following the cessation of a business, which assets were formerly used in that business and are disposed of within three years of cessation; or

(c) shares in a trading company (or a holding company of a trading group) where the individual disposing of the shares has been an officer or employee of that company (or a company in the same group) and owns 5% or more of its ordinary share capital which enables the exercise of at least 5% of the voting rights in that company.

An individual will be able to make claims for relief on more than one occasion, up to a lifetime total of £1 million of gains qualifying for relief.

18.2.14.3 Effect of relief

The effect of the relief is to reduce to 10% the effective rate of CGT on the first £1 million of gains that qualify for relief. This is achieved by reducing the qualifying capital gains by 4/9ths. The qualifying capital gains are the aggregate of gains and losses relating to relevant assets.

EXAMPLES

(Note: the annual exemption has not been included in the following examples, in order to simplify them.)

Sarah sells her trading business and realises gains of £450,000. She has as yet made no other claims for entrepreneurs' relief. On claiming the relief the gains of £450,000 are reduced by 4/9ths (£200,000), leaving £250,000 liable to CGT. This amount is taxed at the individuals' CGT rate of 18%, which means a liability of £45,000. This is the equivalent of an effective 10% tax rate on the £450,000 of gains. Sarah still has the potential to claim the relief against up to £550,000 of qualifying gains at some point in the future.

Gordon sells shares which qualify for entrepreneurs' relief for £1.2 million. He has as yet made no other claims for entrepreneurs' relief. He claims relief up to the maximum £1 million allowed. Thus, £1 million of gains are reduced by 4/9ths (£444,444), leaving £555,556 *plus* the £200,000 (the gains above the relief limit) to be taxed at the individuals' CGT rate of 18%. This creates a liability of £136,000. This is the equivalent of an effective 10% tax rate on the first £1 million (£100,000) plus the standard 18% on the remaining £200,000 (£36,000).

18.2.14.4 'Associated disposal' of business assets

Where an individual qualifies for entrepreneurs' relief on a disposal of shares or securities, relief is also available for any 'associated disposal' of an asset which was used in the company's (or group's) business. For example, if a company director who owns the premises from which the company carries on its business sells the premises at the same time as he sells his shares in the company, the sale of the premises may count as an 'associated disposal' and qualify for entrepreneurs' relief. The relief on an associated disposal is restricted where the asset in question was not wholly in business use throughout the period it was owned.

A similar rule allows relief on an 'associated disposal' by a member of a partnership who is entitled to relief on disposal of his interest in the assets of the partnership. Again, relief is restricted where the asset in question was not wholly in business use throughout the period of ownership.

18.2.15 Death of taxpayer

No capital gains tax is payable when a person dies. The personal representatives of the deceased under the will or intestacy are deemed to acquire the deceased's assets at market value at the time of death. As such, there is neither a gain nor loss. Moreover, all legatees of the estate are deemed to acquire any assets at the base cost of the personal representatives. However, should an asset appreciate in value whilst in the hands of the personal representatives and be disposed of by them to third parties (as opposed to being distributed to legatees), this will result in a gain in the hands of the personal representatives.

18.3 CGT in the business context

Liability to capital gains tax can arise in a variety of situations. The purpose of the following sections **18.4** to **18.7** is to look at the common business scenarios where such liability is likely to arise and to consider the applicability of reliefs and exemptions in such situations.

18.4 Disposals of partnership property

18.4.1 General

When a firm disposes of one of its assets, normal CGT principles apply in determining what gain, if any, the firm has made. There are difficulties involved in applying the normal CGT principles to a partnership context. The premise on which HMRC operates is for each partner to be treated as owning a fractional share of each of the chargeable assets of the partnership (including goodwill) and not, for this purpose, as owning an interest in the business as a whole. When the firm disposes of an asset to an outsider, each partner is treated as making a disposal of his fractional share in the asset.

What follows is concerned with the disposal by a firm of its assets. CGT issues can also arise when partners leave and join partnerships. These are discussed in **Chapter 23**.

18.4.2 Assessment

The assessment and collection of CGT is treated differently from the assessment and collection of income tax. The precedent partner delivers a return to HMRC giving full details of disposals. The assessment is made on the individual partners. Each partner's share in the gain is calculated in accordance with his share in the asset disposed of.

In order to calculate the CGT liability of the individual partners in relation to the disposal of assets it is, therefore, necessary to know the proportions in which assets are owned. This is often referred to as the partners' 'assets surplus ratio'.

18.4.3 Asset surplus ratio

The partnership deed may specify the proportions in which asset surpluses are to be shared. If it does, it is conclusive. If there is no express provision in the partnership deed, the asset surplus sharing ratio is deemed to be the ratio in which profits are shared. It is common for a partnership deed to provide an asset surplus sharing ratio which is different from the profit sharing ratio. For example, the agreement may provide for an individual partner's right to share in an asset surplus to be greater than his right to share in income profits, to reflect the fact that he has made a substantial capital contribution to the firm while contributing comparatively little to earning income profits.

When an asset is acquired by a partnership, each partner's share in the acquisition value is determined by his share in the asset surplus *at that time*. Similarly, in a disposal, each partner's share in the proceeds of disposal is determined by his share in the asset surpluses *at that time*.

EXAMPLE

A and B are in partnership. They share profits equally and have made no special agreement as to sharing asset surpluses. They acquire an asset for £20,000. The acquisition value for each partner is:

A	½	£10,000
B	½	£10,000

They sell the assets for £36,000. The share in the proceeds of the disposal of each partner is:

A	½	£18,000
B	½	£18,000

The chargeable gain of each partner is:

A	£18,000 – £10,000 = £8,000
B	£18,000 – £10,000 = £8,000

Each partner is personally liable for his own chargeable gain and will be assessed for tax at the rates appropriate to his level of income.

18.4.4 Reliefs

If there is a gain realised on the disposal, the exemptions and reliefs already referred to may be available. To the extent that there is a gift element in a disposal, hold-over relief is available to postpone the payment of tax.

A disposal of partnership property in circumstances where the partners intend to re-invest the sale proceeds can attract roll-over relief (under ss. 152–160 TCGA 1992).

18.5 Disposals of shares

18.5.1 Disposals by individuals

A capital profit on the sale of shares by an individual will in most cases attract a liability to capital gains tax and the general principles and reliefs already referred to will apply, with the exception of roll-over (replacement asset) relief under s. 152 TCGA. However, there is a notable exception to this rule when the purchaser of the shares is the company in which the shares were issued. This is dealt with at **18.7**.

18.5.2 Disposals by companies

A disposal by a company of shares it owns in another company will be subject to capital gains. However, the following should be noted:

(a) Companies can claim indexation allowance for the full period of ownership (see **Chapter 19**).

(b) Any capital gain realised by a company will form part of its profits for corporation tax purposes (see **Chapter 19**).

(c) Should the disposal be of a 'substantial shareholding', no charge to tax will arise. A company will be treated as disposing of a substantial shareholding if such shareholding comprises at least 10% of the ordinary share capital and both the selling company and the company in which it owns shares are trading companies and have been for a two-year period prior to disposal. In addition, the shareholding in question must have been owned for a period of at least 12 months in the two-year period prior to the sale.

18.6 Disposals of business assets owned by an investor

18.6.1 Reliefs

It is not uncommon for shareholder/directors or partners to own assets which are used by their respective companies or partnerships. The disposal of such assets may result in a CGT liability for the person concerned.

However, many of the reliefs mentioned above will be available: roll-over (replacement asset) relief; hold-over relief; and entrepreneurs' relief.

18.6.2 Wasting assets

Should the asset have a predictable, useful life of less than 50 years, it will be CGT-exempt in any event. Many such assets do not appreciate in value and are more likely to be sold at a loss, however, so this exemption will then work against the taxpayer, as no allowable loss will be created.

18.7 The purchase by a company of its own shares

18.7.1 The income tax treatment

Where a company redeems or buys its own shares, tax will usually become payable. The amount received from the company is in most cases treated as a dividend (and so is subject to income tax in the hands of the recipient) to the extent that it exceeds the original investment in the company. The return of the original cost of the shares is a capital sum.

EXAMPLE

Purchase Ltd buys back shares from A for £9,000. A originally subscribed for his shares at a nominal value of £1,000. Purchase Ltd is treated as making a dividend of £8,000. A receives the return of his investment of £1,000 at the same price as he paid for it, so there are no capital gains tax consequences (ignoring any items of actual allowable expenditure, etc.). A also receives a dividend of £8,000 which has borne basic rate income tax at source. The consequences of this are as follows:

(a) if the dividend falls to be taxed entirely at basic rate income tax, A need pay no further tax;

(b) if some or all of the dividend falls to be taxed at higher rate income tax, A must account for the balance of the tax due;

(c) if some of the dividend is exempted from tax by falling within A's personal allowance, A will be unable to claim back any of the tax already deducted;

(d) if A has tax-exempt status, for example, as a charity or pension fund, again, as in (c), A will be unable to claim back any tax.

Payments to buy back members' shares are not deductible in calculating the company's profits for corporation tax purposes.

18.7.2 The capital gains tax treatment

Section 219 Income and Corporation Taxes Act 1988 contains provisions excluding such a payment from the definition of a distribution in certain circumstances. Where the payment is so excluded, capital gains tax will be payable on any increase in the value of the shares during the period of ownership (the redemption or repayment is treated as a disposal for CGT purposes as if it were a sale).

A redemption, repayment or purchase by the company is excluded from the definition of a distribution if the company is a trading company and the transaction is made 'wholly or mainly for the purposes of benefiting a trade carried on by the company'. Presumably, the transaction will be made for such a purpose if the object of it was to enable a shareholder of the company who disagreed with the policy of the directors to retire from the business if the company had more capital than it required. A transaction designed to enable the proprietors to take an income tax-free profit would not be covered, and this is reinforced by the further requirement that the main purpose or one of the main purposes of the scheme must not be 'to enable the owner of the shares to participate in the profits of the company without receiving a dividend or the avoidance of tax'. A redemption, repayment or purchase is also excluded from the definition of a distribution if the proceeds are intended to be used (and are used within two years) for the payment of inheritance tax (IHT). The IHT must have arisen on a death and the shareholder must show that undue hardship would have arisen if the shares had not been purchased by the company.

In addition to the basic requirements of s. 219, income tax is only avoided if the following conditions are satisfied:

(a) that the owner of the shares is resident and ordinarily resident in the UK at the time of the purchase;

(b) that he has owned the shares for five years;

(c) that the sale is of a substantial part of his shareholding taking into account any holding of his associates (which terms include close relatives, partners and trustees of certain settlements); and

(d) certain special conditions apply only in the case of groups of companies.

The object of these rules is to ensure that tax avoidance or tax advantages cannot be obtained by a purchase of its own shares by a company, but that 'genuine' transactions should give rise to CGT liability only. It is possible to apply for advance clearance when a scheme to buy back shares is proposed which, if granted, will ensure that putting the proposal into effect will not give rise to an income tax charge.

EXAMPLE

Suppose in the above example the receipt by A fell within s. 219. A would receive a capital sum of £9,000, from which the base cost of his shares could be deducted (ignoring any indexation allowance), resulting in a capital gain of £8,000.

A taxpayer will wish a buy-back to fall within s. 219 if the effect of CGT is a lower income tax charge to tax than would result under rules. There may be, for example, capital losses which could be set off against the gain; or a capital gain may be a lesser amount than an income gain; or the shareholder could claim a valuable relief. Also, whilst most taxpayers will have other income sufficient to use up their personal allowance, if no other chargeable gains are incurred in the tax year in question, the full annual exemption will be available.

EXAMPLE

Five years ago Rehana was allotted 10,000 shares at par in Surface Solutions Limited. The nominal value of each share was £5. Surface Solutions is to buy back 2,000 of Rehana's shares at £15 per share for a total consideration of £30,000. Rehana earns a salary of £42,000.

Income tax position

Capital sum returned	£10,000
Net income received	£20,000
(plus tax credit of £2,222)	
Gross income received	£22,222

Rehana is a higher rate taxpayer, therefore, gross income receipt taxed at 32.5%, less the tax credit, gives an income tax liability of £5,000.

Section 219 alternative

Capital sum received	£30,000
Less:	
Base cost	£10,000
Chargeable gain	£20,000
Less:	
Annual exemption	£9,600

This would leave Rehana liable to pay CGT at 18% on £11,400, giving a CGT liability of £2,052.

18.8 Inheritance tax

18.8.1 General

Inheritance tax (IHT) is payable under the provisions of the Inheritance Tax Act (IHTA) 1984 where there is a *chargeable transfer*. The chargeable transfer is defined as 'any *transfer of value* which is made to an individual but is not . . . an exempt transfer'. A transfer of value is defined as 'a *disposition* made by a person . . . as a result of which the value of his estate immediately after the transfer is less than it would be but for the disposition . . . '. Inheritance tax is payable on the *value transferred* which is the amount by which the value of the transferor's estate is reduced as a result of the disposition.

Transfers of value can be made either *inter vivos* as a result of gifts or sales with a gift element or on death. In this section, we only give an outline of the principal aspects of the tax. The reader is referred to one of the standard tax textbooks for full details of all of the aspects of the tax.

As *inter vivos* gifts and sales at an undervalue can also attract CGT (see **18.2.3**), it is important to consider both capital taxes in such a context. This will be unnecessary on the death of a taxpayer, as only inheritance tax will be payable.

18.8.2 Types of transfer

There are three types of transfer which can give rise to inheritance tax (subject to the availability of any exemptions or reliefs). These are:

(a) a transfer on death which will attract tax at the full rate of 40%;

(b) a potentially exempt transfer (PET) which is an *inter vivos* transfer of value made by an individual as a result of which property becomes part of the estate of another individual or is transferred to certain types of trust. (As such, transfers to companies do not qualify as potentially exempt.) A PET will become fully exempt if the transferor lives for seven years after the transfer. Death within those seven years will result in the transfer becoming chargeable at the rates of tax in force at the date of death. Most likely examples are gifts of cash, real property or shares; and

(c) a chargeable transfer made before death which is immediately taxable but at only half the rates which apply on death; that is, 20%. The death of the transferor within seven years will lead to the transferee becoming liable to tax at the full rates in force at the date of death. There are very few instances of such chargeable transfers, the most likely being the transfer of property into a discretionary trust.

18.8.3 Cumulation

There are only the above two rates of inheritance tax. There is a nil rate band, for 2009/10, of £325,000 and any excess is taxed at the rate of 20% or 40%, depending on the type of transfer—see **18.8.2** above. (The nil-rate band normally increases each tax year—it is estimated that 2% of estates left on death in 2009–10 will be liable for inheritance tax.) However, no transfer can be looked at in isolation. Whether or not the nil-rate band has been used up in relation to a particular chargeable transfer will depend on the total value of all previous chargeable transfers which the transferor has made within the immediately preceding seven years (this includes lifetime chargeable transfers and PETs, which become chargeable, because of death). This process of cumulation will mean that the tax on the present transfer will be calculated as if it were the top slice of a single transfer equal in value to all of the transfers (including the one in question) made during the last seven years.

In a great many instances, the issue of cumulation will not arise and only the total value of the taxpayer's estate will be subject to the nil-rate band. However, this will not be so where any transfers have been made out of the taxpayer's estate prior to death.

EXAMPLE

Example one
Keith dies in June 2009 and the value of his estate at the time of his death is £375,000. If he has made no transfers out of his estate at any relevant time the amount of £50,000 in excess of the nil-rate band will be taxed at 40%.

However, should Keith have made the following transfers, cumulation would have to be considered:

> March 1998—PET of £50,000
> June 2002—PET of £70,000
> February 2005—PET of £100,000

The PET in 1998 is more than seven years before Keith's death, so falls out of the picture. However, the other two PETs are both within seven years of his death, becoming chargeable to tax as a result. The cumulative total of the PETs is £170,000. As this total does not exceed the nil-rate band, no tax is payable on them. However, as Keith's death estate must be cumulated with the PETs, this means that only £155,000 of the nil-rate band will be available to set against his death estate. As such, £220,000 of his death estate will be taxed.

Example two
In real terms, the giving away of PETs is quite likely to reduce the value of the death estate. Therefore, the above rule may not be quite so harsh.

Assume that if Miranda had made no transfers during her lifetime, her estate would have been worth £700,000. On her death in May 2009, £375,000 of her estate would have been chargeable to tax.

If, instead, she had made the following transfers:

> January 2003—PET of £50,000
> August 2004—PET of £200,000

the value of her estate at death could be assumed to be reduced to £450,000.

Therefore, whilst the two PETs become chargeable, thus using up some of Miranda's nil-rate band, her death estate is correspondingly reduced. (Moreover, PETs attract an annual exemption, which may mean a small amount of the estate is free from IHT totally—see 18.8.5.)

Example three
Lifetime chargeable transfers complicate matters. As they are taxable at the time they are made, they must be cumulated with any other chargeable transfers in the previous seven years and then have the nil-rate band applied to them.

Raj, who is still living, has so far made the following transfers:

> March 2004—PET of £150,000
> June 2006—LCT of £183,000
> February 2008—PET of £100,000

His current IHT position is that neither of the PETs attracts any tax. The LCT should be cumulated with any chargeable transfers in the previous seven years (there are none) and have the nil-rate band applied to it. Any excess over the nil-rate band should be taxed at 20%. At this stage, therefore, the LCT bears no tax.

If Raj dies in January 2009, all his lifetime transfers must be re-examined. The effect will be as follows:

(a) The March 2004 PET becomes chargeable and becomes subject to the nil-rate band. Accordingly it will bear no tax.

(b) The LCT must now be cumulated with the March 2004 PET, which means that the revised cumulative total becomes £333,000 and, therefore £8,000 worth of the LCT is now subject to tax at 40%.

(c) The February 2008 PET becomes chargeable and must be cumulated with all chargeable transfers in the previous seven years. The cumulative total at this stage is now £433,000 and all this PET is taxed at 40% as the whole of the nil-rate band is used up.

(d) Raj's death estate must be cumulated with all chargeable transfers in the previous seven years; that is, all the previous three (now) chargeable transfers. As a consequence, the whole of the death estate will also be taxed at 40%.

What should be noted from this example is that it is incorrect to think of a taxpayer only having one cumulative total. Depending on the taxpayer's circumstances, a number of cumulative totals may have to be considered and re-considered as part of the taxpayer's changing IHT profile.

The full rate of 40% only applies where the transfer is made on death or within three years of death. If the transfer is a potentially exempt transfer or a chargeable transfer, which occurs within four to seven years of the death of a taxpayer, a sliding scale applies to determine the value of the transfer which will be subject to tax at the full rates in force at the time of death. This relief operates on the basis of a reduction in the amount of tax which would normally be payable at the full rate as follows:

(a) transfers six to seven years before death—20% of the tax payable;

(b) transfers five to six years before death—40% of the tax payable;

(c) transfers four to five years before death—60% of the tax payable;

(d) transfers three to four years before death—80% of the tax payable.

EXAMPLE

Talbot made a PET of £400,000 five-and-a-half years before he died. He made no other transfers during his lifetime. On his death, the nil-rate band would be applied to the PET and the balance of £75,000 would have to be taxed at 40%. The full tax charge is therefore £30,000. However, only 40% of this is payable as the PET occurred between five and six years before death. The actual liability will be £12,000.

18.8.4 Value transferred

The value of the property transferred plays an important part in the calculation of the liability to inheritance tax. For the purposes of inheritance tax, the value of particular items which have been given away will be the price which the property might reasonably be expected to fetch if it was to be sold in the open market at the time of the gift. However, there is no presumption that the value of the property will be reduced because it was all placed on the market at the same time. The latter reference will be of particular relevance when valuing a large holding of shares in a private company. In addition, there are certain special valuation rules which apply to shares. Quoted stocks and shares are usually valued by taking the lower of the two prices quoted in the Stock Exchange

Daily Official List for the relevant day and adding to it one-quarter of the difference between the lower and the higher quoted prices or, if it produces a lower figure, by taking a figure halfway between the lowest and highest prices at which bargains were struck on the relevant day. The value of unquoted shares will be determined by the normal market value rule but it is sometimes extremely difficult to value such shares accurately. The facts that have to be taken into account include the company's profitability, its dividend record, the level of retained earnings and the value of the assets which the company owns. Should the shares be sold subject to pre-emption rights, the market value will be determined on the assumption that the pre-emption rights did not apply to the hypothetical sale. However, those rights will be assumed to apply to the hypothetical purchaser (which will mean that the value so determined would be the one which a purchaser was likely to pay in the full knowledge that the pre-emption rights will apply to their shares in the future).

Although not exclusively applicable to shares, a further rule which is of particular relevance when valuing shareholdings is the rule relating to 'related property'. This rule recognises the fact that some assets can be more valuable when combined with other assets of the same type than when they are owned individually. Shares which form part of a majority holding in a company will, for example, be more valuable than shares which form part of a minority shareholding. The IHTA 1984 defines a variety of items of property as being related property. This can include any item of property owned by the transferor's spouse at the time of the transfer. If the transfer is made of related property, the property actually transferred and the property to which it is related are valued as a single asset and tax is then calculated on the proportion of the total value which is transferred.

(This textbook does not cover any of the other detailed rules on the calculation of tax, such as the rules relating to gifts with a reservation or changes in values of gifts within seven years of death.)

18.8.5 Exemptions

At the start of this section, we stated that a chargeable transfer was any transfer of value which is not an *exempt* transfer. An exempt transfer will not attract tax and it will not be included in the transferor's cumulative total. The exemptions which can be claimed include the spouse exemption which is available both during lifetime and on death (thus, all gifts, irrespective of value, between spouses are exempt from inheritance tax provided the recipient spouse is domiciled in the UK). An annual exemption of £3,000 per year is available on transfers made before death. If the annual exemption for any year is not used either wholly or partially, the unused part can be carried over for one year but no longer. In addition, small gifts to individuals up to £250 per recipient are exempt.

EXAMPLE

Consider again Keith's estate in the example at 18.8.3. Applying the annual exemption to each PET which becomes chargeable to tax, it will be seen that £6,000 can be deducted from each one, being the annual exemption for the year in question together with the unused exemption from the previous year.

June 2002—PET of £70,000 – £6,000 = £64,000

February 2005—PET of £100,000 – £6,000 = £94,000

As such, the cumulative total of the chargeable PETs at the time of Keith's death is reduced to £158,000, freeing up an extra £12,000 of the nil-rate band to apply against his death estate.

18.8.6 Business property relief

18.8.6.1 General

In addition to the exemptions, the IHTA 1984 also makes various reliefs available which include quick succession relief, agricultural property relief and business property relief. The effect of a relief being available is to reduce the value of the relevant property with a resultant reduction in the amount of inheritance tax payable.

In this section we will look only at business property relief, which is available provided the property was 'relevant business property'. This term is defined as:

(a) property consisting of a business or an interest in a business (and so it includes the interest of a sole proprietor or a partner in a business);

(b) shareholdings in unquoted companies or companies quoted on the Alternative Investment Market;

(c) shareholdings in quoted companies which alone or with other shares owned by the transferor or with related property gave the transferor control immediately before the transfer (control means being able to exercise more than 50% of the votes in general meeting—temporary control will suffice);

(d) land or buildings, or machinery or plant used immediately before the transfer wholly or mainly for the purposes of a company controlled by the transferor or of a partnership of which he was a member;

(e) land or buildings, machinery or plant used immediately before the transfer for the purposes of a business carried on by the transferor and which was settled property in which the transferor had an interest in possession.

The relief on such a property is a reduction in the value transferred of 100% (in the case of property falling within (a)–(b) above) or 50% (in the case of property within (c)–(e) above).

18.8.6.2 'Business'

For the purposes of this relief, 'business' includes a profession or a vocation but does not include a business carried on otherwise than for gain. Agriculture is a type of business and so business property relief may be available to the extent that agricultural relief is not. If the business consists of dealing in securities, stocks, shares, land or buildings or of holding investments, the relief is not available. However, business property relief will be available where the business is the active management of land.

The reduction in value is given on the net value of the business property (that is to say, after the liabilities have been deducted).

Even if the property falls within the categories set out above, relief will not be available unless the transferor has owned the property throughout the two years before the transfer. If property replaces other relevant business property (other than in the case of minority shareholdings), relief is available provided the aggregate period of the ownership of the original and replacement property exceeds two years in the five years before the time of transfer. If the transferee of relevant business property himself makes a transfer of the same property before he has owned the property for two years, this will not prevent the relief being claimed provided the relief was available on the original transfer and one of the transfers was a transfer on death. If property is received on the death of a spouse, the surviving spouse can aggregate the deceased spouse's period of ownership with his own in order to satisfy the two-year period of ownership requirement.

18.8.6.3   Period of ownership

If a business (or other relevant business property) has been owned for two years (or more), business property relief at the appropriate percentage is available on the full value at the time of transfer. There is no obligation to show that particular assets of business have been owned for two years. Having said that, the value of an asset will be excluded from relief if it has not been used wholly or mainly for the purpose of the business throughout the two years preceding the transfer or throughout the period since it was acquired, if later.

18.8.6.4   Anti-avoidance

As a way of preventing taxpayers placing private assets in a business and then trying to obtain business property relief on them, s. 112 IHTA 1984 provides that relief is not available on 'excepted assets'. These are assets which are neither:

(a) used wholly or mainly for the purposes of the business concerned throughout the whole of the previous two years; nor

(b) required at the time of the transfer for future use.

These are alternative requirements. An asset which fulfils either one of the requirements will not be an excepted asset. However, (b) is not available where relief is claimed on an asset used by a company controlled by the transferor or by a partnership of which he is a member.

18.8.6.5   Potentially exempt transfers

Where a transfer is made before death (whether it is chargeable or potentially exempt) and the transferor dies within seven years, the relief is available only if the property originally given or qualifying property representing it has remained as relevant business property in the ownership of the transferee from the date of the transfer to the date of the death of the transferor. If the transferee dies before the transferor within the seven-year period, relief is only available on the death of the transferee if the same condition is satisfied. The property must remain relevant business property in the hands of the transferee. If only a proportion of the property originally given or qualifying property representing it remains in the ownership of the transferee at the date of death, relief is available on the proportion of the property owned at that date. It is sufficient if 'property representing' the original property is in the hands of the donee at the relevant date. It should, however, be noted that:

(a) the whole of the consideration must have been applied on acquiring the replacement property;

(b) replacement property must be acquired within three years after the disposal of the original property; and

(c) the provision applies only to the first replacement and not to subsequent ones.

It is not our intention to deal with the complex rules for determining who is liable to account for inheritance tax to the Inland Revenue on death, nor to consider the rules on the burden or incidence of inheritance tax.

18.8.7   Payment of IHT

Tax on a chargeable transfer made before death must be paid six months after the end of the month in which the transfer is made or, if the transfer is made after 5 April and before 1 October, at the end of April in the next year. Tax in relation to a death is payable six months after the end of the month in which the death occurred. If tax is paid late, interest will be charged.

Inheritance tax on certain types of property can be paid by 10 annual instalments. The instalment option is available in respect of:

(a) land of any description;

(b) shares or securities in a company giving the transferor control of the company immediately before death;

(c) unquoted shares or securities which do not give the transferor control (provided paying the tax in one lump sum will not cause any hardship);

(d) unquoted shares or securities not giving the transferor control in the company, provided at least 20% of the tax paid by the person paying the tax on the shares is either tax on those shares or on those shares and other instalment options;

(e) unquoted shares which did not give the transferor control and the value of which exceeds £20,000, provided they are at least 10% of all the shares of the company or are ordinary shares and at least 10% of the ordinary shares in the company; and

(f) business or interest in a business including a profession or vocation.

Shares quoted on the Alternative Investment Market are still 'unquoted' for these purposes. Control means voting control on all questions affecting the company. The relief is available whether the transfer is on death or *inter vivos* but, in the latter case, the relief is only available if the *transferee* pays the inheritance tax. The instalment option must be claimed by a written notice to the Revenue and the outstanding instalments must be paid off if the assets are sold within the 10-year period.

If the instalment option is available, the first instalment is generally due six months after the end of the month in which the gift has been made. No interest is charged on the tax provided the instalments are paid on time. Although the instalment option does not reduce the amount of tax, the relief is nonetheless beneficial.

The primary liability for IHT on lifetime chargeable transfers falls on the transferor. However, it is also possible for the transferee(s) to meet this liability. If the tax is paid by the transferor, the loss to the transferor will be the value of the gift plus any inheritance tax on it. This will mean that the inheritance tax calculation will be based on the gross loss to the donor. In those circumstances, it will be necessary to 'gross-up' the net gift before the calculation of the tax can be made. If the transferee(s) pay the IHT, no such considerations come into play. This will result in a smaller IHT bill.

The IHT liability arising on death will be met primarily by the personal representatives of the deceased out of the death estate. The liability of the personal representatives is limited to the amount they receive in their capacity as personal representatives.

18.8.8 Partnerships

The IHT legislation contains few provisions dealing specifically with partnerships. According to the general principle of IHT, any transfer of a partnership asset, or of an interest in a partnership, will be a transfer of value by the individual partners if the transfer is by way of gift or there is an element of gift in the disposition.

The transfer will be exempt if it is made between spouses. It will also be exempt if it was not intended to, and was not made in a transaction intended to, confer any gratuitous benefit and either it was an arm's length transaction between unconnected persons or was such as might be expected to be made between unconnected persons.

As a result of this provision, many *inter vivos* transfers which might appear to be transfers of value will escape inheritance tax. For example, when a new partner is admitted and is given a share in the assets without making a payment, there would be a transfer value were it not for this provision. This is considered in **Chapter 23**.

On death, a deceased partner's interest in the partnership will be part of his estate. The position is considered more fully in **Chapter 23** but business property relief (see **18.8.6**) will normally be available.

18.8.9 Shareholdings

The gift of shares may give rise to inheritance tax (and capital gains tax) since inheritance tax is chargeable on the 'loss to the donor's estate'. This normally means the market value of the asset given away, but in some cases the loss is considerably more than market value. For example, if a controlling shareholder gives away enough shares to lose control of the company, the loss to his estate will be very much more than the value of the shares given away.

The most important (but not only) 'reliefs' which will be relevant when shares in a company are given away are 'business property relief' and the instalment option (considered in **18.8.7**).

These reliefs exist because the government recognises that too high a tax burden on the disposal of shares in a company could lead to the break-up of a company as being the only way of raising funds to pay the tax. It should not be forgotten that the general exemptions (such as the spouse exemption and the annual exemption) will be available in respect of business property, as well as the business property relief.

Anybody in business, should consider the possible impact of tax on his family from a relatively young age. It should be clear from the rules described in this chapter that there is a very considerable fiscal advantage in disposing of assets *inter vivos* so as to take account of the fact that the IHT lifetime rates are lower than the death rates, and tax can be avoided altogether if the donor survives seven years after a potentially exempt transfer has been made. Since transfers of value are only cumulated for seven years after they are made (i.e., transfers made more than seven years ago are ignored in calculating the amount of tax), there is an advantage to be gained from making gifts of shares over a considerable period of time rather than all at once. The burden of IHT can also be reduced in the long run by making use of the spouse exemption to ensure that both husband and wife leave enough to take maximum advantage of the nil-rate band that they each have.

 online resource centre   Interactive online exercises (Student Learning Activities) which complement the topics covered in this chapter are available at www.oxfordtextbooks.co.uk/orc/business09_10/.

The corporation tax system

This chapter covers the following topics:

19.1 Introduction

This chapter deals with the corporation tax system, which determines the tax liability of companies. The tax liabilities of those who invest in companies (whether by way of shares or debentures) are considered in **Chapter 21**. The inheritance tax and capital gains tax liabilities of shareholders were considered in **Chapter 18**.

19.2 Calculation of profits—corporation tax

19.2.1 Profits in general

Companies pay corporation tax on their profits. 'Profits' means income profits and capital gains (s. 6(4)(a) ICTA 1988). It is this aggregate profit figure which is assessed to corporation tax. (For the purpose of the tax, unincorporated associations (such as members' clubs), other than partnerships, local authorities and local authority associations, are also taxed as companies (s. 832(1) ICTA 1988).)

Income profits are calculated according to income tax principles (see **Chapter 18**). A company's income receipts are those which fall within definitions in the schedules of the Income and Corporation Taxes Act (ICTA) 1988. (Note: income of sole traders and partnerships is dealt with under the Income Tax (Trading and Other Income) Act (ITTOIA) 2005.) The following are the schedules most likely to be of relevance to a company:

Schedule A	Rents
Schedule D Case I	Profits of a trade
Schedule D Case III	'Pure income' (interest, annuities and annual payments)
Schedule F	Dividends received from shareholdings in companies

Each schedule lays down rules for the deductibility of expenses in calculating income and for the allocation of receipts to a particular tax year. The rules for deduction of expenses which apply for income tax purposes also apply to corporation tax (s. 9 ICTA 1988). There are some exceptions to these rules, particularly in relation to dividends, losses and charges on income. Companies, unlike individuals, do not receive any personal allowances.

19.2.2   Charges on income

A charge on income is defined for corporation tax purposes as an annuity or other annual payment. A charge on income payable out of profits may be deducted from profits liable to corporation tax, provided that it was incurred for valuable and sufficient consideration. Charges should be distinguished from business expenses, which, since the Finance Act 1996, include interest on borrowings. Business expenses are deductible from receipts in calculating income profits rather than from overall taxable profits once calculated. A charge on income is deducted when paid, whereas a business expense is deducted when it accrues due.

19.2.3   Capital allowances

Companies are entitled to claim capital allowances at the same rates as individuals (see **Chapter 22**). Capital allowances of companies are treated as trading expenses of the accounting period in respect of which they are claimed and balancing charges are treated as trading receipts of that period.

19.2.4   Capital gains

Capital gains realised by companies are calculated according to general capital gains tax principles (see **Chapter 18**). However, there are certain key points to note:

- Companies are not entitled to the annual exemption.
- Most reliefs available to individuals are not available to companies, although companies can claim roll-over relief on the replacement of business assets.
- Companies do, however, receive an indexation allowance, which is *no longer* available to individuals and partnerships. (The removal of the allowance for these parties coincided with the reduction, introduced in the tax year 2008/09, of the capital gains tax rate for individuals and partnerships to 18%.)

19.2.5   Indexation allowance

When capital gains tax was originally introduced, no allowance was given for inflation. The result was that, in times of raging inflation, tax would be charged on 'gains' arising as a result of inflation, rather than as a result of a real increase in the asset's value. This unfairness was addressed by the introduction of an 'indexation allowance' which effectively removes inflationary gains from the charge to tax. The allowance is calculated by multiplying the initial and subsequent allowable expenditure by a decimal fraction produced by the following formula:

$$\frac{RD - RI}{RI}$$

where RD is the retail prices index for the month of disposal and RI is the retail prices index for the month in which the expenditure was incurred. (HMRC publishes tables containing the relevant retail price indices.) The resulting figure can then be deducted from the consideration for the disposal, together with any allowable expenditure, to reduce further the actual gain subject to tax.

For all disposals no capital gains tax is levied on gains arising in respect of periods of ownership prior to 31 March 1982. Effectively, companies are treated as having disposed of assets on 31 March 1982 and then immediately re-acquired them at their market value at that date.

19.2.6 'Double taxation'

Retaining appreciating assets in a company can lead to an element of double taxation since, on a sale of the asset, the company pays tax (subject to any relief for replacement assets). The company's gain after tax may be reflected in an increase in the overall value of the company's assets because of the receipt of money from the sale of the asset. This may then cause the value of the shares in the company to increase, which could, in turn, result in a greater gain being realised (subject to exemptions and reliefs) on a disposal of shares by a shareholder.

19.3 Assessment—corporation tax

19.3.1 Basis of assessment

Although income tax and capital gains tax rules are used to calculate the *amount* of profit, the basis of *assessment* for corporation tax is quite different from either of those taxes. For corporation tax purposes, tax is calculated by reference to profits (that is, the aggregate income and capital profits) made in each accounting period of the company (s. 12 ICTA 1988). An accounting period is normally 12 months ending with the company's accounting date: the date to which its accounts are made up. If the accounts are made up for a period of less than 12 months, then the accounting period is also less than 12 months; if for a longer period, special rules apply and the profits are divided on a time basis between two or more accounting periods, none of which may individually be longer than 12 months.

Corporation tax is currently payable nine months after the end of the accounting period so that the date chosen does not affect the length of time between the end of the period and the date of payment. However, large companies—those with annual profits of not less than £1.5 million—are obliged to account for corporation tax on an instalment basis. Such instalments are payable on the 7th and 10th months during the accounting period being assessed, and on the 13th and 16th months thereafter.

EXAMPLE

Wolfe Industrials plc has an accounting reference date of 31 December. In relation to its accounting year ending on 31 December 2008 its corporation tax payments will be payable in July and October 2008 and January and April 2009.

Companies must comply with a 'pay and file' system. This requires companies to estimate their profits and assess their own tax liability, then submit a return together with accounts to substantiate it. Companies have up to 12 months from the end of each of their accounting periods to submit this return but must always satisfy their tax liabilities on the dates set out above. Where under- or over-payments of tax are made, interest (at rates set by statutory instrument) will be payable.

19.3.2 Rates of tax

19.3.2.1 Rates for financial year 2009/10

The rates of corporation tax for the year 2009/10 as determined by companies' profits are set out in the table below. They are announced by the Chancellor of the Exchequer in the annual Budget and legislated annually in the Finance Act. Although companies pay tax on the profits of their own accounting periods, the rates of tax are fixed for financial years, periods starting on 1 April and ending on the following 31 March. Therefore, the financial year 2009 runs from 1 April 2009 to 31 March 2010.

Rate	Company profits (£)
Small companies rate: 21%	0–300,000
Marginal relief applies	300,001–1,500,000
Main rate: 28%	1,500,001 or more

The following paragraphs describe the way in which these rates operate.

19.3.2.2 Main rate

For the financial year 2009, for companies with profits in excess of £1,500,000, the main rate is 28%. This is applied to the entire amount of the profits. A company with profits of £2,000,000 will therefore, before any reliefs are applied, be liable to pay corporation tax of £560,000.

Unless the company happens to make up its accounts to 31 March the profits are apportioned (on a time basis) between two financial years if different rates apply.

EXAMPLE

A company makes up its accounts to 31 December. Its profits for the accounting period ending on 31 December 2008 are £1,600,000—the rate of corporation tax for the financial year 2007 (1 April 2007–31 March 2008) was 30% and for the financial year 2008 (1 April 2008–31 March 2009) the rate is 28%. Corporation tax for the accounting period will be:

£

$$\frac{90}{365} \times 1,600,000 \times 30\% = 118,356$$

$$\frac{275}{365} \times 1,600,000 \times 28\% = \underline{337,534}$$

$$\underline{455,890}$$

19.3.2.3 Small companies' rate

Where a company's taxable profits are between £0 and £300,000, the rate of corporation tax for the financial year 2009 is 21%. This small companies' rate is made under the provision of s. 13 ICTA 1988. As with the main rate, the rate is applied to the total amount of profits within the band. A company with profits of £200,000 would therefore be liable, before any reliefs were applied, for corporation tax of £42,000.

19.3.2.4 Marginal relief

For those companies with taxable profits between £300,000 and £1,500,000, marginal relief is available. The effect of this is to ease the transition between the small companies' and main rates.

The law provides that if taxable profits *including dividends* received fall within the band in which marginal relief applies, they should first be taxed at the main rate of 28%. The resulting liability is then reduced by marginal relief, as seen in the table below. (Should profits including dividends be £300,000 or less, or more than £1,500,000, then marginal relief is irrelevant and the normal rates apply.)

Profits including dividends (£)	Rate of tax
0–300,000	Small companies' rate: 21%
300,001–1,500,000	Main rate: 28% *then* reduced by marginal relief
More than 1,500,000	Main rate: 28%

19.3.2.5   Calculation of marginal relief

Statutory formula

To establish the amount of marginal relief by which tax liability is to be reduced, the following statutory formula must be applied:

$(M - P) \times (I/P) \times$ Statutory Fraction

Where:

M = Higher relevant maximum amount

P = Total profits including non-group dividends

I = Profits excluding non-group dividends

Statutory Fraction = 7/400 (these fractions are set each year by the Finance Act).

The figure resulting from application of the statutory formula should then be deducted from the figure resulting from the application of the main rate to the company's profits, to provide the amount of corporation tax payable.

Marginal tax rates

There is an alternative means of calculating the amount of corporation tax payable where marginal relief is given. It is possible, from the application of the statutory formula, to calculate an effective tax rate to be applied to the profits which fall within the marginal relief band. For 2009, this rate is 29.75%, known as the marginal tax rate.

The following example shows application of both the formula and the marginal tax rate to a company's profits which fall within the marginal relief band. Note that the company in question has not received any profits by way of non-group dividends.

EXAMPLE

Clarke Knitwear Limited has total taxable profits of £600,000 for the accounting year.

£600,000 × 28%   = £168,000

Marginal relief   = (£1,500,000 – £600,000) × (600,000/600,000) × 7/400

= £15,750

Deducting the marginal relief from tax liability at the full rate (i.e., (£600,000 × 28% = £168,000) *less* (£15,750)) gives a figure of £152,250.

Applying the upper marginal rate:

£0 – 300,000 × 21%   = £63,000

£300,000–600,000 × 29.75%   = £89,250

Total tax   = £152,250

Note how the application of the marginal rate produces the same result as application of the statutory formula.

19.3.2.6 Calculation of marginal relief where profits include dividends

Where a company's profits include dividends from another company the situation is more complex. These dividends are not actually taxable in the hands of the recipient company but do have an impact on taxable profits because they must be included in the company's profits total to determine the extent to which a company may benefit from marginal relief. This is why the statutory formula shown above makes a distinction between profits including and not including non-group dividends. The basic effect of the statutory formula is that the higher the proportion of total profits which is made up of dividends, the less marginal relief available for the actual profits taxed.

For the purposes of the formula, dividends do not include dividends paid from another company in the same group as the recipient. It is beyond the scope of this Guide to examine what constitutes a 'group'; suffice it to say that a common example of a payment within a group would be from a wholly-owned subsidiary to its parent. The following example shows the effect which dividends can have on the application of marginal relief.

EXAMPLE

In the financial year 2009, Fallon Limited has trading profits of £300,000 and gross dividend receipts (non-group) of £200,000. Although such dividends will not be taxed in the hands of Fallon Limited, when they are added to the trading profit figure the total amount is £500,000 which means that the trading profit will be subject to the main rate of 28% then reduced by marginal relief.

Applying the statutory formula, the corporation tax liability will be £73,500. This is because tax at 28% on the trading profits of £300,000 is £84,000 and marginal relief reduces this by £10,500 to £73,500. The amount of marginal relief is calculated as follows:

	£
(1,500,000 – 500,000) × 300,000/500,000	= 600,000
600,000 × 7/400	= 10,500

It will be noted that, had the company only had its trading profits of £300,000 in that year, then the small companies' rate would have been payable: 21% of £300,000 = £63,000. It can therefore be seen that dividends, although not actually taxable, have a considerable impact on the company's tax liability.

19.4 Loss relief under the corporation tax system

19.4.1 Introduction

Trading losses of companies are relieved in a number of ways; the scheme of the legislation is very similar to the one which applies for income tax (see **Chapter 17**).

19.4.2 Carry forward

Under s. 393 ICTA 1988, a company can carry forward a trading loss and use it to reduce profits derived from the same trade in future accounting periods. This relief applies to trading profits only; it does not apply to capital gains. (However, note that *capital* losses may be carried forward and offset against future capital gains (see **19.4.5**).) A claim for relief under this section must be made within six years of the end of the accounting period in which the loss was incurred.

EXAMPLE

To illustrate the application of s. 393, the company has an accounting period corresponding with calendar years and its profits and losses are as follows:

	Trade I	Trade II	Capital Gains
	£	£	£
2004	75,000	25,000	Nil
2005	100,000	50,000	Nil
2006	100,000	50,000	20,000
2007	(300,000) loss	50,000	30,000
2008	100,000	50,000	Nil
2009	200,000	50,000	Nil

Under s. 393 the £300,000 loss incurred in Trade I in 2007 can only be carried forward against future profits of that same trade. Therefore, the profits made by Trade I in 2008 and 2009 will be wiped out but the profits from Trade II and the capital gains realised in the years 2007, 2008 and 2009 will all remain taxable.

19.4.3 Use within same accounting period

In addition to or instead of the relief given by s. 393, a company may set off a loss made during an accounting period against any profits of the same accounting period. The claim for relief must be made within two years of the end of the accounting period in which the loss was made. Corporation tax 'profits' include both income and capital gains so a company may set an income loss (from a trade) against a chargeable capital gain. If the loss is not entirely relieved by setting it off against profits of the same accounting period, the company may also make a claim for the unrelieved part of the loss to be set against profits (including capital gains) for the immediately previous accounting period (s. 393A ICTA 1988). A loss cannot be carried back under this provision to a period when the company was not carrying on the business and there are no corporation tax provisions corresponding with s. 381 ICTA 1988 (income tax loss relief for the early years of a new trade). Where relief is being claimed in respect of a loss which has been carried back under this provision, the carried back loss will be taken into account *before* charges on income incurred in the earlier accounting period are deducted; however, any losses made in the earlier year are used to relieve profits before the carried back loss.

In the April 2009 Budget, the Chancellor made additional provision for companies to carry back and set off trading losses against profits of earlier years. This provision extends the current ability (noted above) to relieve losses against profits made in the preceding year, where such losses cannot otherwise be relieved in the year they were suffered. The ability to carry back will be extended from the current one year to a maximum of three, with losses to be applied against later years first. The amount of trading losses that can be carried back—unlimited in respect of the preceding year—will be limited to a maximum of £50,000 per year and to losses of the same trade. This provision will apply to losses made in company accounting periods ending in the period 24 November 2008 to 23 November 2010.

To illustrate the application of ss. 393 and 393A and using the figures set out in **19.4.2**, the £300,000 loss made in Trade I in 2007 can be used to wipe out the Trade II profits and capital gains for that year, resulting in a loss to be carried back of £220,000. Total profits for 2006 amount to £170,000, resulting in £50,000 of the loss being unrelieved. This may then be carried forward against the profits for Trade I in 2007.

19.4.4 Tactical considerations

In deciding which method of relief to use, the company will wish to ensure, so far as possible, that the maximum tax saving is achieved (by setting the loss against those profits which are subject to tax at 28% rather than any lower rate). However, the cash-flow problem of having to meet a tax bill at a time when the cash reserves may be low often means it is preferable not to carry forward the relief but to claim it as soon as possible.

The possibility of carrying forward losses is lost in certain cases where there are substantial changes in both the ownership of the company and in the nature of its trade. This is an anti-avoidance provision designed to prevent the purchase of a company simply to take advantage of its tax losses.

19.4.5 Capital losses

If a company makes a capital loss (calculated in the same way as a capital gain), it may be set off against capital gains of the same accounting period and, if unrelieved, may be carried forward and set off against capital gains of later accounting periods. Although trading losses may be set off against capital gains there are no provisions allowing capital losses to be set off against income profits. Indexation allowances (see **19.2.5**) may operate to reduce losses. Where this occurs, note that the indexation allowance can only be used to the extent that it extinguishes any gain. It cannot create or increase losses.

EXAMPLE

If A disposes of an asset for £60,000 and the base cost for that asset is £45,000, A is left with a gain of £15,000. If the base cost also attracted an indexation allowance of £20,000, this could be used to wipe out the gain, but could not create a loss of £5,000.

19.4.6 Group relief

Section 402 ICTA 1988 makes provision for group relief. In outline, where a company is a member of a group it may surrender its loss to another company in the same group. The latter then deducts the loss from its profits as if it were its own loss. Companies are in the same group, broadly speaking, if one is the 75% subsidiary of the other or both are 75% subsidiaries of a third company.

19.5 Close companies

19.5.1 Definition

A close company is a company controlled by five or fewer participators or any number of participators who are also directors (s. 414 ICTA 1988). 'Participators' are shareholders, loan creditors and certain others entitled to participate in the distributed income of the company. 'Control' includes, inter alia, ownership of a majority of the share capital or a majority of the votes or a right to a majority of the dividends. In assessing control, the rights of 'associates' must be added to the rights of a participator—associates include, among others, the participator's spouse, parents, remoter forebears, children, remoter issue, brothers and sisters. The above definition is only a very brief summary but it is sufficient to show that nearly all private companies are close companies (for example, if a company has nine or fewer shareholders, it must be under the control of some five of them even if none of them is related to each other—it will therefore be a close company unless it falls into one of the small number of cases excluded from the definition).

19.5.2 Taxation considerations

Close companies are subject to certain special tax rules. These are designed to prevent the use of the company as a vehicle for tax avoidance.

If a loan is made to a participator or his associate, then under s. 419 ICTA 1988 the company must pay a levy equal to 25% of the loan within nine months of the end of the accounting period in which the loan was made. This currently means that for every £4 lent an additional £1 must be paid to the Revenue. The levy will be repaid to the company whenever the loan is repaid, waived or written off.

If the borrower pays back the debt in full, no taxation issues arise for the borrower. (except, perhaps, for the fact that any interest which has been forgone or which has been paid at less than the official rate, may result in an income tax liability for the debtor based on that sum). However, if the loan is written off or waived by the company, the borrower benefits from a 'windfall'. As such, income tax will be payable. If the borrower is a basic rate taxpayer, no extra tax will be payable. However, if the borrower is a higher rate taxpayer, the amount written off will be grossed up at the 10% dividends rate of income tax and the resulting sum taxed at 32.5%.

One very important exception is that the above rules do not apply if the amount of the loan does not exceed £15,000 and the borrower owns less than a 5% shareholding in the company.

If a close company provides living accommodation or other 'benefits in kind' for a participator or his associates who are neither directors nor higher paid employees of the company (see **20.3.3(f)**), then the company will be treated as making a distribution (see **Chapter 20**).

If the close company is a 'close investment holding company', the small companies rate of corporation tax will not be available. The company will instead pay corporation tax on its profits, whatever the amount, at the full rate. To fall within this category of close companies, the company must be neither a trading company nor a member of a trading group. Companies which deal in land, shares or securities and companies carrying on property investment on a commercial basis are all treated as trading companies and so outside the scope of this anti-avoidance provision.

Companies are not normally liable to inheritance tax if they make gifts. However, if a close company makes a gift (or other transfer of value) this is deemed to be a gift made by all the shareholders in the company (except those with very small interests) in proportion to their shareholdings. If the shareholders fail to pay inheritance tax on this deemed gift, the company becomes liable (ss. 94–102 and 202 IHTA 1984).

 online resource centre

Interactive online exercises (Student Learning Activities) which complement the topics covered in this chapter are available at www.oxfordtextbooks.co.uk/orc/business09_10/.

Taxation of directors' fees and employees' salaries

This chapter covers the following topics:

20.1 Introduction

One of the largest ongoing expenses of any business is likely to be wage costs. In addition, it is the way in which most people receive a regular income. This chapter considers the taxation treatment of salaries, from the perspectives of both employer and employee. Remember that any type of business can act as an employer. Also, note that employees can be rewarded in ways other than pure salary, such as health insurance or company cars. In most instances, these rewards will result in a tax liability for the employee.

20.2 The employer's perspective

20.2.1 Deductibility of employee remuneration

An employer will wish to ensure that any remuneration or reward paid to its employees will entitle it to claim a pre-tax deduction and reduce its taxable profits. As seen in **Chapter 17**, to be deductible, any expense must satisfy two conditions, namely that the payments must be:

(a) of an income nature as opposed to a capital outlay; and

(b) incurred wholly and exclusively for the purpose of the trade or profession.

Applying this rule, payments that are deductible include the payment of salaries, wages, pension contributions and even lump sum payments in compensation for loss of the employee's office.

The following specific aspects of this general proposition should be noted.

(a) *'Wholly'*

The word 'wholly' relates to quantum, so that excessive payments cannot be deducted. In *Copeman v William J. Flood and Sons Ltd* [1941] 1 KB 202, it was decided that where a payment is held to be excessive, only such proportion of the payment as is reasonable in the light of the employee's work can be deducted.

With regard to pensions, the pension paid to an ex-employee is deductible even if it is paid voluntarily by the employer. In practice most employers who provide pensions do so by setting up a fund managed by an insurance company. Contributions paid into the fund by the employer are deductible as business expenses provided the scheme is a retirement benefit scheme as defined by s. 590 ICTA 1988.

(b) *Compensation for loss of office*

Lump sum payments for loss of office are deductible if they satisfy the conditions set out above, even though they may be one-off payments. In *Mitchell v B. W. Noble Ltd* [1927] KB 719, compensation payments made to directors who were liable to dismissal because of their misconduct but who resigned to avoid bad publicity were held to be deductible on the basis that their retirement was in the interests of the business. Conversely, payments made to former employees to persuade them to enter into restrictive covenants have been held not to be deductible, since the payments were intended to buy off potential competitors and so amounted to a capital payment (*Associated Portland Cement v Kerr* (1945) 27 TC 108 (CA)). This position has now been changed statutorily, such that the payment will be both taxable as income in the hands of the recipient and an income deductible expense for the company (see **20.3.5**). If the employee is redundant and receives a redundancy payment, such payments are deductible and are treated as having been paid on the last day on which the business was carried on if made after the discontinuance of the trade, profession or vocation.

(c) *The provision of benefits*

Many employers provide their employees with benefits over and above their salary, such as company cars, free meals and so on. The cost of providing such benefits will be deductible if the payments are made wholly and exclusively for the purposes of the trade. Thus if cars are provided for salesmen, the outlay will be deductible, but if they are for private use they will only be deductible if they can be regarded as reasonable remuneration.

20.2.2 Social security contributions

Although it is beyond the scope of this Guide to consider the social security legislation in detail, it should be noted that the employer is obliged to make National Insurance contributions in respect of each employee (as well as deducting the contributions of the employee before paying over the net wages). In effect, this means that there is an additional cost to the employer over and above the salary it pays. The employer's contributions are deductible in computing the tax liability of the employer.

20.3 The employee's perspective

20.3.1 Income Tax (Earnings and Pensions) Act 2003

The system for taxation of employees' income is contained in the Income Tax (Earnings and Pensions) Act (ITEPA) 2003. In addition to setting out the basis of the tax charge, it contains provisions which provide for the mechanism by which income tax is deducted at source from an employee's wages and accounted for by their employer to HMRC under the PAYE (Pay As You Earn) scheme—see Part 11 ITEPA. (Contrast this with 'self-employed' income, where recipients must account for tax themselves, normally some time after receipt—see **17.3** for more details.)

Section 6 ITEPA imposes a charge to tax on 'employment income', which is a charge to tax on, inter alia, 'general earnings'. Section 7 ITEPA defines both these terms by reference to s. 62, which states that 'earnings' mean, in relation to an employment:

(a) any salary, wages or fee;

(b) any gratuity or incidental benefit of any kind obtained by the employee if it is money or money's worth;

(c) anything which constitutes an emolument of the employment.

Employment income is taxed in the tax year in which it is received, irrespective of whether or not it is actually earned in that year (see Part 2, Chapter 4, Part 1 ITEPA).

The term 'employment' is clearly important and is defined in s. 4 ITEPA to include a contract of service. Section 5 operates to include 'offices' and 'office-holders' within employment. Neither of these definitions is absolute, so it is worthwhile considering case law for guidance in these areas.

(a) *Office*

Rowlatt J in *Great Western Railway Co. v Bater* [1920] 3 KB 266, said that 'office' meant 'a subsisting, permanent, substantive position which had an existence independent of the person who filled it, which went on and was filled in succession by successive holders', although Lord Wilberforce and Lord Lowry, in *Edwards v Clinch* [1981] 3 All ER 543, felt the definition should be refined. Lord Wilberforce accepted

that a rigid requirement of permanence is no longer appropriate . . . and continuity need not be regarded as an absolute qualification. But still, if any meaning is to be given to 'office' in this legislation . . . the word must involve a degree of continuance (not necessarily continuity) and of independent existence: it must connote a post to which a person can be appointed, which he can vacate and to which a successor can be appointed.

Over the years office holders have been held to include directors of UK companies, NHS consultants, bishops, judges and personal representatives. (Remember that a director may hold the office of director and may simultaneously be an employee, by performing an executive function. (See **20.4** for further discussion of the taxation of directors' salaries.))

(b) *Employment*

Pennycuick V-C said in *Fall v Hitchen* [1973] 1 All ER 368, that, 'unless some special limitation is to be put upon the word "employment" in any given context, the expression "contract of service" appears to be coterminous with the expression "employment"'. The case involved a ballet dancer who entered into a contract having the attributes of a contract of service, in that he was paid weekly regardless of whether a performance was given or a rehearsal attended; the 'employer' paid national insurance contributions on the dancer's behalf as if he were an employee and the dancer worked only for the employer. This contract was therefore assessable, even though it had been entered into in the normal course of carrying on his profession of dancer. Conversely, if it can be shown that the taxpayer's method of earning a livelihood does not consist of obtaining a post and remaining in it (as was the case in *Fall v Hitchen*), but consists of engagements and moving from one engagement to another, he is assessed under ITTOIA (see **Chapter 17**) and not ITEPA, provided the engagements are entered into as part of his profession (*Davies v Braithwaite* [1931] 2 KB 628).

20.3.2 Taxable receipts by employees

A director or other employee who receives salary, wages or a bonus from his employer is obviously assessable under ITEPA. However, rewards for employees, and particularly directors, tend to comprise more than just salary. Perhaps the most common example is that of the company car, but others can have considerable worth, such as loans on favourable terms and subsidised or free living accommodation. Such 'perks' will amount to benefits of money or money's worth and, therefore, will be taxable along with other earnings.

ITEPA contains the 'Benefits Code' in Chapter 2, Part 3, which deals with such benefits and will now be considered.

20.3.3 The Benefits Code

(a) Benefits generally

Benefits from employment generally fall into two categories: either they amount to cash or its equivalent or they amount to the use of something at the employer's expense. An example of the former might be the payment of premiums on private health insurance; an example of the latter would the use of a company car.

Under s. 204 ITEPA, the general rule is that the cost to the employer of providing the benefit will be treated as earnings by the employee. However, a number of specified benefits are subject to their own rules.

(b) Living accommodation

Chapter 5 of Part 3 ITEPA covers this benefit and provides rules on how much an employee is deemed to receive in monetary terms. An employee who occupies premises by reason of his employment is taxed on the greater of either the rent paid by his employer or the deemed 'annual value' of the accommodation less the rent actually paid by the employee. 'Annual value' means the market rent that could be obtained for the premises on the assumption that the landlord will bear the costs of repair and insurance.

EXAMPLE

Scenario one

Employer buys a property for £60,000 to provide accommodation for Employee. Employee pays an annual rent of £4,000 to Employer. The deemed market rent of the property is £10,000 per annum. Employee, therefore, receives a taxable benefit of £6,000—the difference between the deemed market rent and the actual rent paid by the employee.

Scenario two
Employer rents a property for £8,000 per annum to provide accommodation for Employee. Employee pays an annual rent of £4,000 to Employer. The deemed market rent of the property is £6,000 per annum. Employee, therefore, receives a taxable benefit of £4,000—the difference between the actual rent paid by Employer (as it is higher than the deemed rent) and the actual rent paid by Employee.

Where it costs an employer more than £75,000 to provide accommodation for an employee, an employee's liability is calculated on a slightly different basis. In this instance, an employee will be treated as receiving a percentage (based on an official rate of interest in line with mortgage rates) of the amount in excess of £75,000 which the employer has spent on providing the accommodation (so-called 'additional yearly rent'), as well as taking into account any deemed receipt which the employee would normally be taxed upon under the rule above.

EXAMPLE

Employer buys a property for £100,000 to provide accommodation for Employee. Assume the deemed percentage is 5%. Therefore, Employee is treated as receiving additional yearly rent of 5% of £25,000 (the amount over £75,000 paid by Employer for the property) = £1,250.

The deemed market rent of the property is £10,000 per annum and Employee pays an annual rent of £6,000 to Employer.

Employee's total taxable liability for the property is, therefore:

(£1,250 + £10,000) − £6,000 = £5,250.

(c) *Expenses*

Any allowance for expenses payable to an employee will be a taxable benefit, subject to whatever percentage of that allowance is spent on expenses incurred wholly, exclusively and necessarily in the performance of the duties of employment. In which case, such expenses are deductible pursuant to s. 336 ITEPA. For example, if a director has an expense allowance of £1,000 per month and regularly incurs deductible expenses of £800 per month, only the difference will be taxable.

The test for deductibility is stringent, particularly as expenditure has to be shown as necessarily incurred. It is always open to the Revenue to argue that such necessity did not exist.

In many instances, an employee will, instead, incur the expense first and be reimbursed by their employer. This does not normally produce a taxable receipt for the employee, so long as the expense fulfils the test for deductibility. As a sizeable proportion of an employee's expenses claims tend to refer to travelling costs, it is worth noting two specific aspects of the system:

(i) the test for deductibility of travel expenses is less demanding, the rule being that these expenses must be necessarily incurred in the performance of an employee's duties (s. 337 ITEPA);

(ii) in relation to mileage allowance, s. 229 ITEPA exempts from taxation any allowance of 40 pence per mile up to the first 10,000 miles and 25 pence thereafter.

(d) Motor vehicles

As with living accommodation, an employee who is provided with a company car is deemed to receive an annual sum to represent the cash equivalent of the vehicle. This sum can be between 9% and 35% of the list price of the vehicle provided, depending on its carbon dioxide emissions (see Chapter 6, Part 3 ITEPA for full details).

(e) Beneficial loan arrangements

Loans from an employer can be attractive if the rate of interest is lower than that in the marketplace. As such, Chapter 7, Part 3 ITEPA attributes to an employee the value of this difference as earnings. This is done by comparing the actual interest payable by the employee with an official rate of interest, which itself reflects the market rates in force (s. 175(3) ITEPA).

EXAMPLE

Martha is lent £20,000 by her employer. The rate of interest she pays on this to her employer is 2% per annum. As such, she pays £400 interest per annum. Assume that, according to the Revenue's official rates, interest upon such a loan is expected to be 6%; that is, £1,200 per annum. Martha will, as a consequence, be deemed to receive a taxable benefit worth £800.

There are a number of exceptions to this rule, but the one of general application is that, if the aggregate amount owing to the employer by the employee does not exceed £5,000, ITEPA will not bite (s. 180 ITEPA).

Should the whole or part of a loan be written off or released by the employer, the amount released or written off will be treated as earnings (s. 188 ITEPA).

(f) Lower paid employees

Section 216 ITEPA recognises a category of lower paid employees (that is, employees earning less than £8,500 per annum) who receive a more lenient treatment of benefits. For example, expense allowances, company cars and beneficial loans provided to lower paid employees will not be subject to income tax.

To avoid abuse of this system, that is, by paying an employee an artificially low salary and then supplementing this with substantial benefits, the cash equivalent of all benefits received must be included in the employee's earnings total for the purpose of the £8,500 threshold (s. 218 ITEPA).

EXAMPLE

George's remuneration package is made up as follows:

Salary of £6,500 per annum

Company car with a cash equivalent of £1,750 per annum

Expenses allowance of £1,200 per annum.

George's total earnings for the purposes of s. 218 ITEPA are £9,450. As such, George is not a lower paid employee.

Finally, as a rule of thumb, a director will never qualify as a lower paid employee, unless they are a full-time working director with no more than a 5% shareholding in the company and earning less than the specified amount.

20.3.4   Terminal payments

(a)   General principles

The mere fact that the payment is made on the termination of the contract (or the alteration of its terms) does not preclude its taxation under ITEPA, if it is 'something in the nature of a reward for services, past, present or future' (per Upjohn J in *Hochstrasser v Mayes* [1959] Ch 22). As a result of this, sums paid at the end of an employment in accordance with the terms of the employment contract will be taxable since they will represent deferred or advance remuneration (*Dale v De Soissons* [1950] 2 All ER 460). Thus, if an employee is to be paid £10,000 a year for 10 years but under the contract is to receive a lump sum of £50,000 on either the commencement or termination of the term, the sum is fully taxable under ITEPA (see *Williams v Simmonds* [1981] STC 715). However, it is more common for an employee's contract to be terminated and for the employee to be allowed to work out his notice or to be denied this right and paid a lump sum to reflect the money that he would have earned had he been allowed to do so, i.e., a payment in lieu of notice. It is at this point that some important distinctions must be made.

If an employee is allowed to work his notice period or is kept on for the period of his notice, but not allowed to work (so-called 'gardening leave'), the payments made to the employee will be taxable in the usual way. This should be contrasted with the situation where the employee is dismissed without notice and is paid in lieu of notice. Such a payment constitutes damages for breach of contract by the employer, and, as such, will not be treated as taxable as an emolument. Instead it will be taxable under s. 401 ITEPA (see (b) below).

Some employment contracts specifically provide the option for an employer to make a payment in lieu rather than give notice. This is in an attempt to avoid the deeming of a breach of contract, thus preserving many of the terms of the contract, specifically any restrictive covenants. Any payment made under such a provision is taxable as an emolument, as it arises from the operation of the contract.

As such, the exact nature of any lump sum termination payment made to an employee needs careful consideration to determine its status for tax purposes.

(b)   Payments under s. 401 ITEPA

A lump sum payment made to an employee on early termination of the contract by the employer which is not assessable under the general principles may be taxable under s. 401 ITEPA. This taxes a payment on the termination of employment that is not otherwise chargeable to tax (under the general principles). However, the great advantage to the taxpayer of a payment falling within s. 401 is that only if the sum received exceeds £30,000 will any tax be payable and, in such case, only the amount in excess of £30,000 (s. 403 ITEPA).

A common example of a s. 401 payment is a payment in lieu of notice which amounts to damages for breach of contract (see (a) above). This can lead to the unusual situation that an employee who is paid £25,000 in lieu of notice pursuant to a contractual provision will pay tax on this amount, whereas an employee who is paid the same sum, but which amounts to damages for breach, will pay none.

Another example of payments falling within the ambit of s. 401 are ex gratia payments or 'golden handshakes'.

A terminal payment paid to a director near retirement age needs careful consideration, as such a payment may instead be treated by the Revenue as a payment out of an un-approved pension scheme, in which case it will not attract the £30,000 exemption and will be taxed in full under s. 394 ITEPA.

Statutory redundancy payments and, since *Mairs v Haughey* [1993] 3 All ER 801, non-statutory redundancy payments are only taxable under s. 401. However, only genuine redundancy payments are caught. So an attempt to class a payment of less than £30,000 to a director as a redundancy payment to take advantage of the exemption will be closely scrutinised by HMRC. (See Statement of Practice SP 1/94.)

20.3.5 Restrictive covenant payments

If an employee receives a payment in consideration of entering into a restrictive covenant, this is regarded as being a capital outlay by the employer. As such, it should be a capital receipt in the hands of the employee and so not taxable as part of the employee's income. However, s. 225 ITEPA levies income tax on such payments. They are fully taxed in the recipient's hands and the paying employer can deduct them when calculating income profits.

20.3.6 Social security contributions

In the same way that employers must make National Insurance contributions in respect of employee's salaries, employees are also liable to make such contributions. The contributions deducted by the employer from the employee's salary (see **20.2.2**) are not deductible when calculating the employee's tax liability. Employees' contributions are greater than those levied on the self-employed but, in compensation, the benefits available to employees are greater than those available to the self-employed. (The details of the benefits are beyond the scope of this Guide.)

20.4 The proprietors of a business

Some important distinctions need always to be borne in mind when considering the proprietors of a business. First, sole traders cannot earn a salary from their businesses. The profits they make are taxed as a receipt under Income Tax (Trading and Other Income) Act 2005 (see **Chapter 17**). The same applies to partners who are 'true' partners in a partnership. If any such partners pay themselves a salary (in addition to taking any profit share), their total receipts from the business will be taxed in the same way as a sole trader. (See *MacKinlay v Arthur Young McClelland Moores & Co.* [1990] 1 All ER 45 for judicial discussion of this point.) However, 'salaried partners', that is, partners who have no stake in the business in question, are not entitled to any profit share and are remunerated solely by salary (and for whom the title 'partner' is, therefore, somewhat of a misnomer) will be taxed as employees.

The position of a company and its directors is different. As the company is a legal personality separate from its owners and managers, directors who work full-time in the company are treated as its employees and taxed on the salaries they receive. As such, a company pays tax on its profits and directors pay tax on their salaries. With a partnership, there is only the single liability of the partner to tax.

The significance, therefore, of this distinction becomes clear in the context of deductibility. Salaries payable by a company to its directors (as employees) will be deductible from the company's overall taxable profits. 'Salaries' payable to true partners will not be deductible. This does provide the opportunity to manipulate a company's profits by paying directors substantial sums, such that the company incurs little or no liability to corporation tax (although note the discussion at **20.2.1** about excessive salary payments). In many closely held private companies this can be a common method of extraction of profit from the business, although it should be borne in mind that increased salaries will also result in increased National Insurance payments from both the company and its directors (see **20.2.2** and **20.3.6**). By contrast, in a listed public limited company, such manipulation of profit will be prevented by corporate governance rules and will usually be of limited impact due to the substantial profits earned by such companies.

20.5 IR35 companies

Because of the financial and practical burden of the PAYE scheme and National Insurance, employers began to favour an alternative method of rewarding certain staff. Instead of being taken on as employees, the persons in question would create a single shareholder/director company and the 'employer' would then contract with that company for it to provide the services of the shareholder/director (effectively the 'employee'). Payments made to the company by the 'employer' would not be treated as an emolument of the 'employee', but a receipt of the company, thus escaping the PAYE/National Insurance burden on the 'employer'. However, those payments would still amount to a deductible business expense for the paying 'employer'. The 'employee', as a shareholder of the company, could then extract the profits from the company by way of dividend, again avoiding any PAYE/National Insurance obligation, and the corporation tax liability incurred by the company may have been less than the income tax liability on any salary paid direct. (See **Chapter 19** for an explanation of the rates of corporation tax.)

In 1999, Revenue Budget Press Release IR35 was published, explaining that this manipulation of the rules would be prevented in the future. The current legislation is found in ss. 48–61 ITEPA 2003. However, the reference to 'IR35' has remained.

The basic effect of the rules is that in cases where there is, in effect, an employer/employee relationship, payments made into the intermediate company will be treated as deemed employment income of the proprietor of the company and, therefore, subject to PAYE and National Insurance liability in the usual way. This will be the case even if the company pays out no monies to the proprietor or if it pays them out in the form of dividends (in which case there will be set-off between the liability incurred on the deemed payment and the liability on the dividend payment). Should the reader want further details of this very complex area, a recommended starting point is the special website set up by the Inland Revenue—www.hmrc.gov.uk/ir35.

 online resource centre Interactive online exercises (Student Learning Activities) which complement the topics covered in this chapter are available at www.oxfordtextbooks.co.uk/orc/business09_10/.

Taxation of distributions and debenture interest

This chapter covers the following topics:

21.1 Introduction

This chapter deals with the taxation of distributions by way of dividend and of debenture interest. The common factor is that both dividends and debenture interest are income returns on investments made in companies. The tax treatment of each can be contrasted.

21.2 Taxation of distributions by way of dividend

21.2.1 Definition of distribution

A shareholder is liable to income tax on any 'distribution' which he receives in respect of shares. The definition of distribution is complicated but the following types of receipt are the most important:

(a) any dividend paid by the company including a capital dividend;

(b) any other distribution out of assets of the company in respect of shares;

(c) any interest on securities (e.g., debentures) where the interest varies with the profits of the company;

(d) in some circumstances, the issue of bonus shares following a reduction of share capital or the repayment of share capital after a bonus issue.

It should be noted that an issue of bonus shares (that is, shares treated as paid up out of the profits of the company) is not a distribution for tax purposes unless share capital has previously been reduced. However, if the shareholders are given a choice between receiving a cash dividend (which is, of course, a distribution) or bonus shares, those who choose to take the bonus shares are taxed on the amount of cash dividend forgone in almost the same way as if it were a distribution.

When a company redeems or purchases its own shares there is usually a tax liability on the members (see **Chapter 18**).

21.2.2 Tax consequences of the payment of a dividend

The payment of a dividend or other distribution is neither an expense of a company's business nor a charge on its income. The amount of any dividend paid does not, therefore, reduce a company's liability to corporation tax.

21.2.3 Taxation of a recipient of a dividend

21.2.3.1 Corporate recipient

Where a UK company receives a dividend or other distribution from another, the general rule is that these sums are not subject to corporation tax in the hands of the recipient. (However, as was explained at **19.3.2.6**, dividends received may determine the rate at which a company's taxable profits are taxed.)

21.2.3.2 Individual recipient

An individual shareholder who receives a dividend from a company is treated for tax purposes as receiving a sum equivalent to the actual dividend plus a tax credit. The latter is equivalent to 10% of the dividend as grossed up by a tax credit fraction. The current fraction is 10/90.

EXAMPLE

Shareholder receives a dividend of £500. For tax purposes, he is treated as receiving:

The actual dividend	£500
Plus	
10% of £500 grossed up (i.e., £500 plus (10/90 × £500))	£55.56
Total	£555.56

The shareholder is liable to pay tax on this amount. For the tax year 2009/10, the basic tax rate for individuals on dividends is 10% and the higher rate is 32.5%. From 2010/11, there will be an additional rate of 42.5% for those whose income exceeds £150,000.

Dividend income is treated as the top slice of the shareholder's income. Where dividend income falls entirely within the basic rate band of taxable income, the tax credit will satisfy the liability to tax. If dividend income falls entirely within the higher rate band of income, an additional amount of 32.5% of the grossed-up dividend will be due from the shareholder. Where the income cuts across the basic and higher rate bands, the dividend must be apportioned between them and the tax credit deducted from the resulting sum. The balance will be the amount of tax outstanding. Should a shareholder not be liable to tax, there is no ability to claim a repayment of the tax credit.

EXAMPLE

In all the examples which follow, the relevant income tax bands are those for the tax year 2009/10.

Example one

A has taxable income of £15,000 and receives a gross dividend of £555.56 (i.e., £500 cash plus tax credit of £55.56). The total dividend falls within the basic rate income tax band (which is £37,400 for 2009/10). Tax is therefore:

£555.56 × 10% = £55.56

The tax liability is fully satisfied by the tax credit.

Example two

B has taxable income of £38,000 and receives a gross dividend of £1,666.67 (i.e., £1,500 cash plus tax credit of £166.67). The total dividend falls within the higher rate income tax band. Tax is therefore:

£1,666.67 × 32.5% = £541.67

The tax liability is satisfied to the extent of the tax credit, i.e., £166.67. The shareholder is required to pay the remaining tax due of £375. (NB, £375 is equivalent to 22.5% of £1,666.67.)

Example three

C has taxable income of £30,000 and receives a gross dividend of £7,777.78 (i.e., £7,000 cash plus tax credit of £777.78). The dividend falls within both the basic and higher rate income tax bands. Tax is payable as follows:

£7,400 × 10% = £740

£377.78 × 32.5% = £122.78

Total tax payable = £862.78

The tax liability is satisfied as to the extent of the tax credit, i.e., £777.78. The shareholder is required to pay the remaining tax due of £85.

21.3 Debenture interest

21.3.1 Introduction

The tax treatment of interest on debentures will be looked at for two reasons:

(a) it can be contrasted with the tax treatment of dividends;

(b) it may influence whether or not an investment is made into the company by way of equity or debt (loan) funding.

21.3.2 Tax consequences for the paying company

Interest is a 'payment by time for the use of money' (per Rowlatt J in *Bennett* v *Ogston* (1930) 15 TC 374). A payment of interest by a company will usually result in a tax saving to the company because the interest will be a business expense deductible in computing trading profits.

21.3.2.1 Loan relationships

Under s. 81 Finance Act (FA) 1996, a company has a loan relationship where a 'company stands . . . in the position of a . . . debtor as respects any money debt' and the debt 'is one arising from a transaction for the lending of money'. As such, borrowing in the form of debentures comes within the definition.

21.3.2.2 Interest on borrowing for the purposes of trade

Section 82 FA 96 sets out the method by which expenditure resulting from a loan relationship is brought into account: any 'debits', of which the main type is interest, can be treated as income expenses which can be deducted from income profits. Also, charges and expenses incurred in setting up the loan relationship (in this instance, legal or administrative) are treated as debits.

21.3.2.3 Non-trading borrowing

If a company raises money by borrowing but this does not support the trade carried on by the company, interest thereon is treated as a 'non-trading debit'. Such a sum must first be deducted from any 'non-trading credits' (i.e., profits which a company has made from lending money where this is not the trade of the company). If such credits exceed debits, the resulting sum is charged to tax. However, where the situation is in reverse, the company may, very simply, use that deficit and set it off against any profits of the same accounting period or carry it back against any profits of earlier accounting periods (in addition to any deductible sums in **21.3.2.2**).

21.3.2.4 Timing of deductibility

The treatment of payments arising out of loan relationships is determined by their accounting treatment. Consequently, most interest payments payable by a company are deductible on an accruals basis. This means that they are deductible when they accrue due to be paid, rather than when they are actually paid.

21.3.3 Deduction of tax

The company must deduct basic rate income tax from interest which it pays (s. 874 ITA 2007) to individuals. The current rate applicable on all savings and distribution income (other than from dividends) is 20%. (Deduction is not, however, made where interest is short interest or where it is yearly interest paid to a bank in the UK.) When the company deducts tax it must account to the Revenue for the tax deducted. For example, a company borrows £1,000 at 10% interest from an individual. Each year (assuming tax rates remain the same) it will pay £80 to the lender and £20 to the Revenue.

21.3.4 Taxation of the recipient

The gross amount of interest received by a debenture-holder is taxable. As we have just seen, the company usually deducts the 20% tax from the payment so that the amount received is a net amount. To calculate the amount of tax payable it is, therefore, first necessary to calculate the gross amount of interest. This is done by multiplying the net amount actually received by 100/80 (e.g., £80 × 100/80 = £100). If the tax rate changes so will the fraction—the '80' represents 100 minus the rate of tax. Of course, if no deduction of tax has been made at source, this calculation is unnecessary.

The gross amount of interest is investment income in the hands of the recipient and is liable to higher rate tax if the recipient's income is large enough. If the recipient has unused personal reliefs the 20% tax can be reclaimed to the extent that the reliefs are not set against other income.

EXAMPLE

P has taxable income of £30,600 in the tax year 2008/09. He, therefore, has £5,400 of the basic rate band still unused. He received £10,000 gross interest on a loan to a company.

(a) P's net receipt was £8,000 plus credit for £2,000 tax deducted at source by the paying company.

(b) Tax to pay (on gross sum):

£0 – 5,400 × 20%   = £1,080
£5,401 – 10,000 × 40%   = £1,840
                  = £2,920

(c) Tax deducted satisfies £2,000 of the above liability—balance to pay of £920.

online resource centre

Interactive online exercises (Student Learning Activities) which complement the topics covered in this chapter are available at www.oxfordtextbooks.co.uk/orc/business09_10/.

Capital allowances

This chapter covers the following topics:

22.1 Introduction

22.2 Plant and machinery

22.3 Industrial buildings

22.4 Other expenditure which attracts capital allowances.

22.1 Introduction

22.1.1 General

Most businesses will need to acquire fixed assets for use in the business. The depreciation in the value of those assets due to wear and tear arising from their use in the business is not an allowable deduction from the business's profits for income tax purposes, even though their acquisition is essential to the future profitability of the business. However, certain limited types of fixed assets do attract relief in the form of capital allowances which can be deducted when calculating taxable profits. In effect, the allowance is an amount which represents depreciation in the asset in question, calculated according to a fixed formula.

Relief is only available if the capital expenditure has been incurred in respect of the items of expenditure prescribed by the governing statute, the Capital Allowances Act 2001. Under this Act, the principal allowances relate to expenditure incurred on 'plant and machinery' and 'industrial buildings' (although expenditure on other items is deductible under the terms of the Act).

The allowances can be claimed by companies, partnerships or individuals.

Capital allowances are treated as trading expenses incurred in the accounting period in which they are claimed. They are, therefore, deductible from income receipts from the same period.

22.2 Plant and machinery

22.2.1 Definition

The Capital Allowances Act 2001 does not define either 'plant' or 'machinery' and therefore whether the expenditure will attract the allowances will depend on the facts in each case. In *Yarmouth v France* (1887) 19 QBD 647, Lindley LJ said that the term 'plant':

... includes whatever apparatus is used by a businessman for carrying on his business, not his stock-in-trade which he buys or makes for sale; but all goods and chattels, fixed or movable, live or dead, which he keeps for permanent employment in his business.

On the basis of this guidance (which has been followed in subsequent cases), the term 'plant' will not apply to (and so allowances will not be available in respect of) an item which is not: used for carrying on the business; the stock–in–trade of the business; or the premises or place in which the business is carried on. (In addition, the Finance Act 1994 introduced a new Sch. AA1 into the 1990 Act providing that land, buildings and structures cannot be plant.)

A fuller description of the definition of the term is beyond the scope of this Guide.

22.2.2 The allowances

22.2.2.1 Writing down allowance

If the expenditure is incurred on an item of 'plant or machinery', it will qualify for a 'writing down allowance' of up to 20% of the 'qualifying expenditure' in the first and subsequent years. Allowances are then effectively set against profits in the same way as a deductible trading expense, to reduce the tax liability of the business.

The 20% rate was introduced with effect from 1 April 2008 for companies paying corporation tax and 6 April 2008 for businesses subject to income tax. Prior to April 2008, the relevant rate was 25%. Where a business's chargeable period spans a relevant date when the rate changed, then a hybrid rate will operate, effectively calculating allowances by apportioning the chargeable period either side of those dates at the rate in effect for each portion.

The term 'qualifying expenditure' means the original cost of the asset less any allowances already given. The allowance may be claimed in whole or in part by sole traders or partners.

EXAMPLE

Machinery is purchased for £50,000 on 1 January 2009 and the full writing down allowance of 20% is claimed. This would mean that an allowance of £10,000 will be available in the first year of ownership. If the owner of the machinery decides to claim the full 20% allowance in the three subsequent years, the allowance available will be as follows:

	Written down value		Allowance for the year
Second year	£50,000–£10,000 (1st Year WDA)	= £40,000	£8,000
Third year	£50,000–£18,000 (£10,000 + £8,000)	= £32,000	£6,400
Fourth year	£50,000–£24,400 (£10,000 + £8,000 + £6,400)	= £25,600	£5,120

22.2.2.2 Temporary first year allowance

Businesses which invest in plant and machinery in the 12-month period commencing on 1 April 2009 for companies and 6 April 2009 for individuals and partnerships will be able to claim a 40% first year writing down allowance on this expenditure. This one-year temporary increase is designed to encourage and assist investment. Where a business qualifies for the £50,000 Annual Investment Allowance (see **22.2.5.1**), this 40% temporary allowance will apply to any expenditure in excess of that amount. There are certain assets which will not qualify for the temporary first year allowance: these include assets for leasing and cars.

22.2.2.3 Balancing charge or allowance

When the asset is sold at a price which differs from the written down value, there will either be a balancing charge or a balancing allowance on the difference between the sale price and the written down value.

In the above example, the written down value after the fourth year was £20,480 (£25,600–£5,120), so if the machinery was sold for £22,000 there would be a charge to tax of £1,520. This charge is known as the 'balancing charge' and is added to profits for the purpose of calculating tax. This has the effect of ensuring that, taking all the years together, the amount on which relief is finally given is equal to the amount of the actual depreciation.

Should the item be sold for *less* than the current written down value, a 'balancing allowance' will be available as a way of granting relief. So, if the machinery was sold after the fourth year for £18,000, a balancing allowance, deductible from profits, of £2,480 would be given.

Note that a balancing charge can never be more than the total amount of allowance given—any actual profit made on the sale of the asset being liable to capital gains tax, if taxable at all.

The illustration set out above shows that the allowances are of up to 20% of the *unrelieved expenditure* (that is to say, the purchase price less the allowances already taken). Thus, the annual allowance is a percentage of an ever-reducing balance so that it can take many years for the entire expenditure to be set against profits, subject to a balancing charge becoming payable.

22.2.3 'Pooling'

22.2.3.1 General

So far, we have looked at the rules as they apply to the acquisition and subsequent disposal of a single item of plant or machinery. If several items of plant and machinery are owned by the business (as is more likely to be the case) the allowances are given by reference to a 'pool' of expenditure. This will mean that all of the assets in the pool are treated as if they were one asset. The amount of the writing down allowance on the 'pool' of expenditure will be up to 20% of the total of expenditure on machinery and plant less all allowances so far claimed. Where one item included in the pool is disposed of, the sale price of that item is deducted from the written down value of the pool (this deduction being known as a 'balancing adjustment'), so that smaller allowances will be available in later years. A 'balancing charge' will only apply where pooled items are sold for more than the written down value of the whole pool.

Given the change in the writing down allowance rate made in 2008, special rules, including a hybrid rate (see **22.2.2.1** above), will apply to calculate the overall allowances available to businesses who have pools of assets and whose chargeable periods span the relevant date on which the rate changed.

22.2.4 Using the allowances

Writing down allowances are available both in the accounting period in which the asset was purchased and in all subsequent accounting periods during which the asset is owned.

While the system does not lend itself to simplification (especially from the corporation tax perspective), the basic use of a writing down allowance for a company, partnership or sole trader is that of a deductible trading expense. If such allowances exceed income receipts, the loss incurred attracts loss relief in the usual way.

22.2.5 Special rules on plant and machinery

22.2.5.1 Annual Investment Allowance for small and medium-sized businesses

Small and medium-sized businesses (which account for around 99% of businesses in the UK) are entitled to a 100% Annual Investment Allowance (AIA) on purchases of most plant and machinery up to £50,000 in any one year. This allowance will, like other capital allowances, be treated as a trading expense and can thus be set off against income receipts when calculating tax. Where a qualifying business spends more than £50,000 in any one year on plant and machinery, the balance above £50,000 will qualify for standard capital allowances and enter any existing pool of assets. The AIA is designed to encourage investment by providing increased cash-flow benefits.

22.2.5.2 Long-life assets

Plant and machinery which falls within this category attracts a writing down allowance of 10%. Long-life assets are those with a useful economic life of more than 25 years.

This legislation, introduced by the Finance Act 1997, is intended to affect only large concerns. As such, any business which spends less than £100,000 a year on long-life assets is excluded and will still be able to claim the full 20% allowance. Certain cagetories of assets are also excluded, the most relevant being motor cars.

Because these rules result in allowances being claimed at a slower rate than normal, businesses could be tempted to sell off assets prematurely at less than their written down value so as to bring an immediate balancing allowance into effect. The legislation contains provisions to defeat such activity by deeming the sale to have been at the relevant written down value.

22.2.5.3 Leased assets

There are special rules on the availability of capital allowances to the lessor when plant and machinery is bought in order to be leased. There are also special rules for the lessees of equipment. It is important to distinguish between arrangements which are 'pure' leasing contracts, where the title in the assets leased always remains with the lessor, and those which constitute lease-purchase (and hire-purchase) arrangements where the lessee (or hirer) becomes the ultimate owner of the assets, normally upon payment of a final capital sum. In the former case, the lessor will be able to claim writing down allowances; in the latter it will be the lessee. Because of the amount of assets either leased or subject to lease-purchase in the UK, these rules should not be overlooked. The detail of these rules is beyond the scope of this Guide and the reader is referred to one of the standard tax textbooks.

22.2.6 Motor cars

Cars which are used only for business purposes qualify for full writing down allowances. However, cars which are used for private as well as business purposes qualify for a 20% writing down allowance.

22.3 Industrial buildings

22.3.1 Definition

The Capital Allowances Act 2001 allows for allowances to be claimed in respect of the construction and purchase of industrial buildings and structures (such as factories, but not offices) for manufacturing (but not distributive) trades. The Act defines the term 'industrial building' at some length and it can include a mill, a factory and a warehouse. The allowances are not available in respect of the expenditure laid out to acquire the land. Expenditure incurred subsequently when the industrial building is improved can attract the allowances. If part of a building which satisfies the definition of an 'industrial building' is used for non-industrial purposes, the allowance can still be claimed provided expenditure on the non-industrial purpose does not exceed 25% of the expenditure incurred in respect of the whole building.

22.3.2 The allowance

A writing down allowance of 2% (for 2009/10) of the original cost of construction (or purchase) of an industrial building can be claimed for every year when the building is in use. Note that this allowance was originally 4% and is being phased out by 1% each year until March 2011 when it will cease.

22.3.3 Sale of a building

Where the vendor who has been claiming this allowance sells the building, the purchaser can claim a writing down allowance. For nearly all sales after 21 March 2007, this allowance will be calculated on the residual qualifying expenditure of the vendor: the cost of the building to the vendor less the total writing down allowances claimed.

Consider the following example. A taxpayer bought a factory for £200,000 in 2002 and claimed the 4% writing down allowance for each of the first five years of his ownership (giving a total of allowances claimed of £40,000). After five years, in 2007, the taxpayer sold the building for £175,000. Notwithstanding the purchase price, the new owner could only claim writing down allowances on £160,000 (the original £200,000 cost to the vendor less the £40,000 allowances already claimed).

(Prior to 21 March 2007, a regime operated which provided for balancing charges to be levied or balancing allowances to be given to the vendor (see **22.2.2.2** for an explanation of balancing charges). This was varied by the 2007 Budget, as part of a scheme intended to lead to a final withdrawal of the industrial buildings capital allowances scheme by 2011.)

22.4 Other expenditure which attracts capital allowances

The Capital Allowances Act 2001 provides that capital allowances may be available in respect of:

(a) agricultural forestry buildings;

(b) scientific research;

(c) patents and 'know-how';

(d) mines, oil wells, mineral rights, cemeteries, crematoria and dredging; and

(e) hotels.

online resource centre
Interactive online exercises (Student Learning Activities) which complement the topics covered in this chapter are available at www.oxfordtextbooks.co.uk/orc/business09_10/.

Tax consequences of leaving and joining a partnership

This chapter covers the following topics:

23.1 Introduction

In **Chapter 5** we saw that it was possible for an individual to cease to be a partner on the happening of one of the following events:

(a) the dissolution of the partnership;

(b) his retirement or death; or

(c) expulsion from the partnership.

Having considered the legal consequences of the occurrence of these events in **Chapter 5**, we will concentrate in this chapter on the tax consequences (particularly the circumstances in which tax charges can arise). We will only consider the tax exemptions and reliefs where they are of special relevance.

We will also consider the position of a new partner joining the firm, whether or not as a replacement for a deceased, retired or expelled partner.

In this chapter we will not repeat the legal consequences so the reader is recommended to review **Chapter 5** for this information.

Reference is made throughout this chapter to both capital gains tax and inheritance tax. It is recommended, therefore, that **Chapter 18** has been read beforehand.

23.2 Tax consequences of the dissolution of a partnership

23.2.1 Introduction

If a partnership is dissolved by one of the methods explained in **Chapter 5**, the partnership relationship ceases and the assets of the business may be realised. From this will flow various tax consequences.

23.2.2 Income tax

If there is a permanent cessation (on a closure of the business) the relevant closing year rules will be applied (see **17.3.2.3**).

If the partnership has been claiming capital allowances on, for example, the plant and machinery used in the business, balancing charges may be levied if the assets are disposed of for more than their written down value on cessation. Balancing allowances may be claimed if the market value of the assets is less than their written down value.

Finally, if the partnership has made losses, loss relief under s. 89 ITA 2007 in respect of the final tax year of the trade may be claimed. Terminal loss relief will permit the partners to carry back losses made in the final 12 months of the trade against the profits of the same trade during the immediately preceding three tax years or set them off against other income in the year of cessation (see **17.4**).

23.2.3 Capital gains tax

If the partnership property is sold to outsiders following dissolution any gains realised by each partner on the disposal of his fractional share of the assets will be taxable in accordance with general principles. The general principles will also apply when a partner disposes of assets he owns personally but which have been used by the partnership.

23.2.4 Inheritance tax

If the assets of the partnership are disposed of at full market value on dissolution, there will be no reduction in the value of the transferor's estate and, therefore, no transfer of value. If there is no transfer of value there cannot be any IHT liability.

23.3 Tax consequences of the retirement of a partner

23.3.1 Introduction

As we explained in **Chapter 5**, while 'retirement' implies a person retiring from full-time work having reached normal retirement age, in the partnership context 'retirement' simply means leaving the partnership voluntarily so that the age of the 'retiring' partner is irrelevant. In this section we have examined the tax charges which can arise when there is such a change in the partnership.

23.3.2 Income tax

When any partner retires, the closing year rules will apply in order to calculate that partner's final partnership tax liability (see **17.3.3.3**).

23.3.3 Capital gains tax

23.3.3.1 Disposals amongst partners

Where one partner retires from the business he will normally relinquish his interest in the partnership assets in consideration of a capital sum and/or the provision of an income. The retiring partner's present interest in the business is shown on his capital account. He will be treated as making a disposal of that interest to the continuing partners (and to any new partners who are being admitted on his retirement). The continuing (and new) partners will acquire his interest and will thereafter have a greater interest in the business.

Disposals by a firm are subject to the normal CGT principles in determining whether a gain has arisen. However, the lack of a comprehensive body of legislation dealing with the taxation of capital gains realised by partners led to difficulties. HMRC's Statements of Practice D/12, SP 1/79 and SP 1/89 set out the Revenue's view of the way in which general capital gains tax principles apply in a partnership context. The underlying principle on which the Statement of Practice D/12, is based is that each partner is to be treated as owning a fractional share of each of the chargeable assets of the partnership (including goodwill). This concept forms the basis of the rules which follow.

In this section we will consider the capital gains tax consequences which arise, according to the Statements of Practice, when there is a change in the personnel of the partnership (principally on the retirement of a partner or when a new partner is admitted).

EXAMPLE

A, B, C and D share profits (and asset surplus) equally. The assets of the firm were acquired for £60,000. A is retiring and once he has retired, all the profits will be divided equally between B, C and D. The asset-sharing ratio will change as follows:

	Before	After
	£	£
A	15,000 (1/4)	(—)
B	15,000 (1/4)	20,000 (1/3)
C	15,000 (1/4)	20,000 (1/3)
D	15,000 (1/4)	20,000 (1/3)

A has disposed of his quarter interest to the continuing partners and is left with nothing. Each of the continuing partners receives one-third of A's quarter share (i.e., one-twelfth share in the partnership property). They will, naturally, each pay A for such share.

It can be clearly seen from the above example that the retiring partner has made a disposal to the continuing partners. The question then arises of whether or not the disposal has realised a gain (or a loss). Where the assets have not been revalued in the accounts and the retiring partner receives an amount equivalent to the balance on his capital account, he is simply receiving the return of his original capital contribution. There will be no gain and no loss (D/12, para. 4). For example, in the above illustration, if A was paid £15,000 he would realise neither a gain nor a loss.

However, there will be a gain on disposal where assets have been revalued in the accounts (D/12 para. 5). Where assets have increased in value since the date of acquisition the partners may wish to record this increase in the accounts; the process is referred to as a 'revaluation'. The values of the various assets are increased in the accounts and the balances on the partners' capital accounts are increased by a corresponding amount in order to reflect the increase in the worth of the business. A revaluation of itself gives rise to no charge to CGT since there has been no disposal. However, if after a revaluation there is a change in the asset surplus sharing ratio, for example on retirement, the disponer partner will receive more than his original capital contribution and (subject to reliefs) there will be a charge to capital gains tax.

EXAMPLE

The facts are as in the previous example but the partnership decides that prior to A's retirement the assets should be revalued from £60,000 to £90,000. A's share will be worth £22,500. Therefore A will be treated as disposing of assets for £22,500 which were acquired for £15,000, and will have a capital gain of £7,500.

	Before	On revaluation	After
	£	£	£
A	15,000(1/4)	22,500(1/4)	–
B	15,000(1/4)	22,500(1/4)	30,000(1/3)
C	15,000(1/4)	22,500(1/4)	30,000(1/3)
D	15,000(1/4)	22,500(1/4)	30,000(1/3)
	60,000	90,000	90,000

B, C, and D will each be treated as acquiring £7,500 worth of A's share in the assets and therefore their respective base costs will increase from £22,500 to £30,000. They are, therefore, holding assets which have increased in value to them from £15,000 to £30,000. When they realise the assets, there will be a CGT liability.

The members of the partnership, in order to minimise the burden of finding large capital sums, may agree not to revalue assets as and when partners retire. It could be argued that this is a gift by each retiring partner of his share in the increased value of the asset. In the case of a gift (or sale at an undervalue), HMRC can treat the disposal as made for market value unless it was a bargain made at arm's length. In the case of connected persons, transfers are always treated as otherwise than by way of bargains made at arm's length. Partners are normally connected but will not be when transferring property to each other provided the disposal *was pursuant to a bona fide commercial arrangement*. Thus, provided there is some bona fide commercial reason for not revaluing, HMRC will not seek to substitute market value.

Even where the partners are connected other than by partnership (for example, father and son) HMRC has stated that it will only seek to substitute market value where the transaction would not have been entered into by persons who were not at arm's length.

23.3.3.2   Entitlement to reliefs

If a charge to tax arises on the disposal by a partner of his interest in partnership property, the disponer will be entitled to claim the benefit of the CGT exemptions and reliefs in the normal way.

Details of relevant reliefs are given in **Chapter 18**.

23.3.3.3   Goodwill

Goodwill presents particular problems. In recent years partners (particularly in professional firms) who paid for a share in the goodwill of the firm when they were admitted to partnership have agreed not to charge incoming partners for a share (the burden of finding a large capital sum being regarded as too great). The effect of this is that the old partners write off goodwill. It is clear that when an old partner retires and receives no payment for the goodwill he makes a loss on that asset. Many partnerships have argued that the old partners are entitled to make a claim for CGT loss relief when the value of goodwill is written off. (Section 24(2) TCGA 1992 provides that where an inspector is satisfied that the value of an asset has become negligible he may allow an immediate loss.) HMRC resists such claims, taking the view that the goodwill still has a value and does not become negligible simply because the partners choose not to charge for it. However, claims for immediate loss relief have been successful in front of the General and the Special Commissioners. The position is unsettled and the practice varies between inspectors, some being prepared to allow such claims and some not.

23.3.3.4 Payment of annuities

A partnership may agree to pay a retiring partner an annuity. The annuity will be subject to income tax in the hands of the recipient partner. If it is more than can be regarded as reasonable recognition of the past contribution of work and effort by the partner to the partnership, HMRC will treat the capitalised value of the annuity as consideration for the disposal of the retiring partner's share in the assets. An annuity will be regarded as reasonable for this purpose if:

(a) the former partner had been in the partnership for at least 10 years;

(b) the annuity is no more than of his average share of profits in the best three of the last seven years in which he was required to devote substantially the whole of his time to acting as a partner.

23.3.3.5 Disposal of assets owned by partners personally

Where a partner disposes of an asset which he owns personally but which is used by the partnership, the Statements of Practice are not relevant. On such disposals the normal CGT principles are applied to ascertain whether a gain or loss has arisen. Similarly, the disposing partner will be able to claim any relevant exemptions or reliefs.

23.3.4 Inheritance tax

23.3.4.1 Gratuitous benefit

Normal principles of IHT apply in the partnership context. Thus, where a partner sells an interest in the partnership for full consideration there is no transfer of value and therefore no charge to IHT arises. If a partner sells an interest for less than full consideration or transfers it for no consideration at all, prima facie a charge to IHT will arise. However, s. 10 IHTA 1984 provides that a disposition is *not* a transfer of value if it was not intended to confer gratuitous benefit and was either made at arm's length between unconnected persons or, if between connected persons, was such as might be expected to be made between unconnected persons. Partners are not connected persons in respect of transfers between partners of partnership assets pursuant to bona fide commercial arrangements. Thus many transfers which might appear to be chargeable may escape IHT on the ground that there was no intention to confer a gratuitous benefit.

23.3.4.2 Goodwill

It is common for partners to agree that on their retirement (or death) their share of goodwill is to accrue automatically to the other partners without payment. This has the benefit of relieving the partnership of the need to pay for portions of goodwill as and when partners retire. Section 163(1) IHTA 1984 provides that where a person enters into a contract which excludes or restricts the right to dispose of any property the exclusion or restriction will be ignored in valuing the asset when it is next transferred except to the extent that consideration for the exclusion or restriction was given. The effect of s. 163 is that, unless consideration is given for the accruer clause, the clause will be ignored when the goodwill is valued on the transfer to the other partners and the full value of the retiring (or deceased) partner's share in the goodwill will be charged to tax.

23.3.4.3 Business property relief and other reliefs

In the event that an *inter vivos* transaction is regarded as a transfer of value it will be potentially exempt. If the transferor dies within seven years the transfer will be treated as if it had always been chargeable. An interest in the partnership is relevant business property qualifying for business property relief at 100% provided:

(a) the transferor had owned the property for at least two years up to the time of the transfer;

(b) the transferee still owns the property (or replacement property) and it still qualifies as relevant business property.

Where there is a gift of land, buildings, plant or machinery owned by a partner personally but used wholly or mainly for the purpose of the partnership of which he is a member, a reduction of only 50% is available.

The transferor's annual exemption may be available from the tax year of transfer and the preceding tax year, in which case it will reduce the value transferred.

Should a PET become chargeable tapering relief will be available if the transferor survives three years from the date of the transfer. The burden of the inheritance tax will fall on the transferee (unless the transferor provides otherwise in his will). In cases where the potential liability is large the transferee may wish to consider insuring the transferor's life. The option to pay inheritance tax by instalments will be available. The first will be due six months after the end of the month of the transferor's death. Interest will not be payable unless an instalment is late.

23.4 Tax consequences of death of a partner

23.4.1 Introduction

As we saw in **Chapter 5**, under the Partnership Act death causes the automatic dissolution of a partnership, although it is common to provide in partnership agreements that this will not happen. In this section, we look at the tax consequences of the death of a partner.

23.4.2 Income tax

The deceased partner's income will be subject to the closing year rules.

23.4.3 Capital gains tax

The deceased partner's interest in the partnership assets is *acquired* by his personal representatives at market value on the date of death. Since a disposal is a prerequisite for liability to CGT, this means that no CGT is payable on death and that unrealised gains arising during the deceased's lifetime escape the charge to tax.

23.4.4 Inheritance tax

23.4.4.1 General

The estate of a deceased partner will include his interest in the partnership assets. Under s. 4(1) IHTA 1984, the partner is deemed to make a transfer of value on his death and the value transferred is the value of the assets in his estate immediately before his death. Accordingly, subject to exemptions, reliefs and the deceased partner's cumulative total at the date of death, IHT will be payable in respect of the market value of his share in the partnership.

Changes in the value of assets resulting from death are taken into account for IHT purposes. If all or part of the value of the goodwill of the business was personal to the deceased partner the value of the goodwill, and therefore of the business, will fall as a result of the death. The reduced value of the deceased partner's share in the business will then be included in his estate for IHT purposes.

23.4.4.2 Business property relief

Where an IHT liability does arise on death it may be reduced by virtue of the relief for business property given by ss. 103–114 IHTA 1984 (and considered in **23.3.4.3**).

However, there is no entitlement to claim the relief if the assets are the subject of a binding contract for sale at the time of death. A clause in the partnership agreement to the effect that the surviving partners are *obliged* to buy and the personal representatives of the deceased partner are *obliged* to sell the deceased partner's share may have been included in the agreement for sound commercial reasons but it will result in the loss of business property relief. This is because HMRC regard such clauses as amounting to binding contracts (see Statement of Practice 12/80 dated 13 October 1980). If there is no *obligation* to buy and sell, the relief is available and so this difficulty can be avoided by the use of an option arrangement or an automatic accruer clause.

23.4.4.3 Instalment option

IHT attributable to an interest in partnership property can be paid in 10 yearly instalments under ss. 227 and 228 IHTA 1984. The first instalment is due six months after the end of the month of death and no interest is due unless an instalment is late. If the interest in partnership property is sold, all outstanding IHT must be paid off. Where the continuing partners purchase the interest of a deceased partner the instalment option will not thereafter be available to the deceased partner's estate.

23.5 Tax consequences of expulsion from a partnership

In **Chapter 5** we saw that s. 25 of the Partnership Act 1890 provides that the majority of the partners can expel any partner unless a power to do so has been conferred by express agreement between the partners. If the partnership agreement does contain such a power and it is exercised, the tax consequences of expulsion are the same as for retirement.

23.6   Tax consequences of admission of a new partner

23.6.1   Introduction

Although this chapter is primarily concerned with leaving a partnership, the admission of new partners is a topic so closely connected that it seems appropriate to deal with it here.

23.6.2   Income tax

Because partners are treated as notional sole traders for tax purposes, when a partnership starts up, all partners will be equally subject to the opening year rules (see **17.3.2.2**). Accordingly, when a new partner is admitted to an existing partnership, that partner will be treated as if starting up a trade and will initially be subject to the opening year rules, while the original partners will continue to be taxed on the normal current year basis.

EXAMPLE

Y and T are in partnership sharing profits equally. The accounting year end for the business is 30 June. On 1 January 2009, W is admitted to the partnership and will share profits equally with Y and T. W joins, therefore, in the tax year 2008/09.

The tax liability of Y and T for the tax year 2008/09 will be based on profits to the year end 30 June 2008. W's tax liability for his year of joining (2008/09) will, according to the opening year rules, be based upon his profit entitlement from 1 January 2009 to 5 April 2009.

The tax liability of Y and T for the 2009/10 tax year will be based on the share of profits earned during the accounting year ending on 30 June 2009; one-half of profits each up to the date of W's joining and one-third each thereafter.

The tax liability of W for the 2009/10 tax year will be based on W's share of profits for his first 12 months of notional trading, i.e., from 1 January 2009 to 31 December 2009. (This is because the relevant year end in this tax year is not more than 12 months from the date of W's joining.)

For the tax year 20010/11 all three partners will be assessed on a current year basis on profits up to the year end 30 June 2010.

It will be noted that W's tax liability is based upon a certain amount of double taxation; the profits from 1 January 2009 to 5 April 2009 are taxed twice along with profits from 1 July 2009 to 31 December 2009. C may be able to claim overlap relief in respect of this.

If the new partner has to borrow money to raise the funds to buy into the partnership, the borrower will be able to deduct the interest as a charge on his income. The same relief is available if the borrower uses the funds to contribute additional capital to the partnership or to make a loan to the partnership, if it is used exclusively for the partnership's business purposes.

23.6.3   Capital gains tax

A newly admitted partner will acquire an interest in the partnership assets either by purchase or by gift. Thus, for example, if the old partners give the incoming partner a one-third share in profits and asset surpluses, he will acquire one-third of the value of the partnership assets at that date. That value will be his acquisition value.

EXAMPLE 1

A and B, who share profits and assets equally, decide to admit C and to share profits and assets equally thereafter. The partnership assets are shown in the accounts as worth £120,000 at the date of C's admission.

	Before	After
	£	£
A	60,000(1/2)	40,000(1/3)
B	60,000(1/2)	40,000(1/3)
C	—	40,000(1/3)

C's acquisition value is, therefore, £40,000. A and B have disposed of a part of their share in the assets surplus. As discussed above there will be no charge to CGT on such a disposal provided there has been no upward revaluation of the assets in the accounts and provided no payment is made. The old partners are treated as making a disposal for a consideration equal to their capital gains tax cost so that there will be neither a chargeable gain nor an allowable loss at that point. They will carry forward a smaller proportion of cost to set against a subsequent disposal of their assets. HMRC will not seek to substitute market value in such a case since the transaction is likely to be a bona fide commercial transaction where the continuing partners dispose of a share in the asset surpluses but in consideration of the incoming partner covenanting to devote himself to the partnership.

If there has been an upward revaluation in the accounts there will be a potential charge to CGT.

EXAMPLE 2

Taking the same facts as those for the previous example, suppose that the assets are revalued at £180,000 a month prior to C's joining. The accounts would differ as follows:

	Before	After
	£	£
A	90,000	60,000
B	90,000	60,000
C	—	60,000

Both A and B have disposed of one-third each of their entitlement to the assets, such share originally being worth £20,000 (1/3 × £60,000) but which after revaluation stands at £30,000. Each has, therefore, realised a gain (ignoring indexation, etc.) of £10,000. C takes the share of the assets with a base cost of £60,000.

23.6.4 Inheritance tax

Inheritance tax is unlikely to be an immediate problem for a newly admitted partner. However, he might be the recipient of a potentially exempt transfer of value. If so, it is possible that the transfer will become chargeable if one or more of the transferor partners dies within seven years. The donee of an *inter vivos* transfer of partnership property may exercise the right to pay by way of 10 equal yearly instalments, the first due six months after the end of the month of transfer. Interest is not charged unless an instalment is late.

Value Added Tax

This chapter covers the following topics:

24.1 Introduction

24.2 Registration

24.3 Taxable supplies and the charge to VAT

24.4 Accounting for VAT.

24.1 Introduction

Value Added Tax (VAT) is charged on supplies of goods and services made in the UK. Where a person makes taxable supplies in excess of a set limit in any one-year period, he must register with HM Revenue and Customs (HMRC). He must then account to HMRC for VAT on all taxable supplies made. The total amount payable may be reduced by the amount of VAT which he has paid on certain taxable supplies made *to him*.

The liability to pay VAT to HMRC rests on suppliers of goods and services. However, the cost of the tax is actually borne by suppliers' customers (unless they can recover VAT) who are charged VAT on the goods and services they purchase.

VAT is charged in the UK under the Value Added Tax Act (VATA) 1994. The obligation to charge VAT arose when the UK became a member of the European Economic Community in 1973. VAT is the common tax on business turnover within the European Union and should be applied in the same manner in each member State.

24.2 Registration

24.2.1 Turnover limits for registration

Under Sch. 1 VATA 1994, a person becomes liable to register for VAT with HMRC if:

(a) at the end of any month, the value of taxable supplies made during the past year exceeds £68,000; or

(b) at any time, there are reasonable grounds to believe that the value of taxable supplies to be made in the next 30 days alone will exceed £68,000.

If, at the end of any month, a person's taxable turnover in the past 12 months or less exceeds £68,000 but HMRC is satisfied that it will not exceed £66,000 in the next 12 months, that person will not have to be registered.

Where a person makes taxable supplies which do not exceed the relevant turnover limits, he may apply to be registered for VAT on a voluntary basis. The relevant turnover limits for registration are those in force from 1 May 2009 and may be altered in the future.

24.2.2 'Person' for VAT purposes

VATA 1994 requires registration by a 'person'. The latter includes an individual, a body corporate, or a partnership (notwithstanding that the latter has no separate legal personality). A person is only entitled to one VAT registration (irrespective of the number of businesses run) and is therefore liable for VAT on taxable supplies made by *all* of their businesses. There are exceptions to this rule, one being that a company which is organised into several divisions may seek registration for each division.

24.2.3 Registration documentation

A person applying for VAT registration must complete an application form, VAT 1. A partnership must also submit details of all the partners on a Form VAT 2.

24.2.4 Effect of registration

Once registered, a person is liable to account for VAT to HMRC on all taxable supplies of goods and services made in the UK.

24.2.5 De-registration

A person may apply to be de-registered for VAT if he ceases to make taxable supplies or if he can satisfy HMRC that taxable supplies for the next 12 months will not exceed £66,000. This turnover limit for de-registration is that in force from 1 May 2009 and may be altered in the future.

24.3 Taxable supplies and the charge to VAT

24.3.1 Taxable supplies

VAT is charged on taxable supplies of goods and services made in the UK. A taxable supply is one which is made in the course of furtherance of business and is not classified as exempt from VAT under Sch. 9 VATA 1994. (Examples of exempt supplies include most sales of land and buildings, insurance, doctors' services and certain types of education services.)

24.3.2 Rates of VAT on taxable supplies

A taxable supply will be charged at one of two rates: standard or zero. From April 1991 to November 2008, the standard rate of VAT was 17.5%. A temporary reduction in this rate, to 15%, was implemented from 1 December 2008 until 31 December 2009. The standard rate will revert to 17.5% from 1 January 2010 and the examples given below are therefore based on this standard rate.

Zero-rated supplies do not actually give rise to a VAT charge; however, they may allow a person to recover input tax paid on supplies *received by the supplier* (see **24.4.4**).

Zero-rated supplies are set out in Sch. 8 VATA 1994 and include:

Food (except restaurant and hot take-away);

Children's clothing and shoes;

Books and newspapers;

Sales of new houses.

24.4   Accounting for VAT

24.4.1   Charging VAT to customers

A person should start charging VAT to his customers and keep relevant records as soon as he realises that he is liable to register for VAT with HMRC.

24.4.2   Invoice to customers

Once registered, a person will be given a VAT registration number. This must be included on tax invoices sent to customers for supplies of goods or services. The tax invoice should also include the date of supply, type of supply, total amount payable, and the amount of VAT chargeable at the relevant rate. This VAT, charged to customers, will meet the liability to HMRC.

24.4.3   VAT return

A registered person is required to make a VAT return on Form VAT 100 every three months (although monthly or annual returns may be agreed with HMRC). This return determines a person's VAT liability to HMRC: thus a system of *self-assessment* operates. The form must be completed and returned, together with the tax payable, within a month of the end of the three-month period to which it relates. There is an option, for businesses with a turnover of up to £1,350,000, to join an annual accounting scheme. This allows a business to submit a single VAT return each year. The business makes either three (quarterly) or nine (monthly) advance payments to HMRC of the VAT it expects to owe at the end of the year. The business's VAT return is then sent in at the year-end, together with any outstanding VAT payable. If the business has overpaid VAT, it will be returned by HMRC. This scheme is intended to assist businesses in managing cash-flow by making regular payments.

24.4.4   Amount of VAT payable

24.4.4.1   Standard method of calculating net tax due

The amount of VAT payable by a taxable person will effectively be the standard rate of 17.5% as charged on all supplies of goods and services made in the relevant three-month period. This is often referred to as *output tax*, i.e., the amount of VAT charged to customers on supplies *made* by a taxable person.

Output tax may be reduced by *input* tax. This is VAT which the taxable person has paid on supplies *made to* him. However the amount of input tax which can be set off against output tax is limited to such input tax as is attributable to taxable supplies made by that person. Put another way, a taxable person can only set off input tax which relates to supplies which are then used in some way in his making taxable supplies to others.

If a person makes zero-rated supplies, there is no output tax charge. From a customer's perspective, it is as if it is an exempt supply. However, the taxable person is entitled to recover any input tax attributable to zero-rated supplies made by him. This is the benefit derived from zero-rated supplies, compared with exempt supplies.

It should be noted that it is possible, particularly where a person makes predominantly zero-rated supplies, for recoverable input tax to be in excess of output tax. In such cases, HMRC will repay any excess.

The ability to recover input tax and the effect of zero-rated supplies is illustrated in the following examples. The following should be noted:

(a) each example relates to a single three-month VAT period;

(b) the input tax has been assumed to be wholly attributable to the taxable supplies made; and

(c) the supplies received and made figures are shown *exclusive* of any VAT, the latter being shown in a separate column.

EXAMPLE 1

Cost of supplies received	VAT on supplies received (input tax)	Standard rate supplies made	VAT on supplies (output tax)	Net VAT payable
1,000	175	1,600	280	105

EXAMPLE 2

Cost of supplies received	VAT on supplies received (input tax)	Zero-rate supplies made	VAT on supplies (output tax)	Net VAT recovered
1,000	175	1,600	0	175

24.4.4.2   Optional flat rate scheme

HM Revenue and Customs operates a scheme which enables businesses to calculate their net VAT due simply by applying a flat rate percentage to their tax-inclusive turnover (the total turnover generated, including all reduced, zero rate, and exempt income). The flat rate percentage will depend upon the trade sector into which a business falls for the purposes of the scheme. Businesses which can join the scheme are currently limited to those having:

(a) a VAT-exclusive annual taxable turnover of up to £150,000; and

(b) a VAT-exclusive annual total turnover, including the value of exempt and/or other non-taxable income, of up to £187,500.

The aim of the scheme is to ease the administrative burden on small businesses. Those who opt to use the scheme, in most cases, can work out the net VAT due by simply recording their tax-inclusive turnover and applying the appropriate flat rate percentage for their trade sector. Businesses will still need to issue tax invoices to their VAT registered customers, but will not have to record all the details of the invoices issued or purchase invoices received to calculate their VAT. Businesses may be part of both the flat rate and annual return (see **24.4.3**) schemes.

24.4.5   Calculation of tax on VAT-inclusive figure: the VAT fraction

Calculation of standard rate VAT or payable on *VAT-exclusive* figures (as used in the above examples) is comparatively easy. It merely requires calculation of 17.5% of the VAT-exclusive figure.

A figure which combines both the price of the supply *and* the VAT payable on the supply is said to be *VAT-inclusive*. To calculate the VAT element of a VAT-inclusive figure, you need to multiply the figure by a fraction which will provide the equivalent of 17.5% on the VAT-exclusive price. That fraction is 7/47 and is known as the *VAT fraction*. It will obviously change with the standard rate of VAT.

EXAMPLE

The VAT-inclusive price of goods supplied is £2,800.
7/47 of £2,800 = £417.02. This latter figure is the amount of VAT payable.
Therefore, the VAT-exclusive price of the goods is £2,800 − £417.02 = £2,382.98.
(NB 17.5% of £2,382.98 = £417.02.)

---

 online resource centre   Interactive online exercises (Student Learning Activities) which complement the topics covered in this chapter are available at www.oxfordtextbooks.co.uk/orc/ business09_10/.

Insolvency

Bankruptcy

This chapter covers the following topics:

25.1 Introduction

The risk of personal bankruptcy is a spectre which haunts many partners and sole traders. If a partner or sole trader finds that he is unable to pay his debts as they fall due, he may be made personally bankrupt. Thus, the partner or sole trader may be made bankrupt if his liabilities exceed his assets; he faces the same risk if he has insufficient liquid assets to pay his current liabilities even if the value of his total assets exceeds the value of his total liabilities.

It is to avoid this risk that many entrepreneurs choose to trade through a limited company. However, it should not be forgotten that the directors and members of a company may face personal bankruptcy where, for example, a director or shareholder has personally guaranteed a loan to the company or where a director is liable for 'wrongful' trading.

The members or partners may, of course, also find themselves facing bankruptcy as a result of a financial collapse entirely unconnected with the business of their own company or partnership.

The law of bankruptcy is now mostly contained in the Insolvency Act (IA) 1986 together with delegated legislation made under its provisions. The Enterprise Act (EA) 2002 amended the 1986 Act in a number of ways. These changes came into force for the financial year 2004 and:

(a) shortened the period for automatic discharge of most bankrupts;

(b) introduced a new Bankruptcy Restriction Order regime;

(c) imposed a time limit within which a trustee in bankruptcy must deal with a family home; and

(d) introduced a fast track individual voluntary arrangement scheme.

The overall intention behind these changes was to promote a more entreprenurial culture within the UK whilst ensuring that the public remains protected from anyone who is irresponsible or reckless in carrying on their business.

In this chapter we will summarise the law under the following headings:

(a) The procedure for making a person bankrupt.

(b) The appointment, function and removal of the trustee in bankruptcy.

(c) The effect of the bankruptcy order on the bankrupt personally.

(d) The provisions relating to the assets in the bankrupt's estate.

(e) The distribution of the bankrupt's assets.

(f) The duration of the bankruptcy and the discharge of the bankrupt.

(g) The rules governing voluntary arrangements contained in the Insolvency Act 1986.

A debtor who finds himself unable to meet all his debts in full may:

(a) be adjudicated bankrupt; or

(b) have his estate administered by a qualified insolvency practitioner under a voluntary arrangement (see **25.8** below).

25.2 The bankruptcy procedure

25.2.1 Introduction

Bankruptcy proceedings are commenced by the presentation of a petition for a bankruptcy order. The petitioners (who, broadly speaking, simply have to prove that the debtor is unable to pay his debts) are:

(a) a creditor (or creditors jointly) whether secured or unsecured; or

(b) the debtor personally; or

(c) a supervisor of, or a person bound by, a voluntary scheme; or

(d) the Director of Public Prosecutions.

25.2.2 Procedure on a creditor's petition

25.2.2.1 Prerequisites for presentation of a creditor's petition

The court will only entertain a petition presented by a creditor or creditors if certain conditions are satisfied:

(a) The debtor must normally be domiciled or personally present in England and Wales when the petition is presented.

(b) The debt (or debts) which are the basis of the petition must be for a liquidated sum.

(c) The debt (or debts) must amount to at least £750. (This sum can be changed from time to time by statutory instrument.)

(d) The debt must be unsecured. A secured creditor can present a petition but only if he relinquishes his security or petitions only for the unsecured part of the debt.

25.2.2.2 Grounds for presenting a creditor's petition

The petitioning creditor must allege that the debtor appears either:

(a) to be unable to pay; or

(b) to have no reasonable prospect of paying

the debt or debts specified in the petition and that there are no outstanding applications to have a 'statutory demand' set aside. (A 'statutory demand' is a demand in a form which complies with the Insolvency Rules 1986, r. 6.1.) The functions of the demand are described below.

25.2.2.3 Proving inability to pay debt

Before the court will make the order, the debtor's inability to pay his debt or debts may be proved in one of two ways:

(a) by showing that a 'statutory demand' served on the debtor requiring him to pay, secure or compound for the debt to the satisfaction of the petitioning creditor has not been complied with within three weeks;

(b) by showing that execution or other process issued in respect of the debt as a judgment or order of any court has been returned unsatisfied in whole or in part.

25.2.2.4 Grounds on which court may dismiss petition

Once a petition has been presented by a creditor the court may dismiss the petition if it is shown that the debtor can pay all his debts, including contingent and prospective debts; if the creditor has unreasonably refused any offer made by the debtor in response to a 'statutory demand'; or if it is appropriate to dismiss the petition for any reason, including a breach of the rules.

The court *must* dismiss a petition if a 'statutory demand' has been complied with.

25.2.3 Procedure on a debtor's own petition

The debtor himself may present a petition provided he has a connection with England and Wales. Accordingly the debtor must be able to show that he satisfies the requirements set out in **25.2.2.1 (a)** above.

The only ground on which the petition can be based is that the debtor is unable to pay his debts. When presenting the petition, the debtor must lodge a 'statement of affairs' giving full details of his assets, liabilities and creditors. Once presented, the petition can only be withdrawn with leave of the court.

In most cases the court will order an insolvency practitioner to inquire into the debtor's affairs and report on whether the debtor is willing to make a proposal for a composition with his creditors and/or whether the creditors should be summoned to a meeting at which they will consider such a proposal. Having considered the report of the insolvency practitioner the court can, if it considers it appropriate, make a bankruptcy order. Otherwise the voluntary composition will be pursued or the court can issue a certificate of summary administration.

25.2.4 Presentation of a petition by a supervisor of, or a person bound by, a voluntary scheme

The supervisor of, or a person bound by, a voluntary scheme (the details of which are considered below in **25.8**) may base a petition on the following grounds:

(a) that the debtor has failed to comply with his obligations under the scheme (or failure to comply with the supervisor's reasonable requests in connection with the scheme);

(b) that the debtor has provided false or misleading information in connection with entry into the scheme.

25.2.5 Presentation of a petition by the Director of Public Prosecutions

The DPP has power (under the Powers of Criminal Courts Act 1973) to apply to have a person made criminally bankrupt if the person has been convicted of an offence where loss in excess of a specified value has occurred.

25.2.6 Consequences of presenting a petition

25.2.6.1 Restrictions on dispositions

A debtor who is the subject of a bankruptcy petition may be tempted to dispose of property before he is adjudicated bankrupt. The IA 1986 makes void any disposition of property or payment of money made after the presentation of a petition if the debtor is subsequently adjudicated bankrupt unless the court approves the transaction either before or after it takes place.

25.2.6.2 Restrictions on proceedings

The court has power to stay any action, execution or legal process against the debtor or his assets while bankruptcy proceedings are pending.

25.2.7 Making the bankruptcy order

Once the petition has been presented, the court may exercise its discretion to make a bankruptcy order (or, in the case of a petition presented by the debtor personally, to make an interim order so that a voluntary composition with the creditors can be arranged).

25.2.8 Procedure following the making of the bankruptcy order

25.2.8.1 The official receiver becomes receiver and manager of the estate

Unless a trustee in bankruptcy is appointed at the time the bankruptcy order is made, the official receiver (who is an official of the court) will become the receiver and manager of the bankrupt's estate on the making of the order, pending the appointment of a trustee in bankruptcy.

25.2.8.2 Statement of affairs by the bankrupt

The bankrupt must, unless the official receiver dispenses with the requirement, prepare a statement of his affairs within 21 days (although this time limit may be extended by the official receiver). Failure to do so is contempt of court.

When the debtor presents his own petition he must prepare a statement of affairs which is lodged with the petition.

25.2.8.3 Public examination of the bankrupt

At any time after the order is made and before the bankrupt is discharged, the official receiver can apply for an order that the bankrupt be required to attend a public examination of his affairs.

25.2.8.4 Appointment of a committee of creditors

Following the making of the bankruptcy order, a committee of creditors can be appointed by the creditors (unless the official receiver has been appointed as trustee in bankruptcy, in which case the Secretary of State performs the function of the committee).

25.3 The trustee in bankruptcy

25.3.1 Introduction

The IA 1986 provides that the administration of a bankrupt estate should be carried out by a trustee in bankruptcy.

25.3.2 Appointment

The procedure for appointing a trustee in bankruptcy and the date on which his appointment takes effect differ depending on who makes the appointment.

25.3.2.1 Appointment by creditors

If the official receiver is acting as receiver and manager of the bankrupt's estate, he has 12 weeks from the making of the order to decide whether to call a meeting of the creditors for the purpose of appointing a trustee. If he decides to call such a meeting he must notify the creditors within the 12-week period. He *must* call such a meeting if one quarter (by value) of the creditors demand it and if he decides not to call a meeting, one quarter (by value) of the creditors can override his decision. Provided the creditors do not object to no meeting being called, on notifying the court that no meeting will be held, the official receiver automatically becomes the trustee.

25.3.2.2 Appointment by the court

If the order is based on the debtor's own petition, the insolvency practitioner who is appointed to report on the debtor's affairs can be appointed as the trustee.

25.3.2.3 Appointment by the Secretary of State

The Secretary of State has power to appoint the trustee if the creditors fail to make an appointment at their meeting.

25.3.3 Functions of the trustee

The function of the trustee is to get in, realise and distribute the bankrupt's estate in accordance with the provisions of the Act.

25.3.4   Powers of the trustee

The Act gives the trustee wide powers which he may exercise in the course of administering the bankrupt's affairs. He may:

(a) sell any part of the property for the time being comprised in the bankrupt's estate, including the goodwill and book debts of any business;

(b) give receipts for any money received by him;

(c) prove, rank, claim and draw a dividend in respect of such debts *due* to the bankrupt as are comprised in the bankrupt's estate;

(d) exercise in relation to any property comprised in the bankrupt's estate any powers which the Act vests in him as trustee;

(e) exercise all the powers of a receiver appointed by the High Court to enable him to collect or retain the bankrupt's estate;

(f) exercise all the powers the bankrupt could exercise to transfer shares, stock or other property;

(g) exercise extensive powers to require delivery, production or inspection of books, documents and records;

(h) apply to the court for orders directing the bankrupt to do any act in connection with the administration of the estate;

(i) hold property, make contracts, sue and be sued, employ agents, execute documents and do any act which may be necessary or expedient for the exercise of his powers;

(j) disclaim onerous property (e.g., unprofitable contracts).

There are certain further powers which are only exercisable with the consent of the committee of creditors (if there is one) or of the court. These include:

(a) power to carry on the bankrupt's business with a view to a beneficial winding up;

(b) power to mortgage or pledge assets with a view to raising money for the estate;

(c) power to make any compromise or arrangement as may be expedient with the creditors of the estate;

(d) power to require the bankrupt to do any acts in the management or carrying on of the bankrupt's business.

25.3.5   Retirement, removal and release

25.3.5.1   Resignation

A trustee in bankruptcy may resign only if the resignation is accepted either by a creditors' meeting or by the court. Resignation must arise out of ill-health, retirement from practice, conflict of interest or other sufficient causes.

25.3.5.2   Removal

The appointees of creditors can be removed either by the court or by the creditors themselves at a general meeting summoned specially for the purpose.

25.4 Effect of the bankruptcy order on the bankrupt personally

If the court exercises its discretion to make a bankruptcy order against the debtor, he will become an undischarged bankrupt and will be deprived of the ownership of his property.

An undischarged bankrupt suffers certain disabilities; for example, he cannot practise as a solicitor or barrister nor act as a director, nor be involved in the management of a company. Furthermore, an undischarged bankrupt faces criminal liability if he commits one of the offences specified in the 1986 Act. These include making gifts of property, concealing property, and obtaining credit without disclosing the bankruptcy.

25.5 Assets in the bankrupt's estate

25.5.1 Introduction

The trustee in bankruptcy is under an obligation to collect the bankrupt's assets and distribute them among the bankrupt's creditors. In this section, we consider which assets can be claimed by the trustee towards payment of the bankrupt's debts.

25.5.2 Avoidance of dispositions made after the presentation of the petition

Any disposition made by the bankrupt in the period between presentation of the petition and the date the estate of the bankrupt vests in the trustee in bankruptcy is void, unless the court gave prior consent (or subsequently ratifies) the disposition.

25.5.3 Vesting the assets in the trustee

Once the bankruptcy order is made, the undischarged bankrupt is deprived of the ownership of his property.

25.5.4 Bankrupt's family home

Prior to the Enterprise Act 2002, the bankrupt's home vested in the trustee with no time limit within which the latter was required to deal with it. Now the trustee must deal with the bankrupt's interest in the property within three years, failing which it will revert back to the bankrupt unless the trustee:

(a) realises the interest;

(b) applies for an order of sale or possession in respect of the premises in which the interest subsists;

(c) applies for a charging order over the premises in respect of the value of the interest; or

(d) enters into an agreement with the bankrupt regarding the interest.

The three-year period may be extended by application to the court.

25.5.5   Property not available to the trustee

If the bankrupt enjoyed a purely personal right, such as the benefit of the Rent Act statutory tenancy, this is not available to the trustee. The following items are also not available for distribution:

(a) property held by the bankrupt in trust for any other person;

(b) the tools of his trade, as well as such wearing apparel and bedding as is necessary to satisfy the basic needs of the bankrupt and his family;

(c) the personal earnings of the bankrupt to the extent that those earnings are not in excess of what is required to satisfy the reasonable domestic needs of the bankrupt and his family.

25.5.6   Extension of trustee's title to bankrupt's property

The Act gives the trustee power to claim assets which are no longer in the possession or ownership of the bankrupt in the circumstances set out below.

25.5.6.1   Transactions defrauding creditors (ss. 423 to 425)

Grounds

Section 423 IA 1986 can be used to give relief in respect of transactions defrauding creditors. To be within the scope of s. 423 a transaction must be:

(a) a transaction at an undervalue entered into between one person and another; and

(b) be accompanied by the requisite intent, namely that it is done for the purpose of putting assets beyond the reach of a person who is making, or may at some time make, a claim against the relevant person, or of otherwise prejudicing the interests of such a person in relation to the claim which he is making or may make.

Time limit

The transaction which is the subject of an action under s. 423 can have taken place at any time; there is no time limit.

25.5.6.2   Undervalue transactions

If a person who is subsequently made bankrupt has transferred property to, for example, a member of his family or to trustees to hold for the benefit of his family the transaction may be voidable under s. 339 IA 1986.

Grounds on which transaction voidable

If the transaction is at an undervalue and is with a person who is not an associate of the transferor, it is voidable at the instance of the trustee in bankruptcy if the transaction took place within the five years ending with the day on which the bankruptcy petition which ultimately led to the individual being adjudged bankrupt was presented (unless the debtor was solvent at the time of, and despite entering into, the transaction). However, if the individual entered into the transaction at an undervalue within two years of the presentation of the relevant bankruptcy petition, the transaction is voidable irrespective of whether the debtor was insolvent at the time of, or as a result of, the transaction.

Transfer to associate

In circumstances where the transferee is an 'associate' of the transferor, transactions entered into during the period of two to five years preceding the presentation of the petition are presumed, unless it can be *proved* to the contrary, to have taken place at a time when the transferor was insolvent. 'Associate' is defined as the bankrupt's spouse or former or reputed spouse, and, in relation to any of them or the bankrupt, a brother, sister, uncle, aunt, nephew, niece, lineal ancestor or lineal descendant (including relatives of the half-blood, stepchildren, adopted and illegitimate children). A company controlled by the bankrupt or any associate(s), as defined, is an associate.

25.5.6.3 Voidable preferences

A debtor who is in financial difficulties may not only make an undervalue transaction (as described in **25.5.5.2** above) but he may also be tempted to give a 'voidable preference' (s. 340 IA 1986).

Grounds

A 'voidable preference' consists of the debtor doing or suffering anything to be done at a time when he is insolvent which 'has the effect of putting [the person who benefits from the preference] into a position which, in the event of the [debtor's] bankruptcy, will be better than the position he would have been in if that thing had not been done'. Thus, a debtor discharging one of his unsecured, ordinary creditor's debts in full at a time when his assets are insufficient to discharge *all* his debts in full may have given a voidable preference.

If the trustee in bankruptcy considers that a voidable preference has been made, he may apply to the court to remedy the preference. However, an order can only be made where it can be proved that the debtor was 'influenced in deciding to give it by a desire' to improve the position of the creditor. Under these provisions the intention to prefer the particular creditor need not be the *dominant* intention.

Preference given to 'associate'

In cases where the preference is given by an individual to his 'associate' (see **25.5.5.2** above), there is a *presumption* that the debtor was influenced by the desire which would make the preference voidable, unless the contrary is proved.

Time limits

A preference is voidable if it takes place within the two years ending with the presentation of the bankruptcy petition, if the person preferred is an associate, but in other cases the preference is only actionable if it took place in the six months preceding the presentation of the petition.

25.5.6.4 Family homes

The Insolvency Act contains provisions designed to protect the family home of the bankrupt for the benefit of his family (see also **25.5.4**).

If the family home is owned in the sole name of the bankrupt the 1986 Act charges the right of occupation of the spouse of the bankrupt on the interest of the trustee in bankruptcy in the matrimonial home. If an application is made to realise the bankrupt's interest in the house the court will consider certain factors when deciding whether to grant an application for sale of the house. These factors include the creditors' interests, the needs and resources of the spouse, the needs of the children, whether the spouse's conduct contributed to the bankruptcy and all other relevant circumstances. (If the matrimonial home is owned in joint names by the bankrupt and his spouse, the discretionary factors listed above will be taken into account when the trustee applies under s. 30 of the Law of Property Act 1925 to realise the bankrupt's interest.) If the application is made after one year has elapsed since the bankrupt's property vested in the trustee in bankruptcy, the interests of the creditors will be paramount.

If the bankrupt's minor children lived in the home at the time of presenting the petition and when the bankruptcy order was made, the bankrupt cannot be evicted without a court order. The court will consider the creditors' interests, the bankrupt's financial resources, the needs of the children and all the circumstances when deciding whether to make the eviction order. If the application is made after one year has elapsed since the bankrupt's estate vested in his trustee the interests of the creditors will outweigh all other considerations, unless the circumstances are exceptional.

25.6 Distribution of the bankrupt's assets

25.6.1 Distribution procedure

Having realised as much of the bankrupt's assets as possible without needlessly protracting the administration of the estate, the trustee must notify the creditors that he intends to declare a final dividend (or that no dividend will be declared). The notice must also state a final date for the proving of claims (although the court has power, on application by any person, to postpone this date). Subject to any postponement, any creditor who fails to prove by the final date may be ignored in the final dividend.

25.6.2 Order of priority for payment of debts

The distribution of the bankrupt's assets must be made strictly in accordance with the statutory order for payment of debts which is as follows:

(a) secured creditors, who take the mortgaged or charged property in priority to all other claims. However, if the security is insufficient to meet the debt, as far as the excess is concerned, the secured creditor claims as an ordinary creditor;

(b) the administration costs of the bankruptcy paid to the official receiver, the trustee in bankruptcy and others, including professional advisers who have given assistance;

(c) certain sums paid to masters by their apprentices;

(d) the preferential debts which are the same as those relevant on a company liquidation (see **25.8.3**). These debts are calculated by reference to the 'relevant date', which, generally, is the date the bankruptcy order is made (unless an interim receiver is appointed following the presentation of the petition, in which case the date is that on which the receiver is first appointed), and include:

(i) employees' arrears of wages or salary (including time or piece work and commission) for four months prior to the relevant date subject to an overall financial limit prescribed by delegated legislation (currently £800). These sums include sick pay, protective awards, and payments for time off work, such as on trade union work;

(ii) accrued holiday remuneration;

(e) the ordinary unsecured creditors;

(f) statutory interest which will be paid if a surplus remains after all previous claims have been paid. This interest is paid from the date of the order to the date of payment and the rate is the greater of the rate provided for in s. 17 of the Judgments Act 1838 and the rate the bankrupt would have had to pay on the debt if he had not been made bankrupt;

(g) the postponed creditors such as the spouse of the bankrupt who has a provable debt as a result of a loan to the bankrupt spouse;

(h) the bankrupt receives any surplus.

Each class of creditor must be paid in full before the next class receives anything. If the assets are insufficient to meet the debts owed to the creditors of the class, they are paid rateably according to value.

25.7 Duration of the bankruptcy and discharge of the bankrupt

25.7.1 Discharge of the bankrupt

Following the Enterprise Act 2002, from 1 April 2004, the majority of those made bankrupt after this date will be automatically discharged one year after the date of the bankrupt order. The period may even be shorter if:

(a) a bankrupt fully co-operates with the Official Receiver and/or trustee;

(b) creditors do not raise any matters relating to the bankrupt's conduct and affairs which require further investigation; and

(c) the Official Receiver files a notice at the court stating that the investigation of the bankrupt's affairs has been concluded or he thinks an investigation is unnecessary.

A bankrupt will not be discharged if there is a court order suspending his discharge. This could be the case where the bankrupt has not co-operated with the Official Receiver or trustee in bankruptcy.

25.7.2 Effect of discharge

Once the bankrupt has been discharged, he is normally freed from the disqualifications suffered by undischarged bankrupts and from liability to meet his bankruptcy debts.

25.7.3 Bankruptcy Restrictions Order (BRO)

These orders have been introduced as a new civil regime. Where a trustee considers that the bankrupt's conduct has been irresponsible or reckless, the court may make a BRO for a period of between 2 and 15 years, depending on the circumstances of the case. The BRO imposes restrictions which will generally take effect following the discharge of the bankrupt. These will include:

(a) it being an offence for the bankrupt to be involved as an officer or in the management or promotion of a company without the leave of the court;

(b) being unable to obtain credit in excess of £500 without first disclosing the BRO;

(c) only being allowed to trade in their own name or that in which they were adjudged bankrupt.

25.8 Individual voluntary arrangements

25.8.1 Introduction

While formal bankruptcy may be the appropriate method of dealing with many debtors who find themselves in financial difficulties, there will be certain cases where the debtor involved may be able to come to terms with his creditors without involving the full rigour of the bankruptcy procedure. The Insolvency Act 1986 introduced an alternative method by which debtors can come to binding arrangements with their creditors. This allows debtors to propose a composition or scheme of arrangement to creditors. This is known as an individual voluntary arrangement, usually referred to in practice as an 'IVA'. The procedure for this is set out in Pt VIII IA 1986 and is considered further below. In addition, the Enterprise Act has introduced an alternative 'fast track' IVA. This is described in **25.8.7**.

25.8.2 Interim order

25.8.2.1 Application by debtor

If a debtor in financial difficulties wishes to propose a voluntary arrangement to his creditors, he must first apply to the court, even if a petition for his bankruptcy has already been presented, for an interim order to be made. The debtor must have in place an insolvency practitioner who is willing to act in relation to the proposed voluntary arrangement. The latter is known as the 'nominee'.

25.8.2.2 Effect of interim orders

Once the interim order is made, no bankruptcy petition can be presented against the debtor and no other proceedings, execution or legal process can, without the leave of the court, be commenced or prosecuted against the debtor or his assets. (It should be noted that legislation has been proposed to allow a proposal to be made for a voluntary arrangement *without* first applying for an interim order. Obviously, in such a situation, the debtor would not have the benefit of the interim order.)

25.8.2.3 Period of interim order

The interim order is relatively short-lived since it will cease to have effect at the end of the period of 14 days beginning with the day after the order was made, although the court has power to extend the period.

25.8.3 Procedure following the making of the interim order

25.8.3.1 Debtors to provide statements to nominee

After the order has been made the debtor must provide the nominee with a statement giving details of the proposed voluntary arrangement. He must also give a statement of his affairs, which will give details of his assets and liabilities. Failure to do so may result in the interim order being discharged.

25.8.3.2 Nominee's report to court

The nominee is required to report to the court, stating whether the voluntary arrangement has a reasonable prospect of being approved and implemented. In addition, he is required to state whether a meeting of creditors should be called to consider the proposed voluntary arrangements. Should the nominee fail to deliver the report to the court before the interim order expires, the debtor can apply to the court to have the order renewed or extended and the debtor may also apply to have the nominee replaced.

25.8.3.3 Discharge of interim order

If the nominee decides that a meeting of creditors should not be called and the court agrees, the interim order may be discharged.

25.8.4 Consideration of the debtor's proposals

If the nominee has submitted a report to the court recommending that a creditor's meeting be called to consider the debtor's proposals, subject to any directions made by the court, the nominee gives notice of the meeting (at the date, time and place specified in his report to the court) to all creditors of whom he is aware.

At the meeting the proposals will be considered and the proposals may be approved as proposed or with any changes thought appropriate.

25.8.5 Effect of accepting the proposal

Once the proposal is approved, all persons who had notice of the meeting and who were entitled to vote at the meeting (irrespective of whether they did so vote) are bound by the composition or scheme as if they were parties to it. Any creditor who would have been entitled to vote at the meeting, had they been given notice of it, will also be bound by the proposal.

Subject to any challenges within the 28-day period referred to in **25.8.6** below, once the proposal has been accepted, any interim order in force ceases to have effect and any bankruptcy petition which was stayed by the interim order is deemed to have been dismissed (subject to a court order to the contrary).

25.8.6 Challenging the decision of the creditors' meeting

25.8.6.1 Parties who may challenge

Once the creditors' meeting has reported its decision to the court, at any time during the 28 days commencing with the day the report is made to the court, that decision may be challenged by:

(a) the debtor;

(b) any person who was entitled to vote at the meeting;

(c) the nominee (or his replacement).

25.8.6.2 Grounds

The grounds of challenge are limited to the following:

(a) that the composition or scheme accepted by the meeting unfairly prejudices the interests of a creditor; and/or

(b) that there was a material irregularity at, or in relation to, the meeting.

25.8.6.3 Effect of challenge

If the court confirms the challenge, the approval of the meeting may be revoked or suspended. Alternatively, the court may order a further meeting to be held to consider any revised proposal or (if the challenge is based on 'material irregularity' in relation to the meeting) order that the meeting be held again to reconsider the proposal.

Having ordered a further meeting to be held, the court can extend or renew the interim order. However, if the court is satisfied that no revised proposal will be submitted by the debtor, the order to hold a further meeting will be revoked and the approval given at the original meeting will be revoked or suspended.

25.8.7   Fast track IVA

The Enterprise Act has introduced a new fast track post-bankruptcy individual voluntary arrangement scheme. Under the scheme, the Official Receiver is to be the proposed nominee. The proposal for the scheme will be agreed with the Official Receiver and filed with the court, without the need for a creditors' meeting. Instead, the Official Receiver sends the proposal to creditors by post. The latter either agree to or reject the proposal: there is no facility to modify it. Assuming the proposal is approved, the Official Receiver supervises the IVA and notifies the court, which annuls the bankruptcy order.

Company insolvency proceedings

This chapter covers the following topics:

26.1 Introduction

All statute references in this and the following chapter are to the Insolvency Act 1986 except where otherwise stated.

In this chapter we shall deal with the procedures available when a company is insolvent or facing financial difficulties. In the final section of this chapter we shall look at the way in which insolvent partnerships can be subject to the same procedures as companies.

The law relating to these matters is principally contained in the Insolvency Act 1986 together with the Insolvency Rules 1986. However, the Insolvency Act 2000 and the Enterprise Act 2002 made amendments to these regulations and brought about major changes to the insolvency regime in the UK.

The aim of the insolvency elements of the Enterprise Act 2002 was to reform corporate insolvency law. This has been achieved by: streamlining the company administration procedure (see **26.2**) to make it easier to access, quicker, more flexible and fairer; restricting the use of administrative receivership (see **26.4**); and abolishing the Crown's preferential rights to realisations (see **26.8.3**).

The insolvency legislation provides four procedures for companies in financial difficulties.

26.1.1 Administration order

This procedure is directed principally at rescuing companies as going concerns. Following the Enterprise Act 2002, administration may now be commenced without a court hearing, although a number of formalities must be observed.

26.1.2 Voluntary arrangement under the Insolvency Act 1986

This procedure enables a variety of schemes to be implemented (with the agreement of the company and its creditors) to either avoid or supplement other types of insolvency procedure.

26.1.3 Receivership

A receiver is appointed by a lender who holds a charge over some or all of the company's assets. The main responsibility of the receiver is to take control of the company so as to pay off the appointing creditor. However, the law recognises that this may have a considerable and permanent effect on the company and its other creditors. Therefore various statutory powers are granted to the receiver and a number of obligations imposed on him.

Prior to the relevant provisions of the Enterprise Act 2002 coming into force, the majority of receiverships were administrative receiverships (see **26.4.3**). However, this procedure will now only be available in the case of certain specified transactions.

26.1.4 Liquidation (or winding up)

There are two types of liquidation: liquidation by the court (compulsory winding up) and voluntary liquidation. There are many procedural and other differences between these types of liquidation but each is designed to achieve the same thing; that is, the collection and distribution of all the company's assets. The effect of liquidation is that the company ceases to exist as a *commercial* entity. When the liquidation is over the company is 'dissolved'; that is, it ceases to exist as a *legal* entity.

Liquidation by the court is initiated by petition and, in certain circumstances, the appointment of an administrator may still be sought via a court application. There are other elements of all of the above procedures which may require applications to the court at various stages. The High Court has jurisdiction to deal with any such petition or application where the company is registered in England and Wales. This type of business is assigned to the Chancery Division. In addition the county court of the district in which the company's registered office is situated has concurrent jurisdiction where the company's paid-up share capital does not exceed £120,000.

26.2 Administration orders

26.2.1 Background to administration procedure

Administration was introduced in the 1980s as an alternative to winding up. The original procedure involved a relevant party petitioning the court for an administration order on the grounds that the order would achieve one or more of a number of statutory purposes as regards a company in financial difficulties. These included saving some or all of the company as a going concern, obtaining better realisations for creditors than would be achieved on a winding up and seeking a voluntary arrangement. The Insolvency Act provided that, on the making of a petition, a moratorium would come into effect, preventing any further action against the company until the hearing of the petition, unless the court gave leave. Assuming the petition was successful, an administration order would be made and an administrator appointed to take control of the company. The moratorium continued during the period of the order, allowing the administrator 'breathing space' to attempt to achieve the relevant statutory purpose or purposes for which he had been appointed.

A disadvantage of administration was the cost and complexity of seeking an administration order. The petitioner was required to show that the company was either unable or likely to become unable to pay its debts. This had to be supported by a report from an independent insolvency practitioner setting out their reasons for believing that at least one of the statutory purposes could be achieved. These steps, together with the court hearing, may have precluded some companies from pursuing administration as an option where they faced financial difficulties.

The Enterprise Act 2002 introduced a new procedure to allow companies, their directors and floating charge-holders to appoint an administrator without petitioning the court. This enables these parties to pursue administration where historically they might not have done so. (The existing court procedure also remains an option.) In addition, the statutory purposes have been replaced with three objectives, with the primary one being to rescue the company as a going concern. The moratorium on creditor action and flexibility given to the administrator, once appointed, has been retained. The overall aim is to maintain all the benefits of the original procedure whilst making access easier and the procedure faster and fairer. The statutory provisions on administration are now contained in Sch. B1 to the Insolvency Act 1986. Any references below to paragraph numbers are references to paragraphs of Sch. B1.

26.2.2 Persons entitled to appoint an administrator

A person may be appointed as an administrator of a company by:

(a) the holder of a floating charge (para. 14);

(b) the company or its directors (para. 22); or

(c) administration order of the court (para. 10).

Any administrator appointed must be qualified to act as an insolvency practitioner in relation to the company. Once appointed, an administrator is an officer of the court, whether or not appointed by the court.

26.2.3 Objectives of administrator

Paragraph 3(1) requires an administrator to perform his functions with the objective of:

(a) rescuing the company as a going concern; or

(b) achieving a better result for the company's creditors as a whole than would be likely if the company were wound up (without first being in administration); or

(c) realising property in order to make a distribution to one or more secured or preferential creditors.

The three objectives are, in fact, a hierarchy. The first objective is the primary aim of the new administration regime. The administrator is required to perform his functions to achieve that objective unless either it is not reasonably practicable to do so or the objective in (b) would achieve a better result for the company's creditors as a whole. Furthermore, the administrator may perform his functions to achieve the objective in (c) only if he thinks it is not reasonably practicable to achieve either (a) or (b) and he does not unnecessarily harm the interests of creditors of the company as a whole.

Overall, the administrator must perform his functions in the interests of the company's creditors as a whole, subject to performing them as quickly and efficiently as is reasonably practicable.

26.2.4 Appointment of administrator by holder of floating charge

26.2.4.1 Power to appoint

An administrator may be appointed to a company by the holder of a qualifying floating charge over the company's property, as defined in paras 14(2) and (3). The charge in question must be enforceable at the time of the appointment. The holder must first give at least two business days' written notice to the holder of any prior qualifying floating charge or obtain written consent to the appointment from such person. The holder of a floating charge may not appoint an administrator if a provisional liquidator has been appointed or an administrative receiver is in office.

26.2.4.2 Notice of appointment

The appointing charge holder must file with the court a notice of appointment in prescribed form. This must include a statutory declaration by or on behalf of the person who makes the appointment that:

(a) the person is the holder of a qualifying floating charge in respect of the company's property;

(b) each floating charge relied on in making the appointment is (or was) enforceable on the date of the appointment; and

(c) the appointment is in accordance with Sch. B1.

The statutory declaration must be made within a prescribed period.

The notice of appointment must identify the administrator and be accompanied by a statement from the latter:

(a) that he consents to the appointment;

(b) that in his opinion the purpose of administration is reasonably likely to be achieved; and

(c) giving any other information and opinions as may be prescribed.

The administrator may, in making his statement, rely on information supplied by the company's directors (unless he has reason to doubt its accuracy).

26.2.4.3 Time at which appointment takes effect

The appointment of an administrator by a holder of a qualifying floating charge takes effect when the notice provisions set out above have been satisfied.

26.2.5 Appointment of administrator by company or directors

26.2.5.1 Power to appoint

Paragraph 22 gives power to appoint an administrator to a company or its directors to appoint an administrator of that company. This power is restricted if:

(a) the company has been in administration in the past 12 months (para. 23);

(b) the company has been subject to a moratorium in respect of a failed creditors' voluntary arrangement under Sch. A1 in the previous 12 months (para. 24);

(c) there is a pending petition for the winding up of the company (para. 25(a));

(d) an administration application has been made to court and is not yet disposed of (para. 25(b)); or

(e) an administrative receiver is in office (para. 25(c)).

26.2.5.2 Notice of intention to appoint

Directors or companies using the out-of-court route must give at least five business days' notice to any person holding a qualifying floating charge or entitled to appoint an administrative receiver. This notice must identify the proposed administrator and be in the prescribed form. A copy of this notice must also be filed with the court and be accompanied by a statutory declaration that:

(a) the company is or is likely to become unable to pay its debts;

(b) the company is not in liquidation; and

(c) the appointment is not prevented by paras 23 to 25.

The charge-holders to whom notice has been given may either agree to the proposed appointment or appoint an alternative administrator, although a moratorium (as described in **26.2.7.1**) will take effect immediately the notice of intention has been filed at court by the company or directors. [It should be noted that this moratorium can only be lifted with the leave of the court (i.e., as no administrator has yet been appointed, his consent cannot be given).]

If charge-holders do not respond to the notice of intention to appoint, the company's or directors' appointee will take office after the notice period has expired and a notice of appointment is filed at court.

26.2.5.3 Notice of appointment

The administrator takes office when a notice of appointment is filed with the court. An appointment may not be made after a period of 10 business days beginning with the date on which the notice of intention to appoint is filed under para. 27.

The notice of appointment must include a statutory declaration stating that the application meets all the necessary requirements set out in para. 29. It must also identify the administrator and be accompanied by a statement from the latter:

(a) that he consents to the appointment;

(b) that in his opinion the purpose of administration is reasonably likely to be achieved; and

(c) giving any other information and opinions as may be prescribed.

The administrator may, in making his statement, rely on information supplied by the company's directors (unless he has reason to doubt its accuracy).

26.2.6 Appointment of administrator by court

26.2.6.1 Application for administration order

The following may apply to court for an administration order in respect of a company:

(a) the company;

(b) the directors of the company;

(c) one or more creditors of the company;

(d) the justices' chief executive for a magistrates' court (where a fine has been imposed on a company); or

(e) a combination of (a) to (d).

It should be noted that this court route preserves a means of putting a company into administration for creditors without qualifying floating charges (e.g., unsecured creditors).

26.2.6.2 Notice of application

An applicant must, as soon as reasonably practicable after making the application, notify:

(a) any person who has appointed or is or may be entitled to appoint an administrative receiver; or

(b) any person entitled to appoint an administrator by virtue of holding a qualifying floating charge.

26.2.6.3 Effect of application

Where an application has been made but not yet granted or dismissed, or it has been granted but an administration order has not yet taken effect, a moratorium (as described in **26.2.7.1**) takes effect. However, it should be noted that this moratorium can only be lifted with the leave of the court (i.e., as no administrator has yet been appointed, his consent cannot be given).

26.2.6.4 Powers of court

On hearing an administration application the court may:

(a) make an administration order;

(b) dismiss the application;

(c) adjourn the hearing;

(d) make an interim order;

(e) treat the application as a winding-up order; or

(f) make any other order it thinks appropriate.

26.2.6.5 Time at which appointment takes effect

Where the court makes an administration order, the appointment takes effect at the time appointed by the order or, if no time is appointed, at the time the order is made.

26.2.7   Effect of administration

26.2.7.1   Moratorium

Once a company is in administration, creditors may not, without the consent of the administrator or the permission of the court:

(a) take steps to enforce security over the company's property;

(b) repossess goods in the company's possession under a hire-purchase agreement;

(c) commence or continue any legal process against the company or its property; or

(d) exercise a right of forfeiture in respect of premises let by the company.

In addition, no resolution may be passed for the winding up of the company and no winding-up order made.

The object of these rules is to preserve the assets of the company so that an administrator has a better chance of rescuing the company as a going concern.

26.2.7.2   Effect on winding up

In addition to the effect of the moratorium (see **26.2.7.1**), a petition for the winding up of a company will be dismissed on the making of an administration order. While a company is in administration following an appointment by the holder of a qualifying floating charge, a winding-up petition will be suspended (para. 40).

26.2.7.3   Effect on receivership

Administration and administrative receivership are mutually exclusive. As we have seen, notice of an administration application or intended appointment must be given to any person who is entitled to appoint an administrative receiver. An administrator cannot be appointed by a qualifying floating charge-holder, the company or its directors if an administrative receiver is in place. As regards an administration application, the court will dismiss the application if there is an administrative receiver of the company unless either the creditor who appointed the administrative receiver consents or it is shown that his security would be liable to be set aside under ss. 238, 239 or 245 (see **Chapter 27**) (para. 39).

When an administration order takes effect in respect of a company where an administrative receiver is in office (e.g., the creditor who appointed the administrative receiver has consented to the order), that administrative receiver is required to vacate office. During the course of administration, the administrator may require any receiver of any part of the company's property to vacate office.

26.2.8   The administration process

26.2.8.1   Announcement of appointment

The administrator must send notice of his appointment to the company and publish a notice of his appointment in the prescribed manner as soon as reasonably practicable. Notice must also be sent to the Registrar of Companies within seven days of appointment (para. 46(1)) and to the company's creditors.

26.2.8.2   Statement of affairs

The administrator must require a statement of affairs to be prepared (para. 47(1)). This will usually be required from the directors of the company but the legislation allows the administrator to require the others involved in the company's business to provide or contribute to the statement. The statement must be provided within 11 days of the date on which notice of the requirement is received.

26.2.8.3 Powers of administrator

The appointed administrator will run the company and its business with a view to achieving the purpose of administration. The administrator is given power to do anything necessary or expedient for the management of the affairs, business and property of the company (para. 59). His specific powers are those set out in Sch. 1 IA 1986. These include power to sell assets, borrow money, insure, bring and defend proceedings, and appoint agents. The administrator also has powers to dispose of charged property as if it were not subject to the charge (paras 70 and 71) and to dispose of hire-purchase goods as if the rights of the owner were vested in the company (para. 72).

In cases of difficulty, the administrator may apply to the court for directions. The management powers of the administrator override those of the company and its directors: they may not exercise any management powers without the consent of the administrator.

26.2.8.4 Proposals

The administrator is required to prepare proposals for achieving the purpose of administration. These must be sent to the Registrar of Companies, all creditors (so far as he is aware of their claims and addresses) and all members (so far as he is aware of their addresses). The proposals must be sent as soon as reasonably practicable but in any event within eight weeks from the commencement of administration. [This time limit was reduced from three months by the Enterprise Act 2002.]

26.2.8.5 Creditors' meeting

The administrator must hold an initial creditors' meeting within 10 weeks of the commencement of administration. There are exceptions to this requirement (para. 52). No meeting is required where the administrator believes that:

(a) there are no funds available from the insolvent estate for unsecured creditors, outside those flowing from the abolition of Crown preference (see **26.8.3**);

(b) neither the company rescue nor the better result for creditors objective apply (see **26.2.3**); or

(c) that the company has sufficient property to pay each creditor in full.

The creditors may either approve the proposals without modification or approve them with modification to which the administrator consents.

Should the administrator need to make substantial modifications to the approved proposals at any time, he is required to call another creditors' meeting for this purpose.

26.2.8.6 Distributions

An administrator may make distributions to secured creditors and preferential creditors without court permission, and distributions to unsecured creditors with court permission. The administrator may also make payments if he thinks that the payment is likely to assist in achieving the purpose of the administration.

26.2.8.7   Fulfilling the purpose of administration

The question arises as to the practical outcomes of administration. The Insolvency Service (part of the DTI) has stated that 'for administration to be successful it needs to have clear exit routes tied to its purpose'. It is for this reason that the legislation provides that:

- The administrator's proposal may include a proposal for a company voluntary arrangement (CVA) under the Insolvency Act 1986 or a proposal for a s. 425 Companies Act 1985 scheme of arrangement. A company rescue is most likely to involve one of these procedures.

- If the company cannot be rescued, then the administrator will aim to achieve a better realisation of the company's assets than would be achieved on an immediate liquidation.

- Where there are no funds available for the unsecured creditors, the administrator will realise the company's assets and make payments to preferential creditors and fixed and floating charge holders and will arrange for the dissolution of the company simply by sending a notice to the Registrar of Companies.

- If there are funds available for the unsecured creditors, the company will be put into voluntary liquidation, again simply by sending a notice to the Registrar of Companies.

Where the administrator thinks the purpose of administration cannot be achieved, the administrator is required to apply to court.

26.2.8.8   Ending administration

The appointment of an administrator will automatically end 12 months after the date it commenced. However, this may be extended for up to six months with the consent of the creditors or for a specified period by court order.

26.3   Voluntary arrangements

26.3.1   Proposals and nominee's report

The Insolvency Act 1986 seeks to promote agreement between a company in difficulties and its creditors. The directors or (where the company is being wound up) the liquidator or (where a company is in administration) the administrator may make proposals to the company and its creditors. These proposals must, if they are to be put into effect under the Act, nominate a qualified insolvency practitioner to implement them. Where the nominee is not the liquidator or administrator, the person making the proposal (that is, the liquidator, administrator or directors) must submit details of the proposals and of the company's creditors, debts, liabilities and assets to the nominee. The nominee must then submit a report to the court stating whether or not he thinks that meetings of members and creditors should be called to consider the proposals.

26.3.2   Content of proposals

The proposals may be as simple or as complex as the situation of the company demands. In practical terms, the creditors are usually being offered something definite as an alternative to what they might obtain if the company was, for example, to be wound up. Examples of proposals which are commonly made may include one or more of the following:

(a) *Moratorium on repayment of debt*

Creditors are asked not to enforce debts for a specific period of time. The company may be unable to pay debts at present due to cash-flow problems but may expect to be able to pay them in the near future.

(b) *Composition of debt*

Creditors are offered a percentage of their debt in settlement. For example, they might be offered '65 pence in the pound': that is, 65 pence for every pound which the company owes them.

(c) *Debt for equity swap*

Major creditors may be offered the chance to swap their debt for shares in the company. From the company's point of view, the removal of the debt should ease cash-flow problems. The shares will usually give the creditors preferential rights which enable repayment through dividends as soon as profits are available. Such a proposal will often be combined with a fairly radical, general reorganisation of the company's affairs.

26.3.3   Meetings of members and creditors

Where the nominee recommends that meetings should be held he may call the meetings unless the court orders otherwise. Notice must be given to every creditor of whose claim and address the person calling the meeting is aware.

The meetings of members and creditors then consider the scheme, which they may reject, approve or approve with modifications. A simple majority is required at the members' meeting (members having the voting rights attached to their shares by the articles). The position is more complicated at the creditors' meeting but basically the net effect is that the resolution is only validly passed if approved:

(a) by at least three-quarters (by value) of the unsecured creditors; and

(b) by a simple majority (by value) of the unsecured creditors who are not connected with the company.

In relation to (a) only, secured creditors may count in the vote, but only to the extent of the value of their claim which they estimate will *not* be recovered under their security.

The result of the meetings must be reported to the court. The court can reject the scheme on grounds of unfair prejudice or material irregularity.

26.3.4   Implementation of approved scheme by supervisor

Where both meetings approve a scheme the scheme becomes binding on all persons who had notice of the shareholders' or creditors' meeting and were entitled to vote at that meeting together with any creditors who would have been entitled to vote, had they been given notice of the meeting. However, unless he agrees, the scheme cannot affect a secured creditor's right to enforce his security, nor a preferred creditor's preference.

Once approved, the scheme is implemented by the supervisor (who is the same person as the nominee unless the court or meetings decide otherwise).

26.3.5 Relationship between voluntary schemes and administration

The proposal that a voluntary scheme should be implemented does not create a moratorium so that, unless and until the scheme is approved, any creditor can seek payment of his own debt (by court action, petition for winding up, repossession or any other lawful means available to him). Even when the scheme is approved it does not prevent secured creditors enforcing their security. A voluntary arrangement is, therefore, more likely to succeed if a company is first put into administration, thus giving rise to the moratorium. The administrator may then be able to put together a satisfactory voluntary scheme which he can supervise.

26.3.6 Moratorium for small companies

The Insolvency Act 2000 amended the Insolvency Act 1986 as regards the voluntary arrangement procedure for small companies (within the definition in s. 247 of the Companies Act 1985). The directors of these companies may apply for a moratorium of up to 28 days to give them time to put their voluntary arrangement proposal to creditors. The moratorium is similar to that created on a petition for an administration order and will mean that creditors cannot take action against the company's assets during its term. The purpose behind the change in the legislation is to make the voluntary arrangement option more effective and thus attractive to companies in financial difficulties.

To obtain a moratorium, the directors must submit to the nominee the terms of their proposed voluntary arrangement together with a statement of the company's financial affairs. The nominee will then provide the directors with a statement indicating whether or not, in his opinion, the proposal has a reasonable prospect of approval. He will also indicate whether the company is likely to have sufficient funds available to it during the proposed moratorium to enable it to carry on its business, and whether meetings of the company and creditors should be summoned to consider the proposed voluntary arrangement. The directors must then file all the above documents, together with the nominee's consent to act and a statement that the company is eligible for a moratorium, with the court.

26.4 Receivership

26.4.1 Introduction

A receiver is a person who is appointed by or on behalf of a creditor to realise security, such as a charge or series of charges. His principal duty is owed to the party who appoints him; that is, the charge-holder. Whilst receivers may also be appointed by the court, in practice nearly all appointments are made by the charge-holder.

Since 1986, receivers have fallen into two broad categories: receivers appointed under charges over specific assets and administrative receivers, as defined by s. 29(2).

26.4.2   Receivers

A receiver appointed under charges over specific assets derives his powers from the charge under which he was appointed and from certain sections of the Law of Property Act 1925. The latter provides powers to manage, receive income from and sell the property over which the receiver has been appointed. Sometimes this type of receiver will be referred to as a 'receiver and manager', 'fixed charge receiver' or 'LPA receiver'. His role is to deal with the property over which he is appointed in order to realise funds for the party which appointed him. A receiver need not necessarily be a qualified insolvency practitioner.

26.4.3   Administrative receivers

These are defined in s. 29(2) as:

(a) a receiver and manager of the whole (or substantially the whole) of a company's property appointed by or on behalf of the holders of any debentures of the company secured by a charge which, as created, was a floating charge, or by such a charge and one or more other securities; or

(b) a person who would be such a receiver or manager but for the appointment of some other person as the receiver of part of the company's property.

In practice, the person who holds such security will usually be a bank. The bank is also likely to have fixed charges over land owned by the company and certain other assets (e.g., book debts) but these would not prevent it from appointing an administrative receiver given the scope of s. 29(2)(a).

26.4.4   Impact of Enterprise Act 2002 on administrative receivership

The Enterprise Act 2002 effectively abolished administrative receiverships in respect of qualifying floating charges (as defined in para. 14, Sch. B1 IA 1986) created after the date the Enterprise Act came into force. The intention is to promote the out-of-court administration regime (see **26.2.4**). Administrative receivers may now only be appointed by the holders of floating charges created prior to implementation of the Enterprise Act and holders of charges created as part of specific transactions defined in ss. 72B–72G IA 1986. These include capital market arrangements, public–private projects, utility projects, and project finance arrangements. Given these changes, the following paragraphs are only relevant to pre-15 September 2003 and 'specific transaction' floating charges.

26.4.5   Administrative receivers—powers and duties

The administrative receiver, when appointed, effectively replaces the directors in the management of the company. His appointment is, therefore, a matter of great importance to the members, creditors and employees of the company. The law recognises this and so grants powers to and imposes obligations on an administrative receiver which make his position very similar to the position of an administrator. The administrative receiver is chosen by the debenture holder, not by the court, but can only be removed by the court.

26.4.5.1   General powers

An administrative receiver has all the powers conferred on him by the debenture under which he is appointed and also specific powers listed in the Insolvency Act 1986. The statutory powers include power to deal with the assets of the company, take or defend proceedings in its name and power to carry on the business of the company. These powers, listed in Sch. 1, are the same as those granted to an administrator.

26.4.5.2 Disposal of property subject to prior charge

Section 43 gives an administrative receiver power to go to court to obtain an order for the sale of assets free from any security with priority over the debenture under which he was appointed. The court may only authorise the administrative receiver to dispose of such property if it is likely to promote a more advantageous realisation of the company's assets. The court might, for example, authorise such a disposal so as to enable the receiver to sell the business of the company as a going concern. The proceeds of disposal (plus any difference between those proceeds and market value) must be paid to the person who was entitled to the security.

26.4.5.3 Legal position

The administrative receiver is deemed to be the agent of the company (s. 44). Any contract which he makes is, therefore, binding on the company. The agency, however, ends when the company goes into liquidation. Section 44 also makes the administrative receiver personally liable on any contract which he himself makes and on any contract of employment which he 'adopts'. Following the cases of *Paramount Airways* [1994] BCC 172, *Leyland DAF* [2004] UKHL 9 and *Ferranti* [1994] BCC 658, an employee's contract of employment is 'adopted' if he is continued in employment for more than 14 days after the appointment of the administrative receiver (or administrator in the case of administration). The administrative receiver is entitled to an indemnity against personal liability out of the assets of the company and, if the debenture so provides, will have an indemnity from his appointor.

26.4.5.4 Duty to pay preferential creditors

The primary duty of any receiver is to realise the security of the debenture holder who appointed him. A receiver appointed on behalf of a floating charge-holder (whether or not he is an administrative receiver as defined) is, however, under a duty to pay preferential creditors (see **26.8**) in priority to the debt secured by the floating charge.

26.4.5.5 Investigation and report into company's affairs

An administrative receiver is entitled to a statement of affairs from the directors (or in certain cases other officials) of the company. Within three months of his appointment (or longer if the court so directs) he must make a report which he must send to the Registrar of Companies and to creditors.

The report must give details of the events leading to the appointment of the receiver, his dealings with the property of the company, his payments to the creditor who appointed him and to preferential creditors and an assessment of what will be available (if anything) to ordinary creditors.

26.5 Liquidation or winding up

26.5.1 Types of winding up

There are two types of winding up: compulsory liquidation and voluntary liquidation. Compulsory liquidation is initiated by petition to the court. Voluntary liquidation is initiated by a decision of the members of the company. Both types of winding up are designed to bring the existence of the company to an end and to distribute its assets to those entitled to them.

26.5.2 Compulsory winding up

26.5.2.1 Grounds

Compulsory liquidation begins with a petition to the court (Chancery Division or, in some cases, county court—see **26.1.4** above). A petition can be presented on a number of grounds. By far the most common ground is that the company is unable to pay its debts (defined in s. 123). A company is treated as being unable to pay its debts if:

(a) a demand for payment, in the prescribed form (a 'statutory demand'), for more than £750 (this figure may be changed from time to time by regulations) has been left at the company's registered office and the company has neglected to pay the debt, or to secure or compound for it (that is, agree to a reasonable compromise) to the reasonable satisfaction of the creditor for three weeks; or

(b) execution or other process issued on a judgment, decree or court order is returned unsatisfied; or

(c) it is proved that the company is actually unable to pay taking into account contingent and prospective liabilities; or

(d) it is proved that the value of the company's assets is less than the amount of its liabilities taking into account contingent and prospective liabilities.

Apart from inability to pay debts there are other grounds on which a company may be wound up. These are, however, seldom resorted to and are not considered in this Guide save that the 'just and equitable' ground is considered briefly in **Chapter 10**.

26.5.2.2 *Locus standi*

A petition for compulsory winding up may be presented by the company itself, any creditor or creditors (including contingent or prospective creditors), any contributory or contributories (the term 'contributory' includes the members of the company and certain former members) and, in very limited circumstances, by the Department of Trade and Industry. In practice, the overwhelming majority of petitions are presented by creditors.

26.5.2.3 Court's discretion to refuse order

Even where a creditor has proved grounds for winding up, the court has a discretion to refuse to make an order winding up the company. An order will normally be refused where:

(a) the petitioning creditor (together with any supporting creditors) is owed £750 or less. This is by analogy with the rule whereby a statutory demand for more than £750 can be used as proof of inability to pay debts;

(b) the majority by value of the creditors oppose the winding up of the company.

26.5.3 Voluntary winding up

26.5.3.1 Commencement

By s. 84 a company can be wound up voluntarily if:

(a) a special resolution to wind up is passed; or

(b) an extraordinary resolution is passed to the effect that the company should be wound up as it cannot continue in business because of its debts (that is, the company is, in effect, insolvent).

The winding up commences from the date of passing the appropriate resolution. A notice of the resolution must appear in the *London Gazette* within 14 days of its being passed.

26.5.3.2   Types of voluntary winding up

There are two types of voluntary liquidation; a members' voluntary winding up and a creditors' voluntary winding up.

Members' voluntary winding up

This form of liquidation is utilised if the company is solvent. Within the five weeks immediately preceding the date of the resolution (or on that date but before the resolution is actually passed) the directors (or the majority of them if more than two) make a statutory declaration, setting out the company's assets and liabilities, and stating that they have made a full enquiry into the company's affairs and are of the opinion that the company will be able to pay its debts in full within 12 months of the commencement of the winding up. The declaration must be delivered to the Registrar within 15 days after the day the resolution was passed.

Creditors' voluntary winding up

If no such 'declaration of solvency' is filed, the winding up is a creditors' winding up. A meeting of the creditors must be called for a day not later than the 14th day after the day on which is held the meeting at which the members pass the winding-up resolution. Notice of the meeting must be posted to the creditors at least seven days before the creditors' meeting and the meeting must also be advertised in the *Gazette* and at least two newspapers.

Conversion from members' to creditors' voluntary winding up

During the course of a members' voluntary winding up, it may become clear that the company will be unable to pay its debts within 12 months of commencement of the winding up. If this happens the liquidator must report the fact to the creditors, call a creditors' meeting and convert the liquidation into a creditors' voluntary winding up.

26.6   Liquidators

For all forms of liquidation, any liquidator appointed must be a qualified insolvency practitioner.

26.6.1   Compulsory liquidation

When a winding-up order is made, the official receiver of the court becomes the liquidator of the company and continues in office until someone else is appointed (s. 136(2)). The official receiver may summon meetings of creditors and contributories with a view to the appointment of a liquidator. He must either do so or give notice that he intends not to do so within 12 weeks of the winding-up order and may be required to call such meetings by one quarter (by value) of the creditors.

Where meetings of creditors and contributories are held, each meeting may nominate a liquidator. If the same person is nominated by each meeting, he becomes the liquidator. If different people are nominated, the creditors' nominee takes office unless a creditor or contributory successfully applies to the court for the appointment of the contributories' nominee (either alone or jointly with the creditors' nominee) or of some other person.

26.6.2 Creditors' voluntary winding up

As we have already seen, in a creditors' winding up a meeting of creditors must be held within 14 days of the meeting (of the members) at which the winding-up resolution was passed. The creditors may nominate a liquidator at their meeting. He will then become liquidator of the company but any director, member or creditor may apply to the court for the appointment of the members' nominee (either alone or jointly with the creditors' nominee) or of some other person.

The members will often have appointed a liquidator at the meeting at which the resolution for creditors' winding up was passed. Such a liquidator is entitled to act until the creditors' meeting is held but during that period his powers are restricted to collecting the company's property, disposing of perishable goods or other goods which may decline in value and taking other steps to protect the company's assets.

26.6.3 Members' voluntary winding up

The liquidator is appointed by the members in general meeting.

26.6.4 Functions of liquidators

The function of the liquidator of a company is to collect in the assets of the company and to pay their value to those creditors who are entitled according to the statutory order for payment (see **26.8**). If there is anything left after all creditors have been paid their debts and interest, the surplus goes to the members. If there are two or more classes of shares some members may have priority over others in claiming the surplus.

Sections 165 and 167 give liquidators extensive powers to assist them in performing their functions. These powers include:

(a) power to pay any class of creditors in full;

(b) power to enter into a compromise or arrangement with creditors (this can be made binding without the agreement of all the creditors in certain cases provided that the voluntary arrangements procedure (**26.3**) is used);

(c) power to compromise claims to which the company is entitled; (The liquidator can only exercise the above powers with the sanction of an extraordinary resolution in the case of members' winding up, of the court, a committee of creditors or creditors' meeting in the case of creditors' winding up and of the court or committee in the case of compulsory winding up.)

(d) power to bring or defend legal proceedings;

(e) power to carry on the company's business for the purpose of beneficial winding up; (Sanction is required in the case of compulsory winding up only.)

(f) power to sell the company's property;

(g) power to execute documents (including deeds);

(h) power to borrow on the security of the company's assets;

(i) power to act through agents;

(j) power to do 'all such other things as may be necessary for winding up the company's affairs and distributing its assets'.

(No sanction is required for items (f) to (j) in any type of winding up.)

26.6.5 Proceedings against the company

It would obviously be unfair if one creditor could start an action after the liquidation had begun and so obtain priority over the other creditors. Therefore, once an order for compulsory winding up has been made, no action can be started or proceeded with unless the leave of the court is obtained (s. 130). In addition, at any time between presentation of the petition and the making of the order, the company, or any creditor or contributory, can apply to have any action pending against the company stayed (s. 126). Furthermore, any execution, attachment, sequestration or distress started after the commencement of a compulsory liquidation is void. However, if the attachment or execution was begun before presentation of the petition, it can only be avoided by the liquidator if it was completed after commencement of the liquidation. This last provision also applies to voluntary liquidations, the operative date being the date the resolution to wind up the company was passed.

With regard to voluntary liquidations, the liquidator, any creditor or member, may apply to the court to have actions stayed. Such a stay is not granted automatically although, if the action is begun after the date of passing the resolution to wind up an insolvent company, it will normally be granted.

26.7 Collection and distribution of assets in liquidation

26.7.1 Property of the company

26.7.1.1 Power to sell or charge

The liquidator has power to sell or mortgage the property and to satisfy the claims of the various people entitled in the company's liquidation (see **26.6.4**).

26.7.1.2 Power to disclaim

An important power of the liquidator in relation to the company's property is the right of disclaimer given by s. 178. The section gives the liquidator power to disclaim any of the company's property which consists of unprofitable contracts, or other property that is unsaleable or not readily saleable.

26.7.2 Assets in the hands of the company

26.7.2.1 Assets held on trust

The creditors of an insolvent company are entitled to payment from its assets. They are not entitled to any assets of which the company is the legal owner but which it holds on trust for a third party. This has been held to apply in certain cases where a company holds cash for its customers. In *Re Kayford Ltd* [1975] 1 All ER 604, the company put money received from mail order customers into a special trust account from which it only made withdrawals when goods were delivered to the customers. When the company went into liquidation it was held that the money in the account belonged to the customers whose orders had not been fulfilled and so was not available to the liquidator.

26.7.2.2   Assets subject to retention of title

Many suppliers of goods supply goods under contracts which contain retention of title clauses. These are clauses which state that the vendor retains title to the goods supplied until the purchaser pays for them. Such clauses have been considered in a number of reported cases (the leading case is *Aluminium Industrie Vaasen BV v Romalpa Aluminium* [1976] 2 All ER 552). Their effect varies depending on the exact wording which is used and on the circumstances of the case. A straightforward reservation of title clause is effective in ensuring that the vendor, not the liquidator, is entitled to the goods (or the proceeds of their further sale) if the company becomes insolvent. However, clauses which have tried to extend the unpaid vendor's rights (for example, by purportedly transferring them to newly manufactured goods only partly consisting of the goods which he originally supplied) have generally failed. (For the powers of an administrator to dispose of goods despite a retention of title clause see **26.2.5.1**.)

26.8   Entitlement to assets

26.8.1   Introduction

The principal duty of the liquidator of a company is to collect in and distribute the assets to those creditors entitled and to meet the costs of the procedure. In a large majority of cases there will be insufficient funds available to pay all the creditors in full. The question therefore arises as to how, to whom and in what order the company's assets (or monies realised from the sale of such assets) are to be paid.

In the majority of liquidations of any size, there is a high likelihood that there will be charged assets. Given that the standard form of floating charge will seek to cover all assets of a company, present and future, it will often be the case that the majority of assets available to a liquidator will fall into the class of charged assets. In such a case, the only free assets potentially available would be any amounts recovered through actions taken by the liquidator (see **Chapter 27**).

With this in mind, the best approach to understanding relevant entitlements is to look at those parties who have an interest in the assets of an insolvent company and, in each case, examine their legal entitlement.

26.8.2   Creditors with fixed charges

Creditors with fixed charges are entitled to payment out of the charged assets before those assets are used for any other purpose. As between creditors with fixed charges over the same assets, their priority to assets is governed by registration under s. 395 CA 1985. (It should be remembered that a fixed charge takes priority over any floating charge, even if the latter is created and registered first, unless the floating charge prohibited the creation of later fixed charges ranking in priority to it and the fixed chargee had notice of this prohibition when he took the charge.)

If the security of a fixed charge is inadequate (that is, the value of the charged assets is less than the amount of the debt), the chargee may claim the balance of its debt as an ordinary creditor (or under any valid floating charge in its favour). If the debt is over-secured (that is, the value of the charged assets is more than the amount of the debt), the chargee will be paid in full and the balance will be available for other creditors.

The costs of realising fixed charge assets should be paid out of the amounts realised from the sale of such assets.

26.8.3   Costs of winding up

The principal rules on how the expenses of a winding up are to be paid are set out in section 176ZA of the Insolvency Act 1986, which came into force in April 2008. The Insolvency (Amendment) Rules 2008 provide additional detail. The expenses of a winding up should be paid out of the assets of the company available for the payment of general creditors. In so far as these are insufficient, the expenses will be paid out of assets subject to any floating charge created by the company. (The latter can include any amounts recovered through actions taken by the liquidator.) The effect of section 176ZA is therefore to give priority to the expenses of a winding up over the claims of floating chargeholders.

In terms of the costs of any legal proceedings which a liquidator seeks to take to recover property—i.e., litigation expenses—the priority provided by section 176ZA is not automatic: the liquidator must first obtain approval from the relevant floating charge-holder. If this is not forthcoming, the liquidator may seek approval from the court. Approval is not required if the litigation expenses are unlikely to exceed £5,000.

Finally, note that section 176ZA IA 1986 does not affect the ring-fenced assets for unsecured creditors under section 176A IA 1986 (see **26.8.5.2**).

26.8.4   Preferential creditors

After payment of costs and expenses, the next category of creditor is the preferred creditor. Categories of preferential debts are defined in Sch. 6 IA 1986. These categories have been reduced in number by the Enterprise Act 2002, which abolished the Crown's preferential rights. Originally, the Crown had a claim to certain amounts due to HMRC and in respect of social security contributions. These funds will now be available for creditors further down the order. The remaining categories of preferential debts are:

(a) Wages owed to an employee in respect of the four months before the relevant date up to a maximum of £800 per employee (this figure may be varied from time to time by statutory instrument). Certain categories of holiday pay are also preferential.

(b) Money lent to an employer so as to enable it to pay debts in category (a) above and which was in fact used for that purpose. (Thus a bank is a preferential creditor if it allows an employer to overdraw a 'wages account' so as to keep on the workforce in the four months before the relevant date.)

The 'relevant date' is usually the date of the winding-up resolution or order (as applicable) or date of appointment of a receiver.

Preferential creditors (to the extent of their preference) are entitled to payment in full before ordinary creditors or holders of floating charges receive any payment—see s. 40(2) as regards receiverships and s. 175 as regards liquidations. If the assets are insufficient to pay the preferred creditors in full they rank equally *inter se* and so each is paid the same proportion of the preferred debt.

26.8.5   Creditors with floating charges

Creditors with floating charges will fall to be paid out of charged assets, following re-payment of amounts owed to fixed charge-holders, costs and expenses relating to any *receiver* appointed to realise the charged assets and preferential claims in any such re-ceivership. (This assumes a receiver had been appointed prior to a subsequent liquid-ation.) In addition, as seen above in **26.8.4**, where there are insufficient free assets to pay preferential claims in a liquidation, charged assets can be applied to pay preferential claims.

The Enterprise Act 2002 changed the position of creditors who take floating charges over the assets of a company which enters into liquidation, administration or receivership.

26.8.5.1   Pre-Enterprise Act 2002 floating charge-holders' position

For creditors who took floating charges over the assets of a company prior to 15 Septem-ber 2003, they were (and continue to be) entitled, following payment of sums owed to preferential creditors, to sums realised from the assets the subject of their charge until their debts were fully satisfied. Any monies remaining following such payment would be available for unsecured creditors.

26.8.5.2   Current position

Following the Enterprise Act coming into force, s. 176A IA 1986 provides that, in rela-tion to assets secured by floating charges created after 15 September 2003, a liquidator, administrator or receiver is to make a prescribed part of the company's net property available for the satisfaction of unsecured debts. The way in which this prescribed part of the company's net property is to be calculated is set out in the Insolvency Act 1986 (Prescribed Part) Order 2003. The calculation is as follows:

(a) where the company's net property does not exceed £10,000 in value, 50% of that property;

(b) subject to the limit stated below, where the company's net property exceeds £10,000 in value the sum of—

(i)   50% of the first £10,000 in value; and

(ii)   20% of that part of the company's net property which exceeds £10,000 in value.

The value of the prescribed part of the company's net property to be made available for the satisfaction of unsecured debts of the company pursuant to s. 176A shall not exceed £600,000.

The prescribed part is not to be distributed to the holder of a floating charge except in so far as it exceeds the amount required for the satisfaction of unsecured debts. There is an exception to this rule where the relevant office-holder believes that the cost of mak-ing a distribution to unsecured creditors would be disproportionate to the benefits.

(Remember, following **26.8.2** above, that the costs of realising a fixed charge asset should be paid from the proceeds of such assets. Therefore, there will be an apportion-ment of costs between fixed and floating charge assets in those cases where both types of charge have been taken.)

26.8.6   Unsecured creditors

These creditors, sometimes referred to as ordinary creditors, rank behind preferred and secured creditors save to the extent of the provision made for them by s. 176A (see **26.8.5**). They rank equally *inter se*, that is, equally as between themselves in proportion to their respective debt. They would be paid out of free assets or any funds available from charged assets following payment of all prior claims (i.e., fixed chargeholders, preferential creditors and floating charge-holders).

26.8.7   Interest on debts

Once all creditors have been paid in full any surplus is first used to pay interest on debts from the date of liquidation. This interest is paid to all creditors equally regardless of whether their debts ranked equally for payment.

26.8.8   Shareholders

Any surplus after payment of debts and interest goes to the members according to the rights attached to their shares. As with unsecured creditors, they would be paid out of free assets or any funds available from charged assets following payment of all prior claims (i.e., fixed charge-holders, preferential creditors and floating charge-holders).

26.9   Dissolution

Once winding up is complete the company may be dissolved. This is achieved in the following ways:

(a) In compulsory liquidation the liquidator gives notice to the Registrar of Companies that he has completed the winding up. The company is then automatically dissolved three months later.

(b) In voluntary winding up the liquidator holds a final meeting and files certain returns with the Registrar of Companies. The company is then automatically dissolved after three months.

(c) The Registrar may dissolve a company by striking it off the register in certain circumstances where the company has ceased to trade.

26.10   Application to partnerships

26.10.1   Introduction

Care must be taken to define the precise nature of insolvency in relation to a partnership. It is possible for an individual partner to be bankrupt without the partnership being insolvent. Equally, it is possible for a partnership to be insolvent without any of the partners being bankrupt. Finally, a situation could exist where a partnership was insolvent *and* some or all of its partners bankrupt. A distinction must be maintained between an insolvent partnership and bankrupt partners since applicable procedures and the rights of the creditors of each will vary according to which you are dealing with. The provisions of the Insolvency Act 1986 relating to bankruptcy (see **Chapter 25**) will apply to individual bankrupt partners. In the case of an insolvent partnership, specific provisions of the Insolvency Act 1986 which apply to companies can also be applied to a partnership, as a result of the Insolvent Partnerships Order 1994.

26.10.2 Insolvent Partnerships Order 1994

26.10.2.1 Winding up as an unregistered company

The Insolvent Partnerships Order 1994 (the 'Order') provides that an insolvent partnership may be wound up as an unregistered company under the Insolvency Act. A petition may be brought by a partner or a creditor. If it is thought that debts will not be met from the assets of the firm, the Order allows bankruptcy petitions against individual partners to be brought in conjunction with the petition to wind up the partnership.

26.10.2.2 Priority of creditors on a winding up of a partnership

Under the Order, priorities operate as in the case of an insolvent company, with preferred and secured creditors having priority over ordinary creditors. However, the situation becomes more complex where a partnership is being wound up and bankruptcy petitions are being brought against individual partners. In this situation, there are effectively two sets of creditors, those of the partnership and those of the individual partners. The Order provides for the following priorities in such a situation:

(a) Partnership creditors must first seek to satisfy their claims from the partnership property.

(b) Creditors of individual partners must first look to the personal assets of those individuals.

(c) Should there be insufficient partnership assets, partnership creditors may seek to satisfy their claims from the personal assets of the individual partners. In such a situation, their claims are apportioned amongst the individual partners and *rank equally* with those of the creditors of those individual partners.

(d) Should creditors of individual partners find that those partners have insufficient assets to meet their claims, they may look to the partnership property. However, they can only do so *after* all the claims of partnership creditors have been met.

26.10.2.3 Disqualification

The Order applies certain provisions of the Company Directors Disqualification Act 1986 (see **9.5.2**) to partners of an insolvent partnership. A court may therefore, following a petition of the Secretary of State for Trade and Industry, find that a partner's conduct was such as to make him unfit to be concerned in the management of a company. If this is the case, the partner can be disqualified for a period of between 2 and 15 years from being involved in the management *of a company*. Such disqualification does *not* prevent him becoming involved in another partnership.

26.10.2.4 Administration and voluntary arrangements

The Order also provides that partnerships may be the subject of administration or enter into a voluntary arrangement with their creditors.

 Interactive online exercises (Student Learning Activities) which complement the topics covered in this chapter are available at www.oxfordtextbooks.co.uk/orc/business09_10/.

Liabilities arising from insolvency

This chapter covers the following topics:

27.1 Wrongful trading

27.2 Transactions at an undervalue and preferences

27.3 Transactions defrauding creditors

27.4 Floating charges.

In this chapter we will look at a number of rules which enable insolvency practitioners to claim assets which are not held by the insolvent company itself. You should note that the ability to take action under some of these rules is limited only to a liquidator, or a liquidator or administrator.

27.1 Wrongful trading

Under s. 214, the directors of a company which is being wound up may be made liable, by the court, to contribute to the assets of the company if they are found to be guilty of wrongful trading.

27.1.1 Grounds

A person is guilty of wrongful trading where:

(a) the company goes into insolvent liquidation;

(b) that person knew or ought to have concluded (at some time before the commencement of winding up) that there was no reasonable prospect that the company would avoid going into insolvent liquidation; and

(c) that person was a director of the company at that time.

27.1.2 Defence

A defence is available to a director who shows that he took *every* step with a view to minimising the potential loss to the company's creditors as he ought to have taken. However, in judging whether this defence is available, the court applies a combined objective and subjective test in examining the knowledge and actions of the director. They are taken as being those of a reasonably diligent person having both:

(a) the general knowledge, skill and experience that may reasonably be expected of a person carrying out the same functions as are carried out by the director in relation to the company; and

(b) the general knowledge, skill and experience that that director has.

The steps which a director must take to avoid liability for wrongful trading will vary depending on the circumstances of the case.

27.2 Transactions at an undervalue and preferences

Certain transactions which a company has entered into may be set aside on the ground that they are transactions at an undervalue or preferences. An application to the court by the liquidator is required for such transactions to be set aside. (The same rules apply in administration save that the application is then made by the administrator.)

27.2.1 Transactions at an undervalue

A transaction at an undervalue (s. 238) is a transaction where the company makes a gift to any person and receives either no consideration or consideration worth significantly less than the consideration provided by the company. However, a transaction cannot be set aside if it was entered into in good faith for the purpose of carrying on the company's business and at a time when there were reasonable grounds for believing that the transaction would benefit the company. For this reason a transaction cannot be set aside when the company sells stock or other assets at a reduced price so as to overcome cash flow problems.

27.2.2 Preferences

A preference (s. 239) is given if the company does anything or suffers anything to be done which puts a creditor, or a surety or guarantor of a debt of the company, into a better position on an insolvent liquidation than he would have been in if that thing had not been done. Examples of preferences include payment in full of a debt to a particular creditor who would only have received partial payment on winding up or the giving of security to a creditor. A transaction cannot be set aside as a preference unless the company was influenced in deciding to give the preference to a person by a desire to put that person into a better position on liquidation than he would have been in if it had not been done. Such a desire is presumed where the preference was given to a connected person (defined in s. 249), which includes any director of the company. (This presumption is rebuttable: *Re Fairway Magazines* [1993] BCLC 643.) Where payment was made or security was given to a creditor because he was threatening proceedings or otherwise insisting on payment he will usually be able to show that there was no desire to put him in a better position on liquidation. This will be on the grounds that the company was merely responding to genuine commercial pressure.

27.2.3 'Relevant time' requirement for transactions at an undervalue and preferences

Undervalue transactions and preferences can only be set aside if they were entered into at a 'relevant time'; that is, when both of the following requirements are satisfied:

(a) in the case of a transaction at an undervalue, the transaction takes place within two years before commencement of winding up or presentation of the petition for administration or, in the case of a preference, within six months before that date (unless the preference was made to a connected person in which case the period is extended to two years); and

(b) in the case of either an undervalue or preference, the company is insolvent at the time of the transaction or becomes insolvent as a result of the transaction. Where a transaction at an undervalue has been entered into with a connected person, insolvency is presumed unless it can be disproved.

27.2.4 Court can make order as it sees fit

Where it is shown that a transaction can be set aside as a transaction at an undervalue or preference the court can make such order as it sees fit for restoring the position to what it would have been if the transaction had not been entered into. This could include, for example, ordering the person who entered into the transaction or who received the preference to return property or its value to the company. The position of a bona fide purchaser for value is, however, protected.

27.3 Transactions defrauding creditors

Sections 423–425 contain further provisions by which transactions at an undervalue can be set aside. The application of these is not restricted to liquidation or administration and the undervalue transaction can be set aside whenever it was made. However, the person who applies to the court to have the transaction set aside must show that the company in entering into the transaction did so with the purpose of putting assets beyond the reach of that person.

27.4 Floating charges

Under s. 245, a floating charge is prima facie invalid if:

(a) it was made within 12 months before the presentation of a successful petition for winding up or for an administration order or before the passing of a winding-up resolution; and

(b) it was made at a time when the company was unable to pay its debts or became unable to do so as a result of the charge.

Where the company has created a floating charge in favour of a connected person the charge is prima facie invalid if it was made within *two* years before the petition or resolution. The charge is prima facie invalid in such a case even if the company was (and remained) solvent when the charge was created.

A floating charge created within the time limits (and so prima facie invalid) is, however, valid to the extent of:

(a) consideration for the charge consisting of money paid or goods and services supplied to the company at or after the creation of the charge; and

(b) consideration consisting of discharge or reduction of any debt of the company at or after the creation of the charge; and

(c) interest on (a) and (b) above.

EXAMPLE

Montrel Limited has a fully extended, unsecured overdraft with its bank, owing the latter £20,000. In September 2006, the bank agrees to extend the overdraft to £35,000 providing Montrel Limited grants the bank a floating charge to secure all sums due to it. Montrel does so, as it requires £15,000 to enable it to pay wages and money owing to HM Revenue and Customs. Two months later, Montrel, having drawn down the £15,000 but not repaid any money to the bank, becomes insolvent as a result of a winding-up petition.

The floating charge was given to the bank within 12 months of a successful petition for winding up and Montrel was unable to pay its debts at the time. As a result, it is prima facie invalid. This would have the result that the bank would rank as an unsecured creditor in Montrel's liquidation for the sum of £35,000. However, under the criteria above, the charge will be valid to the extent of the consideration for the charge supplied to the company consisting of money paid at or after the creation of the charge, namely the £15,000. The result of this is that the bank will, in Montrel's liquidation, rank as:

(a) a secured creditor (under the floating charge) for £15,000; and

(b) an unsecured credtitor for £20,000.

Section 245 is designed to prevent a company benefiting a creditor by giving a charge for existing debt. The exceptions are designed to ensure that a company may still give security in order to obtain money or supplies even though in some difficulty. This should not in principle cause any harm to existing creditors.

 online resource centre
Interactive online exercises (Student Learning Activities) which complement the topics covered in this chapter are available at www.oxfordtextbooks.co.uk/orc/ business09_10/.

Additional topics

A debenture document

This chapter covers the following topics:

28.1 Introduction

In this chapter we will look briefly at some of the terms which might be found in a debenture document. Before reading this chapter you will find it useful to read **Chapter 11** again.

Debentures vary enormously. We will be looking at one type of debenture only; that is, a debenture which is given by a company in return for a loan by a bank. This type of debenture will contain different provisions from a debenture which is designed to secure a long-term loan from people who want to invest money in a company but who prefer a fixed return rather than the possibility of a variable dividend which would be produced by an issue of shares.

A debenture is likely to contain clauses dealing with the following matters:

(a) the amount of the loan (which may be fixed or variable);

(b) a promise by the company that it will repay the loan on a fixed date and/or on the happening of certain events;

(c) a promise by the company that it will pay interest at a fixed or variable rate;

(d) a charge or charges over some or all of the company's assets—this may include floating as well as fixed charges;

(e) clauses designed to protect the position of the lender (e.g., by giving the lender power to appoint a receiver).

In the rest of this chapter we have given examples of the sort of clauses which may be found in debentures of this type. They are not taken from the debenture of any particular bank. They are provided for the purposes of illustration only so that students may get an idea of what the different clauses in the debenture are for. In practice those who draft debentures for banks will (quite rightly) wish to cover every possible contingency in their debentures. The clauses which they draft are, therefore, usually much fuller than the illustrations given below.

28.2   Terms relating to repayment and interest

The debenture will include a promise by the company that it will repay to the bank the amount which is lent to it. Frequently the debenture will relate to any money which the company owes to the bank. In this case the debenture is mainly designed to secure the repayment of an overdraft by the company. The repayment clause will then refer to something along the lines of 'all monies or other liabilities actual or contingent now or in the future owed by the company to the bank on any account or for which the company may for any reason be or become liable to the bank now or in the future'. Usually provision is made for payment 'on demand', i.e., as soon as the bank asks for it.

If none of the money secured by the debenture consists of a long-term loan (so that the sums secured all relate to variable amounts such as overdraft, interest and bank charges) there will often be a promise to pay a fixed small amount. The clause might, for example, include a term under which the company 'covenants to pay to the bank the sum of one pound (£1) on demand'. Such a provision ensures that the agreement between the company and the bank is not discharged if the company temporarily pays off its overdraft so that the bank temporarily is owed nothing.

There will be a promise to pay interest. In the case of the type of loan we are considering (i.e., a loan by a bank) this will usually be a promise to pay a variable rate of interest on any money outstanding from time to time. This clause could refer to a particular way in which interest is to be calculated (e.g., that it should be a certain number of percentage points above the bank's base rate from time to time). However, the more usual provision is to say that the interest is to be calculated 'in accordance with the bank's usual practice'. Provision may also be made for the rate to be agreed between the parties if possible. Such provisions might at first sight seem rather vague. However, the practice of banks in relation to various classes of loans can be determined objectively if it becomes necessary to do so. The bank is also protected by the fact that if the company does not pay the interest which it is asked to pay, the bank can always call in the whole loan. The company also has the right to redeem the loan by paying the bank, if it can afford to do so.

28.3   Terms relating to security

It is possible to have an unsecured debenture. However, the type of bank debenture which we are examining in this chapter is pointless unless security is given by the borrowing company to the bank. Before it will lend or allow an overdraft the bank will wish to be satisfied that the company is and is likely to remain solvent. Before it will lend or allow an overdraft the bank will also wish (in most cases) to be satisfied that the company's assets are sufficient security for the loan. This will require the bank to consider two matters:

(a) What is the value of the assets offered as security?

(b) Is the company free to give security over the assets?

Valuation is a question of fact. As far as security is concerned the bank will wish to know what other charges the company has already created over its assets. This information will be available from a company search (see the requirements as to registration in **Chapter 11** and as to searches in **Chapter 15**).

28.3.1   Mortgages and fixed charges

The first type of security which the bank will wish to consider is charges over the valuable assets of the company. A legal mortgage of any land which the company may own is likely to be viewed as the best security which the bank can take in most cases. This mortgage will be supplemented by a fixed charge over later acquired land (freehold and leasehold) which the company may acquire. This charge will be an equitable charge as a legal mortgage of land to be acquired in the future is not possible. The debenture will often also say that the bank can insist on the company executing a legal mortgage of any future acquired land once it is acquired and that the title deeds are to be deposited with the bank in the meantime. For most purposes a specific equitable charge is as good as a legal mortgage so this adds little to the bank's security.

The mortgage will require the company to insure the property and to keep it in a good state of repair.

The debenture will also usually provide for security by way of fixed charge over any shares which the company owns in other companies.

The debenture will also frequently contain a fixed charge over the company's goodwill. This is not necessarily a very valuable security as the goodwill is itself often of rather questionable value, especially as the security is only likely to be enforced if the company is in financial difficulties.

Modern debentures often contain a fixed charge over 'the book debts and other debts of the company'. Book debts are the sums owed to the company by, for example, its customers. In effect the fixed charge over book debts says that the bank is entitled to collect the money due to the company in order to discharge the company's own debt to the bank. The law recognises that such a charge is possible but there are technical problems regarding the charge as a fixed charge if the company is free to deal with its book debts as it wishes. The debenture will, therefore, provide that when payment of the debts is received by the company the money must be paid into the company's account at the bank and that the company is not to be free to assign or otherwise deal with its debts.

In light of the decisions of the Privy Council in *Agnew v IRC* [2001] 2 BCLC 188 and the House of Lords in *Re Spectrum Plus Ltd: National Westminster Bank plc v Spectrum Plus Ltd* [2005] 2 BCLC 269, it is highly questionable if a fixed charge over book debts can ever be achieved because of the level of restraint and monitoring required to be exercised by the chargeholder over the realisation of book debts.

Finally, the bank will also look to take a fixed charge over any other assets of the company which are permanent in nature, for example, large items of machinery. Because of the restrictions on the use and sale of assets owned by the borrower that mortgages and fixed charges impose, they are unsuitable security over assets of a transient nature, for example, vehicles and stock. The more suitable security in relation to these assets is a floating charge, which will be discussed next.

28.3.2   Floating charges

As we saw in **Chapter 11** a company can create a floating charge over any of its assets. This is a charge which allows the company to deal with the assets even though they are the subject of the charge. This has the benefit of giving the company flexibility while at the same time giving the bank some sort of security. The problem from the bank's point of view is that the charge is of uncertain value until the security crystallises. In order to reduce this problem it is usual to provide that the company is not free to sell the whole of its undertaking without the consent of the bank. There will also be provision stating that the bank can give notice of crystallisation. This is a clause which says that the bank may 'give notice to the company converting the floating security into a fixed charge in relation to any assets specified in the notice'.

The company will normally be prohibited from creating any later charge ranking in priority to the floating charge. Such a provision is necessary as without it the company is free to charge the floating charge assets by way of specific charge. This does not invalidate the floating charge but clearly if the assets are now subject to a fixed charge which will take priority, the value of the floating charge as a security is greatly reduced.

The company will usually also be required to insure the floating charge property.

28.4 Clauses designed to give the lender further protection

28.4.1 Personal guarantees

If the bank is not satisfied with the security which the company can provide, it may well require personal guarantees from the directors of the company, in addition to the security given by the company.

28.4.2 Appointment of a receiver

One of the clauses which will be contained in the debenture will allow the bank to appoint a receiver. (Note that in respect of most floating charges created on or after 15 September 2003, as a result of the Enterprise Act 2002, administrative receivers (see **Chapter 26**) may no longer be appointed.) The function of the receiver is to realise assets for the bank, pay it off and then return the company to the directors. In practice the company may well be wound up after the receivership as the receiver will have withdrawn many of the assets of the company. The powers and duties of a receiver are dealt with in **Chapter 26**.

Shareholders' agreements

This chapter covers the following topics:

29.1 Introduction
29.2 Advantages of a shareholders' agreement
29.3 Drafting a shareholders' agreement
29.4 Legal limits on the use of shareholders' agreements
29.5 Enforcing the agreement.

29.1 Introduction

In this chapter we will look at shareholders' agreements. These are agreements between shareholders about how their company should be run. The company is also sometimes joined as a party in the agreement so that it too will be bound by the terms (the company cannot, however, override its statutory powers in this way). In particular they are likely to contain terms under which the shareholders agree how they will vote on various issues which may be raised at company meetings. For example, each shareholder might agree to support the re-election of the other shareholders as directors.

Shareholders' agreements are only likely to be effective in the case of companies with a small number of shareholders. If an agreement about how members will vote is to be effective it must usually be made by at least enough members of the company to ensure that a majority of the votes at any meeting will be cast in accordance with the agreement. If there are many members it will be difficult to get a large number of them to enter into a contract. Remember also that the contract (like any other contract) is only enforceable by and against those who are parties to it, so the effectiveness of the agreement is much reduced if a large number of members are not party to it.

29.2 Advantages of a shareholders' agreement

29.2.1 Secrecy

The agreement, unlike the articles, is not open to inspection by the public.

29.2.2 Protection of interests

A shareholders' agreement can protect the interests of some of the members in ways which cannot be easily achieved by the articles. In particular, unless the company provides for different classes of shares, all the shareholders have to be treated alike. If this is not what is desired then it may be much simpler to give one shareholder exceptional rights in a shareholders' agreement. For example, it may be intended that one person (perhaps the founder of the company) should remain a director throughout his life. This is quite difficult to achieve in the articles because the shareholders have a statutory right to remove a director from office. Added voting rights may effectively give a director an invulnerable position (see, for example, *Bushell v Faith* at **9.5.1.4**) but these rights will be attached to the shares and so will pass to the director's successors in title unless very cumbersome arrangements are made. A shareholders' agreement can achieve this very simply if the shareholders agree to vote for X each time his re-election as a director is in issue and to vote against any resolution to remove him from office.

29.2.3 Difficulties of enforcing articles

Although the articles of a company are deemed to be a contract between the company and its members, many cases have decided that this does not mean that each individual member is entitled to enforce compliance with every term of the articles. Generally only those terms which relate to the membership rights of the shareholder can be enforced. If the terms are included in a shareholders' agreement then any party to the agreement can enforce it in full. Furthermore a shareholders' agreement can be enforced simply by means of an action by one shareholder against another. If a shareholder seeks to enforce a term in the articles he will normally have to sue in a representative capacity.

29.2.4 Veto

A shareholders' agreement may give each individual party to it a veto over any proposal which is contrary to the terms of the agreement. In this way a shareholder may be protected even though he only has a small number of shares. However, such agreements should not be lightly entered into. Each shareholder will wish to have a veto against any decisions which he thinks are inappropriate, but he should remember that the other parties will also have the same veto powers (unless he is able to negotiate them for himself alone).

29.3 Drafting a shareholders' agreement

The uses to which shareholders' agreements are put and consequently the clauses which are included in them vary greatly depending on the circumstances which lead to the particular agreement. In this paragraph we will examine some of the main types of provision which may be included.

29.3.1 Appointment of directors and service contracts

The agreement will frequently require all the parties to the agreement to vote in favour of any resolution which reappoints any of them to be a director of the company. It should then also include a term requiring each party to the agreement to vote against any resolution for the removal of any of the parties from the office of director. If it is decided to include such terms, then it may also be appropriate to consider whether there should be any time limit; for example, it might be for a fixed period of time, or it might only apply until each director reaches a specified age.

This clause might also provide for remuneration of the directors and approval of their service contracts for specified or indefinite periods exceeding five years.

29.3.2   Approval for policy decisions

The articles of almost all companies including those (the vast majority) which use Table A as the basis of their articles, provide that business decisions are to be taken by the directors. It would usually be quite inappropriate for articles to provide that the shareholders are to have power to run the company's business. However, if there are particular issues which the shareholders have agreed to as matters of policy, these could be included in a shareholders' agreement. The agreement might, for example, require the agreement of the parties before any new ventures could be undertaken by the company, or before the company could expand the area of its operation. This would be reinforced by an agreement that the parties would vote against any attempt to circumvent such an agreement, and would take whatever steps they could to prevent these things from happening without such approval.

29.3.3   Issue of shares and protection of voting rights

One of the main purposes for which a shareholders' agreement may be used is to protect the shareholders from 'watering' of their interests. This occurs where new shares are issued and a shareholder does not get some of the shares. For example if a shareholder now has 40% of the 1,000 shares which have been issued, he has enough shares to block a special resolution. If a further 1,000 shares were issued and he got none of them then his interest would be reduced to 20% and so (unless the voting rights were changed) he would lose the power to block a special resolution. To prevent this from happening pre-emption rights may be included in the shareholders' agreement.

The considerations here are similar to those in relation to pre-emption rights contained in the articles of a company which we considered in **Chapter 14** (and remember that there are also statutory pre-emption rights in limited circumstances; see **11.2.3**). In some cases it may be more appropriate to include pre-emption rights in a shareholders' agreement. This would be so, for example, if the shareholders wished to keep the existence of the pre-emption rights secret or if they were to apply only to some of the shareholders.

An issue of debentures or other borrowing by the company will not affect the powers of the shareholders to vote in respect of their shares. However, the effect of borrowing will be to reduce the amount of profit available for potential dividend payments to the shareholders. It may, therefore, be appropriate for the clause to require the approval of the parties for borrowing above a certain figure.

A clause in a shareholders' agreement could be drafted so as to require approval of the parties to the agreement for any issue of shares or other reorganisation of capital. This would go further than a simple pre-emption right as it would effectively give the parties a right to veto issue of shares, not just a right to insist on taking some of the shares themselves. Alternatively the clause could provide that the existing shareholders would be bound to make further investment in certain circumstances specified in the clause. Obviously a shareholder should not undertake such an obligation lightly in case he does not have the resources to meet his obligation when it arises.

29.3.4 Withdrawal from the company

One of the principal features of company law is that a shareholder (unlike a partner in a partnership) is not normally allowed to withdraw his investment. This is the idea of maintenance of capital which we saw in **Chapter 11** (we also saw the limited exceptions in **Chapter 12** under which a company can redeem or buy back its own shares). A shareholders' agreement can be used to allow a shareholder an opportunity to leave the company and to take out his capital. For example, the agreement will often include a clause requiring a shareholder to offer his shares to the other members pro rata if he wishes to sell. As in the case of a pre-emption right on transfer contained in the articles (see **Chapter 14**), this clause will contain valuation provisions which will be designed to ensure fairness to both the selling member and the buying member.

A simple pre-emption right will not, however, ensure that the shareholder can sell his shares. He must offer them to the other members but they may not wish to buy. In this case the member is unlikely to be able to sell to an outsider, as there is likely to be a restriction on the right to transfer either in the articles or in the shareholders' agreement. It is possible to include a term whereby the shareholder who wishes to get out of the company has a right to insist that the other members of the company will buy his shares. Such a clause should only be entered into if the finances of the potential purchasers are likely to be strong enough to be able to comply with the agreement.

29.3.5 Payment of dividends

Although it is not likely to be one of the commonest clauses to be found in a shareholders' agreement, it is possible to include a term which will either require the payment of dividends or which will restrict the payment of dividends. A clause which purported to require payment of dividends other than out of accumulated realised profits (after deduction of accumulated realised losses) would be unenforceable as such payments would be illegal.

29.3.6 Restrictive covenants

Restrictive covenants may be included in a shareholders' agreement. This sort of term might be appropriate where a shareholder has brought particular expertise to the company and the other shareholders wish to preserve that expertise for the company. If such a clause is included it is likely also to appear in any service contract which the shareholder has with the company (for example where he is a director as well as a shareholder). Restrictive covenants are void on grounds of public policy unless they are reasonable in area and time.

29.3.7 An arbitration clause

Like many commercial agreements the shareholders' agreement will often include an arbitration clause so that any disputes which arise out of it can be resolved without the need for action in the courts.

29.4 Legal limits on the use of shareholders' agreements

29.4.1 Power to alter the articles

A company has a statutory power to alter its articles by special resolution. A shareholders' agreement cannot take this right away. However, it can provide that members are personally in breach of contract if they vote in favour of an alteration which is contrary to the terms of the agreement: see for example, *Russell v Northern Bank Development Corporation* [1992] 1 WLR 588.

29.4.2 Directors' duties

The directors of a company have a fiduciary duty to the company. A shareholders' agreement could not lawfully permit the directors to breach this fiduciary duty. Furthermore directors have a number of duties which are of a public nature (particularly in relation to insolvent companies). A shareholders' agreement could not authorise or direct the directors as to how they are to perform their functions. For example, a director would be liable for failure to make statutory returns to the Registrar of Companies even if his shareholders' agreement purported to require this. Similarly a director could not absolve himself from liability for wrongful trading on the basis of a shareholders' agreement.

29.5 Enforcing the agreement

A shareholders' agreement is a contract. Each party provides consideration by agreeing to abide by the terms of the agreement. It follows from this that if the agreement is broken, the other parties can claim damages. The agreement can also be enforced by an injunction which requires a shareholder who is a party to it not to vote in a way contrary to the terms of the agreement. It may also be enforced by a positive injunction requiring a shareholder who is a party to it to vote in accordance with its provisions.

Sale of a business to a company

This chapter covers the following topics:

30.1 Introduction

A sole trader or partnership may decide, for a variety of reasons, to incorporate the business. If this step is taken, although the business will remain unchanged, the incorporation will give rise to a number of tax and other problems. In this chapter, we will consider these problems and how they can be avoided, or at least mitigated. As we shall see, the tax rules are the most important in this area, since if they are not appreciated the payment of an unexpected tax bill can cause very serious cash flow problems. As an aid to understanding these problems, it is helpful to bear in mind that when the trader (which for these purposes includes partnerships) incorporates the business, it is transferred to a separate legal entity, the company. This means that the trader ceases to trade as an unincorporated business and disposes of the business and its assets to the company. The fact that the former proprietor or proprietors own the company and operate the business in exactly the same way as before is immaterial since the members and the company are distinct legal entities (*Salomon v A. Salomon & Co. Ltd* [1897] AC 22).

It may therefore come as a surprise to many traders who incorporate their businesses to discover that incorporation can lead to the payment of income tax, capital gains tax and stamp duty. In this chapter these tax liabilities will be considered in turn.

30.2 Income tax

30.2.1 The closing year rules

Of the possible tax liabilities which can arise, the one which may cause the most difficulties, if it is not provided for, is the liability to income tax. Transferring the business to the company means that the unincorporated trader has permanently stopped trading, with the result that the closing year rules of assessment will apply. (See **17.3.2.3** for an explanation of the closing year rules.)

30.2.2 Loss relief

If a loss is made in the final 12 months' trading, it can be carried across against income from another source under s. 64 ITA 2007, and any unabsorbed loss carried back and set against the profits of the three tax years immediately preceding the year of incorporation, taking later years before earlier ones (s. 89 ITA 2007). If, having made use of both provisions, there is still an unabsorbed loss, it cannot be used by the company. However, s. 86 ITA 2007 permits the former proprietors, provided they sold the business in exchange wholly or mainly for shares in the new company, to set the remaining loss against income received from the company while they continue to own the shares. They must reduce earned income (such as directors' fees) before investment income (such as dividends).

Although it may appear strange that a loss-making business should be incorporated there may be sound reasons for doing so. For example, the business may be entering a temporary period of recession and the trader may want to protect himself from personal liability for future debts, or the loss may have been deliberately created by claiming capital allowances in respect of items of plant and machinery bought shortly before incorporation.

30.2.3 Capital allowances

Whether or not the purchase of an item attracting capital allowances has created the final year loss, the trader's capital allowance position is the remaining income tax point which needs to be considered. The rules relating to capital allowances have already been considered (see **Chapter 22**). The important point to be considered in the context of incorporating a trader's business, is that the transfer to the company, even if the purchase price is to be paid in shares, will be a disposal. If the capital allowances already claimed exceed the amount by which the assets have actually depreciated in value, HMRC has a right to levy a balancing charge. This means HMRC recovers the tax lost as a result of the over-deduction of allowances. Thus there can be another additional income tax bill arising on the incorporation. However, it is possible to ensure that the transfer of plant and machinery is not to be regarded as a discontinuance of the trade for the purposes of capital allowances provided:

(a) the trader and persons connected with him (which includes partners) are the majority shareholders in the new company; and

(b) an election is made to the effect that if there is no discontinuance, there is no disposal and the balancing charge does not arise. The result is that the new company takes over the trader's capital allowance position and makes the appropriate claims for writing-down allowances in respect of the, as yet, unallowed expenditure.

30.3 Capital gains tax

30.3.1 The disposal

The incorporation of the old business not only means there is a discontinuance for income tax purposes, but that there is also a disposal for CGT purposes. This disposal arises because the business, its assets and connections (i.e., goodwill) are being *sold* to the company in exchange for shares. This is a chargeable disposal within the Taxation of Chargeable Gains Act (TCGA) 1992 and the trader will be liable for any gain that is realised.

This liability cannot be avoided by the company issuing shares of a purely nominal value in exchange for the assets, as HMRC has a right to substitute the market value of the assets in such circumstances. This gain could be considerable, especially if the business is successful and was set up several years previously. However, a number of reliefs operate in these circumstances which will be looked at in turn.

A business owner has essentially three options as to how his capital gains tax situation is managed on an incorporation:

(a) transfer the entire undertaking as a going concern in return for shares in the new company and claim roll-over relief;

(b) transfer certain assets for full value and pay the tax on those and keep other assets and allow the company to use such retained assets;

(c) transfer certain assets either for nil consideration or at an undervalue and claim hold-over relief in respect of those and keep other assets and allow the company to use such retained assets.

Option (b) requires no explanation as it does not involve a specific relief, but options (a) and (c) will be looked at in turn.

30.3.2 Relief under s. 162 TCGA 1992

30.3.2.1 The basic rule

Section 162 TCGA 1992 applies where a person (not being a company) 'transfers to a company a business as a going concern, together with the whole assets of the business, or together with the whole of those assets other than cash, and the business is transferred wholly or partly in exchange for shares issued by the company to the person transferring the business'. The section permits a deduction to be made from the gain arising when the business and its assets are disposed of. Section 162(4) provides that this deduction is the gain reduced by the fraction A/B, where A is the 'cost of the new assets' (that is, the value of the shares issued to the former owner), and B is the whole of the consideration received by the former owner in exchange for the business. Thus, if the former owner transfers a business with assets worth £100,000 to the new company and receives £90,000 worth of shares and £10,000 worth of debentures in exchange, his gain will be reduced by the fraction £90,000/(£90,000 + £10,000), i.e., 9/10ths. This means that the former owner only pays tax on 1/10th of the gain realised on the disposal of the business; the remaining 9/10ths are, however, taxable when he disposes of the shares at some time in the future. If he only receives shares, the whole of the tax liability on the gain would be postponed in this way, or 'rolled-over' as the Act describes it.

It should be noted that the relief only applies to the former owner and his tax liability. The company's acquisition price of the assets will be their full market value at the date of the disposal.

30.3.2.2 The assets transferred to the company

Although these rules may appear complex at first sight, two simple requirements can be extracted from them. First, to claim the relief at all, the whole of the assets of the business (other than cash) at the date of incorporation must be transferred to the company, and secondly, the relief may only be claimed in full if the consideration received was entirely in the form of shares. Provided these conditions are satisfied, the effect of s. 162 is that the former owner acquires the shares at a value equal to his original acquisition price of the assets that have just been transferred to the company, so tax is only paid when they are later sold or given away. Since s. 162 relief can be obtained so easily by following these rules, it may seem strange that a number of traders choose not to take advantage of the relief and actually retain ownership of certain assets which they subsequently allow the new company to use (whilst still transferring the bulk of the business assets to the new company). There is, however, a good reason for this, which is to avoid the 'double capital gains tax charge', which is a problem where companies own appreciating assets, such as land or buildings. If a company owns such an asset and disposes of it realising a gain, the company will pay corporation tax on that gain. The post-tax gain will then increase the value of the company's assets, which in turn has the effect of increasing the value of the shares. This will result in the shareholder making an increased gain, and so paying more capital gains tax, on a later disposal of the shares. Retaining the asset in the former owner's hands ensures that there is only one capital gains tax charge if the asset is disposed of. It may also produce a stamp duty saving (see **30.6.5**).

30.3.2.3   Method of payment for assets

Even if HMRC is convinced that all the assets comprised in the business have been transferred, the relief can only be claimed in full if the company 'pays' for the assets in shares. As has already been explained, if the consideration is wholly or partly in debentures and/or cash the roll-over relief is wholly or partly denied to the former owner.

It is much more common, however, for the former owner to be paid in shares and debentures (the reason being that, as a shell, the company will have no cash with which to make the purchase). Debentures have advantages for both the holder (in the form of security of both capital and income) and the company (in the form of a pre-tax deduction in respect of the interest payments), and these advantages may compensate the former owner for partial loss of capital gains tax relief. It should be remembered that receiving part of the consideration in debentures means a proportionate part of the gain is taxable, but this taxable gain could be reduced or wiped out by the annual exemption. This has the attraction of reducing any future taxable gain and also of ensuring that the owner does not lose the benefit of the annual exemption for the year of incorporation.

30.3.3   Relief for gifts of business assets (s. 165 TCGA 1992)

Section 165 gives 'hold-over' relief where an asset used by the trader in his trade, profession or vocation is transferred to a company, provided the transaction is not a bargain at arm's length. This means that if the asset is 'sold' at an undervalue, or even given to the company, the trader and the company can elect that the company acquires the asset for a consideration equal to the trader's acquisition cost (if there is an outright gift) or the sale price (if there is a sale at an undervalue). The effect of the relief is to postpone the payment of tax until the asset is disposed of, when the *company* will be liable to pay the tax, not the trader.

In contrast to the relief under s. 162 TCGA 1992, this relief operates even if not all assets are transferred simultaneously. It does, therefore, have the advantage of flexibility.

30.3.4   To retain or not to retain

It will be seen that there is no simple answer to the question of whether or not to retain assets. However, a number of matters can be borne in mind:

(a) The choice to retain an asset will result in the denial of relief under s. 162 TCGA 1992. The other possible relief under s. 165 TCGA 1992 will, however, still be available for other assets which are transferred. It should be remembered that this relief, in effect, puts the gain into the hands of the company.

(b) If the intention is that an appreciating asset is to be disposed of in the near future and replaced, then either the proprietor or the company may still be entitled to roll-over relief under s. 152 TCGA 1992.

(c) If the intention is that an appreciating asset is to be disposed of and *not* replaced, then which party is to realise the gain requires careful consideration. The proprietor, as an individual, is subject to CGT at 18%. The company will pay at an effective rate of between 21% and 28%, depending on its profits, but may also claim indexation allowance. Therefore, the use of either s. 162 or s. 165 to first put the asset into the hands of the company may produce an immediate benefit. If, however, the proprietor has accumulated capital losses or could realise the same, it may be sensible for him to realise the gain.

(d) The prospect of a double charge to tax may be more imagined than real, especially if the intention is that the proprietor will retain the shares for several years. Also, to substitute a single asset for a number of shares provides greater scope for tax planning as an asset will normally have to be sold in toto, whereas fractions of a shareholding can be disposed of over a period of time. Therefore, the use of s. 162 relief may produce a number of benefits in this regard.

(e) Stamp duty will play an important part in the decision. The retention of assets or their transfer for nil consideration, so as to claim s. 165 relief, will ease the stamp duty burden. However, a balance has to be struck between this and capital gains tax to ensure the best saving for the owner. Stamp duty is looked at in detail below.

30.4 VAT

If the trader is registered for VAT, VAT may be chargeable on the transfer of the assets unless the business is transferred as a going concern (s. 33 Value Added Tax Act 1983). Any decision to retain assets in the hands of the proprietor for reasons explained above may, of course, prejudice the availability of this exemption.

30.5 Stamp duty/stamp duty land tax

30.5.1 Introduction

The purchaser of certain assets, in this case, the newly formed company, should always consider whether or not such a purchase triggers a charge to stamp duty or stamp duty land tax. A limited number of transactions need to be considered as follows.

(a) *Stamp duty*

The transfer of shares and certain transactions involving partners and partnership property are subject to stamp duty.

(b) *Stamp duty land tax*

Transactions involving land and real property (both freehold and leasehold) are subject to stamp duty land tax.

As regards the incorporation of a business, stamp duty is, therefore, irrelevant. No existing shares in the newly formed company are being transferred; there is simply an allotment of them to the proprietor. However, as most transactions are likely to involve a property element, stamp duty land tax will have to be looked at.

30.5.2   Stamp duty land tax

Stamp duty land tax (SDLT) applies to the acquisition of both freehold and leasehold interests in land. Therefore, the transfer of the property of the business to the new company may attract SDLT.

Unlike stamp duty, SDLT is not a charge on documents, but is a charge on transactions. As such, within 30 days of the completion of the relevant transaction, a land transaction return (form SDLT 1) must be completed and sent to HMRC together with any SDLT payable. In return the company will receive a certificate of evidence of the same. Without this, title to the property cannot be registered.

It may be thought sensible, therefore, for the owner of the business to retain the freehold or leasehold and, instead, grant a lease or sub-lease, respectively. SDLT, however, is also payable on the grant of any lease for seven years or more or of a lease for less than seven years, if SDLT is due at 1% or more on that lease. (See **30.5.3** next for details of SDLT rates.)

30.5.3   The stamp duty land tax rates

The amount of stamp duty land tax payable is ad valorem; that is, based on the value of the property interest transferred. In respect of the purchase of a freehold interest in business property, SDLT rates are as follows:

Purchase price	SDLT rate
£150,000 or less	0%
£150,001 to £250,000	1%
£250,001 to £500,000	3%
Over £500,000	4%

In respect of the grant or assignment of a leasehold interest in business property, SDLT has to be calculated both on the rent payable and any other consideration, most likely any premium. It is beyond the scope of this work to consider the detail of these complex calculations. However, by way of brief summation, the greater the rent payable and the longer the term of the lease, the larger the SDLT burden.

30.6   Subsidiary matters

The tax matters already dealt with will, of course, be important to the former owner but there are a number of other points that must not be overlooked.

30.6.1   The transfer and employment law

Historically, the general rule was that the transfer of the business terminated the contracts of employment of all the employees and, if common law and statutory claims against the business owner were to be avoided, the employees had to be notified of the transfer and offered employment with the new company on the same, or suitable, terms before the transfer took place. However, as a result of the Transfer of Undertakings (Protection of Employment) Regulations 1981 (SI 1981/794) and their recent replacement by Transfer of Undertakings (Protection of Employment) Regulations 2006 (SI 2006/246), this is no longer the case, since reg. 4(1) of the 2006 Regulations provides that a 'relevant transfer' shall not terminate a person's contract of employment and the contract shall have the effect after the transfer as if it had originally been made between the employee and the transferee. (A 'relevant transfer' is defined in reg. 3(1) as including 'a transfer of an undertaking, business or part of an undertaking or business situated immediately before the transfer in the United Kingdom where there is a transfer of an economic entity which retains its identity'.) Thus, if a business is transferred to a company, the employees are treated as if their contracts had originally been made with the new company, which takes over all the trader's rights, powers, duties and liabilities under the employment contracts. Therefore, the employee's period of continuous employment is preserved, as are any pre-existing rights against the old employer for breach of contract or duty. As a result, the new employer could be faced with liability for a constructive dismissal arising from the old employer's breach, for example, and should obtain suitable indemnities.

While these regulations do not prevent an employee bringing a claim against the trader if there is a substantial change made in his working conditions, no action can be brought simply because the identity of the employer has changed, unless the employee shows the change to be significant and to his detriment.

Regulation 5 does not enable the fact of the transfer to be kept from the employees. Regulation 10 imposes an obligation on the transferor to inform and consult with appointed employee representatives.

30.6.2 The transfer and company law

In addition to the matters that always arise on the formation of a new company, one special problem particularly relevant to this kind of transfer must be considered. On the assumption that the transferor of the business will be a director of the new company, the consent of the members in general meeting will almost certainly be needed to the purchase by the company of the assets. Section 190 CA 2006 requires such consent to be obtained if a director sells to (or buys from) the company a non-cash asset or assets of the 'requisite value', which means assets worth £100,000 or representing at least 10% of the company's assets (subject to a minimum value of £5,000). If the consent is not obtained, the transaction is voidable at the instance of the company and the director will have to account to the company for any profit made and indemnify it for any loss or damages arising. In order to obtain the necessary consent, a general meeting of the company will have to be held immediately after incorporation and before the transfer takes place.

Furthermore, the transferor must make sure that the new company's name is displayed in all relevant places, e.g., websites, registered office, place of business, stationery and other publications and that its letters, order forms and websites contain the required information, i.e., country of registration, registered office and registered number.

30.6.3 The transfer and other miscellaneous matters

Further practical points to be dealt with include the following:

(a) The local inspector of taxes must be notified that there is a new employer for PAYE purposes as well as there being a new company liable to corporation tax.

(b) If the business's turnover exceeds the threshold for VAT registration, its VAT registration must be cancelled and the company must apply to have itself registered. In order to ensure there is no gap in the VAT registration it is advisable to cancel the old one after the company's registration has been confirmed.

(c) The consent of a landlord to the assignment of a lease must be obtained. If the new company is taking over responsibility for hire-purchase contracts, the consent of the finance house must be obtained.

(d) The former owner can bring his personal liability to existing creditors to an end by entering into a contract of 'novation'. However, the consent of the creditors is required. As a counterpoint to this, the owner may still be asked to guarantee liabilities which have been assumed by the new company; for example, indebtedness to a bank and those under a lease.

(e) The company must take out appropriate insurance cover and have any vehicles transferred into its own name.

Limited liability partnerships

This chapter covers the following topics:

31.1 Introduction

31.2 Key elements of LLPs

31.3 Factors influencing choice

31.4 Conclusion.

It is recommended that the concepts governing both partnerships and companies have been studied and understood before reading this chapter. In particular, as most of the regulation which governs companies governs limited liability partnerships (LLPs), it is recommended that the reader has a working knowledge of the regime which covers companies before considering LLPs.

31.1 Introduction

The popularity of private limited companies as business media can be attributed to one thing: the availability of limited liability for the owners and managers. However, the trade-off is public disclosure of much of what the company does, together with a complex regulatory regime. For this reason, the medium of a partnership can still be an attractive choice in certain circumstances, particularly for professional firms.

However, one of the major disincentives to setting up in business through the medium of a partnership is the exposure which each partner faces to liabilities of the partnership. Not only is each partner personally liable for all liabilities (either contractual or tortious) of the partnership, there is also no limit on such liability. This has been a source of considerable concern to large professional partnerships, where the work undertaken can be advising on matters running into millions of pounds. With clients becoming increasingly litigious in relation to their advisers, the threat of a massive (and potentially ruinous) claim is ever present.

It was against this background that the concept of LLPs was introduced by the Limited Liability Partnerships Act (LLPA) 2000, which came into force on 6 April 2001. It is important to note that the Act merely provides a framework and that certain detail can be introduced by regulations made by the Secretary of State (ss. 14–17 LLPA 2000). Therefore, it is crucial that reference is made to such regulations. The key regulations in existence are the Limited Liability Partnerships Regulations 2001. It should be noted at the outset that the LLPA 2000 does not replace the regime for partnerships under the PA 1890. It is still possible, therefore, to operate a business as a 'traditional' partnership. In addition, LLPs are available to any type of business and not limited to professional partnerships.

The key rationale for the creation of LLPs is to allow entrepreneurs the protection of limited liability, while preserving the flexibility of the partnership structure. As such, LLPs can best be described as a hybrid of both companies and partnerships. However, as will become apparent, they owe much more to the former than the latter. (This is reinforced by the fact that s. 1(5) LLPA 2000 categorically states that the law of partnerships does not apply to LLPs.) Additionally, the Limited Liability Partnerships (Application of Companies Act 2006) Regulations 2009 extend the effect of many provisions of the Companies Act to LLPs.

31.2   Key elements of LLPs

31.2.1   Limited liability

Third parties who deal with LLPs will contract and deal with the LLP as a distinct legal entity (s. 1(2) LLPA 2000). This is in contrast to partnerships, where the partners and the partnership are one and the same. This means that any recourse the third party has will be against the LLP entity and its assets rather than the partners themselves. That much is straightforward. What is more difficult is just how partners can limit their liability. Section 1(4) LLPA 2000 states that members of an LLP shall contribute to the assets of the LLP in the event of its being wound up as is provided for by the Act. Unfortunately, the Act makes no further provision in this regard. However, the expectation is that partners will guarantee to contribute a fixed sum in the event of insolvency, as do members of a company limited by guarantee. Therefore, it is feasible that partners' liability could be limited to as little as £1.

However, it is perhaps an over-simplification to imagine that those involved in LLPs will never incur any form of personal liability. Although the issue is not clear-cut, the view is that liability for negligent misstatement will still attach to the errors of a partner. This is particularly germane in the instance of a professional LLP, such as a law or accountancy firm. As such, whilst the partnership as a whole may not bear the liability for negligent advice, the individual who gave that advice may be liable.

31.2.2   Creation

An LLP is very much like a company in that it will have to be registered with the Registrar of Companies and a certificate of incorporation will be issued as proof of this fact (ss. 2 and 3 LLPA 2000). To achieve incorporation, details of the LLP must be entered on form LLP2 and submitted to the Registrar of Companies with a fee of £20. The basic contents of the form are:

(a) the signatures of two or more persons associated with the business;

(b) name of the LLP (which must end with the words 'Limited Liability Partnership' or 'LLP');

(c) a statement about the intended location of the registered office and the actual address of the same;

(d) the names and addresses of those persons who are to be involved with the business.

This shares similarities with the procedure for registration of a company. However, one major difference is that there is no specimen constitution which an LLP can adopt (as the Model Articles for companies), nor must the LLP register its constitution with Companies House as a matter of public record.

31.2.3   Unlimited capacity

Section 1(3) of the LLPA 2000 states that an LLP has unlimited capacity, in the same way that companies formed under the CA 2006 have unrestricted objects. However, a distinction seems to be that companies still have the option of restricting the scope of their objects in the constitution (s. 31 CA 2006). This possibility does not appear to be available to LLPs.

31.2.4   Members and designated members

In the preceding paragraphs reference has been made to 'partners' in LLPs. Strictly speaking, this is incorrect. The persons involved in an LLP will be classed as 'members', thus drawing another parallel with companies.

The initial members of the LLP are those who signed the incorporation document. Further members can join the LLP with the consent of the then current members.

There must be a minimum of two members in an LLP. Should the number fall to one and remain so for at least six months, the benefit of limited liability will cease and the remaining member will be liable together with the LLP for all debts and liabilities incurred during that period. This requirement excludes the availability of LLPs for sole traders. It also puts LLPs at a disadvantage as compared to private limited companies, which can allow their membership to fall to one, should the situation ever arise.

There is a special class of members known as 'designated members', as specified by s. 8 LLPA 2000. The incorporation document will have to contain details of such members. Their key responsibility is in relation to ensuring that the LLP's accounts are signed off and filed with the Registrar of Companies.

31.2.5   Disclosure requirements

As with companies, the *quid pro quo* for limited liability is public disclosure. The key filing responsibilities of an LLP are:

- the filing of accounts;
- the filing of an annual return;
- the notification of changes to the membership;
- the notification of changes in designated members;
- the notification of a change to the registered office.

31.2.6   Relationship of members with the LLP, each other, and third parties

31.2.6.1   LLP

Every member is an agent of the LLP (s. 6(1) LLPA 2000). As such the common law fiduciary duties that an agent owes to a principal would appear to apply to members of an LLP. It is beyond the scope of this text to consider the relationship between an agent and its principal, but the basic parameters will be that the member:

(a) Must act in good faith towards the LLP.

(b) Must not put himself in a position of conflict with the LLP.

    (c) Must not profit personally from his position.

    (d) Must make full disclosure of information which is of legitimate interest to the LLP.

Note, however, that whilst much of the Companies Act does apply to LLPs, the statutory duties which apply to directors are not imposed on members of an LLP. The rationale for this is that members of an LLP cannot be equated with directors due to the absence of a distinction between the owners of an LLP and its management.

This agency relationship presumably also means that members acting with either actual or apparent authority have the power to bind the firm, although the Act does not make this point explicitly. What the Act does do, however, is provide an exception to this basic rule, which is akin to the 'unless' exception in s. 5 PA 1890. Thus, if any member is acting without authority and the person he is dealing with either knows that he has no authority or does not know or believe him to be a member, the LLP will not be bound by the acts of the member.

Persons ceasing to be members of LLPs can still operate as its agents until either the third party is notified of the fact or notice is sent to the Registrar of Companies.

LLPs are also liable for the wrongful acts or omissions of individual members, when acting in the course of the LLP's business (s. 6(4)) to the same extent as the member. The LLPA 2000 is silent on the meaning of 'wrongful acts or omissions'. This will likely include tortious acts, and it may also include criminal acts.

More difficult still is the issue of ownership by the members of a stake in the LLP. Shareholders in a company can point to an asset which represents their holding in the company. Similarly, partners in a 'traditional' partnership have a direct proprietorial stake in the assets used by the partnership or at least a claim in their proceeds of sale (see *Popat v Schonchhatra* [1997] 3 All ER 800). However, with LLPs, the separation between the legal entity and its owners exists, without any legal mechanism being in place to record ownership. Therefore, if an LLP uses its funds to buy an asset, that asset is owned by the LLP. However, in substance, the members will be of the view that it is their money which has been used and, therefore, the property is theirs. Furthermore, profits made by the LLP will be profits of that entity, but must be available to the members.

Regulation 7, para. (1) of the Limited Liability Partnerships Regulations 2001 provides that members are entitled to share equally in the capital and profits of the LLP, which borrows heavily from s. 24(1) PA 1890. Section 24(1) operates to allocate the entitlements of partners and does not act as a basis for determining ownership. There is no reason to assume that reg. 7, para. (1) should be treated differently. As such, it is arguable that in neither the LLPA 2000 nor the Limited Liability Partnerships Regulations 2001 is there an absolute statement about the rights of ownership which members enjoy in an LLP. Also, because of the effect of s. 1(5) LLPA 2000 it is not possible to treat members of an LLP as equivalent to partners in terms of their legal status.

That the law is silent on this issue is perhaps a grave oversight. Therefore, to ensure certainty, members will have to enter into arrangements with their LLPs to provide for these issues. The exact nature of such a relationship will have to be determined carefully, as will what comprises a member's share in the LLP, what a member may or may not do with that share and any specific entitlement of a member when they leave the LLP.

31.2.6.2 Each other

As stated above, members of LLPs are free to organise their internal affairs as they wish. This is the flexibility of the existing partnership regime which the Government has wished to preserve. Doubtless the basis for any such agreement will be pre-existing partnership deeds, although these obviously cannot be left unamended. Should such an agreement not be in place, the default provisions in the Limited Liability Partnership Regulations 2001 can be relied upon. However, many of these will not be satisfactory for all but the simplest of LLP arrangements.

Of particular interest is the ability of members of an LLP to bring a claim for unfair prejudice under s. 994 CA 2006. However, this may be more of a theoretical possibility than real if an LLP agreement exists, for two reasons:

(a) The members can agree to exclude the possibility in the LLP agreement.

(b) In any event, the agreement may be comprehensive enough to deal with all internal disputes, excluding the need to assert unfair prejudice.

31.2.6.3 Third parties

Essentially there is no relationship between members of LLPs and third parties. Therefore, unlike in a partnership, issues of liabilities of a business following a member after retirement do not arise. However, as has been mentioned already, it is possible that, in certain circumstances, individual members may find themselves liable in tort to third parties, particularly when giving professional advice.

Also, there may be instances where due to the principal/agent relationship between an LLP and its members, a member may be held liable for breach of warranty of authority to an outsider.

31.2.7 Taxation

The principle of separate legal personality is not maintained as far as taxation is concerned, so an LLP is not a taxable person. Instead, as with partnerships, it is the members who are taxed as profit centres.

31.2.8 Impact of other Acts

Sections 14–16 LLPA 2000 allow for the Secretary of State to make provision for company and insolvency law to apply to LLPs. This has been done primarily through the regulations already mentioned. However, other regulations exist which deal with accounting and audit issues, such as the Limited Liability Partnerships (Accounts and Audit) (Application of Companies Act 2006) Regulations 2008. As such, large tracts of the Companies Act 2006, the Company Directors Disqualification Act 1986 and the Insolvency Act 1986 apply to LLPs. As a general rule, it is safe to assume that much of the legislation which applies to companies and their directors applies equally to LLPs and their members, for example:

- The choice of an LLP's registered name is subject to the same controls and restrictions as a company's registered name. Furthermore, LLPs are subject to the same disclosure requirements about registered names as companies.

- LLPs' accounts have to be audited in accordance with the Companies Act 2006 to give a true and fair view of the business.

- Charges granted by LLPs over their assets have to be registered at Companies House.

- Members of LLPs can face disqualification orders, such that they can be neither members of other LLPs nor company directors.

- Insolvent LLPs are subject to the same insolvency regime as companies and their members will find themselves subject to the same scrutiny as directors of insolvent companies, for example, they could commit wrongful trading.

31.3 Factors influencing choice

There will be two instances where the question of choosing an LLP arises: as part of a business start-up or existing partnerships considering conversion. When considering LLPs, it should always be remembered that their resemblance to traditional partnerships is an exception rather than a rule and that it is better to think of them as corporate structures.

The authors consider that there is very little likelihood of the members of an existing company wishing to alter its status to that of an LLP, as this will alter fundamentally their relationship with each other and their business medium, with no corresponding benefit.

31.3.1 Business start-up

One easy decision can be made at the outset, when advising on the appropriate business medium. If only one person is to be involved in the venture, neither a partnership nor an LLP is possible. Thereafter the basic rules about choice of business medium (as set out in **Chapter 32**) apply and, whilst there are three possible formats to choose from, the basic choice is between a corporate entity (company or LLP) or a partnership. In turn, this means a choice between limited liability, public disclosure, substantial regulations and compliance and unlimited liability, absolute secrecy and very limited compliance. This distinction is, however, blurred when taxation is considered, because LLPs do share the taxation regime of partnerships rather than companies.

If a decision is made in favour of a corporate entity, then some of the distinctions to be drawn are as follows:

(a) The decision-making regime within an LLP can be as simple or as complex as the members wish. There is no such choice with companies. However, the two-tier decision-making process within companies (that is, directors and shareholders) may allow for greater flexibility in power-sharing.

(b) Raising capital is still likely to be easier through a company, because of the flexibility inherent in shares as an investment mechanism. If, however, the business is likely to remain close-knit and to rely primarily upon its initial members for finance, this may not be a disincentive to choosing an LLP.

(c) Within the framework of a company there is more scope for leaving profits within the company or paying them out. Within an LLP, profits earned are taxed in the hands of the members, irrespective of whether or not they are drawn out.

(d) The regime for companies is relatively clear and well understood, whereas the regime governing LLPs may throw up unforeseen problems as it matures.

(e) It is relatively inexpensive to set up a company and considerable precedents exist for many permutations of articles. Whilst an LLP members' agreement is not a requirement of law, clients would be ill-advised not to have one. The length and complexity of such documents may result in a considerable initial cost burden.

31.3.2 Conversion from partnership to LLP

Much of what has just been discussed will be relevant in this situation also. However, a number of other issues may have to be considered, such as:

(a) *The cost of conversion.* The re-draft of any existing partnership deed may be a lengthy and costly process. In addition, there is the practical issue that every existing partner should sign the incorporation document and it should contain their addresses. In a professional partnership of, say, more than 100 partners worldwide, this would pose logistical problems.

(b) *The cost/management of disclosure.* Notification must be made every time a member either joins or leaves and every time a member's address changes. Again, in large partnerships this is an extra burden of bureaucracy. Moreover, having such details on the public register may be regarded as undesirable by some.

(c) *Disclosure of financial information.* For professional partnerships, the disclosure of accounts is seen by many to be a major disincentive to adopting LLP status. Also, the accounts of a partnership are prepared for the purposes of internal consumption and those of HMRC, whereas the accounts of an LLP will have to conform to the standards and requirements set out in the Companies Act 2006 (and related regulations).

(d) *Borrowing.* When a bank lends to a partnership, it can take comfort from the fact that the individual estates of the partners will be available to meet any shortcomings in the assets of the firm. Such comfort would be removed if conversion to an LLP took place. To overcome this, banks may ask individual partners to act as guarantors of the LLP, thus partially eroding the benefits of limited liability.

(e) *Leasehold property.* Many of the same issues for banks arise in relation to any leases the partnership may hold.

(f) *Novation of key contracts.* Contracts with the existing firm will have to become contracts with the LLP.

(g) *Ownership of assets.* As mentioned in **31.2.5.1** it would appear that members of an LLP will own part of the LLP, rather than the LLP's assets direct. Conversion will, therefore, require the transfer of the business of the firm into the hands of the LLP. However, the LLP cannot offer shares in return, as would happen if a partnership were to convert to a company. It makes no sense for the LLP to pay the partners cash for the assets, as this would involve the LLP borrowing money effectively to return every partner's capital contribution. Instead the consideration for the sale is best treated as the corresponding share which each member will enjoy in the LLP. Note that this transfer will be a tax-neutral event, as the sale to the LLP will not be treated as a disposal for capital gains tax purposes. Moreover, in most circumstances, no stamp duty will be payable.

31.4 Conclusion

The rationale behind LLPs is admirable and they go some way to providing a middle ground between companies and partnerships. However, what is unfortunate is that they are the product of an amalgamation of two regimes, rather than being the product of completely fresh thinking. In many ways they owe more to companies than they do to partnerships and this lack of clear water between the two media may mean that the choice of a limited company is preferable, especially when the latter is a much more mature entity. Statistics do show an upward trend in new registrations, however. For example, in the DTI report *Companies in 2002–2003*, the total number of LLPs registered as at 31 March 2003 was around 4,500. In the same report for the following year, this figure had increased substantially to nearly 7,500. Current statistics indicate that around 30,000 LLPs have been registered. There can be no doubt that, amongst the professions, the LLP route is becoming increasingly preferred. However, average statistics for new incorporations of companies stand in excess of 350,000 per annum, so the company would appear to be still the main business medium for the time being.

Choice of business medium

This chapter covers the following topics:

32.1 Introduction

The purpose of this chapter is to make a comparison between companies, on the one hand, and partnerships or sole traders on the other, with a view to explaining the various factors which ought to be taken into account when a choice is made between the two business media.

Once these comparisons are understood, **Chapter 31** should then be considered to understand how the further possible choice of a limited liability partnership should be assessed. As limited liability partnerships fall somewhere between companies and partnerships, it is essential that either side of the spectrum of choice is considered first.

The choice will first be made when a new business is set up, but should be kept under review as circumstances (and the law) change. For the sake of clarity, the differences between companies and partnerships are considered under various headings. It is important to realise that in making a choice each factor should be taken into account. In particular cases one factor may outweigh all the others, but generally each medium has some advantages and some disadvantages so that often the choice will be a difficult one.

32.2 Risk of capital

All business involves a risk of capital. The degree of risk obviously varies considerably depending on the nature of the business, the economic climate and the skill of the people running the business. The amount of capital which is at risk also varies considerably—some types of business require a great deal of capital, others very little.

One advantage of a company over a partnership is that a company can be formed with limited liability. This means that the shareholders must contribute the amount unpaid on their shares, but no more, if the company goes into liquidation when it is insolvent. In the vast majority of cases the shares will be fully paid, so that no contribution towards the company's debts has to be made. However, the shareholders will lose their shares when the company fails so that, realistically, the limit to their liability is what they have invested in the company. A shareholder who is also a director will also lose his livelihood. A director (including a shadow director) may also become personally liable in certain circumstances when the company is wound up (see **Chapter 26**).

If a partnership becomes insolvent, each of the partners is jointly and severally liable for all the debts of the partnership. This means that they stand to lose not only what they have invested in the business but also any other property which they own. The liability of partners is, therefore, unlimited in amount. The partnership agreement may make provision as to how losses are to be shared between the partners but this does not prevent creditors claiming in full from a rich partner whose poor partners are unable to pay their share of the loss.

At first sight limited liability would seem to be an enormous advantage to the proprietors of a business in every case. However, there are at least two circumstances where limited liability is not very significant:

(a) *Where there is little risk of substantial loss of capital*

The clearest example of this is a business involving the giving of advice, such as a consultancy. The proprietor expects to make profits by providing expertise in return for payment; comparatively little is required in the way of capital expenditure on equipment and the running costs of the business will be small. In many cases the biggest potential loss will be claims for damages if bad advice is given to clients and this can be covered by insurance.

(b) *Where the proprietor risks everything he owns in the business*

If the proprietor's only assets are what he has invested in the business, he will effectively lose everything when the business fails whether it is a company or partnership. (This is, of course, only true while all the capital remains in the business, so that limited liability will become relevant once the proprietor starts to take profits out of the business on a large scale.)

Limited liability afforded by incorporating a business can sometimes be made illusory by the directors of the company having to give guarantees. Many businesses rely on borrowed money. A bank lending to a small company will often require a personal guarantee from the directors or shareholders, so that if the company cannot repay the loan the bank has further security. Guarantees may also be required from the landlord of any premises which a company may lease. These will primarily be in respect of the company's obligations to pay rent, but may also cover performance obligations, such as those requiring a tenant to keep the property in good repair.

Limited liability is most significant (and can realistically be achieved) where there is a substantial risk of loss of capital invested and the proprietor (or one of the proprietors) has private wealth not invested in the business. In such cases limited liability may be so desirable that it far outweighs any other consideration and, therefore, the business must be run as a company.

32.3 Expense

Certain expenses must inevitably be incurred when a company is formed. These include the Registrar's fee on incorporation and the cost of preparing the memorandum and articles. If a partnership is formed these expenses need not be incurred since there are no registration requirements. However, in most cases the partners will want a properly drawn up partnership agreement and will wish to instruct a solicitor to draw it up for them.

It is difficult to make any general comparison between costs of formation, since they will depend largely on the complexity of the proposed memorandum and articles or partnership agreement. The legal fees payable for formation are about the same in both cases where the documents have to be drafted by a solicitor. However, a company can be bought 'off-the-peg' from a law stationer for around £50 (including the Registrar's fee), which will be less than the cost of drawing up a partnership agreement of similar complexity.

In addition to legal advice, the proprietors of a new business will often wish to seek advice from accountants. Again, the amount payable for the advice will depend on the complexity of the advice given rather than the business medium used. Similarly, certain printing costs will be incurred for business letter paper. These expenses are only *necessary* in the case of a company (which must comply with the provisions of the Companies Act relating to the name, number and address of the company), but in the case of a partnership printed letter paper will normally be used even though it is not required by law.

After formation the major administrative costs of a business will again depend on the complexity of the business. However, in respect of accounts a company is at a disadvantage when compared with a partnership. All types of business will wish to keep accounts and prepare final accounts annually. Nearly all businesses will wish to pay a qualified accountant to draw up these accounts (if only so as to make sure that advantage is taken of tax reliefs and exemptions). A company, however, must draw up the accounts in a particular way. This means that the accounts must in some respects show more information than the accounts of a partnership and for a small business this may involve considerable extra cost. (It should be remembered that the partial exemption of 'small' companies from accounting requirements applies only to the published accounts—full accounts must be prepared for the members.) Furthermore, once the accounts have been produced they must be audited by an independent qualified accountant. This means that a company must incur two lots of accountants' fees annually, whereas a partnership need only incur one.

A company is also required to prepare an annual return and to pay a fee on filing it with the Registrar. The Companies Act also requires many other returns to be filed from time to time (e.g., particulars of directors, charges and address of registered office); although fees are not payable on the filing of these returns, their preparation will add to the running costs of the business if it is a company. Many company directors will not feel able to deal with these matters themselves and so will have to hire a qualified company secretary or take legal advice.

The running costs of a company will be more than those of a partnership although the difference is not likely to be great enough to be significant, except in the case of small businesses.

32.4 Management

The Companies Act lays down certain rules as to the management structure of companies. A company is, for example, required to have at least one director and a secretary. Certain obligations are imposed on these officials in relation to filing returns. However, a company is entitled to lay down in its articles rules as to management of whatever type it chooses. A partnership may also establish its own rules for management of the business. The Partnership Act 1890 lays down certain presumptions (e.g., that, in the absence of contrary agreement, decisions are taken by a majority vote of the partners except in a limited number of cases where unanimity is required). The partners are free to vary these presumptions by agreement or by a course of dealings. Both types of business medium are, therefore, entitled to choose a management structure which is suitable for the particular case.

32.4.1 Internal flexibility

After a suitable management structure has been chosen it may need to be changed because of changed circumstances. In the case of a company, changes to the articles require a special resolution (i.e., a 75% majority of the shareholders). However, many changes of management structure can be made without a change in the articles. Thus if the articles are in the usual form, the maximum number of directors can be increased and new appointments can be made to the board by an ordinary resolution (simple majority of shareholders) and a managing director can be appointed by the board. The board may also decide on its own procedures for taking decisions and may delegate decision-making powers as and when necessary. If it is considered that the structure is too flexible, the articles may provide for special resolutions in circumstances where an ordinary resolution would otherwise be sufficient (except in the case of removal of directors from office, where an ordinary resolution is always sufficient (s. 303 CA 1985)). The articles may also restrict the powers of the board and require the approval of the members in general meeting for major decisions. An extreme degree of inflexibility can be achieved, if desired, by including in the memorandum provisions which could have been included in the articles and by making these provisions unalterable.

In the case of a partnership, the agreement between the partners can be altered. This normally requires the approval of all the partners so that the 'constitution' of a partnership is more rigid than that of a company. However, if, when the partnership agreement is drawn up, it is decided that a greater degree of flexibility is required, the agreement can provide for alteration by a majority (without unanimous agreement), either in general or in particular cases.

It is, therefore, possible for either business medium to have a very flexible or a very rigid management structure, as the proprietors wish.

32.4.2 Security of tenure

Just as the profits of a partnership are divided between the partners so, in the case of most small companies, the profits will be divided between the directors. Security of tenure as a partner or director is, therefore, of vital concern to the proprietors of a business.

A director is always subject to removal by an ordinary resolution of the members. However, a director who has the majority of votes (or a majority of votes on a resolution for his removal—see *Bushell v Faith* [1970] AC 1099, at **9.5.1.4**) is effectively irremovable.

A director who does not have a majority of votes but who has a service agreement may be entitled to substantial compensation if removed from office, and so to that extent may be protected.

In the case of a partnership, removal of a partner will, subject to contrary agreement, involve the dissolution of the partnership. At first sight this would seem to put a partner in a stronger position than a director. However, in practice, this is not necessarily so. In some cases it will be possible for some of the partners to get rid of one of their colleagues and then set up a 'new' business after the dissolution, which will in effect be a continuation of the old business. This will be possible particularly if those who remain own the premises where the business is carried on. The position of a junior partner is not, therefore, necessarily stronger than that of a director who is not in control of the company.

The practical reality of the situation is that if a director or partner is vital to the business he cannot be removed without bringing the business to an end. However, where a director or partner is really no more than a senior employee, he can be removed on payment of any compensation provided for in his service contract or in the partnership agreement. A director, but not a partner, may also be entitled to compensation for unfair dismissal or redundancy.

32.4.3   Succession to the business

The articles of a company may restrict the right to transfer shares, thus preventing a shareholder from selling out or giving away shares to anyone he pleases. Such restrictions may be coupled with pre-emption rights given to the other shareholders. Alternatively, shares may be freely transferable. It is, therefore, possible to make provision for succession in advance, provided that sufficient thought is given to the problem at the time when the articles are drafted. Similarly, a partnership agreement may make provision for bringing in new partners and for payment to the existing partners on leaving. If no other provision is made, unanimity is required for the admission of a new partner. Since the partners have to be able to work together in running the business, it is unlikely that they would be willing to allow admission of new partners without such agreement.

It is, therefore, possible to lay down rules for succession with either type of business medium. In practical terms the problem of succession is one which can only be solved if suitable purchasers can be found or if suitable donees willing to carry on the business are available. It is generally easier to achieve succession in the case of a company, since the sale of a majority shareholding passes control to the purchaser. The majority shareholder will usually be free to sell out since he is in control of the board who will, therefore, approve any transfer of his shares unless there are any pre-emption rights.

32.5   Publicity

A company is required to make a considerable amount of information, including annual accounts, available to the public. A partnership is not required to make such information available. A desire to keep the affairs of the business secret may influence some businessmen to prefer a partnership to a company, but it is not likely to be a major factor in most cases, especially since the partners will, in practice, be required to show their accounts to any prospective lender.

32.6　Taxation—trading profits

The reader is advised to have read **Chapters 17** to **24** before reading the rest of this section.

32.6.1　Companies

A company has a choice as to how to use its profits—they may be used to pay dividends interest, or directors' fees, or they may be retained in the business. Each of these four possibilities has different tax consequences. Generally speaking, the payment of directors' fees is the most tax-efficient use of profits, and for a small, private company most of the profits will normally be used for this purpose for non-tax reasons anyway. This is because the directors must be compensated for the work that they do for the business and often little profit will be left over for other purposes.

Where profits are sufficiently large, however, a company can be used as a means of tax planning by deciding to retain profits or pay dividends. Retained profits are liable to corporation tax at between 21% and 28% (depending on the size of the profit). The rate can be kept down to 21% if sufficient is paid in directors' fees to keep the profits within the small companies' rate band. This rate of tax may be somewhat less than the director/ shareholder's rate of income tax (which may be 40%). However, the future consequences of capital taxes must also be taken into account. The accumulated profits will be reflected in the value of the shares in the company so that, on a disposal of shares a higher CGT and/or IHT may be payable, thus reducing the effectiveness of the income tax saving resulting from retention of the profits.

As dividends are non-deductible for the paying company and will be made out of after-tax profits, their payment may be seen as inefficient from a tax perspective. However, such payments do not incur any National Insurance liability for either the company or a director, so there may be some important comparisons to be made between dividend payments and increased directors' salaries or bonuses. A decision to pay dividends may, of course, be taken for non-tax reasons, since it is the only way to provide a shareholder who is not also a director employee with a return on his investment.

32.6.2　Partnerships

A partnership offers less scope for tax planning in relation to income profits than a company. All the income profits are taxed as income of the partners whether they are actually paid to them or are retained in the business (unless a capital allowance is available). To the extent that profits are withdrawn from the business a partner is in the same position as a director receiving directors' fees—both pay income tax on the sums that are received.

It used to be the case that the preceding year basis for partnerships was an incentive against forming a company on the start–up of a business venture. However, because of the change to the system, any new business will now be immediately taxed on a current year basis. However, it should still be borne in mind that a payment of a salary to a director will suffer an immediate deduction for tax under the PAYE system, whereas drawings by a partner will not.

To the extent that profits are retained in the business, a partner pays the same tax as if the profits had been withdrawn. This will be an advantage when compared with a company where the partner's rate of tax is less than the rate of corporation tax, and a disadvantage when it is more.

32.6.3 Conclusion

It is, unfortunately, not possible to come to any general conclusions about which business medium is the more suitable from the point of view of income taxation. Probably in most circumstances there is now little to choose between the two. This is partly the result of the fact that relatively small differences now exist between the rates of tax applying to individuals and companies. In any case, in most businesses, substantially all the profits will be used to pay directors' fees or will be withdrawn by the partners. Where profits are sufficiently large that there is a real possibility of tax planning, the greater flexibility provided by the system of company taxation may be advantageous.

32.7 Interest relief

A payment of interest by an individual must generally be paid out of taxed income. However, in some cases interest paid may be deducted from income before it is assessed to tax as a 'charge on income' (so that tax relief is available on the interest payment). This relief is available where money is borrowed to buy an interest in a partnership. Relief is also available where money is borrowed to buy shares in a close company provided that either:

(a) the shares give the borrower a 'material interest' (i.e., more than 5% of ordinary share capital or a right to more than 5% of the income); or

(b) the borrower owns some shares and, from the time when he used the loan until the time when the interest was paid, he was working for the greater part of his time in the management or conduct of the company.

32.8 Capital gains

A company pays corporation tax at an effective rate of between 21% and 28% on any capital gain which it makes. The disposal of assets by a partnership gives rise to tax at the appropriate rate for the individual partners, which is 18%. However, a company and its proprietors suffer two disadvantages in respect of capital gains. First, the profit made on the disposal of a capital asset (after payment of tax) will be reflected in the value of the shares in the company and further capital gains tax will be payable on disposal of those shares. For example, an asset is purchased by a company for £10,000 and sold for £20,000. Tax of (say) £2,100 will be paid, leaving a net profit after tax of £7,900. This profit will be reflected in the value of the shares so that if they are disposed of, a further gain of £7,900 will be taxed. Secondly, a company is not entitled to an annual exemption, whereas in the case of a partnership each partner is entitled to an annual exemption for the first £9,600 worth of gains during each tax year.

In addition to the above, companies may be able to use the indexation allowance in respect of capital gains, to reduce the gain on which tax is charged.

32.9   Inheritance tax

32.9.1   Close companies and anti-avoidance

A company cannot normally be used as a means of avoiding IHT, since gifts by a close company are attributed to the shareholders in the company (s. 94 IHTA 1984). Nearly all small companies come within the definition of a close company. Similarly, gifts of partnership assets will be liable to tax as gifts of the individual partners. Inheritance tax is, therefore, generally a neutral factor in the choice of business medium.

32.9.2   Business property relief

Prior to 6 April 1996, one potential taxation disadvantage of incorporation was that *any* partnership share would attract 100% business property relief on its subsequent transfer but a shareholding of less than 25% would only attract 50% relief. After this date the situation changed and along with it this curious distinction. Any shareholding in a private company will attract 100% business property relief (see **18.8.6**).

There is, however, still a difference in the relief given where an asset is owned by an individual partner or shareholder but used by the partnership or company. A partner whose private property is used by his partnership is entitled to relief of 50% when he gives the property away. Similar relief is available to a shareholder but only if he owns shares which give control of the company.

32.10   Pensions and social security

There are a number of ways in which people in business may provide for their retirement. The most favourable method from the tax point of view is an 'exempt approved occupational pension scheme'. Such a scheme affords generous tax relief on contributions by both employers and employees and further relief from capital taxes to the managers of the scheme. Its purpose is to provide a pension and, in some cases, a lump sum on retirement. Such schemes are not available to the self-employed (such as partners). Partners are able to get the relief by means of a personal pension. Contributions are deductible from taxable income up to a certain percentage of relevant earnings depending on the age of the contributor. However, the relief is limited to the appropriate percentage of £102,000 in the case of partners whose income exceeds this figure.

Social security also operates differently in respect of employees and the self-employed. Contributions must be made by both employer and employee in respect of an employed person; a self-employed person must contribute at a rate higher than the employee's contribution but lower than the employer's and employee's contributions combined. The benefits to which an employed person is entitled are correspondingly higher than those to which a self-employed person is entitled.

32.11 Raising finance

Whilst there are numerous partnerships which have bank borrowings, as a general rule companies are treated as a more attractive proposition as borrowers, because of their ability to grant floating charges, which in turn gives the lender greater security.

A corporate structure also makes the introduction of new investment capital easier. An investor in a partnership will ideally have to be made a partner, if he or she is to own a stake in the business. This can be disruptive for the existing management structure of the partners and also has the downside for the investor in that henceforth he or she will have unlimited liability for the debts of the partnership. Taking on a new shareholder in a company can have no disruptive influence on its management, since the roles of shareholder and director can be kept separate, and the investor only stands to lose the value of the investment and nothing further. Also, an equity investor in a company has greater flexibility in their exit from such an investment, in that they can sell all or part of their shareholding to existing shareholders, third parties (subject to any terms of pre-emption in the articles of association) or back to the company itself. With a partnership share the only truly feasible exit is to sell it in its entirety to existing partners.

An investor can, of course, simply lend money to a partnership. However, there will be no capital growth in such investment, as there would be with becoming a partner and taking a partnership share. A shareholding, particularly if it has voting rights, will normally always have the possibility of capital growth.

32.12 Conclusion

It is not possible to lay down any hard and fast rule as to which business medium is the more beneficial since there are too many variables. In a significant number of cases the desirability of limited liability will indicate company formation as the only real possibility. Where limited liability is not of great importance, the tax factors will be more significant. Generally speaking, a company will be more likely to be required where profits are large and a partnership where they are small, but really the only sound advice is that each case must be determined according to the particular circumstances and the particular wishes of the partners of the business.

Treaty of Rome, Articles 81 and 82

This chapter covers the following topics:

33.1 Introduction

Articles 81 and 82 relate to the competition policy of the European Community. They are among the most important provisions of the Treaty. The object of the Treaty is to ensure that there is a free market which enables goods to move freely between the member States. Article 81 furthers this objective by outlawing certain agreements which prevent, restrict or distort competition within the Community. Article 82 prohibits abuse of a dominant position in the common market or a significant part of it in so far as it may affect trade between member States.

In addition to the provisions of the Treaty itself regulations have been made by the Council of Ministers and by the Commission which supplement the provisions of the Treaty. The Court of Justice of the European Community and the Court of First Instance have also been called upon to develop a considerable body of case law relating to the competition policy of the Community.

The Council of Ministers has granted wide powers to the Commission in relation to competition law. In particular the Commission both makes policy decisions and enforces them (as to enforcement, see below). Parties aggrieved by a decision of the Commission are entitled to appeal, on points of law, to the Court of First Instance, and ultimately from there to the Court of Justice (ECJ) of the European Community itself.

On a purely national level, Articles 81 and 82 have influenced competition regulation in the UK through the Competition Act 1998, hence its inclusion in this chapter.

33.2 Article 81

Article 81(1) prohibits:

all agreements between undertakings, decisions by associations of undertakings and concerted practices which may affect trade between member States and which have as their object or effect the prevention, restriction or distortion of competition within the common market.

Agreements are defined as including informal agreements which may fall short of being contracts. The concept of a 'concerted practice' is even wider. This has been held to include any case where 'practical co-operation' between undertakings (i.e., businesses) have been set up in opposition to the concept of competition. An example of a concerted practice is where different undertakings keep their prices in line with each other. The fact that prices have risen at the same time is not, however, sufficient to prove a concerted practice. There must be evidence that the activities of the undertakings involved are such as to distort the market.

Decisions by associations of undertakings include such things as price fixing by trade associations. Decisions which have the effect of fixing prices are subject to Article 81 even if they are not binding on the members of the association, provided they are likely to be complied with at least to the extent that the free market will be affected.

It should be noted that what is prohibited is any agreement which may *affect trade between member States*. This does not, however, mean that an agreement which is made between undertakings in only one member State is automatically valid. An agreement between undertakings which only relates to activities within one country may indirectly prevent other companies from entering that market from a different member State.

33.2.1 Vertical agreements

A vertical agreement is one between undertakings at different levels within the market. For example a manufacturer's agreement with a wholesaler or a wholesaler's agreement with a shop are vertical agreements. Examples of vertical agreements include agency agreements and supply agreements. Such agreements may fall foul of Article 81. (For further discussion of such agreements, please see **Chapter 35**.)

33.2.2 Horizontal agreements

Horizontal agreements are made between undertakings which are at the same level of the economic chain. For example, an agreement between two manufacturers is a horizontal agreement. These agreements are unlikely to be valid in view of the provisions of Article 81.

For example in *Heintz van Landewyck Sàrl v Commission* (Cases 209/78, etc.) [1980] ECR 3125, an instruction from a trade association representing tobacco manufacturers in Belgium and Luxembourg was held invalid. This was on the basis that the trade association was able to give directions which were binding on its members. This case also decided that Article 81 can apply to non-profit organisations (such as the trade association) if they are carrying on economic activities.

33.2.3   Article 81(3)

Article 81(3) provides an exemption from the basic rule contained in Article 81(1) where the operation of the rule would be inconsistent with the more general principles of competition law. Article 81(3) may exempt an agreement if it:

contributes to the improvement of the production or distribution of goods or to promoting technical or economic progress, while allowing consumers a fair share of the resulting benefits, and . . . only imposes restrictions on the parties which are indispensable to the attainment of these objectives and does not allow the parties concerned the possibility of eliminating competition within the relevant product market.

33.2.4   Is it possible to avoid falling foul of Article 81?

Article 81 is widely drawn so it is not possible to contract out of it. However, there are a number of effective exemptions.

33.2.4.1   Agreements of minor importance

The Commission has itself issued a notice on Agreements of Minor Importance ([2001] OJ C368/07) which lays down guidelines allowing small-scale agreements in circumstances where a similar agreement on a larger scale would be void. Put very simply, where the parties to a horizontal agreement own in aggregate no more than 10% of the market share for the product in question and no more than 15% each of the market in relation to a vertical agreement, the agreement falls outside the ambit of Article 81. When it is difficult to class an agreement as vertical or horizontal, the 10% threshold applies.

The market share test is an attempt to quantify which arrangements may not amount to an appreciable restriction of competition. The notice also recognises that agreements between undertakings which exceed these thresholds may still not appreciably restrict competition.

Certain restrictions within agreements, however, will remove the benefit of the notice, even if the market share thresholds are not exceeded. The most likely type of restriction is any attempt to fix sale prices. These exceptions from the notice are complex and reference should always be made to the specific detail of the notice when considering the effect of a particular restriction.

The notice also makes reference to the fact that certain agreements may not be capable of appreciably affecting *trade* between member States. These are agreements between small and medium-sized enterprises (SMEs). An SME is defined as an undertaking which has fewer than 250 employees and which has either an annual turnover not exceeding EUR 50 million or an annual balance sheet total not exceeding EUR 43 million.

33.2.4.2   Article 81(3)

We have already seen that Article 81(3) itself provides for exemption where the agreement is beneficial. Until 1 May 2004, an undertaking which believed that its agreement should be exempt under that provision could apply to the Commission for an individual exemption which confirmed the exempt status of the agreement.

Such applications were not a straightforward matter and it often took several years for a decision to be made. In reality, very few such exemptions were officially given.

Instead, the Commission normally responded by way of a 'comfort letter', which was best regarded as an 'administrative' rather than 'legal' clearance.

Because of the pressures which the previous system was under and in light of the expansion of the EU from 15 to 25 member States, this system of notification was ended from 1 May 2004. This change was part of a major alteration in the way the Commission deals with competition policy. Further discussion of these changes is to be found at **33.4**.

33.2.4.3 Block exemptions

A system of block exemptions has been devised by the Commission. This provides that certain types of agreement are not to be regarded as infringing Article 81. In relation to each type of agreement the Commission will usually produce lists of contract terms which will be regarded as acceptable in such agreements ('the white list') and terms which will exclude the agreements from the block exemption ('the black list'). All block exemptions are limited in time, allowing the Commission the option of renewing, reviewing or, indeed, withdrawing them at given times.

Until quite recently, six block exemptions were in existence, each one targeting particular arrangements. From 1 June 2000, those which applied to exclusive distributorship agreements, exclusive purchasing agreements and franchise agreements were supplanted by Regulation (EC) 2790/99, which operates to provide exemption from the effect of Article 81(1) to various types of vertical agreements. (Other block exemptions cover specialisation agreements, research and development agreements and technology licensing. It is beyond the scope of this Guide to consider these.)

Vertical agreements are those which are entered into between businesses at different levels in the production and distribution chain and which govern the circumstances under which those businesses buy and sell goods and/or services.

However, the exemption will only apply when the market share of the supplier or the buyer (where the agreement has exclusive supply obligations) does not exceed 30%. Market share of the supplier is calculated on the basis of the market sales value of the goods or services in question sold by the supplier, which are regarded as interchangeable or substitutable by the buyer, by reason of the price of the goods or services, intended use and characteristics. Market share of the buyer is based upon the market purchase value of the relevant market.

The relevant time period for calculation of market share is that in respect of the previous calendar year.

The Regulation anticipates that such market share may fluctuate and provides that:

(a) if market share increases beyond 30% up to 35%, the exemption will continue to apply for a period of two calendar years after the year in which the first increase over 30% occurred;

(b) if market share increases beyond 35% the exemption will continue to apply for a period of one calendar year after the year in which the first increase over 35% occurred.

The vertical agreements block exemption differs from other block exemptions in that the traditional 'white list'/'black list' approach is not followed. Instead, vertical agreements between parties who fall below the 30% market share threshold will fall within the exemption, provided they contain no prohibited clauses. The main clauses to consider are:

(a) restrictions on the buyer's, i.e., the distributor's, ability to determine its sale price. However, the supplier is free to set a maximum or recommended sale price.

(b) restriction of the territory into which the buyer may sell. An exemption to this is the restriction of active sales into an exclusive territory reserved for the supplier or allotted by the supplier to another buyer. This is to facilitate the creation of exclusive distribution networks. Passive sales, i.e., when the buyer is approached by a potential customer outside the territory, cannot be prevented.

Clauses having the above effect will take an agreement outside the block exemption. However, it is also important to note that certain clauses, whilst not prejudicial to an agreement as a whole, will themselves not benefit from the block exemption. If such clauses prove to be severable, then the remainder of the agreement will stand within the block exemption. Very simply, such provisions are:

(a) direct or indirect non-competition clauses which are operative for more than five years;

(b) clauses which restrict the buyer from manufacturing, purchasing or selling competing goods or services for more than one year after termination of the agreement in question.

There is no need to notify an agreement for the block exemption to apply. As such the key role of the lawyer when drafting and negotiating vertical agreements is, where possible, to produce something which falls within the exemption and to advise on the consequences of proposed clauses which would prevent this (assuming, of course, that the market share test is satisfied).

33.3 Article 82

Article 82 provides:

Any abuse by one or more undertakings of a dominant position within the common market or in a substantial part of it shall be prohibited as incompatible with the common market in so far as it may affect trade between member states.

Notice that Article 82 (unlike Article 81) may be infringed by one undertaking acting alone. The key requirements here are that there must be a dominant position in the market and that that position must have been abused. The ECJ has decided that a dominant position is one which 'enables the undertaking [or undertakings] to prevent effective competition . . . by giving it the power to behave to an appreciable extent independently of its competitors, customers and ultimately of its consumers' (*United Brands Co. v Commission* (Case 27/76) [1978] ECR 207). To be actionable the dominance must exist in a particular market. This is sometimes defined as the relevant product market which means the market for the goods in question together with any other goods which are effective substitutes for the goods in question.

Article 82 itself provides a list of activities which may be regarded as an abuse. This list is not intended to be exhaustive:

(a) imposition of unfair prices or trading conditions;

(b) limiting production markets or technical development to the prejudice of consumers;

(c) discriminating between different trading parties;

(d) by including terms in contracts which are collateral to the subject of the contract.

The abuse which is prohibited by Article 82 might also constitute a breach of Article 81. The two Articles are not designed to be mutually exclusive.

33.4 Enforcement of competition policy

33.4.1 Direct effect

The provisions of Articles 81 and 82 have 'direct effect' in each of the States of the EC. This means that they are part of the law of each of the member States (in the UK as a result of the European Communities Act 1972). If there is any conflict between the provisions of EC law and the pre-existing UK law the EC law is to prevail. This means that UK courts must recognise and give effect to the competition law of the Community.

Agreements made in the UK which according to the principles of contract law may be valid, may be rendered void as a result of the competition law of the Community. In some cases, however, it may be possible for an English court to apply the principle of severance; that is, the court may be able to declare the clause in the agreement which offends competition law to be void, but uphold the rest of the contract. Whether the court can do this depends on the principles of English law. The traditional approach is that the court will not order severance if to do so would effectively require a re-writing of the agreement, either because the offending part cannot be separated within the agreement or because it is so fundamental to the agreement that to sever it would amount to imposing a new contract on the parties.

In addition to the possibility of action by another party to the contract it is also possible for third parties to sue under either Article if they have suffered loss. The position in English law is not entirely clear, but it would seem that the court can impose an injunction or award damages for breach of 'statutory' duty (see *Garden Cottage Foods v Milk Marketing Board* [1984] AC 130).

In light of the recent changes in the administration and enforcement of EC competition law as set out in **33.4.2** following, it is likely that national courts will assume a role of increased importance.

33.4.2 Enforcement by the Commission

For over 40 years, EC competition law was the remit of the Commission. Originally, when the EU was made up of a small number of member States, this was a sustainable system. However, with the continued expansion of the EU, this centralised system could no longer effectively fulfil its role.

The publication of a White Paper in 1999 on modernising competion law ([1999] OJ C132) signalled the intention of the Commission to move away from this position and to devolve its powers to member States. This process culminated in Regulation 1/2003, which came into force on 1 May 2004 and replaced Regulation 17/62.

The main effect of the new system is that the Commission be able will focus its (limited) resources on policing major infringements of competition law and will no longer be involved in adjudicating on the status of commercial arrangements. As was explained at **33.2.4.2**, under the previous system, an exemption from the prohibition of Article 81(1) was only available by applying to the Commission under Article 81(3).

This requirement has now disappeared and agreements which fulfil the requirements of Article 81(3) will be deemed to benefit from the exemption automatically. National Competition Authorities (NCAs) and national courts now have the power to decide upon the applicability of Article 81(3). However, such decisions will, in essence, be after the fact, due to the absence of any notification system and are likely to happen either as part of an NCA investigation or of litigation. Parties entering into agreements will have to assess their status at that time (presumably with professional input). They will also have to review the continued applicability of Article 81(3) to such agreements to take into account changes in the parties and changes in the market. Of course, should an agreement fall within a block exemption or be of minor importance, the applicability of Article 81(3) will be irrelevant.

One exception to the lack of notification procedure is that the Commission has reserved the right to provide informal guidance on novel or unresolved issues. The details of this system are yet to be worked out, but the availability of such guidance should be seen as the exception rather than the norm.

One possible objection to the system as it now stands is that member States may be inconsistent in their application of Articles 81 and 82. To address these concerns, a cornerstone of the new system is co-operation and co-ordination between the Commission, NCAs and national courts in the form of the European Competition Network. For example, each NCA must submit to the Commission drafts of intended decisions at least 30 days before the decision is to be adopted. By doing so, the Commission is able to detect differences in approach between NCAs. In addition, a national court is able to ask the Commission for information and opinions which may aid it in reaching a decision and the Commission itself may intervene in court proceedings to express its views on the issues before the court.

As under the previous system, to fulfil its role, the Commission has the power to carry out inspections at a company's offices (so-called 'dawn raids'), but such powers have been widened to allow it to search other premises, such as private houses and vehicles. In addition, any NCA may itself carry out such an inspection to establish any breach of Article 81 or 82 and the Commission may instruct an NCA to carry out such an investigation.

Should the Commission make a finding of infringement of either Article 81 or 82, it may order the undertakings involved to cease such infringement. To this end, it may impose behavioural or structural remedies on the relevant undertakings. As their description suggests, a behavioural remedy will normally involve a modification to commercial activities, whilst a structural remedy will normally involve the divestment of elements of a business. Structural remedies, therefore, can only be imposed when no behavioural remedy would be effective or where a behavioural remedy would be more burdensome than a structural one. As an alternative to these remedies, the undertakings concerned may offer commitments about future behaviour, etc., to the Commission which meet its concerns. In this case, the Commission can order that the commitments are binding on the undertakings for a specified period of time.

The Commission also has the power to impose fines of up to 10% of turnover in the preceding business year of any undertaking found infringing either Article 81 or 82. The size of the fine will be determined, inter alia, by the gravity and duration of the infringement. Additional daily fines may also be imposed as a way of compelling undertakings to desist in any infringement. These may not exceed 5% of the average daily turnover of the undertaking concerned in the preceding business year.

33.5 The Competition Act 1998 and the Enterprise Act 2002

33.5.1 Introduction

As was explained in the introduction to this chapter, UK competition law is now heavily influenced by that of the EC. Moreover, when considering the potential anti-competitive nature of a client's actions or commercial arrangements, national laws cannot be forgotten. As such, we now turn to the UK system.

The Competition Act (CA) 1998 received Royal Assent on 9 November 1998 and came fully into force on 1 March 2000 at which date the Resale Prices Act 1976, the Restrictive Trade Practices Act 1976 and the bulk of the Competition Act 1980 were repealed. The purpose of the Act was to modernise competition law in the UK and to address many of the criticisms which had been levelled at the piecemeal legislation which had previously existed.

The introduction of the Enterprise Act 2002 has brought about further changes and enhancements to the UK competition regime. One particular change is to the administration of competition matters. Historically the Director General of Fair Trading (DGFT) had responsibility for enforcing competition policy through the Office of Fair Trading (OFT). The Enterprise Act abolished the position of DGFT. Instead, all the functions, rights and liabilities of the DGFT are now assumed by the OFT. In furtherance of this, the OFT became a recognised statutory body which operates as a limited company. (See **33.5.2.8** for further discussion of the Enterprise Act.)

33.5.2 The Competition Act prohibitions

33.5.2.1 General

The prohibitions are known as Chapter I and Chapter II prohibitions. Chapter I of the Act is concerned with anti-competitive agreements and Chapter II is concerned with abuse of a dominant position within the market. Put simply, Articles 81 and 82 of the Treaty of Rome have been transposed into UK legislation. However, the Act does not replace them, rather, its prohibitions run in parallel with those of the EU. As such, only agreements which affect trade within the UK and the behaviour of undertakings dominant in the UK will be governed by the Act. There is, however, an obligation on the courts pursuant to s. 60 to interpret the Act in accordance with principles of EC competition law.

The effect of an agreement does not have to extend across the whole of the UK. If an agreement is only intended to operate in part of the UK, that will be sufficient.

33.5.2.2 Chapter I prohibition

Agreements between undertakings which may affect trade within the UK and have as their object or effect the prevention, restriction or distortion of competition within the UK are caught by this prohibition (s. 2 CA 1998). Any such agreement will be void, or, if the offending terms are severable from the rest of the agreement in question, those terms. In addition, the parties concerned may face fines of up to 10% of their UK turnover.

It is proposed that only agreements which have an *appreciable* effect on competition will be prohibited. It is thought that only if the joint market share of the parties to the agreement in question exceeds 25% will an agreement have an appreciable effect. It is anticipated that this will take many agreements outside the prohibition. However, if the purpose of any agreement is price-fixing, resale price maintenance or market sharing, the issue of appreciability is irrelevant.

A further exception is a category of agreements identified in the Act as 'small agreements' (s. 39 CA 1998). If an agreement is 'small', no fine will be imposed in respect of it. A small agreement is defined in the Competition Act (Small Agreements and Conduct of Minor Significance) Regulations 2000 (SI 2000/262) as being an agreement between parties whose joint turnover does not exceed £20 million. However, all price-fixing agreements fail to qualify.

It is important to note that for the purposes of the Act, if an agreement is intended only to operate in a part of the UK, that part will constitute the UK. It is unnecessary for an agreement to be shown to have an appreciable effect on competition across the whole of the UK. Similarly, in this instance, market share presumably need not be assessed on a UK-wide basis, so it may be a mistake to assume that agreements between small local undertakings are not caught by the Act.

33.5.2.3 Chapter II prohibition

Conduct by one or more undertakings which amounts to the abuse of a dominant position in a market which may affect trade within the UK or part of it is caught by this prohibition (s. 18 CA 1998). Taking a lead from EC law, a 40% market share can be viewed as dominance.

Undertakings which infringe the Chapter II prohibition may be requested by the Office of Fair Trading to modify or cease such conduct. They may also be fined in the same way as for a breach of the Chapter I prohibition. There is an exception to this second sanction if the conduct is of 'minor significance' (s. 40 CA 1998). Conduct of minor significance is the activity of any undertaking whose turnover is less than £50 million.

33.5.2.4 Chapter I exemptions

As well as the possible exclusion due to lack of appreciability discussed above, there are four main exemptions to this prohibition:

(a) Individual exemption granted by the OFT—must be applied for. This may take two forms: either the agreement does offend the prohibition, but will be exempted because of some perceived greater benefit (akin to Article 81(3) exemption) or confirmation that the agreement does not, in fact, offend against the Act.

(b) Under any block exemption pursuant to the Act which are made by statutory instrument.

(c) If an agreement qualifies for the benefit of any EC block exemption. This is the case even if the agreement has no effect on inter-state trade within the EU. As such, it is possible to draft an agreement, the effect of which will be limited to the UK, to comply with a block exemption and gain exemption from the Act. The Act does, however, reserve the right to withdraw the benefit of this exemption if the OFT sees fit.

(d) If the agreement constitutes a vertical agreement, pursuant to The Competition Act 1998 (Land and Vertical Agreements Exclusion) Order 2000. The Order contains a definition of vertical agreement which borrows heavily from that contained in Commission Regulation (EC) 2790/1999 (see **33.2.4.3**). However, the major difference is that no 30% market share threshold features in the Order. No vertical agreement which contains a price-fixing arrangement benefits from the exclusion.

33.5.2.5 Chapter II exemptions

The main exemptions to Chapter II are contained in Schs 1 and 3 to the Competition Act. The Act also reserves the right for the Secretary of State to make amendments to these Schedules. The reader is recommended to consult these for the full picture.

It is also possible to apply to the OFT for guidance as to whether or not the Chapter II prohibition is infringed.

33.5.2.6   Enforcement

The Act grants the OFT powers to search premises and seize documents, etc., as part of the conduct of any investigation into breaches of the Act. In addition, failure to produce documents when requested, the destruction of documentation during an investigation and providing false or misleading information are criminal offences. If such offences are committed by a body corporate, but with the consent or connivance of, or through the neglect of, any director, secretary or manager of that body corporate, that person also commits a criminal offence.

33.5.2.7   Civil liability

Whilst the Competition Act is not explicit on this point, it is understood that third parties affected by breaches of either the Chapter I or Chapter II prohibitions will have a claim in damages. This is presumably by analogy with the concept of breach of Article 81 entitling a third party to bring a claim, because of its direct effect. Although it is equally possible that a claim can be based on the more 'traditional' ground of breach of statutory duty.

33.5.2.8   The Impact of the Enterprise Act 2002

The Enterprise Act has increased the significance of UK competition law control in three ways:

(a) The Act provides for the creation of the Competition Appeals Tribunal. Persons affected by breaches of either the Chapter I or II prohibitions (or breaches of Article 81 or 82) may bring a claim for damages before this new tribunal.

(b) The Act renders the dishonest operation of a cartel a criminal offence, punishable by both a fine and imprisonment. Put simply, a cartel is an arrangement between at least two undertakings to fix prices, limit supply or production or to divide up markets, so long as those undertakings operate at the same level in the supply chain (s. 188).

(c) Directors of companies which breach the competition provisions of either the Competition Act or the Treaty of Rome may face directors disqualification proceedings (s. 204).

 online resource centre   Interactive online exercises (Student Learning Activities) which complement the topics covered in this chapter are available at www.oxfordtextbooks.co.uk/orc/business09_10/.

The right of establishment, the right to provide services, and the free movement of goods

This chapter covers the following topics:

34.1 Introduction

In this chapter we will examine two closely related rights established by European Community law. These are the 'right of establishment' and the right to provide services. The right of establishment is the right of a national of one member State to set up business in another member State. The right to provide services is a right to do business in another member State in ways which fall short of setting up a business. Under Articles 48 and 55, the right of establishment and the right to provide services are extended to 'companies or firms formed in accordance with the law of a member State and having their registered office, administrative centre or principal place of business within the Community'.

We will also examine the related issue of the free movement of goods within the European Community as enshrined in Articles 28 and 30 of the Treaty of Rome.

34.2 Establishment and services

Article 43 provides (in part):

. . . restrictions on the freedom of establishment of nationals of a member State in the territory of another member State shall be abolished . . . such . . . abolition shall also apply to the setting up of agencies, branches or subsidiaries by nationals of any member State established in the territory of any member State.

> Freedom of establishment shall include the right to take up and . . . manage undertakings in particular companies or firms . . . under the conditions laid down for its own nationals by the law of the country where such establishment is effected . . .

Article 49 provides (in part):

> . . . restrictions on freedom to provide services within the Community shall be . . . abolished . . . in respect of nationals of member States who are established in a State of the Community other than that of the person for whom the services are intended.

Services are defined as services 'normally provided for remuneration'.

These provisions effectively mean that nationals of all member States are to be treated as being on the same footing as far as doing business in any member State is concerned. A French national is, for example, free to set up business in the UK either on his own account, in partnership or through the medium of a company. Furthermore it would be illegal in terms of Community law for UK law to discriminate against him in respect of such a business.

However, companies formed in a member State are effectively excluded from this right unless their business is established in one of the member States. The reason for this is that such a company is not really an economic entity within the Community.

In addition, it should equally be possible for a business based in the Netherlands to offer services to customers in Italy or Spain.

Whilst at the edges the differences between providing services and establishment are blurred, the simple distinction is that establishment carries with it a sense of integration and permanent physical presence, which provision of services does not require.

34.3   Limitations on the rights of establishment and provision of services

The fundamental freedoms outlined above have often brought Community law into conflict with national laws. For example, a member State may not be prevented from allowing nationals of other member States to set up a company within its jurisdiction, but what if the requirements of incorporation were stringent enough to be a considerable barrier to such activity? Alternatively, should an Italian electrician wish to provide services in another member State, would it be acceptable for the other State to demand that the electrician take an aptitude test before working there?

The case law which has built up has answered these questions by concluding that national law which restricts the freedoms afforded by Articles 43 and 49 will only be justifiable if:

(a) it is applied in a non-discriminatory manner;

(b) it achieves justifiable means, which are in the general interest;

(c) it is no more than is necessary to achieve those means.

Two particular cases will be considered to illustrate how these conditions apply.

In *Centros Limited v Erhvervs- og Selskabsstyrelsen* (Case C-212/97) [1999] ECR I-1459, a company had been incorporated in England by two Danish nationals. The intention was not for the company to trade in England, but to trade in Denmark. An application to the Danish authorities to set up a branch in Denmark was refused, the main objection being that to allow such activity would circumvent the law in Denmark on minimum share capital, which was more stringent than that in England and Wales. In substance, this was 'incorporation though the back door'.

The ECJ held that the refusal of the Danish authorities was unlawful and contrary to the principle of freedom of establishment. The right to form a company in one member State and then set up branches in others is an inherent aspect of such freedom. The Danish authority's argument that requiring minimum paid-up capital was the only appropriate way of ensuring creditor protection was rejected. The Court was particularly swayed by the fact that, if the company in question had had a trading history in the UK, its application to register a branch would have been successful, exposing Danish creditors to risk in any event.

In *Commission v Germany* (Case 205/84) [1986] ECR 3755, rules governing insurance were under scrutiny. German law required that all providers of insurance in Germany had to be permanently established in Germany and also had to be authorised. The Commission challenged these requirements. The German state attempted to justify such rules by claiming that, due to the special nature of insurance, particularly the need for certainty that any claim will be met, considerable public protection issues arose.

The Court decided that direct insurers could be compelled to be established in Germany, but that requiring co-insurers to do the same was disproportionate. Regarding authorisation, the Court felt that this was justifiable, although it had never been argued before it that member States were not entitled to exercise any supervision of insurance business. The fact that directives for the insurance sector also required member States to create and maintain systems of authorisation was influential in the Court's decision.

34.4 Free movement of goods

34.4.1 Introduction

In order to open up markets within the European Community and to allow traders the opportunity to market their goods 'on a level playing field', there was included in the Treaty of Rome Article 28, the effect of which is to remove barriers to the sale of goods across and within all member States.

This Article covers all measures taken by member States, including not just those emanating directly from government but also from institutions or bodies which have governmental or legislative approval or backing (*R v Royal Pharmaceutical Society of Greater Britain* [1989] 2 All ER 758).

34.4.2 Article 28—restrictions on imports

Article 28 states that 'quantitative restrictions on imports and all measures having equivalent effect shall . . . be prohibited between member States'.

It will be noted that the wording covers both measures which are prohibitions or restrictions of themselves (quantitative restrictions) and measures which amount to or have as their effect a prohibitive or restrictive effect on imports (measures of equivalent effect). For example, the Article will equally defeat an import ban on matches as it will a provision requiring that all imported matches be sold in metal, fire-proof containers. (Although it could be argued that the latter measure is for the protection of the consumer—see **34.4.5**.)

34.4.3   The 'Dassonville' formula

The case of *Procurer du Roi v Dassonville* (Case 8/74) [1974] ECR 837 established the following definition of measures of equivalent effect:

All trading rules enacted by member States which are capable of hindering directly or indirectly, actually or potentially, intra community trade . . .

The adjective 'capable' is important. The measure in question need not have an immediate effect on intra-Community trade. Thus, Article 28 has a wide ambit and can be used to challenge the validity of a great many measures at a national level which, although not aimed at partitioning markets or not amounting to protectionism on the part of a member State, in some way demonstrate this characteristic. In the remainder of this chapter we shall look at whether or not there are any limitations on this far-reaching rule.

34.4.4   The *Cassis* principle—treatment of measures of equivalent effect

Measures of equivalent effect need not necessarily be aimed specifically at imported goods. For example, a law of a member State requiring all alcoholic drinks to be sold only in half litre bottles, irrespective of where they are produced, could hinder trade in drinks because drinks companies wanting to import into that country would have to have specific bottling facilities to comply with such legislation. Although not necessarily so in this example, legislation of this kind may be based on sound, objectively justifiable reasoning, such as the protection of public health or the consumer.

As such, the ECJ has acknowledged the fact that certain laws should be upheld even if they appear contrary to Article 28. What the court devised has become known as the '*Cassis* principle', which draws a distinction between legislation which is applicable to all goods wherever their origin ('indistinctly applicable') and that which applies only to imported goods ('distinctly applicable') (see *Rewe Zentral AG v Bundesmonopolverwaltung für Branntwein ('Cassis de Dijon')* (Case 120/78) [1979] 3 ECR 649). Any restriction which is *indistinctly* applicable will only offend against Article 28 to the extent that the restriction it seeks to impose is out of proportion to the ends it is trying to achieve. In other words, if these ends can be achieved by lesser methods which have a reduced impact on inter-State trade, the relevant legislation will be caught by Article 28. (The treatment of distinctly applicable restrictions is covered by Article 30—see **34.4.6**.) This so-called 'rule of reason' has been applied in cases where the legislation under scrutiny was concerned with:

(a) fiscal supervision;

(b) protection of public health;

(c) fairness of commercial transactions;

(d) defence of the consumer;

(e) protection of the environment;

(f) protection of culture.

The facts of *Cassis de Dijon* provide a useful example of how this rule operates. The German authorities had prevented the importation of the French liqueur, Cassis de Dijon, due to its alcohol content being less than legislation allowed for beverages of that type. (Fruit liqueurs had to have a minimum alcohol content of 25%; Cassis contained between 15 and 20% alcohol.) This was a requirement applying to all such drinks, irrespective of their origin. However, it was clear that its effect was to prevent the sale of certain alcoholic drinks in Germany and, thus, was contrary to Article 28 (or Article 30, as it then was numbered).

The German government put forward a justification for this rule on the grounds of consumer protection and public health, that is, it ensured that the public knew such drinks would always have a minimum alcohol content and, therefore, be of a high quality and higher alcohol content in drinks would encourage sensible drinking. The Court's view was:

> . . . requirements relating to the minimum alcohol content of alcoholic beverages do not serve a purpose which is in the general interest and such as to take precedence over the requirements of free movement of goods . . .

The same ends could be achieved by clear labelling of products to ensure that the customer was fully informed of the characteristics of the product being bought. Moreover, other drinks with much lower alcohol content, such as wine and beer, were freely available, so the public health argument was unsustainable.

34.4.5 The practical effect of Article 28

Perhaps a surprising (but inevitable) effect of Article 28 has been its use as a defence in certain prosecutions involving the regulation of trading in member States, those involving Sunday trading laws in the UK being a good example (see *Torfaen BC v B&Q plc* (Case 145/88) [1989] ECR 765 and *Stoke-on-Trent and Norwich City Council v B&Q plc* (Case C-169/91) [1992] ECR I-6635). This led to the ECJ in the case of *Keck and Mithouard* (Joined Cases C-267 & 268/91) [1993] ECR I-6097 attempting to redefine the impact of *Dassonville* to allow greater freedom for member States to regulate trade on a national level without concern for Article 28. The decision distinguishes between 'requirements to be met' by goods, such as those relating to size, designation, labelling and packaging, and those rules which govern 'selling arrangements'. When considering a 'requirements to be met' issue, one must still consider *Dassonville* and, if caught, must then consider the impact of the '*Cassis* principle'. However, 'selling arrangements' will prima facie not come within the ambit of *Dassonville*, provided that those arrangements apply to all affected traders equally and do not involve discriminatory treatment between domestic and imported products. As such, it is less likely that traders will be able to rely upon Article 28 to challenge or avoid prosecution under national selling regulations. (In the *Keck and Mithouard* case itself, the parties had been prosecuted under a French law which governed predatory pricing and were claiming invalidity of such law. The ECJ's view was that such a law did not offend Article 28.)

In summary, when considering measures of equivalent effect, the following questions should be borne in mind:

(a) Does it constitute a selling arrangement? If so, there must be evidence of discrimination against imported goods for Article 28 to bite.

(b) Is the measure distinctly or indistinctly applicable? If the latter is the case, the rule of reason will apply and the proportionality of the measure to the aim it is intended to achieve must be considered. If the former, one of the exemptions within Article 30 must be proven.

This Article will now be considered.

34.4.6   Article 30—derogation from Article 28

In addition to the 'rule of reason', Article 30 allows member States to derogate from Article 28 on the following grounds:

(a) public morality;

(b) public policy;

(c) public security;

(d) protection of health;

(e) protection of national treasures;

(f) protection of intellectual property rights.

Such grounds are narrowly construed and any member State must be able to justify objectively any ban or restriction it is imposing.

By far the most relevant of the above to businesses is that relating to intellectual property. Whilst it is beyond the scope of this book to look at such a topic in any detail, brief explanation should be given.

By way of example, suppose that a company in one member State manufactures compact discs. It owns copyright in those recordings. It arranges to have those discs sold in another member State by a different company but this company decides to re-import the discs back into their country of origin where they are not available. Such an action would constitute breach of copyright and could, therefore, be prevented by the manufacturer. However, such action is contrary to Article 28, and so must fall within the ambit of Article 30 to be justified. In such a case, the ECJ decided that derogation from Article 28 only extends to protection of the actual intellectual property itself and action beyond this will not be permitted (see *Deutsche Grammophon GmbH v Metro-SB-Grossmärkte GmbH* (Case 78/80) [1971] ECR 487).

This is a complex and sophisticated area of law and the reader is first recommended to become familiar with the basic concepts of intellectual property and then to consult the relevant texts for a full explanation. However, a rule of thumb with regard to this area is that:

(a) Once the intellectual property owner has permitted its goods which are the subject of the intellectual property rights onto the market in any member State, its rights are said to be 'exhausted' and any attempt to use such rights to prevent importation of those goods into another member State will contravene Article 28.

(b) There is nothing, however, to prevent an owner of intellectual property exercising its rights to prevent blatant infringement by counterfeiters, etc.

 online resource centre   Interactive online exercises (Student Learning Activities) which complement the topics covered in this chapter are available at www.oxfordtextbooks.co.uk/orc/business09_10/.

Business contracts—agency or distributorship agreements

This chapter covers the following topics:

35.1 Introduction

It is in the very nature of running a trade or business, whether it is run as a partnership or through a company, that the proprietors of the business will deal with 'outsiders'. The most important group of 'outsiders' are the customers of the business who buy its goods or services. They are not, however, the only 'outsiders' with whom the business must deal.

While many businesses will deal direct with their customers (particularly businesses which involve supplying services directly to the customers), some businesses enter into contracts with intermediaries to whom they supply goods which the intermediaries sell on to the ultimate purchasers.

Of all the wide range of contracts businesses can enter into, the ones which we will look at in this chapter are the contracts with such intermediaries. Depending on the nature of the arrangement with the intermediary, the contract may be either an agency or a distributorship (or marketing) agreement.

Before we look at these agreements in more detail, it is worth considering why a business might enter into such arrangements. At first sight, it might appear to make more financial sense for the supplying business to deal directly with its ultimate customers rather than through an intermediary who will, obviously, be looking to make a profit on the transaction. The reasons why it would in fact make commercial sense to use the intermediary will depend on the nature of the supplier's business and its reasons for considering using an intermediary. For example, a manufacturer of goods may not have the finance to support, or the expertise to run the retail outlets it needs to sell its goods to the general public. Alternatively, a supplier may have decided that there is a wider market for its goods, but that it lacks the necessary knowledge of the new market to be able to exploit the opportunity. In these types of circumstances the most sensible way for the supplier to reach its ultimate customer, or to expand its business, is to use an intermediary with the necessary facilities or expertise.

35.2   An agent or a distributor?

When setting up the relationship with the intermediary, the supplier will need to decide whether he wishes to appoint an agent or a distributor. So what is the difference between an agent and a distributor?

In brief, the agent will represent the supplier when seeking, negotiating and concluding contracts with the ultimate purchaser of the goods. Even though the ultimate purchaser may deal principally (or even exclusively) with the agent, the contract created will be between the supplier and the ultimate purchaser (assuming that the supplier is fully disclosed as the principal of the agent). In this circumstance, the agent will usually take a fee for each contract concluded and the risks, financial and commercial, will be borne by the supplier.

Conversely, a distributor will buy the goods from the supplier and then re-sell them to the distributor's own customers, with the return the distributor seeks from the arrangement represented by whatever profit he can make on the re-sale. Given that the distributor will be bearing the financial and commercial risk involved in finding the ultimate purchaser, the profit margin the distributor adds when re-selling the goods may be greater than the commission which an agent would charge. This will have the effect of increasing the ultimate sale price of the supplier's goods. This in turn may have an adverse affect on the marketability of those goods if a supplier's principal rivals in the particular market are able to sell at lower prices (because, for example, they have the necessary resources or expertise to be able to sell directly to the ultimate purchaser). Where a distributor is involved, the supplier will have no direct contractual relationship with the purchaser (since the contractual relationship will be between the distributor and the ultimate purchaser), but this will not necessarily protect the supplier from liability for defective goods.

Whichever type of intermediary arrangement the supplier decides to opt for, it is sensible to set out the terms of the arrangement in a written agreement. The written agency agreement will define the authority and duties of the agent and set out the agent's rights as against the supplier. The structure of a distribution agreement will be different to reflect the fact that the distributor buys the goods outright from the supplier. Perhaps the key provisions in a distributorship agreement relate to the restrictions on competition which each party to the agreement wishes to impose on the other.

Once the supplier has taken the decision to use an intermediary, the supplier's business objectives will determine which of an agency or distributorship arrangement is most appropriate. An agency arrangement will be appropriate where the supplier wants to retain control of the terms of sale of his products, where direct contact with the customer is important (for example, where only the supplier can provide specialist after-sales service) or where the supplier wants to retain control over the purchasers of his products or services. Conversely, a distributorship arrangement will be attractive where the supplier is selling products which require little or no direct contact with the ultimate purchaser or where the supplier is trying to break into a new market. In the latter case, a distributorship arrangement could be especially attractive as the agreement can impose an obligation on the distributor to make an agreed volume of purchases thus, in effect, guaranteeing the supplier a market. In return, the distributor will be given rights to re-sell the supplier's goods. Whether those rights are exclusive or not will depend on the nature of the distributorship agreement but, obviously, an exclusive right to re-sell a highly valued product could be extremely valuable to the distributor.

One problem with both agency and distributorship arrangements is that by their very nature they can restrict competition. The national and EC competition rules, therefore, may have an impact on the terms of the arrangement into which the principal or supplier and the agent or distributor can enter.

In the rest of this chapter, we will look at the provisions relating to agency and distributorship arrangements dealing with each arrangement separately. We will look firstly at the different types of arrangements which can be created under agency or distributorship agreements, then at the legal rules (including competition rules) which can have an impact on such agreements and finally at some common provisions to be found in agency and distributorship agreements.

35.3 Agency agreements

35.3.1 Types of agency agreement

The key aspect of an agency agreement is that the agent is merely an intermediary between the supplier (his principal) and the supplier's customer, the agent's acts being regarded as those of the supplier (his principal). While the agent may be closely involved in concluding the contract, he will not usually be a party to the contract, nor will he acquire rights or obligations under it. Having said that, there are a number of different types of agency agreement into which the principal and agent can enter. The agent's powers can be limited merely to seeking 'contracts' for the supplier (the agent in those circumstances is commonly called a 'marketing agent'). It is perhaps more common for the agent to be appointed as a 'sales agent' in which case the agent will have power to enter into contracts on behalf of his principal. The powers of a 'sales agent' can be determined by the agreement between the two parties and the most common types of arrangements are:

(a) *An exclusive agency agreement*

As the title implies, the agent has exclusive rights to represent the principal and the principal cannot appoint other agents to represent him. The exclusivity may apply worldwide or be limited to particular territories.

(b) *The sole agency arrangement*

The principal is barred from appointing other agents (again on a worldwide or territorial basis) but is free to seek customers directly himself.

(c) *The non-exclusive agency agreement*

Under this form of agreement, the principal can appoint other agents and seek customers himself.

35.3.2 The regulation of agency agreements

35.3.2.1 The general rules

Prior to 1 January 1994, the regulation of the principal–agent relationship was largely a matter of agreement between the parties as the common law imposed limited rights and obligations on either side. The Commercial Agents (Council Directive) Regulations 1993 (SI 1993/3053) (which came into effect on 1 January 1994) made radical changes to the old position (see **35.3.2.2** below).

Under the common law, the duties owed by an agent to his principal included the duties:

(a) to obey the principal's lawful instructions;

(b) to act within the limits of the authority given to the agent by the principal;

(c) to use reasonable diligence and care;

(d) to avoid conflicts between the agent's interests and those of his principal;

(e) to disclose all material facts to the principal and not to reveal confidential information; and

(f) to account to the principal for any property or money belonging to the principal under the agent's control.

The common law duties imposed on the principal include the obligation to pay the agent remuneration and/or commission and the agent's expenses as well as giving the agent an indemnity against losses incurred while acting within the scope of the agent's authority.

The agent's responsibilities in relation to contracts which he helps to conclude on behalf of his principal will depend on whether the customer, the third party, was aware that the agent was acting as such. If the customer knows the agent is acting as such for a 'disclosed principal', the contract will be between the principal and the third party *provided* the agent was acting within the scope of his actual or ostensible authority. If the agent was acting within the scope of his authority, he would not be liable in respect of the contract; only the principal can sue or be sued on it. If the agent was acting outside the scope of his authority the agent will be liable unless the principal has ratified the contract.

In circumstances where the agent is acting for an 'undisclosed principal' (that is to say the third party is unaware of the agency arrangement), both the agent and his principal can sue or be sued under the contract (provided the agent was acting within the scope of his authority). If the 'undisclosed principal' informs the third party of the agency arrangement, the third party will have a choice of either continuing to regard the agent as the other party to the contract or regard the contract as being with the agent's principal (which has the effect of relieving the agent of any liability).

35.3.2.2   The Commercial Agents (Council Directive) Regulations 1993

General

These Regulations (SI 1993/3053) regulate most commercial agency arrangements where the agent is required to perform any part of his duties anywhere in the EC. The freedom of principals and agents to agree the terms of their relationship have been severely curtailed by the Regulations since many of the Regulations are mandatory and cannot be overriden by contrary agreement. Not only do the Regulations apply to agency arrangements (called 'agency contracts' in the Regulations) entered into on or after 1 January 1994, they also apply to arrangements in existence on 1 January 1994.

As their title suggests, the Regulations implemented EEC Council Directive 86/653 on the co-ordination of laws of member States relating to agents. As such, this Directive may be of relevance when interpreting the Regulations. Also, all other member States, therefore, have their own similar implementing legislation. This may be relevant when considering the issues raised in the next paragraph.

Jurisdiction and territorial application

The Regulations apply to the activities of commercial agents in Great Britain (not to Northern Ireland where separate, but identical, Regulations apply) unless the parties have agreed that the agency contract should be covered by the law of another EC country. Therefore, an agency contract under which the agent is based in Great Britain and will perform his duties in Great Britain will be governed by the Regulations unless the agency contract provides that the law of another EC country is to govern the agreement. That situation could arise where the principal is from an EC country other than Great Britain and in those circumstances the relevant legislation from the other EC country will apply to the agreement. If the commercial agent is to perform his duties in a country outside the EC, the Regulations will be irrelevant. The position is somewhat complicated where a British principal appoints a commercial agent to act in another EC country and the governing law of the contract is that of England. The Regulations would seem not to apply because the agent is not performing his duties in Great Britain. In addition, it would appear that the regulations of no other country can apply because of the governing law clause.

Until quite recently, there was no solution to this unsatisfactory problem. However, it was remedied by the introduction of the Commercial Agents (Council Directive) (Amendment) Regulations 1998 which brought about a change to the 1993 Regulations. The effect of the change was twofold:

(a) It is possible for parties to choose a governing law from another member State, in which case, an English court is obliged to apply that chosen law. (This assumes, of course, that the English court has jurisdiction to hear the matter.)

(b) Where the governing law is that of England and Wales, but the agent is to perform his or her duties outside Great Britain in another member State, a court must still apply the Regulations, so long as the relevant regulations of that member State allow the contract to be governed by law from a jurisdiction other than that in which the agent is to perform his or her duties.

Commercial agents

The Regulations apply to 'commercial agents' and the term is defined as 'a self-employed intermediary who has continuing authority to negotiate the sale or purchase of the goods on behalf of the principal or to negotiate and conclude the sale and purchase of goods on behalf of and in the name of that principal'. There were differing views among the commentators on the Regulations as to whether this definition of a 'commercial agent' was intended to mean that the Regulations only apply to individuals. Probably, the better argument is that the Regulations are applicable to a 'commercial agent' whether an individual, a partnership or a company.

In *AMB Imballaggi Plastici v Pacflex* [1999] 2 All ER (Comm) 249, the defendant, Pacflex, attempted to construe itself as an agent, in order to substantiate a claim for compensation on termination of its contract with the claimant. At no stage in the proceedings was the argument put forward that the defendant did not qualify as an agent, because it was a company. In fact, the defendant failed in its argument on other grounds, namely that it was not acting 'on behalf of' the claimant, but, rather, was buying and selling for itself only.

Application of the Regulations

The Regulations apply to any agency contract whether oral or written. However, the Regulations provide that a number of 'agents' should be excluded from the coverage of the Regulations, including:

(a) an officer of a company or an association (not just company directors) acting as an 'agent' of the company or association;

(b) a partner authorised to enter into binding commitments on behalf of his partners or his fellow partners;

(c) any insolvency practitioner acting as such;

(d) a commercial agent whose activities are unpaid; and

(e) commercial agents whose activities as such are considered to be secondary (the criteria for determining whether the activities are 'secondary' are very wide and are contained in the Schedule to the Regulations).

Duties of the principal and agent

Regulation 3 sets out the duties of the commercial agent to his principal and cannot be contracted out of. The agent is required to look after the interests of his principal and to act dutifully and in good faith. In particular, the agent must make proper efforts to negotiate and, where appropriate, conclude the transactions he is instructed to take care of, to communicate to his principal all necessary information available to him and to comply with reasonable instructions given by his principal.

The duties of a principal to his commercial agent are set out in reg. 4 and cannot be contracted out of. The regulation imposes an obligation on the principal to act dutifully and in good faith in his relations with his commercial agent. Furthermore, the principal must provide his commercial agent with necessary documentation relating to the goods concerned, obtain for his commercial agent the information necessary for the performance of the agency contract and notify the agent (within a reasonable period) once he anticipates that the volume of commercial transactions will be significantly lower than that which the commercial agent could normally have expected. Finally, the principal is required to inform his commercial agent (within a reasonable period) of his acceptance or refusal of, and of any non-execution by him of, a commercial transaction which the commercial agent has procured for him.

Remuneration and commission

If the parties to the agency contract have not agreed a level of remuneration or commission, the Regulations provide that the agent will receive the amount which it is customary to pay to agents marketing the types of goods or services concerned in the same geographical area. In the absence of any such custom and practice, the agent will receive 'reasonable remuneration taking into account all aspects of the transaction'. The Regulations contain detailed provisions determining how commission is to be calculated and when it is to be paid. However, these do not apply if the agent is not remunerated, whether wholly or in part, through 'commission'. 'Commission' is defined as 'any part of the remuneration of the commercial agent which varies with the number or value of business transactions'.

Under reg. 7 (which can be contracted out of), the agent is entitled to receive commission transactions concluded during the period covered by the agency agreement where the transaction has been concluded as a result of his actions or where the transaction is concluded with a third party who he previously acquired as a customer for transactions of the same kind. The agent will also be entitled to commission on transactions concluded during the period covered by the agency contract where he has an exclusive right to a specific geographical area or to a specific group of customers where the transactions have been entered into with the customer belonging to that area or group. It is normal to deal with the situation covered by reg. 7 in the agency agreement and so the provisions of this regulation are likely to come into play only when the parties have, for whatever reason, omitted to deal expressly with this issue. (See *Kontogeorgas v Kartonpak* (Case C-104/95) [1996] ECR I-6643 where the scope of Article 7 was crucial as the agreement was silent on the point.)

It is perhaps more likely that the parties may have failed to agree on the agent's entitlement to commission on transactions concluded **after** the agency contract is terminated. Regulation 8 (which can be contracted out of) covers this situation and provides that the commercial agent will be entitled to commission. In the circumstances if the transaction is mainly attributable to his efforts during the period covered by the agency contract and if the transaction was entered into within a reasonable period after that contract terminated or (provided commission would have been payable under reg. 7 if the contract had been entered into during the agency contract) the order of the third party reached the principal or the commercial agent before the agency contract terminated.

Under reg. 10, 'commission' becomes due as soon as, and to the extent that, either the principal has executed the transaction, or the principal should, according to his agreement with the third party, have executed the transaction or the third party has executed the transaction.

Provision of information
Regulation 12 requires the principal to supply the agent, each quarter, with a statement of the commission due and the 'main components used in calculating the amount'. The agent will be entitled to demand that he be provided with all the information and records which are available to the principal which he needs in order to be able to check the amount of commission due to him.

While the Directive does not require agency agreements caught by the Regulations to be in writing, reg. 13 gives both sides the right, on request, to a signed document from the other party setting out the terms of the agency contract, including any variations made subsequent to their original entry into the agency contract.

Termination
Arguably, the most important provisions of the Regulations relate to terminating agency contracts, in particular the provisions introducing minimum notice periods and compensation for termination of agency contracts.

The Regulations make no provision for notice where an agency contract for a fixed term is terminated on the originally agreed date. However, if the fixed term agreement continues to be performed by both parties after the fixed term has expired, the agreement is converted into an agency contract for an indefinite period and the minimum notice period set out in reg. 15 will apply.

If reg. 15 applies, either party can terminate it on giving notice which will be at least one month during the first year of the contract, two months during the second and three months during the third and each subsequent year. Regulation 15 is mandatory and so it is not open to the parties to agree shorter periods of notice but they may agree longer periods of notice (although reg. 15(3) provides that, in those circumstances, the period of notice to be observed by the principal must not be shorter than that to be observed by the agent). Where a fixed term agency agreement is converted into an indefinite term one under reg. 14, the notice period set out above will apply. The original fixed period must be taken into account in the calculation of the period of notice.

As we have explained, agency agreements in existence before 1 January 1994 (when the Regulations came into effect) are covered by the Regulations. Commentators on the Regulations have taken the view that the duration of the agreement prior to that date should be taken into account in calculating the minimum notice period.

Post-termination indemnity or compensation
Regulation 17 sets out the rules relevant when determining if the commercial agent is entitled to any compensation on the termination of the agency contract. The EC

Directive which the Regulations implement gave member States two alternatives with regard to compensation when implementing the Directive in the national legislation. The member States could either provide for an 'indemnity' for the agent (of a maximum of one year's commission, calculated by reference to an historic average) to which the agent would be entitled if he had substantially enhanced the goodwill of the principal's business or for 'compensation' for the agent for damage suffered as a result of the ending of the agency relationship.

Regulation 17 permits the principal and agent to choose whichever of 'indemnity' or 'compensation' they prefer (although if the agency agreement is silent on the point, the agent will receive 'compensation' rather than 'indemnity').

Regulation 17(3) provides that the commercial agent should be entitled to an indemnity if and to the extent that:

(a) he has brought the principal new customers or has significantly increased the volume of business with the existing customers and the principal continues to derive substantial benefits from the business with such customers; and

(b) the payment of this indemnity is equitable having regard to all the circumstances and, in particular, the commission lost by the commercial agent on business transacted with such customers.

Assuming that the commercial agent is entitled to an indemnity, the amount of the indemnity shall not exceed a figure equivalent to commission for one year calculated from the commercial agent's average annual remuneration over the preceding five years. If the contract goes back less than five years, the indemnity should be calculated on the average for the period in question. (The fact that the commercial agent is entitled to an 'indemnity' does not prevent him from seeking damages for breach of contract.)

So far as the 'compensation' alternative is concerned, reg. 17(6) provides the commercial agent should be entitled to compensation for the damage he suffers as a result of the termination of his relations with the principal. Such damage shall be deemed to occur particularly when the termination takes place in either or both of the following circumstances, namely circumstances which:

(a) deprive the commercial agent of the commission which proper performance of the agency contract would have procured for him whilst providing his principal with substantial benefits linked to the activities of the commercial agent; or

(b) have not enabled the commercial agent to amortise the cost and expenses that he had incurred in the performance of the agency agreement on the advice of his principal.

The commercial agent loses his entitlement to indemnity or compensation if, within one year following the termination of his agency contract, he has not notified his principal that he intends to pursue his entitlement.

These rights to indemnity of compensation can also arise where the agency agreement is terminated as a result of the death of the commercial agent.

The rights to payment of indemnity or compensation are, however, excluded where:

(a) the principal has terminated the agency contract because of the commercial agent's default, which would justify immediate termination of the agency contract because of the commercial agent's failure to carry out all or part of his obligations under the contract or where exceptional circumstances arise; or

(b) the commercial agent has himself terminated the agency contract, unless the termination is justified by circumstances attributable to the principal or on the grounds of age, infirmity or illness of the commercial agent in consequence of which he cannot reasonably require to continue his activities; or

(c) the commercial agent, with the agreement of his principal, assigns his rights and duties under the agency contract to another person.

The grounds for excluding these payments are set out in reg. 18.

Both concepts of compensation and indemnity for agents are somewhat alien to English jurisprudence. This is perhaps not surprising when the concept of compensation has its origins in the French legal system and the concept of indemnity in the German. For these reasons, in the Scottish case of *King v T. Tunnock Ltd* (2000 SC 424), the court took its lead from French law in calculating compensation due to an agent and in *Moore v Piretta* [1999] 1 All ER 174 an English court was prepared to be influenced by German law when calculating an indemnity payment.

What is perhaps unfortunate is that, whilst most member States, when implementing the Directive, opted for either indemnity or compensation, the UK was prepared to allow both possibilities to co-exist. Not only has this meant that two new concepts have had to be imported and understood into UK jurisprudence, it has also led to a system which produces potentially two markedly different results. In the *Tunnock* case the main factors which the court believed it had to take into account were that:

(a) compensation represents the price the principal must pay for buying-out the agent's share in the goodwill which attaches to the agency arrangement;

(b) the normal level of compensation is two years' commission.

This is somewhat at odds with an indemnity, where the cap of one year's commission applies. So, for instance, in the *Piretta* case, the indemnity calculation produced a figure of £92,000, which was then capped at just under £65,000. However, it is clear from the wording of reg. 17 that compensation and indemnity are expected to produce different results.

The English courts have not been so definite as the Scottish and have been reluctant to follow the benchmark of two years' commission, presumably believing this to be too generous to agents. For example, in *Barret McKenzie v Escada (UK) Ltd* [2001] ECC 50, the judge expressed doubt about the suitability of the approach taken in the *Tunnock* case. Further, in *Ingmar GB Ltd v Eaton Leonard Inc.* [2002] ECC 5, the court accepted the potential validity of benchmarking compensation payments at two years, but expressly reserved the right to deviate from this and, in fact, did so.

Most recently, in *Lonsdale v Howard and Hallam Ltd* [2006] EWCA Civ 63, the Court of Appeal emphatically rejected any reference to the practice of other national courts prior to the Directive coming into existence. Moore-Bick LJ, delivering the judgment of the court, explained that the Directive should be considered a piece of EC legislation in its own right. The judge then went on to examine the wording of the Directive and held that the purpose of reg. 17(6) was to provide an agent with compensation for the loss of the agency business, which included whatever goodwill attached to it. The 'two year' rule should, therefore, not even be considered as a useful guideline. As a consequence, it was appropriate to consider the state of the principal's business at the time of termination. The consequence for the agent in this instance was that, as the principal's business was in serious decline, the judge at first instance was correct to make an award of £7,500, rather than an amount of nearly £20,000, based on two years' gross commission, which was sought by the agent.

Clearly this decision produces a fairer system than one based upon a crude mathematical presumption. However, it does mean that each case must be considered on its own facts and any benchmark for starting negotiations between principal and agent has disappeared.

The parties to the agency contract have to agree at the start of the contract whether 'indemnity' or 'compensation' within reg. 17 would be paid at the end. Therefore, they will have to take a view on this important issue on the basis perhaps of little or no information. The clear limit on the amount of indemnity may make it attractive to many principals, especially as the right to indemnity only arises if the agent has brought in new customers or 'significantly increased' the volume of the principal's business. Therefore, the agent has to have grown the principal's business to get an indemnity, whereas the right to compensation would be available if the agent has merely maintained that business. It is obviously simplistic to suggest that there is a general rule of thumb which can be applied. The principal and agent will have to take into account all the surrounding circumstances, which may justify reaching a different conclusion.

Settlement of disputes

The parties may not derogate from the compensation and indemnity provisions to the detriment of the commercial agent before the agency contract expired (reg. 19).

Restraint of trade clauses

Any restraint of trade clause in any agency contract will be valid only if and to the extent that:

(a) it is concluded in writing;

(b) it relates to the geographical area or group of customers and the geographical area entrusted to the commercial agent and to the kind of goods covered by his agency under the contract; and

(c) it is for not more than two years after the termination of the agency contract.

The regulation which deals with the restraint of trade clauses (reg. 20) goes on to provide that 'nothing in this regulation shall affect any enactment or rule of law which imposes other restrictions on the validity or enforceability of restraint of trade clauses or which enables the court to reduce the obligations on the parties resulting from such clauses'. Therefore, the existing common law rules on restraint of trade (which require that any such clause must be reasonable as between the parties and not against the public interest) will still apply to such clauses in agency contracts.

35.3.2.3   The competition issues

The EC rules

It will be remembered that Article 81 prohibits agreements which restrict or distort competition and which affect trade between EC member States. The nature of terms commonly found in agency agreements (for example, provisions relating to customers, trading terms, limitations on the agent's ability to handle competing products, etc.) are such that agency agreements in theory can fall foul of Article 81. However, two things are likely to assist. First, the agreement may be of minor importance (see **34.2.4.1**). Secondly, the Commission has produced guidance on the relevance of Article 81 to agency agreements in its guidelines on the applicability of the block exemption for vertical agreements (see **34.2.4.3**).

The guidelines explain that the key factor to be considered is the financial and commercial risk borne by the agent in relation to the contracts it arranges for its principal. If the agent bears no such risks, it is to be treated as an integral part of the principal's activities and, accordingly, the relationship between the agent and principal can have no anti-competitive effect. In essence, therefore, if the agent acts as no more than a 'middle-man', Article 81 will not apply.

Should an agent, however, be regarded as commercially independent of its principal, Article 81 may apply. First, therefore, the agreement may benefit from the exemption in Article 81(3). If there is doubt about this, the next possible 'safe harbour' is the block exemption for vertical agreements. Clearly if the agreement has not yet been drafted, it would be worth doing so to take advantage of the block exemption. The 30% market share criterion must, of course, be satisfied.

The UK rules

The UK competition regime was examined at **34.5**. (The reader is advised to consult this section first.) It will be remembered that Chapter I of the Competition Act operates in much the same way as Article 81 of the Treaty of Rome, albeit on a UK level only. As such, the first consideration must be jurisdictional. As a rule of thumb, should the impact of the agreement be felt outside the UK, for example either the agent or the principal is based outside the UK in another member State, then EC rules should be considered first.

Should the Competition Act be relevant, because of the effect of s. 60 of the Act, the applicability of Chapter I will be decided upon in much the same way as Article 81 to an agency agreement under EC rules. As such, a 'true' agency agreement (see *The EC rules* above) will fall outside the prohibition altogether. A 'non-genuine' agreement will have to be considered in the light of the Vertical Agreements Order. If it amounts to a vertical agreement (and it is likely that it would), subject to any price-fixing arrangements, Chapter I will fail to bite. If it does not, the agreement must be shown to have an appreciable effect on competition in the UK for it to be prohibited, again subject to any price-fixing arrangements.

35.3.2.4 The provisions of agency agreements

In this section we will look, in outline, at the key provisions which could be included in such agreements. It should be remembered that the Commercial Agents (Council Directive) Regulations 1993 (SI 1993/3053) give each party the right to a written statement of terms (reg. 13) and render void any post-termination restrictive covenant which is not in writing (reg. 18).

Appointment and authority

When appointing the agent, the agreement should set out the extent of the agent's authority. Is the agent to have authority to sell the products covered by the agreement with all powers necessary to market the products, negotiate terms and enter into contracts on behalf of the principal? (In other words, is the agent to be a 'sale agent'?) Alternatively, is the agent to be a 'marketing agent' and so only have power to promote the products and solicit orders which have to be passed back to the principal?

The subject matter of the agreement: goods or services

The 'products' which are the subject matter of the agency agreement, whether they be goods or services, need to be clearly defined. What is to happen if circumstances merit a change in those goods and services? Can the principal change them unilaterally or does the agent have to agree to such changes?

Customers, territory, and exclusivity

It is usual to restrict the agent's appointment to finding customers in a defined territory or to a specified type of customer.

The agency agreement can give exclusive or non-exclusive rights to the agent for the defined territory. If the agency is to be exclusive, the principal will agree not to appoint another agent in the teritory but may wish to reserve the right to supply existing (specified) customers in the territory. The agent will usually agree not to seek orders for the products from the customers outside the specified territory.

Duration

The agreement can be either for an indefinite term or for a fixed period. If it is for an indefinite term, the 1993 Regulations impose minimum notice periods (or up to three months). If the agreement is for a fixed term but continues beyond the agreed termination date, it will be regarded as being for an indefinite period and the Regulations' provisions relating to minimum notice periods will apply.

The duties of the agent

Irrespective of the duties imposed on agents by common law and by the 1993 Regulations, the agent's duties will usually be set out in full in the agreement. This will normally include an obligation on the agent to use its best endeavours to promote a market product in the territory, and to seek and (if the agency is a sole agency) accept orders, on the principal's standard terms and conditions. Although the common law will imply obligations to act in good faith and obey all the principal's reasonable lawful instructions, they should be expressly stated. A variety of more specific obligations can be imposed, including the obligation on the agent to make its status clear to all potential customers, a prohibition on the agent incurring liability for representations or warranties on the principal's behalf, save as authorised and a prohibition on making secret profits.

The rights and duties of the principal

As with the agent, the common law and the 1993 Regulations impose a number of duties on the principal (including the obligation to act towards the agent in good faith). The agreement will give or impose a number of additional rights and duties on the principal. The principal will normally want the ability to change the goods or services (and their price) which are the subject of the agreement. The principal will also want the right to approve any expenses incurred by the agent which are to be reimbursed by the principal as well as the right to inspect the agent's books. The agent will want the reassurance that the principal has taken all the necessary steps to ensure the quality of the goods or services being provided, that the principal maintains appropriate product liability insurance and can perform its contracts with third parties.

Commission

Should the parties fail to agree on the amount of commission paid under the agency agreement, the 1993 Regulations give the agent the right to the remuneration customarily paid to agents dealing with the same goods and services in the same geographical area. The Regulations do not, however, specifically provide what is the amount of the commission to be paid. Having said that, it is usual for agency agreements to cover the question of commission and it is usually in the form of a percentage of the net invoice price of the goods sold through the agent or of cash received by the principal from those sales. The commission provisions should determine when commission becomes due (usually once a principal has been paid by the customer) and for the date on which the commission should be paid. If the agent is a sales agent, the agent may reserve the right to retain the commission from the payments in which case the agreement will contain strict provisions dealing with how the payments should be accounted for.

Termination

In addition to providing minimum notice periods for indefinite term agreements, if the Regulations apply to a particular case, they provide for agents to receive compensation or indemnity on termination, irrespective of whether or not the principal is in breach. In any event, the principal will want to reserve the right to terminate early (either summarily or on notice) if the agent is in breach of contract, is declared bankrupt or insolvent, purports to assign the agreement or is likely to become unable to perform the contract.

Restrictive covenants

The principal may want to protect his business interests by imposing such a covenant on the agent. Under English law, the covenant will be enforceable if the principal has an interest worthy of protection and the restrictions (as to time, subject matter, geographical area, etc.) are considered to be reasonable as between the parties at the date the restriction is imposed and not against the public interest.

Other provisions

Agency agreements commonly also include a variety of other provisions including those relating to:

(a) intellectual property;

(b) confidentiality;

(c) assignment;

(d) force majeure;

(e) notices;

(f) governing law and jurisdiction.

35.4 Distributorship agreements

35.4.1 Types of distributorship agreement

35.4.1.1 Exclusive distributorship agreements

The distinguishing feature of such agreements is that they give the distributor the exclusive right to sell the product in the territory covered by the distributorship agreement. The supplier will be prevented from selling the goods in the relevant area either on his own account or through agents or other distributors.

The Office of Fair Trading in the UK and the European Commission favour this form of distributorship agreement for a variety of reasons. Exclusive distributorship arrangements are considered to encourage competition between different brands of the same type of goods. This is because knowing that he is the only source of a particular brand of goods within his territory will encourage the distributor to market those goods heavily and the supplier's wish to establish itself within that area will encourage it to maintain the continuity of supply. Furthermore, appointing an exclusive distributor means that the supplier of each brand of goods only has to deal with one entity in the region and thus avoid the necessity for maintaining a potentially expensive network of dealers. Exclusive distributorship arrangements will usually mean that there are a number of brands of the same product competing vigorously against each other. The effect of this will be to benefit members of the public, who will have access to a wider choice of goods at more competitive prices.

35.4.1.2   Sole distributorship agreements

The key difference between a sole distributorship agreement (although the term 'sole' is not a term of art here) and an exclusive one is that while the distributor under a sole distributorship agreement will be the only distributor with whom the supplier will deal in a particular territory, the supplier is *not* prevented from continuing to sell its products in the territory on its own account. In return, the distributor will commonly agree to regard the supplier as his sole supplier of the type of goods which are the subject of the agreement.

The economic benefits of an exclusive distributorship agreement do not apply to a sole distributorship agreement and so these types of agreements are not so favourably treated by the Office of Fair Trading and the European Commission.

35.4.1.3   Non-exclusive distributorship agreements

Under such an arrangement, the distributor merely takes the supplier's products. The distributor has no exclusive rights to those products, so that the supplier can appoint other distributors in the same territory, nor is the supplier prohibited from selling its own products on its own account in the territory.

Again, the economic benefits of exclusive distributorship agreements do not apply to non-exclusive ones, and so the Office of Fair Trading and the EC Commission do not look upon them as favourably as exclusive arrangements.

35.4.1.4   Selective distributorship agreements

The distinguishing feature of such an arrangement is that the supplier limits the number of distributors he will appoint in a particular territory so that the distributors who enter into such an agreement will not be given exclusive rights to deal with the supplier's goods.

A selective distributorship arrangement may not encourage as much inter-brand competition as an exclusive distributorship arrangement, and so they are less favourably treated by the UK and EC competition authorities than are exclusive arrangements. Nevertheless, they will be permitted, subject to satisfying certain conditions which are set out in **35.4.3.2** below.

35.4.2   The competition issues

Much of what was said at **35.3.2.3** with regard to agency agreements can be repeated here. The first consideration is again a jurisdictional one. Having established which regime applies, the following issues need to be raised in respect of an agreement.

EC regime

If there is a possibility that the agreement in question infringes Article 81, consideration must be given to the following questions:

- Is the agreement of minor importance?
- Does the agreement in question comply with the block exemption on vertical agreements or can it be so drafted to comply?
- Does the agreement automatically benefit from the exemption in Article 81(3)?

If the answer to all the above questions is in the negative, then the agreement will be void and the parties thereto subject to the possibility of fines.

UK regime

As the UK position is somewhat more lenient, the agreement will very likely fall within the vertical agreements order and, therefore, be exempt from the effect of Chapter I. In the unlikely event that this is not the case, the appreciability test should be applied to establish the effect of the agreement on competition within the UK. In both these instances, the key feature will be the absence of price-fixing or resale price maintenance.

35.4.3 The provisions of exclusive distribution agreements

In this section we will look, in outline, at the key provisions which could be included in such agreements.

35.4.3.1 Exclusivity

The very nature of such agreements are that they should grant exclusive rights to the products to the distributor, and the rights and obligations imposed on both sides of the agreement must be clearly stated. Care should be taken when drafting these provisions to ensure that the block exemption for exclusive distributive agreements applies (see above).

35.4.3.2 Term

If a supplier is using the exclusive distributorship agreement as a way of establishing its products in a new territory, it will obviously want to ensure that the distributor he chooses is encouraged to put in the necessary marketing effort to achieve the supplier's aim. Accordingly, the supplier will probably want to offer the distributor a long-term contract while reserving for himself the right to terminate the agreement if, for example, there is a major structural or financial change to the distributor adversely affecting the promotion of the supplier's goods. The distributor will probably also be keen to enter into a long-term arrangement with the supplier as it will ensure continuity of supply of the goods. However, from the distributor's viewpoint, such long-term arrangements can have their problems; for example, if the supplier tries to impose an obligation of a heavy 'minimum purchase commitment' on the distributor.

Furthermore, should the agreement be for a fixed term the distributor will probably want to include a provision giving him the right to extend the term provided the arrangements specified by the agreement are working satisfactorily. He will want to do this as a way of protecting his investment if he has spent time and money promoting the supplier's goods. The distributor will not want to face the risk of the supplier switching the distributorship arrangement to another, cheaper distributor after the initial effort of establishing the product in the territory has been made.

35.4.3.3 Minimum purchase commitment

A distributorship agreement can be a way of guaranteeing a market for some at least of the supplier's products and many exclusive distributorship agreements contain a provision to this effect (whether setting a minimum purchase requirement for each year of the agreement or over the whole term of the agreement). Such a requirement can be unattractive to a distributor who will not only have to lay out funds to promote the goods, but may also have to lay out funds to buy stocks before the market in the goods has been properly established.

35.4.3.4 Territory

The area which the agreement will cover should be specified and obviously should be realistic given the resources and expertise of the distributor.

35.4.3.5 Price, payment, title and delivery

Most agreements will provide for an agreed price for the goods to be supplied at the start of the term of the agreement but the supplier will usually reserve the right to increase the price subsequently to cover increased manufacturing costs and the like. If this right to increase the price is entirely at the discretion of the supplier, the distributor can find himself in an extremely difficult financial position, especially where he is subject to a minimum purchase commitment. Therefore, distributors try to limit the rights of the supplier to increase prices to inflation-linked rises, or increases in the cost of production, as well as trying to ensure that the prices can only be increased at fixed intervals (say, annually).

Whatever the price agreed may be, the supplier will want to ensure he receives payment before he loses control of the goods. One device which is often incorporated into these agreements is a provision permitting the supplier to retain title of the goods until full payment has been received.

From the distributor's point of view, he will need to ensure that the goods are delivered on time to mesh in with his own distribution schedules. The distributor will usually try to include in the agreement a provision enabling him to claim damages from the supplier for late delivery.

35.4.3.6 Trade mark and patents

The agreement should include provisions dealing with whether the distributor must sell on the goods using the supplier's trade mark or whether the distributor can re-brand them. Similarly, there must be protections built into the agreement to cover the situation where there is any allegation of an intellectual property right infringement (usually in the form of an indemnity given by the supplier to the distributor in such circumstances).

35.4.3.7 Restrictive covenants, warranties and exclusion clauses

The supplier will often want to protect himself from the distributor taking advantage of any knowledge acquired in the course of the distributorship agreement. The nature of the restrictive covenants which the supplier will want to impose will depend on the circumstances, but might include preventing the distributor acting as a distributor for competing goods produced by a rival supplier (but whether such a provision will be enforceable will depend on the nature of the restriction).

The distributor may be willing to rely on the warranties given by the Sale of Goods Act 1979 but the supplier will usually give express warranties (subject to exclusion clauses usually limiting or excluding altogether a supplier's liability for any loss of profits the distributor suffers).

35.4.3.8 Other clauses

There may be a variety of other clauses which the parties will want to consider, such as obligations imposed on the distributor in relation to marketing, reporting, providing adequate technical backup, taking out appropriate insurance, seeking any necessary approvals, dealing with assignment of the benefit of the contract and disputes.

35.4.3.9 Other types of distributorship agreements

The terms of the other types of distributorship agreements (see **35.4.1** above) will often be broadly similar to those found in exclusive distributorship agreements, save that the terms creating the exclusive nature of the arrangement will, obviously, not apply.

Developmental questions

The following questions are designed as an aid to your learning. They should not be looked on as specimen examination questions, the answers to which should be memorised. In fact, many of the questions do not have an absolute answer. However, by thinking about them, you should develop a greater understanding and insight into the topics raised.

Partnerships

1. The partnership relationship is one of utmost good faith. Why is this? Try to think of three examples from the Partnership Act which support this relationship.

2. Peter imports wine and sells it on by mail order. Peter has a website and also advertises occasionally in the local and national press. Peter has limited storage facilities, so he has an arrangement with his friend Bernard to store the greater percentage of his stock with him for £800 per month. Because of this arrangement, Bernard very often has to process orders which Peter receives. Bernard, therefore, receives 7% of the retail price of every case of wine which he processes.

   Consider whether or not Peter and Bernard are in partnership together.

3. If you were considering joining a partnership, what sorts of enquiries would you make about the partnership business and why?

4. Gill, Peake and Kani operate a partnership together. They have no written agreement between them, but there has always been an understanding that they will share profits equally and will all contribute equally to the capital of the partnership. Should Peake wish to leave the partnership, what options are available to her?

5. Consider the difference between partnership liabilities and partnership losses and the different rules in the Partnership Act for dealing with them.

6. A, B, C and D are in partnership. X is hoping to join the partnership, but wishes to limit his exposure and would like the following clause added to the partnership agreement which already exists between A, B, C and D:

   At no time shall X be responsible for any debts or liabilities of the Partnership either existing at the time X joined the Partnership or incurred subsequent to that date and as a consequence no action, claim or proceedings shall be brought against X for such debts or liabilities.

   How effective will this clause be in achieving X's aims? Consider how you would re-draft the clause to make it more effective, if possible.

Companies

1. Your client is joining a company as finance director. She is being appointed to the board of the company and will also enter into a contract of employment as finance director.

   - As her solicitor, advise her as to the practical differences between being appointed to the office of director and entering into a service contract. What rights and duties arise from each?

   - Now put yourself in the position of the solicitor advising the company.

   - What board and shareholder resolutions would have to be passed to facilitate the appointment of the new director and the entering into of the contract of employment?

   - What documents would have to be sent to Companies House following the appointment?

2. The concept of maintaining capital exists to protect both creditors and shareholders. In what ways is this concept embodied in the Companies Act 2006?

3. What are the practical implications of converting from a private to a public company limited by shares, both as regards the conversion itself and the ongoing obligations? What are the potential advantages and disadvantages?

4. Hamford plc is buying the entire issued share capital of Torpress Limited. To facilitate the purchase, Hamford plc is borrowing £4,500,000 from a bank. To secure this loan, the bank will take security over the assets of Torpress Limited once it is owned by Hamford. What issues arise from this proposal to grant security?

5. In what ways does the Companies Act 2006 seek to control the activities of company directors?

6. Atlantra Limited has issued all of its authorised share capital. Three new investors have each agreed to purchase 10,000 £1 ordinary shares at a price of £3.70 per share.

   - What resolutions would have to be passed by: (a) the board; and (b) the shareholders, in order to facilitate the purchase of shares?

   - What documents would have to be sent to Companies House following the purchase?

   - What effect would the purchase of shares have on Atlantra's accounts?

Taxation

1. Consider why capital allowances exist. Why are different capital allowances available for, on the one hand, plant and machinery and, on the other, industrial buildings?

2. Consider the following examples and decide whether or not the receipt/expenditure in question is of an income or capital nature and its taxation consequences, if any:

   (a) Bradford Decorating Supplies Limited, a wholesaler of decorating products, sells 3,000 rolls of wallpaper.

   (b) John sells his holiday cottage in Devon for £125,000.

(c) Chris receives 150 ordinary shares in Eastern Optics Limited as a gift from her aunt, Josephine.

(d) Barry, a jeweller, sells a diamond ring for £4,500.

(e) Compton Homes Limited sells a property on a new housing development it is building.

(f) Wizard Cars Limited, a car dealership, buys a car from a member of the public.

(g) Hollington Furniture Warehouses Limited carries out refurbishment and improvement of its three furniture salesrooms for a total cost of £750,000.

3. Wheatcroft Plumbing Services is a business operated by Stephen Wheatcroft as a sole trader. It is in its third year of trading and has just recorded a trading loss. What taxation options are there for Stephen in respect of the loss?

4. Explain the purpose and effect of the application of marginal relief in the calculation of corporation tax.

5. Can a company benefit from the application of the rules on VAT?

The European Community

1. Your client manufactures gardening equipment, including secateurs, lawn edgers and hedge trimmers. It wishes to export these products to Italy and has discovered that any such goods with a cutting blade have to be packaged so as to be totally inoperable at the retail stage. They must also bear a warning sign or tag (in Italian) explaining that the products contain dangerous, sharp blades and that extreme caution should always be exercised in their use.

Your client wishes to know how far it must comply with these requirements, if at all.

2. How would your answer to 1. above differ if the requirements in question only applied to imported goods?

3. Is there any difference from a UK and EC competition perspective between an agency and a distributorship agreement?

4. Car Discounters plc ('Discounters') and Autosave Limited ('Autosave') both operate car supermarkets in the UK. Discounters has three sites in the North West of England and Autosave has two sites in the North East of England and one near Edinburgh. The managing directors of both companies have informally agreed not to set up sites that compete with each other's existing sites. They have also agreed that, for the next three years, Discounters will only expand by opening a maximum of two sites in the West Midlands and Autosave will only expand by opening one site in the East Midlands and one in Glasgow.

What legal consequences arise out of the arrangement described?

Insolvency

1. Explain, giving practical examples, the objectives of the Enterprise Act 2002 as regards the development of the law on personal bankruptcy and corporate insolvency.

2. What benefits remain in taking security over the assets of a company following the Enterprise Act 2002?

3. Greenmark Limited is in financial difficulties. It owes its creditors amounts totalling £834,000. The largest (and only secured) creditor is a bank, which is owed £478,000, and has asked for a meeting with the company to assess the available options. The company receives £120,000 from its largest debtor. The board of the company meets to consider how to apply this amount.

   As solicitor to the company, advise the board as to its options.

   If you were a solicitor advising an individual director rather than the company, would your advice differ?

4. In what ways does: (a) the intent of a company; and (b) the relationship between that company and the other party to the transaction, have an impact on the ability of an insolvency practitioner to apply successfully for an antecedent transaction to be set aside?

Index